Nietzsche's Kind of Philosophy

Finding His Way

RICHARD SCHACHT

The University of Chicago Press
Chicago and London

The University of Chicago Press, Chicago 60637
The University of Chicago Press, Ltd., London
© 2023 by The University of Chicago
Published 2023
Printed in the United States of America

32 31 30 29 28 27 26 25 24 23   1 2 3 4 5

ISBN-13: 978-0-226-82285-3 (cloth)
ISBN-13: 978-0-226-82286-0 (e-book)
DOI: https://doi.org/10.7208/chicago/9780226822860.001.0001

Library of Congress Cataloging-in-Publication Data

Names: Schacht, Richard, 1941– author.
Title: Nietzsche's kind of philosophy : finding his way / Richard Schacht.
Description: Chicago ; London : The University of Chicago Press, 2023. |
    Includes bibliographical references and index.
Identifiers: LCCN 2022022549 | ISBN 9780226822853 (cloth) | ISBN 9780226822860 (ebook)
Subjects: LCSH: Nietzsche, Friedrich Wilhelm, 1844–1900. | BISAC: PHILOSOPHY /
    Individual Philosophers | PHILOSOPHY / General
Classification: LCC B3317 .S363 2023 | DDC 193—dc23/eng/20220708
LC record available at https://lccn.loc.gov/2022022549

♾ This paper meets the requirements of ANSI/NISO Z39.48-1992 (Permanence of Paper).

Nietzsche's Kind of Philosophy

To Judy
My everything

Contents

Preface

Nietzsche has been a preoccupation of mine since I first made his acquaintance as an undergraduate at Harvard in the early 1960s. At that time, in Harvard's Philosophy Department, he was not considered to be a real philosopher at all, let alone one worth taking seriously. The situation I encountered as a grad student in the department at Princeton in the mid-1960s was essentially the same, even though Walter Kaufmann was there. Kaufmann, who both encouraged and furthered my interest in Nietzsche, was his most prominent Anglophone champion at the time; but that is one of the reasons why Kaufmann himself was never taken seriously as a philosopher, either in the professional mainstream or in his own Princeton department.

Kaufmann's Nietzsche, while emphatically not a proto-Nazi, was proclaimed instead to have been an existentialist. But that, in analytic circles, was not much of an improvement, even though it did serve to help de-Nazify him. The analytic philosopher Arthur Danto's surprising 1965 book *Nietzsche as Philosopher*[1] found little admiration or traction either among his analytic colleagues or among their existentialist foes. My own interest in Nietzsche was similarly neither understood nor shared by my colleagues at the University of Illinois during my early years there, but it was at least tolerated (if not encouraged)—though I thought it prudent to defer active pursuit of that interest until after I was tenured.

Today there are few in the profession who are disposed to deny that Nietzsche was a philosopher, even though there continue to be many in the analytic mainstream who remain unconvinced that he was one who is worth taking seriously—except perhaps negatively: as an exemplar of the kind of danger he himself took to be what he called "the advent of nihilism." Yet there are also now many, even in analytic circles (as there long have been in the interpretive or "Continental" tradition),[2] who regard him has having been not only a philosopher deserving of the name, but moreover an interesting and perhaps even important one, well worth talking about and taking seriously in a positive way.

But if so, what sort of philosopher was he? If Nietzsche was indeed a philosopher, what is the character of his philosophical thinking? What kind of philosophy was *his* kind of philosophy? Although he was largely unknown or ignored during his productive lifetime (to his great dismay), that has certainly changed. But he has been read and understood in a variety of radically different ways, by both admirers (ranging from aesthetes to Nazis) and detractors (of numerous persuasions). Many of these depictions have been caricatures and even travesties that need not be taken seriously; but those of philosophers of note in both the interpretive and analytic traditions are very nearly as disparate.

For Heidegger and Jaspers, for example, Nietzsche was a transitional thinker between the metaphysical tradition and their own (very different) kinds of post-metaphysical "philosophy of *Existenz*" (human "existing"). For Sartre and Camus, he was a kindred existentialist spirit. That is basically how Kaufmann influentially portrayed him—and beyond that, perhaps also as a bit of a pragmatist. For post-existentialist French thinkers (such as Foucault and Derrida) and their Anglophone followers, what he was instead was an early or proto-poststructuralist and deconstructionist, and indeed a kind of anti-philosopher, who repudiated not only traditional modes of metaphysical-philosophical thinking but philosophy itself. That basically was how Richard Rorty regarded him.

For Danto, on the other hand, and subsequently for many of those in the analytical philosophical community who took their cues from him concerning "Nietzsche as philosopher," Nietzsche was a sometimes analytically minded philosophical nihilist and "moral terrorist," who could be read—both for fun and for critical profit—as a proto-analytical critic of metaphysics, religion, conventional morality, and much else. But that was pretty much the extent of Danto's presentation and appreciation of him.

More recently, it has become common for philosophers in the mainstream of that tradition to read Nietzsche (or the part of him they deem worth taking seriously) as subscribing to something like the newly fashionable scientistic naturalism that is one strand of analytical philosophy. Others in that tradition (Alasdair MacIntyre and Bernard Williams among them) have found him to be important in other ways relating to their own interests and concerns, but have provided only limited readings of him that do not begin to do justice to the full range of his philosophical thinking.

While bits and pieces of Nietzsche can be and have been used to justify these and other such characterizations and interpretations, it has long seemed to me that Nietzsche is best conceived rather differently than in any of these ways: namely, as a kind of "naturalistic" thinker, broadly construed. That was one of the general themes of the first of my Nietzsche books (my 1983 *Nietzsche*),[3] as well as the leitmotif of my second (*Making Sense of Nietzsche*),[4] and that is true of this one as well. Both what I mean by this and my case for it (as a general characterization of Nietzsche's thought) receive a further elaboration and defense here.

My own general characterization of Nietzsche as a "naturalistic" or "naturalizing" thinker of course needs to be filled in, elaborated, and supported if it is to be meaningful and more persuasive than any of the others mentioned and on offer—including others going by the same name. That is what I mean to be doing in this book, in a variety of ways. And I mean to be taking my cues from what we find Nietzsche saying and doing in his philosophical works, both comprehensively and more specifically read and considered.

Indications of the general character and agenda of his philosophical thinking are provided by Nietzsche himself in the vivid language he uses to title his books and label some of his chief concerns. Summarizing his thought in his own (German) terms, in a single sentence, I would say the following of it: It centers on the *entgöttlicht* reconsideration of the *Menschlich*, in the aftermath of the *Tod Gottes* and in the *Dämmerung* of all *Götzen*, with close attention to both the ubiquity of the *Allzumenschlich* and the possibility of the *Höher-* and *Übermenschlich*, in the intellectually *redlich*, philosophically sophisticated, and dis-"illusioned" manner of the *Freigeist* and *fröhlichen Wissenschaftler*, and the likewise positively de-"moralized" manner of one who is *Jenseits von Gut und Böse*, at once *Antichrist* and *Antinihilist*, and who recognizes that everything about human reality and valuation has a *Genealogie* and now requires *Umwertung*— all by way of preparing the way for a *Philosophie der Zukünft* that would further contribute not only to the better *Erkennen* and *Begreifen* of human reality and possibility but also to *Wertschaffen*, to *Lebenserhöhung*, and to the kind of *Lebensbejahung* that finds expression in his *Zarathustra*.

But what does all of this mean? One could simply translate Nietzsche's German terms and say, reasonably and correctly enough, that what it means, in English, is this: Nietzsche's kind of philosophical thinking centers on the *de-deifying* reinterpretation of the *human*, in the aftermath of the *death of God* and in the *twilight* of all *idols*, with close attention to both the ubiquity of the *all-too-human* and the possibility of the *higher* human and *supra-human*, in the intellectually conscientious, philosophically sophisticated, and positively dis-"illusioned" manner of the *free spirit* and *joyful inquirer*, and the likewise positively de-"moralized" manner of one who is *beyond good and evil*, at once *anti-Christian* and *anti-nihilistic*, and who recognizes that everything about human reality and valuation has a *genealogy* and now requires *revaluation*—all by way of preparing the way for a *philosophy of the future* that would further contribute not only to the better *comprehension* of human reality and possibility, but also to *value creation*, to *life enhancement*, and to the kind of *life affirmation* that finds expression in his *Zarathustra*.

But the fact that Nietzsche's German terms have English counterparts that generally suffice for translational purposes, and the fact that his German terms have commonly accepted German meanings and (at least in some cases) recognizable philosophical uses, even together, do not take us very far. Neither of these facts implies that those who can make appropriate sense of the sentences in the English translations of his writings they read, or even also knows enough German and enough about German philosophical usage, know all they need to know to understand Nietzsche's philosophical thinking, concerns, and undertakings. That further requires, at a minimum, an intimate familiarity with the whole range of his published writings that bear upon any given topic or issue, and with his own uses of the terms in question (and others related to them)—preferably in his German as well as in translation—which often take on meanings that are quite distinctive and differ significantly from those of standard usages and common renderings.

In short: what is needed is not only a comprehensive interpretation of his thought, but also two sorts of readings of his writings on which to base it: *extensive* readings of his various major overtly philosophical works, and *intensive* readings (mindful of his German) of what we actually find in them when we look at what he explicitly says with respect to more or less specific topics and broader issues in the range of works in which he deals with them. That is my project here.

This book begins with a prologue (chapter 1), in which I elaborate upon the previous paragraphs. It is followed by a series of five chapters, each focusing on one of Nietzsche's most important works: *Human, All Too Human*; *Joyful Inquiry*; *Thus Spoke Zarathustra*; *Beyond Good and Evil*; and *On the Genealogy of Morality*, with an eye to what they say and show about his kind of philosophy at those junctures. *Zarathustra* is a special case; but each of the chapters on the other four works includes both a general discussion of the work and a close examination of one (or, in the case of *Beyond Good and Evil*, several) of its parts, as a significant example of the kind of thing he does in it.

I then move on, in the second half of the book, to consider the appropriateness of a number of familiar rubrics that are often applied to Nietzsche's kind of philosophy, in the light of the understanding of it that the first half is intended to develop and cultivate—Nietzsche as nihilist? Existentialist? Individualist? "Free spirit"? Naturalist? Each of these discussions also serves as an opportunity to explore the aspects of his thinking that relate to the rubric in question.

My focus throughout is upon Nietzsche's philosophical thinking, primarily as it is to be encountered in a broad range of the writings that he either published or left prepared for publication. One thing I do not do much of in either part of this book is something I did quite a lot of in my 1983 *Nietzsche*: namely, cite and make interpretive use of relevant material that is to be found in Nietzsche's *Nachlass*. I continue to consider that material to be well worth discussing, but I consider it more important this time to make my cases for my readings without relying upon it.

Another thing I do not do here is to attempt an interpretation of Nietzsche's philosophical thinking as comprehensive and systematic as in that earlier book. I feel no need to do that again, because I consider that book to do it well enough—and to complement as well as reinforce the sorts of things I say and do here quite well.

The philosophical Nietzsche literature has grown enormously in the past half century, and has become not only vast but also profuse. Nietzsche's philosophical thinking and texts have come to be given many different sorts of treatments, just as they have been made use of in many different ways, within as well as beyond the philosophical community and its various post-Kantian traditions. One of my aims here is to provide readers with a broad text-based grasp of what he is doing and thinking that will enable them to cope with that burgeoning and diverse literature.

A third thing I do not do here is to take up and respond explicitly and specifically to various contributions to that literature on the matters I discuss. That would have been quite simply impossible to do in a responsibly thorough way in a book of this sort. As the (far from complete) bibliography indicates (and it is confined to monographs), everything I discuss in this book has been discussed by many others in the decades following the appearance of my 1983 *Nietzsche*—not only in monographs, but in the vast number of anthology essays and periodical articles published since then, which continues to grow.

Attempting to take explicit account of it all, or even of that fraction of it with which I am most in agreement or disagreement on various matters, would require turning every chapter into a book itself. Moreover, I have no doubt that, at least for many of the readers I hope to have, efforts along those lines would not have been appreciated, and would have been an unhelpful (as well as unwelcome) distraction. And they would have had the inevitable consequence of "datedness." (Books featuring extensive references to and discussions of that sort have a very short half-life.)

This book simply is not a book of that sort—a book that engages the broadly or very recent literature on some specific topic or aspect of Nietzsche's thought. As Nietzsche said of his *Thus Spoke Zarathustra*, in its subtitle: it is "A Book for All and None." Its sort of engagement is of a different kind, and is twofold. First: it is that of a would-be "educator" for those wanting to understand Nietzsche's kind of philosophy on its own terms—a guide who brings to this challenge a lifetime of engagement with Nietzsche's texts and thought.

And second: mine is the engagement of one who cares deeply about philosophy and its future, and Nietzsche's potential importance in that context—and who finds it worrisome that certain unhelpful tendencies in that very (recent Anglophone philosophical) literature are coming to be dominant and even normative. I refer in particular to the tendency to try to read and understand Nietzsche in terms of the conventions in the recent philosophical literature on various matters being debated as though he were a participant in them; and to the tendency to suppose that writing about any aspect or feature of his philosophy ought to take the form of "engagement with the recent literature" relating to it.

By its very nature, as well as overtly, this book is intended to serve as a call for a large-scale reconsideration of the character of Nietzsche's kind of philosophy, and of the suitability to it of what is often being done in its name. That includes the elevation to a norm of the above-mentioned kind of engagement, and the morphing of the understanding and pursuit of his kind of philosophy in the directions of models of analytic and scientistic thinking that are of dubious appropriateness to what we find Nietzsche actually doing. And the book is further intended to be read and understood as my own attempt to contribute to that reconsideration—in general terms, in the first chapter, and then by way of the two sorts of strategy pursued in the two parts of the book that follow it.

For those who have come to expect and prefer ground-level engagement with the literature, the similarities and differences between my accounts and others on offer that matter to them will not need to be pointed out. A number of the chapters were initially prompted by issues raised or positions taken by other interpreters, or were originally written for symposia to which others also contributed. I have for the most part reframed them here to make Nietzsche's treatments of the issues that concern him my focus, rather than what others have said about them. Discussions of these issues in the literature deserve to be read; but it is what Nietzsche himself says and does in his texts that are of abiding interest, and are most deserving of explicit attention.

I have tried to make my discussions of Nietzsche and the conclusions and characterizations I draw from them persuasive to others in philosophy who think and write about "Nietzsche as philosopher," and to those in other disciplines with interests in his philosophical thinking that are as serious as my own. Yet I also have tried to write in a way that will make the contents of this book accessible and engaging to readers of other sorts—to philosophers and students of any philosophical persuasion and orientation who have an awareness of Nietzsche as a "person of possible interest" to them, and to a wider readership as well, both within and beyond academia. That is because I consider Nietzsche to be a thinker and writer who both aspired to and amply warrants attention in all of these circles. (That, too, is worth bearing in mind, as one seeks to understand his kind of philosophy.)

My discussions are intended to keep the reader's attention on stages and aspects of Nietzsche's philosophical thinking as it is on display in his primary philosophical writings from *Human, All Too Human* onward, as seen through the prisms of my readings of them. It is my hope that they will continue to reward that attention for as long as such readings of Nietzsche on such matters are of interest.

This book has been a long time in the making. It is my hope that it will be a significant contribution to the understanding and appreciation of Nietzsche's kind of philosophy and philosophical thinking.

Explanations

Throughout this volume, I shall refer to Nietzsche's writings and designate citations from them by way of either abbreviations or acronyms of my preferred English-language renderings of their titles (see the following reference key). Nietzsche made it easy for those citing him in any language and edition of his works by numbering the divisions and parts of most of them, and (in his "aphoristic" writings) Arabic-numbering the "aphorisms" (as it has become customary to call the numbered sections—some very short, others quite long— of which most of his published writings consist). I use these numberings (as is common in the Nietzsche literature), rather than page numbers, to identify passages cited or referred to, resorting to using his section titles only where he did not number them.

I cite passages from Nietzsche's writings in English translation, sometimes my own but more often using as points of departure Walter Kaufmann's or R. J. Hollingdale's familiar translations. I retranslate portions when I deem different renderings to be preferable to theirs. (I have tried to keep my renderings consistent, at least within chapters; but they sometimes vary between chapters.) Where the exact words Nietzsche uses seem to me to matter to the understanding of what he is saying, and the renderings are my own, I frequently cite the original German words or phrases, to show what I am re-rendering (usually in brackets). At times, when it seems appropriate, I simply use the German originals in place of any English renderings, especially when they present translation problems, and I think readers will have become sufficiently well acquainted with them to understand them. (For example: *Mensch* and *Wissenschaft*.)

Nietzsche is very fond of emphasizing words when he wishes it to be understood that they are to be read with emphasis. In English that is most commonly done by italicizing. In Nietzsche's German, however, it is most commonly done by way of extra spacing between each letter of an emphasized word. That cannot be done here. Following common English-language Nietzsche-literature practice, I give his German words in italics when they are *not* to be read with emphasis, and use standard lettering when they *are* to be read with emphasis— the exact opposite of what we and I do when writing in English (as in the previous two clauses of this sentence). I trust that readers will soon catch on, and will read sentences cited in both languages with appropriate emphasis or lack thereof.

In the following reference key I provide a guide to the various short ways (acronyms or key identifying title words) of citing and referring to Nietzsche's writings that I shall be employing. My aim is to simplify these uses and mentions of his writings, making them sufficiently clear without constantly repeating the full titles of the works.

The German titles of some of Nietzsche's books have such obvious English renderings that they are used by everyone who translates them or refers to them in English. But that is not true of all of them; and as translations multiply (and those of Kaufmann and Hollingdale cease to be taken for granted), a variety of renderings of some of them are now to be seen. My choices are those I have (in some cases rather recently) come to favor, for reasons of both accuracy and aptness. In all cases it should be obvious to readers which of his books I am talking about, even to those who are accustomed to other versions of them. I have shown some of the greater variants in the reference key.

I would strongly recommend that English-speaking readers who have (or think they may come to have) a real interest in Nietzsche consider acquiring at least the first six volumes of the Colli-Montinari (De Gruyter) paperback *Kritische Studienausgabe* (Critical Student Edition) of Nietzsche's published writings, and keep it at hand—along with English translations of these works and a good German-English dictionary—as they read this volume (and, for that matter, as they read translations of his writings and other studies of them), even if their knowledge of the German language is minimal. (Making use of them is one good way of becoming more knowledgeable of and comfortable with the German language in general, as well as with Nietzsche's uses of it—which is of great value to anyone who is serious about understanding his philosophical thinking.)

The Colli-Montinari edition of Nietzsche's complete works is the authoritative "critical edition" of them in the original German. It exists in two versions. Both are published by Walter de Gruyter (Berlin and New York). The official hardcover and electronic version is *Nietzsche Werke: Kritische Gesamtausgabe*, commonly cited by the acronym "*KGW*" (*K* for Kritische, *G* for Gestamtausgabe, *W* for Werke, i.e., "Critical Complete Works Edition"). A much less expensive paperback version is also available, and is the print edition that is most commonly used: the *Kritische Studienausgabe*, commonly cited by the acronym "*KSA*" (*K* for Kritische, *S* for Studien, and *A* for Ausgabe, i.e., "Critical Study-Edition").

Note: In both of these versions, Nietzsche's original German spellings are preserved. They include some older spellings that are no longer in use, and have not been for quite some time. (For example: the word for "part" that Nietzsche spelled "*Theil*" is now spelled "*Teil*"; and his "*Morgenröthe*"—the title of the second work in his "Free Spirit" series that we know as "*Daybreak*" or "*Dawn*"—is now "*Morgenröte*") As is usually done these days, I use the modernized versions of the words in question, which therefore diverge occasionally for those that appear in the *KGW* and *KSA*.

Reference Key

The following is a key to acronyms, abbreviations, English titles, German titles, alternate English titles and original date of writing for texts referenced in this book.

Acronym	Abbreviation	Full Title (English, with German below)	Written
A	(None)	The Antichristian	1888
		Der Antichrist, published 1895	
		(aka The Antichrist)	
BGE	Beyond	Beyond Good and Evil	1886
		Jenseits von Gut und Böse	
BT	Birth	The Birth of Tragedy	1872
		Die Geburt der Tragödie	
CW	Wagner	The Case of Wagner	1888
		Der Fall Wagner	
D	(None)	Daybreak	1881
		Morgenröte	
		(aka Dawn, Dawn of Day)	
EH	(None)	Ecce Homo [Behold the Man]	1888
		Ecce Homo, published 1908	
GM	Genealogy	On the Genealogy of Morality	1887
		Zur Genealogie der Moral	
		(aka On the Genealogy of Morals)	
HH	Human	Human, All Too Human	1878
		Menschliches, Allzumenschliches, version/vol. 1	
HH	Human	Human, All Too Human	1879–80
		Menschliches, Allzumenschliches, vol. 2, incl. WS	
JI	Inquiry	Joyful Inquiry, Books 1–4	1882
		Die fröhliche Wissenschaft	
		(aka The Gay Science; Joyful Wisdom)	
JI	Inquiry	Joyful Inquiry, Book 5	1887

Acronym	Abbreviation	Full Title (English, with German below)	Written
SE	Schopenhauer	Schopenhauer as Educator	1874
		Schopenhauer als Erzieher, included in UR	
UDH	History	On the Uses and Disadvantages of History for Life	1874
		Vom Nutzen und Nachtheil der Historie für das Leben,	
		included in UR	
		(aka The Use and Abuse of History)	
UR	Reflections	Unfashionable Reflections	1874
		Unzeitgemässe Betrachtungen, includes SE and UDH	
		(aka Untimely Meditations; Unmodern Observations)	
TI	Twilight	Twilight of the Idols	1888
		Götzen-Dämmerung, published 1889	
TL	Truth	On Truth and Lies in a Nonmoral Sense	1873
		Über Wahrheit und Lüge im aussermoralischen Sinn	
		(aka On Truth and Lie in an Extra-Moral Sense),	
		unfinished and unpublished Nachlass manuscript	
Z	Zarathustra	Thus Spoke Zarathustra	1883–85
		Also Sprach Zarathustra	
		(aka Thus Spake Zarathustra), parts 1–2, 1883; 3, 1884;	
		4, 1885 (1892); part 4 printed privately by Nietzsche in	
		1885; published by his sister in 1892 (after his collapse).	
WS	Wanderer	The Wanderer and His Shadow	1880
		Der Wanderer und sein Schatten, included in HH II	
WP	(None)	The Will to Power	(1883–88)
		Der Wille zur Macht,	
		posthumously selected material from N.'s notebooks	
		of 1883–88; published by others in multiple editions,	
		beginning 1901	
KGW	(None)	Nietzsche Werke: Kritische Gesamtausgabe, ed. Colli and	
		Montinari	
KSA	(None)	Nietzsche Werke: Kritische Studienausgabe, ed. Colli and	
		Montinari	

Introduction

This book is intended to contribute to an understanding of Nietzsche as a philosopher, and of his kind of philosophy. Its first part, "Nietzsche Becoming Nietzsche," is preceded (in chapter 1) by a general discussion of the problem and task of coming to understand his philosophical thinking. I regard (and characterize) this chapter as a kind of "prologue" to what I do in both parts of the book. I then go on to discuss five of his most significant philosophical books—*Human, All Too Human* (chapter 2); *Joyful Inquiry* (chapter 3 and addendum to chapter 5); *Thus Spoke Zarathustra* (chapter 4); *Beyond Good and Evil* (chapter 5); and *On the Genealogy of Morality* (chapter 6)—and the "Nietzsches" (plural, even though related) that one encounters in them. These five works span the dozen years of his brief but intense philosophical life, and together represent much of the fruit of it. If there is anything deserving of being called "his kind of philosophy," it has to be found (and should be on display) in some or all of these books.

I believe that it is important for anyone interested in Nietzsche's ideas and his kind of philosophy (his kind of naturalism included) to have an awareness of the character and content of these major works from the outset, before coming to any conclusions about various ways of regarding and understanding him. Generalizations about the kind of philosopher he was and about his thinking need to be informed by attention to what he is saying, doing, and thinking in the range of these works. So my question in this first part of this volume is: What sort of philosopher does Nietzsche show himself to be in each of the works discussed?

There is no substitute, of course, for familiarity with each and all of these works themselves. For readers who are new to any of them, these first chapters should be particularly helpful, by giving at least a sense of each of them.

And for those who are acquainted (and even well acquainted) with them, those chapters should be useful as reminders of what Nietzsche does in them, as that bears upon the understanding of the kind of thinker we encounter in each of them, at their junctures in his brief philosophical life.

I

The first work I discuss, *Human, All Too Human* [*Menschliches, Allzumensch-liches*, henceforth *Human* or *HH*], was also the first of Nietzsche's overtly and self-consciously philosophical published works. Its first version (now its first volume) was published in 1878; two supplements to it, the second of which (*The Wanderer and His Shadow*) was initially published separately in 1880, were subsequently added (and became its second volume). The result was the version of the work as we now know it—double the length of its first version, and by far the longest of his books. It shows us the sort of philosopher Nietzsche had become—and in effect had made himself into—at that point, as he transitioned out of his identity as a classical philologist at Basel, and ventured into print, already quite sure of himself.

It was an auspicious beginning. The author of this relatively early work was also in some ways Nietzsche at his most engaging—and insightful. There has long been a tendency to read him backward, looking at his pre-*Zarathustra* philosophical writings and thinking through the lenses of his better-known (and considerably later) *Beyond Good and Evil* (1886) and *On the Genealogy of Morality* (1887)—and also with certain interpretations and appropriations of him in mind. But a very different Nietzsche comes into view if one can put all of that out of mind for a while, and look at this remarkable inaugural work with fresh eyes. It is a good way to begin a reconsideration of his kind of philosophy.

Unlike Nietzsche's previous writings (his early *The Birth of Tragedy* and the four monographic essays that followed it), and also unlike the works of most other philosophers, *Human* is an arrangement of hundreds of aphorisms (remarks or paragraphs on various subjects, few as long as a single page). It is also an impressive work, in size, range, and originality. Much of it is philosophical only in a rather broad sense, and a fair amount of it is not recognizably philosophical at all; but that is the sort of thinker Nietzsche was at that point, and to no small extent remained—his preference for an aphoristic style included. His kind of philosophical thinking was then (and subsequently) nourished by his thinking about a great many things relating to human life and human reality—many of them cultural, social, linguistic, psychological, and eventually human-biological and physiological as well.

The third chapter deals with *Joyful Inquiry* [*Die fröhliche Wissenschaft*, henceforth *Inquiry* or *JI*; commonly known as *The Gay Science*, the title of the Kaufmann translation]. The first four-part (or four-"Book") version of this work (1882) was the culminating work of Nietzsche's "free spirit" [*Freigeist*] series of writings, and of his pre-*Zarathustra* philosophical development. (A fifth part or "Book," resuming the project of the earlier work, was added to an expanded version of it five years later, and is discussed in an addendum to chapter 5, on *Beyond Good and Evil*, just after which it was published and so with which it is usefully paired.) On its back cover he himself characterized the series (which began with *Human*) as having the "common goal" of presenting "a new image and ideal of the free spirit" [*ein neues Bild und Ideal des Freigeistes*].

But this work was more as well: a very important illustration of the kind of "free-spirited" philosophizing that Nietzsche had come to both advocate and undertake as his own by that point in his intellectual and philosophical development. Its third part or "Book" is of particular importance because of his explicit coupling of the "death of God" idea and phenomenon with the ideas and tasks of both the de-deification (*Entgöttlichung*) of our understanding of "nature" and the "naturalizing" (*Vernatürlichung*) of our interpretation of our human reality ("*uns Menschen*" [us humans])—which he then proceeds to illustrate.

The title Nietzsche gave this book, *Die fröhliche Wissenschaft*, suggests that it may be appropriate to characterize his kind of philosophy at this point as a kind of "*Wissenschaft*"—commonly translated as *science*, but really meaning "cognitive inquiry or discipline" more generally. It is a rubric that embraces a wide variety of kinds of inquiry and thinking, exemplified for him not only by what "scientists" as we ordinarily think of them do (in the "natural sciences" in particular), but by such disciplines as history, mathematics, and his own previous field (classical philology), as well as philosophy—and so, for him, what *he* does in that work itself.

Its actual title, *Die fröhliche Wissenschaft*, is something of a mystery. It may have been suggested to him by an Italian phrase, *la gaya scienza*, associated with the late-medieval poet-minstrel troubadours, which did not appear in the work's first edition, but which he added on the title page of its second edition, perhaps as a kind of resonant or playful epigraph. In any event, it inspired what has become the commonly used English version of its title, *The Gay Science* (as Kaufmann rendered it in his generally favored translation). But that warrants comment, and needs parsing.

The *Wissenschaft* (literally, "knowledge craft") we encounter in this work is Nietzsche's enlightened, secular, post-metaphysical "naturalizing" kind of philosophical thinking at this point in its development (natural-science-allied but not -driven). And by characterizing it as *fröhlich* [joyful], he contrasts its high-spiritedness with the grimness of the Schopenhauerian pessimism and other philosophical tendencies he was seeking to counter. I have chosen to render its title in English as *Joyful Inquiry*, because the kind of inquiry we encounter Nietzsche pursuing here is not for the most part of the "scientific" sort at all, as that term has come to be understood. Rather, this "*Wissenschaft*" is chiefly knowledge-pursuing inquiry of several other sorts (which our word "science" therefore misrepresents). "*Wissenschaft*," both in German and for Nietzsche, includes the sciences, but does not simply mean "science." It means knowing-directed inquiry more generally.

Nietzsche's monumental four-"part" [*Teil*] *Thus Spoke Zarathustra; A Book for All and None* [*Also Sprach Zarathustra*, 1883–85; henceforth *Zarathustra* or *Z*], and the kind of thinker he shows himself to be in it, obviously warrant careful attention. I give it that attention in chapter 4, in which my focus is not upon all of the many things Nietzsche has Zarathustra *say* and *undergo* here, but rather on what more broadly Nietzsche as the work's creator is *doing* here. This is a work—a literary-philosophical creation—very different from the others; and it stands in a different relation to his philosophical thinking and concerns than the others do. To the very end, Nietzsche considered it to stand apart from, and above and beyond, all the rest—as he makes clear by the singular extravagance of what he says about it in his reflections on each of his books (in "Why I Write Such Good Books") in *Ecce Homo*.

Nietzsche does give literary expression to some of his philosophical ideas in the course of *Zarathustra*'s four parts, and applies some of them to a wide range of human phenomena and human situations. Yet its philosophical content, conceived as analytical and interpretive thinking, does not seem to warrant his own very high estimation of its importance. That importance, as he conceived of it, would not seem to be of the same sort as that which he accorded to any of his other, more straightforwardly philosophical works, ideas, analyses, critiques, and interpretations.

In this chapter I attempt to illuminate its different sort of importance—for Nietzsche, and perhaps for us as well. If I had given this chapter a subtitle, it would have been "Nietzsche as Educator," echoing the title and basic idea of his most philosophically interesting early monograph, *Schopenhauer as Educator*. But it also has to do with something more: namely, his attempt to *engage in* the very sort of activity that he contends, in his very next book (*Beyond Good and Evil*), is to distinguish the "future philosophers" he envisions from the kind of "free-spirited philosopher" he had been up to this point. The difference has to do with what he calls "value creation" (and promotion); and what that requires and involves is *sensibility transformation*, of the sort that *Zarathustra* is intended both to exemplify and itself to foster.

Beyond Good and Evil [*Jenseits von Gut und Böse*; henceforth *Beyond* or *BGE*] and its author are the subjects of chapter 5. Nietzsche published nothing other than *Zarathustra* in the interval between the first edition of *Joyful Inquiry* (1882) and this work four years later (1886). During those intervening years, however, in addition to writing the four parts of *Zarathustra*, he also amassed a wealth of material in his notebooks that he drew upon extensively in the flurry of writings he published or readied for publication in the final three years prior to his collapse in January 1889. It was with *Beyond* that he resumed his more straightforwardly philosophical writing.

In this book Nietzsche undertook to reflect upon both the kind of philosopher he had been and the kind of "philosopher of the future" he saw a need for, who would be that kind of ("free-spirited") philosopher *and more*, as is hinted by its subtitle: "Prelude to a Philosophy of the Future." Its main title (*Beyond Good and Evil*) signifies not only a repudiation of the sort of morality that is based on a good-versus-evil dichotomy, but also of a moralizing approach to philosophical interpretation and evaluation more generally. That work is therefore obviously a key text for the topic of Nietzsche's kind of philosophy—particularly in view of the fact that so little time remained to him to develop and pursue it.

Beyond is also of great importance for the understanding of Nietzsche's "will to power" idea, about which he has more to say here than he does in any of his other post-*Zarathustra* published writings. It also is in this work that he makes at least a beginning of a moral philosophy that reflects non-polemically and philosophically upon morality and moralities, both as human phenomena and with an eye to their actual and possible uses—to both the detriment and the enhancement of human life. In that respect *Beyond* comes closer to indicating the kind of moral philosophy that he would have replace what has previously passed for "moral philosophy" than he does anywhere else—including his *Genealogy*. And he also makes the beginning of an attempt to develop a new sort of political philosophy, revolving around a much broader conception of the political than his rather conventional previous conception had been—and a beginning of its practical application that is both problematic and disconcerting.

It is what Nietzsche has to say about what he has in mind with respect to the "*and more*" of the "new philosophers" and "philosophy of the future" in relation to the kind of philosopher and philosophy that he had previously been preaching and attempting to practice, however, and that underlies that broader conception and its application, that matters most for my purposes in this book. And it is what I have to say about that question—both in this chapter and in chapter 10—that may pose the most interesting problem with respect to his kind of philosophy: What should we make of it?

The philosophically productive time remaining to Nietzsche after *Beyond* really amounted to little more than the next year (1887). The increasingly frantic final year that followed was devoted to a remarkable but philosophically thin series of polemics, as Nietzsche sought one last time to settle scores with targets that his previous efforts had not sufficed to lay to rest—Christianity, Wagner, and a host of philosophical and cultural "idols" from Socrates to the fads and fashions of his own day. And then, perhaps sensing that his time was running out, he literally dashed off (in a mere three weeks!) the brief review of his life and works that is his philosophical-autobiographical *Ecce Homo* [*Behold the Man*—namely, himself].

But 1887 was a remarkably and importantly productive year for Nietzsche. It included substantial new prefaces to all of his pre-*Zarathustra* books, and a resumption of the project of *Joyful Inquiry*, in the form of an important fifth "Book" (part) he added to the initial four (along with a new preface). The best known (and arguably most important) of his late works, however, was a book of the same year that Nietzsche characterized both as a sequel to what he had to say about morality and moralities in *Beyond* and (in its subtitle) as a kind of "polemic": *On the Genealogy of Morality* [*Zur Genealogie der Moral*; henceforth *Genealogy* or *GM*]. This work and its author are the subjects of chapter 6, the last chapter in the first part of this book. It is in some respects the most impressive of Nietzsche's books, both philosophically and psychologically speaking. It consists of three "essays"—and they are actual essays (designated as such—*Abhandlungen*) rather than topically grouped sets of aphorisms, even though he numbers their sections in a somewhat aphoristic way.

In these essays we see Nietzsche pursing several central topics on his emerging philosophical agenda in a more sustained manner than is on display anywhere else in his mature philosophical writings. They pertain both to his manner of reckoning with certain types of broadly "moral" (or moral-psychological) phenomena, and to his thinking with respect to the intersection of the investigation of these phenomena and his kind of philosophical anthropology. (By that I mean: his project of a naturalizing but also historically developmental reinterpretation of human reality.) They were intended to help prepare the way "genealogically" for his "revaluation of values" (and more specifically of moralities and their valuations), which he left barely begun. But they themselves are not what he meant by the "revaluation" of the "moralities" and "moral" phenomena he selects for discussion. They exemplify important parts of his philosophical thinking with respect to such phenomena, and to human reality more generally; and as such they are among the best guides to its understanding we have.

These five chapters are by no means the whole story of "Nietzsche Becoming Nietzsche" as I would have that phrase understood. They are important parts of a larger story. For additional parts of it, I would refer interested readers to my similar discussions of several of his other works that I believe also to be of considerable significance for the understanding of his kind of philosophy.[1]

II

I have given the second half of this book the title "Nietzsche Becoming—What?" In its five chapters a variety of rubrics are discussed, which are commonly (but very differently) thought to be apt characterizations of Nietzsche's thinking. These are framed as discussions of questions posed by these labels: "Nihilist?" "Existentialist?" "Individualist?" "Naturalist?" And (Nietzsche's own contribution to the list) "*Freigeist* [Free Spirit]?"—an expression that, in his hands, becomes a kind of stage name for *fröhliche Wissenschaftler*.[2]

My general question in this second part of the book is: To what extent does Nietzsche show himself to be a kind of philosopher to whom one or another of these familiar labels may appropriately be applied—and if so, how so? My readings of Nietzsche in relation to the aptness of these diverse characterizations suggest varying verdicts (mainly and decidedly mixed). But I believe the questions to be worth asking and addressing, because the explorations of these questions here, taken together, are helpful in pursuing the larger questions of Nietzsche's kind of philosophy, and of the kind of philosopher he both called for and attempted to be—as well as useful, in the cause of laying to rest certain commonplace distortions that impede their understanding.

The first of them (chapter 7, "Nietzsche as Nihilist?") begins with a succinct statement of my understanding of Nietzsche on the "Nietzsche and nihilism" question. My basic point is that the answer to the question of whether "nihilism" is an appropriate and helpful rubric with which to frame and characterize Nietzsche's philosophical thinking is neither yes nor no—or rather, it is both. In a nutshell: I take him to be a nihilist with respect to absolutes of any sort, but not more generally. On the contrary: I consider him actually to be a kind of modest (non-absolutist) *realist* and *cognitivist* in many domains and contexts, for whom there is much about and within the bounds of human reality that admits of comprehension, and a good bit about the world in which we find ourselves as well.

I then proceed to make a case for that understanding of him by undertaking a substantial review of what he is doing (and saying, with respect to knowing and knowledge) in his philosophical writings from beginning to end—thereby showing him to have been nothing like a radical nihilist for whom there are no tenable versions of the very ideas of "reality," "truth," and "knowledge," at any point along the way. (I further observe, or at any rate contend, that the same sort of case—mutatis mutandis—could be made against his construal as the same sort of radical nihilist with respect to all versions of the very ideas of value and meaning, his anti-*metaphysical* nihilism in all such matters notwithstanding.) This review also provides an occasion to comment usefully on the various philosophical tasks he takes on in the course of these writings—which is very relevant to my general topic in this book.

I next (in chapter 8, "Nietzsche as Existentialist?") pose and respond to the same sort of question with respect to the rubric(s) of "existentialism" or "*Existenz*-philosophy." The former was the then-popular rubric used to reintroduce Nietzsche to the post–World War II generations both in the Anglo-American world and in Europe; and as an antidote to his appropriation by the Nazis and Fascists in the previous generation and its widespread acceptance by their opponents, it was strategically useful. The idea of its appropriateness lingers on; and it is an idea that is well worth addressing. What kind of "existentialist" or "existential philosopher," if any, does Nietzsche show himself to be? Answering this question requires a consideration of the character of existentialism and its more substantial parent *Existenz*-philosophy (philosophy of human "existing"), and then of Nietzsche's concerns and thinking, to see whether the shoe fits. It also requires a contrasting preliminary statement of my sense of how and what Nietzsche thinks philosophically, to the extent that these matters admit of this sort of generalization and summarization.

The next chapter (chapter 9, "Nietzsche as Individualist?") takes up the question of whether (as is often supposed) the rubric of "individualism" comes any closer to capturing the thrust of Nietzsche's thinking with respect to human reality, and more specifically with respect to his conception of the "higher" sort of humanity of which he often speaks (and has Zarathustra speak). Nietzsche is often thought to have championed a highly "individualistic" type of human being and human life—sometimes conceived romantically, sometimes existentialistically, and sometimes fantastically (for example, of the sort subsequently popularized by Ayn Rand).

In this chapter the appropriateness of this idea in any such version is considered, and is shown to be a misunderstanding of Nietzsche's very real interest in the human possibility of various sorts of individuality, and in their assessment in relation to other sorts of human possibility. Human individuality, for him, turns out to be nothing intrinsically valuable at all simply per se, and when valued in that way is very much in need of "revaluation." However, he does consider some forms of it to be conditions of the possibility of the "higher" spirituality that is central to his conceptions of life enhancement and the *übermenschlich*, to which he attaches the greatest of human importance; while others are features of many of the expressions and forms that such "higher" humanity may take.

The penultimate chapter (chapter 10, "Nietzsche as 'Free Spirit'?") gives a reading and discussion of what Nietzsche has to say with respect to a rubric of his own providing: that of the *Freigeist* or "free-spirited" thinker. He himself applied it to the series of works of his pre-*Zarathustra* years that began with *Human*, and continued to employ it self-referentially subsequently (in *Beyond* in particular). In *Beyond*, however, Nietzsche also gives clear indications that it is a rubric that does not suffice to characterize the "philosophy of the future" to which (or of which) *Beyond* is styled a "prelude." And it further does not capture the character of the kind of "new philosopher" he had come to envision—and perhaps saw himself as anticipating, at least in aspects of his own efforts from *Zarathustra* and *Beyond* onward.

In this chapter I explore both this rubric (as Nietzsche himself employs it) and its limitations (as he had come to see them) as a possible way of framing and understanding his own kind of philosophy. I make the important further point that, even for the later Nietzsche, his kind of philosophy not only had been of that "free-spirited" sort (prior to *Zarathustra*), but expressly remained so—even as it became significantly more ambitious as well. I conclude by considering what more he would seem to have had in mind.

In the final chapter (chapter 11, "Nietzsche as Naturalist?"), I expand upon the topic of Nietzsche and naturalism that is broached on a number of occasions in previous chapters. This is an issue of the utmost importance for the understanding of Nietzsche's kind of philosophy, precisely because—on my view (and that of many others)—his kind of naturalism and his kind of philosophy, while not one and the same topic, are intimately related. The very fact that Nietzsche clearly shows himself to be *a kind of* naturalistic thinker in his writings from beginning to end also shows that he did not consider what he has to say with respect to truth, knowledge, nihilism, perspective, and interpretation to bar the way to any such kind of thinking.

The real question, therefore, is *what sort* of naturalistic or "naturalizing" thinker he was, with respect to human reality in particular. The central contention of this chapter is that Nietzsche's kind of naturalism, while intended to be science-friendly and scientifically informed, is also *not* to be understood *scientistically* (which is to say: taking its cues from the natural sciences, both methodologically and substantively). I then go on to flesh out the idea of his kind of naturalism that the rest of his thinking leaves room for, suggests, and in a sense requires, to do justice to the interest in and understanding of human reality and possibility that are on display throughout his writings. It is that very display that I take to make the positive case both for my reading of what the basic character of his kind of naturalism is, and for the extrapolation and elaboration of it that I offer.

Prologue

Toward Understanding Nietzsche

Hört mich! Denn ich bin der *und* der. *Verwechselt mich vor allem nicht!* [Hear me! For I am *thus* and *thus*. Above all, do not turn me into something else!]
Ecce Homo, Preface:1

Nietzsche ends the first section of his preface to his *Ecce Homo* with these words, italicized and with an exclamation mark. He certainly has been *heard*. But has his exhortation here been *heeded*? It is quite possible that no philosopher before or since has been so diversely understood—and, I would say, so often *verwechselt*, "mistaken," in the sense of mis-taken, "taken for" or turned into something else (for example: a fascist, an existentialist, a nihilist, a moral terrorist, a poststructuralist, a deconstructionist, and, more recently, a scientistic naturalist). And by this I mean not just Nietzsche the human being, and Nietzsche the thinker, but also his philosophical thinking. And beyond that, *his kind of philosophy*, which has been *verwechselt* far more frequently than he could have imagined.

To be sure, Nietzsche himself was partly to blame, owing to the manner in which he wrote, the excesses of his rhetoric, and the temptations to misunderstanding with which his writings are filled. But I would say that more of the blame lies in the readiness and even eagerness of so many of his interpreters—friends and foes alike—to see what they *want to see* in him, and in his "philosophizing" [*Philosophieren*], and to exploit him selectively and interpretively for their own purposes.

I have my own views concerning the general contours of Nietzsche's philosophical thinking, as it developed in the course of his brief philosophical life. I also have views on many of the things he discusses, as well as on the meanings of his many key terms and passages in his writings. I will not attempt to expound and argue for any of these things in this "prologue" (even though I will make some mention of them). That is what I will be doing, in several ways, in the rest of this book.

What I *will* be doing in this first chapter is something rather different, that should be of interest to anyone faced with the challenge of "making sense of Nietzsche" (the title of an earlier book of mine). I shall be talking about ways of *reading and using Nietzsche* that can help with this task. I will be distinguishing between several ways of reading him, and will be suggesting that what I call a *comprehensive reading* is needed—as an antidote to *all* of those "-ist" and "-istic" distortions of him, and as the key to understanding his kind of philosophy and his philosophical thinking.[1]

I

From the outset of his self-consciously philosophical writing, in the initial one-volume 1878 version of *Human, All Too Human* [henceforth *Human* or *HH*],[2] Nietzsche thought of himself as calling for, announcing, and attempting himself to become a *new sort* of philosopher, engaged in a *new kind* of philosophy. That is all the more reason why he needs to be read in ways that will help us guard against and counter the *Verwechsel*-ing he anticipated and feared.

Nietzsche's kind of philosophy was always a "work in progress." It emerged and developed over a very short period of time, and without the benefits—but also without the detriments—of anything more than a passing acquaintance with philosophy as the academic discipline it was in his place and time. He was, relatively speaking, a philosophical autodidact, who became seriously interested in philosophy as something he needed to *do* in the mid-1870s, attempting to equip and school himself to take on the kinds of issues and problems that had come to matter to him. He had come to realize that these issues and problems were (broadly speaking) philosophical in nature. And he carried on his philosophical reformation and self-education both in private (in notebooks he began to keep very early on) and in public (in print), beginning overtly with that first installment of *Human* that appeared in 1878 (begun two years earlier), while he was still a philologist academically at Basel, six years after his pre-philosophical but philosophically auspicious first book *The Birth of Tragedy* [1872; henceforth *Birth* or *BT*]. But those efforts and this development ended all too soon, with his career-ending collapse less than a dozen years later.

My question here, briefly put, is this: how can we best go about trying to understand Nietzsche as a philosopher—of *his kind of philosophy*, and of *his philosophical thinking*? And my first suggestion is that a good way to begin is with Nietzsche himself. How can we *make use of him* to help us *make sense of* him? The obvious general answer to this question is: by looking at and paying attention to both *what he tells us about* his writings and thinking, and also *what he shows us*. But how would he have us follow his injunction not to *verwechsel* him as we do so? His explicit answer is, in a way, very simple: he wants us to *read him*.

But what he means by that is not so simple. He wants us to *learn to read him*, in *the ways* that he *needs to be read* in order to be understood, fully and justly. In short: he wants us to *learn* to read him *"well"* [gut]. So he exhorts us, at the end of his 1886 preface[3] to *Daybreak* [*Morgenröte* ("D")]: *"learn* to read me well" [lernt *mich gut lesen*]. That is, he says: learn to *"read well"* [gut *lesen*]—as his first discipline, philology, teaches one to do. And he parses *gut lesen* here as: "to read slowly, deeply, looking cautiously before and aft, with reservations, with doors left open, with delicate eyes and fingers" (*D* P:5). To this he adds, at the end of his 1887 preface to *On the Genealogy of Morality* [*Zur Genealogie der Moral*; henceforth *Genealogy* or *GM*], that this kind of careful and thoughtful reading is both especially *necessary* and particularly *difficult* for readers unfamiliar with the "aphoristic form"—his own professed and favorite form of writing.

This difficulty is compounded by the fact that, while a good many of the numbered sections in which most of his books consist have the compactness and epigrammatic quality supposedly characteristic of aphorisms, a good many others do not. They instead are paragraph-length or even page-length *reflections* of a frequently related but also relatively self-contained nature. Yet even these longer reflections share with genuine aphorisms the characteristic of being distinct observations, rather than clearly connected sequential paragraphs in a sustained line of thought. They typically make (and sometimes elaborate) a *point* of some sort on some topic, but need (and are intended) to be thought about in conjunction with other points on the topic, both in the same book parts and elsewhere. This makes reading most of Nietzsche's books a very different experience—and challenge—from reading chapters in a typical philosophical monograph. And what makes understanding both his kind of philosophy and his philosophical thinking even more challenging is that he wrote no definitive treatises, and instead gives us almost nothing more than these bits and pieces, leaving it to us to try to figure out what to make of them collectively.

Nietzsche says, in his preface to *Genealogy*, that the required sort of reading is a kind of "art" or acquired skill; and "one thing is necessary above all if one is to practice reading as an *art* in this way [. . .]: *das Wiederkäuen*"—that is, *rumination* (literally, "chewing again"). By this he means: *chewing over* his many point-making remarks on various topics, in a given book's parts and elsewhere, trying to grasp their specific points and their collective upshot. And that is not the way most people read. Nietzsche underscores the importance he attaches to this thought both by emphasizing the words *das Wiederkäuen* and by making it literally his "last word" in this preface. It is a figure of speech, but it is a powerful and suggestive one. This is the kind of reading he says he hopes for and *needs*; and it is for that rare kind of reader, with that kind of intellect and conscience, that he is saying he writes. "Therefore," he rather ruefully observes earlier in the same sentence, "it will be some time before my writings are 'readable' " (*GM* P:8).

<h2 style="text-align:center">II</h2>

But *what* of Nietzsche's writing is to be subjected this "ruminating reading," and how? He does make one important comment and suggestion, earlier in this very same section of his preface to *Genealogy*. What he is doing and saying in this book—and presumably in his other books after *Thus Spoke Zarathustra* [*Also Sprach Zarathustra*; henceforth *Zarathustra* or *Z*] as well—should be "clear enough," he says, if "one has first read *my earlier writings*," with suitable care and close attention (*GM* P:8; emphasis added).

This is a significant point. One of the most important things one needs to do, to understand both Nietzsche's thinking and his kind of philosophy, is to bear in mind what he says and does in his *pre-Zarathustra* works, when reading his *post-Zarathustra* works from his last few years. And he quite certainly is referring here not only to *The Birth of Tragedy*, but even more importantly to what he called his "*Freigeist*" or "free spirit" series, from the first volume of *Human* to the first version of *Joyful Inquiry* [*Die fröhliche Wissenschaft* (1882); henceforth *Inquiry* or *JI*].[4]

Moreover, I suggest, one should *try not* to read these earlier books through the optics of Nietzsche's later writings. They should be read on their own, as points of his previous arrival, as well as points of departure that his later works presuppose. And they also should be read both for what he *says about* the kind of philosopher he is trying to be, *and* to see the kind of philosopher *he shows himself to be* at each of those points, from *what he does* in the books in question. For the kind of philosopher he *shows himself to be* is of crucial importance to the understanding of what he *means* by the terms and phrases he uses. (For example: what he means by the "historical philosophizing" [*historische Philosophieren*] he calls for at the outset of *Human* is shown and exemplified by what he chooses as his topics in the rest of the volume, what he does with them, and how he does it. And what he *means* by "*uns Menschen zu* vernatürlichen" [to *naturalize* ourselves] at the outset of Book 3 of *Inquiry* [*JI* 109] is likewise shown and exemplified by what he goes on to discuss and pursue in the rest of that Book[5] and work.)

Each of Nietzsche's major post-*Zarathustra* writings, I further suggest, should be read and interrogated in this way as well—not just for the specific content of the various things he discusses in them, but also for what *they* each reveal about the kind of philosopher he *took himself* and *shows himself* to be. I have in mind, in particular, *Beyond Good and Evil* [1886; henceforth either *Beyond* or *BGE*], the added fifth Book of *Inquiry* (1887), *Genealogy* (1887), and *Twilight of the Idols* [1888; henceforth *Twilight* or *TI*]. None of these works and instances of Nietzsche as philosophical author, by themselves, is definitive of his kind of philosophy; but they all must be taken into account. All of these "authors" are "Nietzsche"; but they are not all of the same mind, and their differences as well as their similarities are well worth noting—and ruminating.

This kind of attention to the full range of Nietzsche's major philosophical works is a part of what I mean by a *comprehensive reading* of him as a philosopher. But there is more to it than that. I will now indicate what I take to be other parts of it—which might also be thought of as other *resources* for understanding him and his kind of philosophy with which he in effect provided us. They all are differently problematic, but I consider them to be significant nonetheless.

Several of them are self-interpretive. Both the most fascinating and the most problematic of them (owing to the deteriorating condition of its author) is of course *Ecce Homo* (*EH*), Nietzsche's "last word" on himself and his books. (Its Latin title literally means "behold the man"!)[6] One certainly must read it, and take much of it seriously—at least as grist for the mill of his interpretation and understanding; but one certainly also should not accept it at face value, and as definitive and authoritative, in seeking to make the best possible sense one can of him as a philosopher. It is as much self-*presentation* as it is self-interpretation; but I consider it to be of value for the light it sheds on the question of what he saw himself—or wanted us to see him—as having tried to do in his various works.

Nietzsche also published and left for us a number of other self-interpretive reflections, rather similar in nature, but less problematic in this respect. I refer to the rich set of forewords (*Vorworten*) and prefaces (*Vorreden*) to his pre-*Inquiry* books that he wrote retrospectively in 1886, and with which he then continued to provide his post-*Zarathustra* books (including the expanded second version of *Inquiry*). These remarkable writings do not settle the question of how to understand him and his kind of philosophy in the works discussed; but I do consider them to be valuable reflections, which we are fortunate to have. Nietzsche clearly intended the retrospective ones to be read and heeded by future readers of those books, to help them—but also at times to try to *steer* them—in their understanding not only of his situations, concerns, and intentions in writing them, but also of their contents. For that reason, I believe that these prefaces, and the corresponding sections of *Ecce Homo*, are best read by those new to Nietzsche not *before* but rather *after* reading the books on which he is commenting.

III

At this point a general comment about reading and understanding Nietzsche is in order. Nietzsche did not provide us with treatises working out the main lines and details of settled positions on these matters. But he did much more than just state views and move on. He left us with a wealth of remarks and reflections relating to topics and issues that were on his mind and philosophical agenda—ranging from human reality and the world in which we find ourselves, to truth and knowledge, to morality and value, and to many and various *instances* of all of them—in his (mainly aphoristic) books both before and after *Zarathustra*.

It is very tempting—and is a temptation to which many of Nietzsche's interpreters and readers have succumbed, friends and foes alike—to hunt for and seize upon vivid and sweeping quips he makes—for example, "There is no truth," and "There are no facts, only interpretations"—and to regard them as positions and views to which he is committed, without qualification and across the board. But to understand him at all well, one must do the very opposite: namely, look at the *many* things he wrote—in his main philosophical works in particular—that relate to the issue or topic in question.

By this I mean not only things Nietzsche states expressly and directly about something or other—for example, about "truth," or "knowledge," or "morality," or "value," or "the world," or "*der Mensch*" [the human].[7] I mean also *uses he makes* of the associated language, and his comments and reflections on phenomena that fall within the orbits of these topics. And my point is that developing an understanding of him that does anything like justice to him as a philosopher is no simple or easy matter, achieved by reading a handful of passages on any such topic and taking them at face value. It requires exploring and taking into account this whole wealth and profusion of what he has to say that *bears upon* them in his various writings—and trying to get a sense of the breadth, depth, and character of *his thinking* concerning them, in both its broad currents and its more specific contours and applications. This is an argument for a *comprehensive* reading of him.

This comment applies not only to Nietzsche's writings before and after *Zarathustra*, but also extends, in a way, to that monumental work itself. There is nothing said on any topic addressed in that work that should be supposed to encapsulate Nietzsche's thinking concerning it. *Zarathustra* is at once very different from his other books (and from the kind of philosophical endeavors he pursues in them), and also significantly connected with his larger concerns and undertaking that found expression for him in both of those ways. Yet it is by no means clear what that connection is, and how both the kind of work *Zarathustra* is and elements of its content relate to the concerns of his *Freigeist* series (or to those of such earlier writings as *The Birth of Tragedy* and *Schopenhauer as Educator*), on the one hand, and to those of *Beyond* and subsequent writings, on the other.

What *is* clear is that, to the end, Nietzsche remained convinced of the importance of this work, both humanly and philosophically. And I would say that no account of his philosophical thinking can be considered to do justice to it that cannot make sense of that conviction, and of the human realities and possibilities that he puts in play in that work—of life enhancement, life affirmation, and value creation in particular. *Zarathustra* looms too large in the middle years of the brief decade of his philosophical life to be ignored. And it powerfully resists certain simplistic caricatures of his thought—even though it all too easily gives rise to others.

Zarathustra also is perhaps the most notable instance of yet another sort of resource Nietzsche provided to those who seek to understand him. In it he employs an idiom and literary devices quite different from those he employs in his more straightforwardly philosophical writings, to illuminate these and others of his most salient ideas that figure significantly in his subsequent writings. Other cases in point are the "Prelude in German Rhymes" with which he prefaced the 1882 version of *Inquiry*; the "Songs of Prince Vogelfrei" [which means "free-as-a-bird"], with which he concluded its 1887 expanded second version; the "Epigrams and Interludes" he placed in the middle of *Beyond*; and the "Aftersong" with which he concluded that work.

In this connection it is also worth noting that Nietzsche took *music* very seriously, both personally and philosophically, and made much of it as a human phenomenon of the highest order throughout his life. He loved music-making—piano playing in particular—and composed a remarkable amount of piano music in his early years, including a good many *Lieder* [songs]. Prose poems he called "songs" are central and climactic in *Zarathustra*. And Nietzsche often calls upon the phenomenon of music—and its artistic companion, dance—to serve as evidence and illustration of points he wants to make. His kind of philosophy, in his hands, and like his important conceptions of "the Dionysian" and "value creation," might be said to be animated by (in his phrase) "*der Geist der Musik*" [the spirit of music].

There is some aptness in Alexander Nehamas's choice of the phrase "life as literature" as the subtitle of his well-known *Nietzsche: Life as Literature*.[8] to convey what he takes to be the central theme of Nietzsche's thinking. But

I would say that "life as music" would be an even better choice for that purpose—
and it has the advantage of his having actually used the phrases "the music of
life" [*die Musik des Lebens*] and "insofar as life is music" [*insofern Leben Musik
ist*] in the course of explaining "Why we are no kind of idealist" [*Warum wir
keine Idealisten sind*] (*JI* 372; see also *JI* 373). Here and elsewhere he delights in
making it clear that one does not understand him if one does not understand
that for him music is the key to some of the most important questions of both
philosophy and life. Knowing this about him and bearing it in mind is a paradigm instance of "making use of Nietzsche to make sense of Nietzsche."

IV

Next: there is, of course, Nietzsche's *Nachlass*—the great mass of written material he "left behind" (the literal meaning of *Nachlass*), much of it in notebooks
he kept, that has now been published in its entirety, and dwarfs the totality of
his books in word count. The questions of how to regard this material, and of
what uses can and should (and should not) be made of it, have long been debated. I consider it to be another problematic but valuable resource that can
contribute significantly to the understanding of Nietzsche's kind of philosophy.

In my 1983 *Nietzsche*, I made considerable use of some of this material that
had been selected and published after his death, and had become readily available at the time under the title *The Will to Power* in English translation. I subsequently became and remain much more cautious about making use of this
material; but I continue to subscribe to the basic tenets of the position on the
matter that I took in a paper published in my *Making Sense of Nietzsche*[9] (chapter 7) under the title "Beyond Scholasticism: On Dealing with Nietzsche and
His *Nachlass*."

My position, in brief, was and remains that, while the *Nachlass* material
settles nothing, and cannot be supposed to represent Nietzsche's *considered
conclusions* about anything, it also has considerable value for the light it sheds
upon *his philosophical thinking*, and the ways in which he approached and
grappled with the issues we find him dealing with in his books. As I like to put
it: the notebooks in which much of the *Nachlass* material is to be found might
be thought of as Nietzsche's "philosophical *workshop*," in which he carried on
his philosophical experiments, worked on his philosophical projects, and tried
out many ideas and lines of thought, returning to and reworking some drafts
repeatedly. Versions of some of it found their way into the books he published,
while much did not—although more might have, had his productive life not
been cut so short.

Nietzsche's very early collapse, in his mid-forties, left many unanswerable questions. They include: which sketches and drafts of ideas and lines of thought to be found in his notebooks would he (or even might he) have pursued and included in further books (the extensive body of material on "nihilism," for example), and which both was and would have remained abandoned (as some appears to have been). But there is one thing that may safely be said about what is in the *Nachlass*: it all was *something he was thinking about and thinking*—at the time he wrote it down, as he wrote it down, and when he returned to it to revise and rework some of it. And as such, it represents a further boon for those looking for *help from Nietzsche* to gain further insight into his philosophical concerns and thinking, and into his kind of philosophy, supplementing what can be gained from his published writings. Availing oneself of this material is a further part of the conception of a "comprehensive reading" of Nietzsche that I am advancing and advocating.

V

Another such boon Nietzsche might be said to have provided, for non-German readers who tend to make use of translations, is *his German text itself*—provided that they have a fair knowledge of German. This boon is greater for those who have an awareness not only of the dictionary definitions of German terms he uses, but also of their standard nineteenth-century German-philosophical senses. And it is greater still for those who have become acquainted with Nietzsche's ways of using German words and phrases that he not only utilized but seized upon and shaped to his purposes, giving them further meanings in his texts *as he chose to use them*. A few examples will suffice to make this point: *Wissenschaft* is an obvious one,[10] as are *Moral*, *Sittlichkeit*, *Genealogie*, *Übermensch*, *Wille*, *Macht*, and *Geist*.

Consulting Nietzsche's German texts is often essential to enable the reader or interpreter to correct for liberties translators have taken, and to see where and what problematic choices they may have made in their renderings of his German words. I will give a single example to drive this point home. The grand climax of Part Three of *Zarathustra* is the second "*Tanzlied*" [Dancing Song], with its famous and dramatic twelve-line (stroke-of-midnight) proclamation "*Oh Mensch! Gieb Acht!* [Give heed! That is: "Listen!"]," followed by its elaborating "*Ja- und Amen-Lied*" [Yes and Amen Song], each verse of which is followed by the refrain "*Denn ich liebe dich, oh Ewigkeit!*" [For I love thee, O eternity!]. Its central ringing message is that, "deep" as the woe and misery of life and the world is, there is something deeper still, that is capable of overriding it. What is it?

The word Nietzsche's long-canonical American translator Walter Kaufmann

used (followed by his British counterpart, R. J. Hollingdale) to translate Nietzsche's German word is "joy." This brings to mind—as Kaufmann meant it to[11]—
the "joy" [*Freude*] famously celebrated by Schiller and Beethoven. And that
state of intense delight is what generations of English-speaking readers have
supposed was Nietzsche's chosen candidate to bear the weight of his deepest
insight into the answer to the pessimism that gives the last word to suffering.
But what he names here is not *Freude*. It is—*Lust*! And while *Lust* has a derivative use meaning something like "delight" or "joy," its primary meaning refers not simply to *that* sort of pleasurable state that human beings are capable
of experiencing. It is a word naming a different sort of capacity altogether, an
instance of which is the kind of powerful sexual *desire or craving* that the word
"lust" now brings to mind in modern-day American English.

That word in English once had the same broader range that *Lust* still has
in German, and certainly still had in Nietzsche's time, covering powerful desires or cravings more generally—and designating *this* general sort of affective phenomenon (rather than any particular instance of it). And that is surely
a significant part of what Nietzsche has in mind here: *strong desire*—even if
also the kind of exhilaration that is associated with its avid pursuit and consummation. The kind of "joy" the German word *Lust* can be used to designate might be thought of as the state of delight that can *accompany* or be a
part of any sort of it *in full flower*, when something deeply and strongly desired is in prospect or being relished ("enjoyed" intensely). And, so understood,
it is reasonable to suppose that the *Lust* Nietzsche is invoking in that important moment in *Zarathustra* is that complex phenomenon, rather than (mere)
"joy." At the very least, the very fact that he chose to use this word (rather than
Freude or any other) is something one needs to be aware of, and ought to
prompt one to wonder what to make of it.

I might add that, in this instance as in many others, the translation word
choice makes an interpretive difference—just as it would have made a difference if the word Nietzsche had chosen to say what he meant had been *Freude*
rather than *Lust*. And *Lust* understood as the affective/experiential phenomenon of (powerful) *desire* (and its consummation) suggested above seems to
me to be a much more plausible candidate for the role he gives it in this passage than *Freude* would have been. For it names a very basic sort of human
capacity that can endow things with meaning, and can experientially override
and surmount the debilitating "woe and misery" to which it is here contrasted.

This illustrates the importance of checking the German and taking it into
account (if one is able to do so), and cases are legion. And this example not
only shows what a valuable and important resource Nietzsche's German can
be, but also argues strongly for those writing about Nietzsche to provide the

German words he uses together with their chosen English renderings. So, for instance, even if Kaufmann was determined to translate *Lust* as "joy," it would have helped—and been truer to Nietzsche as well—if he had made the lines read: "Joy [*Lust*], deeper yet than agony," and then—after "Woe implores: Go!"—"But all *Lust* wants eternity!" Because that would have made it clear that what Nietzsche is talking about here is *Lust*, the meaning of which—for Nietzsche here—needs looking into and taken very seriously, particularly in view of the tremendous importance it has for him, as that which makes ecstatic "life affirmation" humanly possible.

VI

Consulting the German texts of Nietzsche's writings that he himself prepared for publication is also essential if one is to be aware of what he did and did not emphasize, in the forms of emphasis and punctuation in use in German publishing conventions of which he extensively and at times creatively avails himself. He was very particular about these things. They frequently affect the ways he means what he is saying to be taken—which translators often do not even try to convey, and have difficulty conveying when they do. Moreover, if use is being made of *Nachlass* material, it is important for readers and interpreters to be aware of the extent to which the notes in question are well formed or fragmentary.

Paying close and serious attention to the German texts and Nietzsche's German is an instance of the different sort of reading that is commonly referred to as *close reading*, which the philologist in Nietzsche highly esteemed. But the primary instance of "close reading" is simply paying very close attention to the terms he uses, the ways in which he uses them, and the things he uses them to say, whether in analyses and descriptions or in interpretations, diagnoses, and explanations. I myself am an advocate and practitioner of such readings, *as well as* readings of the "comprehensive" sort. In my larger scheme of things, I maintain that Nietzsche needs to be read *both* comprehensively *and* closely with the *Wiederkäuen* [rumination] of which he speaks. But they are different sorts of *Wiederkäuen*.

The two together combine to constitute what might be called a *Gesamtlesen* or "total reading" of Nietzsche. But for certain purposes—such as mine on many occasions in this book and elsewhere—it is *comprehensive* reading that is most needed, with close reading in supporting and refining roles. It is particularly desirable to counter the supposition that he must be some sort of "-ist"—such as an "existentialist" or a "pragmatist" or a "deconstructionist" or a "naturalist"—and that what needs to be disputed and settled is *which one* of them (or some other such "-ist") he is, or most closely resembles. Nietzsche simply is not that kind of philosopher, of any sort.

This is something that it takes good comprehensive reading to make clear. At times he says things that make him sound like he is each and all of these things, and more; but that only shows that he actually is none of them. A comprehensive reading of Nietzsche, availing oneself of all of the resources I have noted, is conducive to a much more *nuanced understanding* of both his kind of philosophy and his philosophical thinking than is common among his readers and in the literature. It also makes possible a recognition that he himself was a much more *nuanced thinker* than he is commonly taken to have been.

A comprehensive reading is needed for other reasons as well. Nietzsche often announces or calls for certain philosophical *tasks and projects* that are intelligible in a general sort of way, but leaves open *how they are to be carried out*, and how they may need to be supplemented to do justice to their subjects and topics: "de-deifying" and "naturalizing," for example, and interpreting and reinterpreting, evaluating and revaluating, and the varieties of developmental and genealogical thinking and analysis that he calls for from *Human* onward. For Nietzsche those ancillary *implementing* questions are questions that cannot (or at any rate should not) be decided in advance, dogmatically or aprioristically, but rather must be worked out as such inquiries proceed.

VII

One thing more: I would contend that, to understand Nietzsche's thinking and kind of philosophy, one must consider more than his various *critical* proclamations with respect to things philosophers previously have thought and done, or commonly suppose and aspire to do. It is at least as important to take account of what he himself *goes on to say and do*, in his various writings contemporaneous with or subsequent to those stricture-suggesting passages. His practices are often at odds with what he might seem to be preaching, in his more radical-sounding moments. It is possible, of course, that he was simply a hopelessly incoherent thinker; but it is also possible—and, to my mind, more plausible and preferable—to suppose that it is not his settled intention to preclude as much as one might think; that his preaching is to be understood in the light of his practices; and that the tendencies of his developing thinking are best understood in the light of both.

This is another reason for reading him comprehensively—and, when doing so, being attentive to the sorts of things he offers throughout his writings as examples of what he has in mind; to the sorts of language he shows himself to be prepared to continue to use or to devise; and to the sorts of issues he shows himself to take seriously, post- as well as pre-*Zarathustra*, his pronouncements possibly notwithstanding. Reading him comprehensively is a crucial antidote to ways of understanding him and his pronouncements that are piecemeal, myopic, and therefore simplistic and misguided.

The philosophical Nietzsche I have come to know, through my many years of reading him comprehensively as well as closely, is certainly an adventuresome, unconventional, and at times distressing thinker and writer in a number of respects. But he is not as wildly radical in the main currents of his thought as some take him to be. He is, in short, a better, more sophisticated, and more deeply interesting philosopher than many suppose him to be. This Nietzsche is not merely an iconoclast who undertakes not only to demolish all philosophical idols, but also to put an end to the very idea of philosophy as a cluster of significant forms of *inquiry aspiring to comprehension*.

Nietzsche is fundamentally something more and different: a Nietzsche who would be both herald and inaugurator of a "philosophy of the future" that has a very substantial positive agenda, on the far side of the *Götzen-Dämmerung* (idols-waning) he heralds and promotes, the "death of God and all gods" he announces, and the "de-deification" of everything that needs it, beyond the awakening from the metaphysical dream of eternal truths and values and immutable essences and realities that he would have us renounce once and for all. And also beyond the seductiveness of the twin dangers that may seem all too tempting to those on the rebound from the loss of that dream: nihilism and scientism.

Nietzsche's kind of philosophy, as I have come to understand it, is or should be a powerful alternative and antidote to both of those temptations. It is a reconsidering, reassessing, reinterpreting, and revaluing kind of philosophy, which revolves around his strong interest in a number of large problems and issues, to which he returns again and again, in both his various books and his notebooks.

The general challenge Nietzsche attempts to meet is the challenge of rethinking human reality and the world in which we find ourselves, in a de-deifying, de-moralizing, and post-metaphysical way that makes the best sense we can of them and does the best justice we can do to them. And the broad central problem of his philosophical enterprise, as I see it, is *der Mensch*—the problem of *human reality and possibility* itself, supposing *der Mensch* to be a piece of nature and kind of living creature that has *come to be* all of the things it both generally and variously is, with all of the *supra*natural (that is: no longer merely natural) abilities and possibilities it has come to have. His kind of philosophy—his "philosophy of the future"—is the kind of multifaceted inquiry that will be needed for this task, and for the most to be made of it.

VIII

This anthropological optic, I suggest, provides a general frame for Nietzsche's rethinking of many of the other philosophical "problems" that remain, and to which he persistently returned, after setting aside various previous ways of conceiving of and dealing with them. One in fact is what might be called the problem of *die Moral*, morality and moralities, with "morality" being conceived as a variety of human phenomena—some pathological, others not—having a *normative* character, and with the concept and phenomenon of normativity itself an issue that needs to be rethought. Another such problem, of positive as well as critical interest to Nietzsche, is that of *religion*—that is, various religions and sorts religiousness, similarly conceived. And a third is that of *art*—arts, artists, and artistic experience—that is at least as multifarious, and as significant, as any other cluster of human phenomena.

Other "problems" of the same general sort are the problems of *value*—values, valuation, and value creation—that arise in a whole different way with the demise of the illusion of absolute values, and the more general problem of culture. On the other hand, Nietzsche was also powerfully interested in a cluster of problems of a very different sort, which arose for him in the aftermath of the abandonment of "metaphysical philosophy" in favor of the "historical philosophizing" that he calls for and attempts to undertake. These are the problems of what is now to be made of and done with the ideas of *truth*, *knowledge*, and *Wissenschaft*—and of the intellectual reality of the various emerging and developing *Wissenschaften* (cognitive disciplines).

To understand and appreciate Nietzsche's kind of philosophy, one must take his interest in all of these topics and issues seriously, as he pursues it and as it develops throughout the range of his philosophical writings. And that, I believe, requires both of the kinds of readings I have been discussing—comprehensive readings in particular, although supplemented by close readings.

I contend that a critical criterion of the viability of any interpretation of any aspect of his thinking is whether it can be *squared with* a comprehensive reading of him *that makes sense*. It should count against a proposed interpretation of some aspect of his philosophical thinking if it *does not fit*, at least in a general sort of way, with what he is saying and doing in his philosophical writings *after*—as well as before—the main texts on which that interpretation is most centrally based.

IX

The same is true, I suggest, with respect to a variety of broad *issues*, that arise both *for Nietzsche, in* his philosophical thinking, and *for us, concerning* his philosophical thinking. I will conclude by mentioning and commenting on two much-discussed cases in point (on each of which there are chapters below): the issues of Nietzsche's thinking as it relates to *nihilism* and to *naturalism.* These are commonly framed as the questions of whether he *was* (or *was not*) a philosophical "nihilist," and *was* (or *was not*) a philosophical "naturalist." I suggest that neither of these questions deserves a straight answer, and that the issues need to be framed differently—as the issues of "*Nietzsche and nihilism,*" and of "*Nietzsche and naturalism.*" These issues then resolve themselves into questions relating to what *he had to say* about "nihilism" and "nihilists," and *about* "naturalism" and "naturalists," and questions relating to what sort(s) of "nihilist" and "naturalist" he might appropriately be said *to have been* and to have *not been*—perhaps at different points in the course of his philosophical life.[12]

These issues and questions are good examples of those that call for a comprehensive reading of Nietzsche that extends to his notebooks—and, in particular, those from his post-*Zarathustra* years. (That is not something I do in the chapters on each of them below; but what I say in those chapters draws upon my having done so in my *Nietzsche.*) In the case of "nihilism," the *Nachlass* is where most of his reflections on nihilism are to be found. Their sheer quantity shows how very much it was on his mind during those last years of his productive life; and the tone of the relatively few mentions of it in his published writings of those years show how apprehensive he was about its advent as a cultural as well as intellectual phenomenon and philosophical stance. But his notes show him to be favorably disposed toward only some of its forms.

And we have more to go on, where the question of his own stance in relation to them is concerned, than just those notes and remarks. We further have the *stands he takes* on the matters at issue in his books, and considers (without explicit reference to it) in other notes. Moreover, we also have all that he is prepared to *go on doing* and *affirming* philosophically notwithstanding his seemingly nihilistic repudiations, showing that he does not subscribe to sorts of nihilism that would rule them out.

Nietzsche may well have been a nihilist of *some* sort; but he cannot possibly have been a nihilist of *all* of the sorts that he himself discusses, and quite certainly *was not* some of them in any settled way. To be able to say any more than this, of an all-things-considered nature about his apparent tendency, one must be guided less by particular pronouncements—especially in the notebooks—than by a very comprehensive reading of his published writings, sensitive to what he *is doing* as well as says he is doing, the language he uses, and the terms and concepts he employs, supplemented by the consideration of related notebook material sensitive to the same issue. These are matters I pursue in the first chapter of the second half of this book (chapter 7).

X

The "Nietzsche and naturalism" issue likewise can best be dealt with, I would say, in the same sort of way. The crucial question here, too, is: If Nietzsche may appropriately be said to have been *some sort* of "naturalist," or to have in effect subscribed to some kind of "naturalism," *what sort* of "naturalist" was he, and *what kind* of naturalism was *his kind* of naturalism? Or perhaps: what *kinds* (plural) of naturalism were *his kinds* of naturalism at various points along his way, from *Human* to *Inquiry* and onward? On my comprehensive reading of him, *his* kind of naturalism is not a *doctrine*, but rather a kind of broad surmise or *proposition* and a general *program*. His post-religious, post-metaphysical, *and* post-nihilistic conjecture and proposition is that everything that is *more than merely natural* is something that a piece of nature has *become*, out of its own resources, happenstances, interactions, and their resulting dynamics.

And his associated program? That, I suggest, was his multifaceted endeavor to make the best case he could for this proposition, notably by thinking up hypothetical but plausible accounts of how the crown jewels of our humanity—various human intellectual and "spiritual" [*geistige*] phenomena—could have originated and developed in that sort of mundane bootstrapping way. For their very possibility may be taken to show that these undeniably real human phenomena have no necessary supernatural or metaphysical presuppositions (and therefore implications) as *conditions of their possibility*—even if the specific accounts he suggests may be historically problematic.

Their point is to show that *some such* entirely this-worldly and even mundane developmental "genealogies" for such phenomena are conceivable, thereby obviating the need for anything of the sort to make sense of their emergence. Nietzsche's word for this program in *Inquiry* is *vernatürlichen* (*JI* 109): the "natural-*izing*" of our understanding of these phenomena, and so of ourselves as *Menschen*—of our human reality as a metamorphosis of our originally merely "natural" reality. And he leaves it entirely open for the exploration of such phenomena to determine how radically they have come to depart from those characteristic of the latter.

The kind of reading of Nietzsche that is needed to pursue this issue—the issue of his kind of "naturalism"—involves more than examining what he has to say directly, in his books from *Human* onward, about *der Mensch*, the "translation of *der Mensch* back into nature," and *der Mensch* as a creature that has "become" *what* it is and *as* it is in the course of human events. It is a reading that centers on his published writings, onward, but extends into familiarity with what he experimentally wrote and did in his notebooks as well.

Such a reading also involves taking account of things like what he means by a *Geschichte der moralische Empfindungen* [History of Moral Sentiments] (in *Human*), a *Naturgeschichte der Moral* [Natural History of Morality] (in *Beyond*), and a *Genealogie der Moral* [Genealogy of Morality]. It also needs to be informed and guided by *what* Nietzsche *does* in his reflections on these matters, and *how* he does it in these books. It should consider, for example, what he does (and how he does it) in *Inquiry* immediately after his call for *historische Philosophieren* at its outset. More broadly, it should involve taking account of all that he shows *his* kind of "naturalism" *does not preclude* him from treating as actual aspects of human reality and possibility, even though what is most significant about them is beyond the purview of natural-scientific comprehension and explanation.

A comprehensive reading of Nietzsche reveals the inappropriateness of imputing an austerely scientistic naturalism to him, his own occasional austere pronouncements notwithstanding. That sort of naturalism simply cannot be *squared with* too much that he says and does in both his earlier and his later writings, and so is quite simply implausible. A comprehensive reading makes it clear that his kind of naturalism—which he nowhere defines and articulates specifically—has to be thought of as an expansive and open-ended one, that does not presume to know or legislate the limits to the emergently possible, the range of concepts that their emergence may call for and warrant, and the sorts of values that their development may engender.

A conception of Nietzsche's kind or version of naturalism, if he can be said to have and advocate one, further must at the very least be reconciled with that part of his thinking that expresses itself in the attention and emphasis he gives to culture, music, and the literary arts; in the artistic-creative dimension of his conception of "higher humanity"; and in his idea of value creation and his *Zarathustra* project. And his naturalism should be understood as one that takes these human realities and possibilities as seriously as he himself does—which is to say: one that incorporates them without caricaturing them, draws upon them in its developing understanding of what human reality and possibility have become, and aspires to make sense of the fact that we have come to be capable of such things. (I elaborate upon that understanding of his naturalism in chapter 11.)

PART I

Nietzsche Becoming Nietzsche

The Nietzsche of *Human, All Too Human:*
A Book for Free Spirits

MENSCHLICHES, ALLZUMENSCHLICHES:
EIN BUCH FÜR FREIE GEISTER

Lack of historical sense [*historischem Sinn*] is the hereditary failing [*Erbfehler*] of all philosophers [. . .]. But everything has become [*ist geworden*]; there are *no eternal facts* [*ewigen Tatsachen*], just as there are no absolute truths [*absoluten Wahrheiten*]. Consequently what is necessary from now on is *historical philosophizing* [*historische Philosophieren*], and with it the virtue of modesty.
Human, All Too Human, I:2

Human, All Too Human is the monument of a crisis. It is subtitled "A Book for *Free* Spirits": almost every sentence marks some victory—here I liberated myself from what in my nature did not belong to me.
Ecce Homo, "Books," HH:1

With these last remarks Nietzsche began his own reflection—in his autobiographical *Ecce Homo* (1888)—on this remarkable collection of almost 1,400 aphorisms, published in three installments, the first of which had appeared in 1878, ten years earlier (*EH* "Books," *HH*:1). The crisis to which he refers was first and foremost a crisis of multiple dimensions in his own life. The first installment of *Human, All Too Human,* which he subsequently came to refer to as its first volume [*Erster Band*], was the product of a period of devastating health problems that necessitated his resignation in 1879 from his professorship in classical philology at Basel University. (Two supplements, which he initially published separately—as *Vermischte Meinungen* [*Miscellaneous Opinions*] and *Der Wanderer und sein Schatten* [*The Wanderer¹ and His Shadow*]—but subsequently republished together as its second volume [*Band*], appeared during the next two years.) *Human* also marked Nietzsche's transition from the philologist and cultural critic he had been into the kind of philosopher and writer he then began to be.

Fraught as that transition was for Nietzsche, the crisis to which he refers was above all a crisis in his personal and intellectual development; and although that crisis was very much his own, it presaged the larger crisis toward which he came to see our entire culture and civilization moving, in consequence of what he subsequently came to call "the death of God."[2] In Nietzsche's own case, this crisis was precipitated not only by his deepening appreciation of the profound and extensive consequences of the collapse of traditional ways of thinking, but also by his growing recognition of the insufficiency of the resources of both the Enlightenment and romanticism to fill the void. The three installments of *Human* are no less important for the insight they yield into the kind of struggle in which Nietzsche was engaged than they are for the many sparks that flew in the course of his efforts to find a new and better way to go on.[3]

I

I shall begin with some contextualizing. Nietzsche's mid- to late nineteenth-century European world did not appear to be a world headed for crisis. The ordeals, horrors, and dramatic changes of the twentieth century that were to come were largely unimagined (and indeed unimaginable), even to Nietzsche, who was far more prescient than most. (His prescience extended even to the point of his deeming the advent of air travel to be inevitable [*HH* I:267]!) In 1876, when he began working on the material that was published two years later in what is now the first volume of *Human*, Europe was again at (relative) peace. It had been ten years since the Austro-Prussian War that had left Prussia dominant in Central Europe. German unification under Prussian leadership had been achieved in 1871, and the new Prussia-centered German *Reich* appeared to be thriving, with Emperor Wilhelm I on the throne and Otto von Bismarck at the helm.

Everything seemed to be coming along very nicely for Western civilization in general, Europe in particular, and Germany more specifically. It was the heyday of European imperialism, with India recently incorporated into the British Empire, and much of the rest of the non-Western world coming under European sway. The industrial revolution was sweeping all before it, and capitalism was triumphant. New technologies and modes of transportation and communication were transforming Western societies. (Nietzsche himself must have been among the very first philosophers to own one of the newly invented typewriters—although owing to his failing eyesight it proved to be of little use to him.) Despite the success of conservative elements of European societies in retaining their social position and political power, forces preparing the way for their eventual dislodgement by more popular forms of social, cultural, economic, and political organization were gathering.

The physical sciences were advancing spectacularly; and while the influence of Karl Marx and Sigmund Freud had yet to be felt, the social and historical disciplines were maturing, and the biological sciences were coming on strong. Charles Darwin already loomed large. His *Origin of Species* had been published in 1859, and his *Descent of Man* in 1871. Germany, flush in its new identity as a nation and making up for lost time, was emerging as an economic, political, and technological powerhouse, as well as the world's new leader in many of the sciences. It also continued its century-long dominance in philosophy, with ever-mutating forms of idealism, neo-Kantianism, naturalism, and materialism competing in the aftermath of Hegel.

The basic tenets of Christianity and its morality were largely taken for granted. Various forms of the Christian religion, enjoying official state status in many countries and the unquestioning allegiance of the vast majority of their populations, seemed immune to serious challenge. The arts, literature, and music were flourishing as well, in Germany as elsewhere in Europe. In 1876 the frenzy surrounding the composer Richard Wagner rose to new heights, with the opening of Bayreuth, and the performance of the first complete four-opera cycle of Wagner's monumental *Ring of the Nibelung* (with Nietzsche in attendance).

Yet Nietzsche was convinced that all was far from well. He was repelled by the popular culture and blustering new social, economic, and political world burgeoning around him, and could no longer take seriously the intellectual and religious tradition associated with it. By 1876 he also found himself increasingly estranged from the newly fashionable alternatives to that tradition that its critics and rivals had been touting, including his erstwhile idols and mentors Arthur Schopenhauer and Wagner himself (in person). Everywhere he looked, even at those things and thinkers supposedly representing the pride of our culture and the zenith of humanity, what he saw was not only far from divine but—as he came to put it—all too human.

II

Nietzsche had long yearned—and continued to yearn—for a "higher" or elevated form of humanity with a worth great enough to warrant the affirmation of life even in the absence of any transcendentally supplied meaning, and the preponderance of the all-too-human. This yearning found its initial rather convoluted but impassioned expression in his first book, *The Birth of Tragedy* (1872). During the next few years, however, Nietzsche came to the hard realization that the attainment of such a higher humanity was by no means at hand, or even at all likely, unless something could be done to advance it—something more (and different) than had been done by Wagner, on whose operatic "rebirth of tragedy" Nietzsche had initially pinned his hopes.

He next gave this yearning another very different and more thoughtful—although again rather strangely framed—expression two years later, in his important essay *Schopenhauer as Educator*. His new answer, articulated quite eloquently in that essay, was dedication to the *enhancement of culture* (with Wagner demoted somewhat, from the status of savior to that of "exemplar" of cultural creativity and excellence).

But Nietzsche soon recognized that such dedication would come to naught without a new sort of "enlightenment," more sophisticated (and without illusions) in every way—scientifically and psychologically as well as historically and intellectually. The desired enhancement of human cultural life (and of human life itself) required an uncompromising examination of everything human and all too human that at once stands in our way and is our point of departure, and a soberly realistic stock-taking of what there is to work with in undertaking to foster that enhancement deliberately and wisely. The idea and ideal Nietzsche seized upon at this juncture, as his new form of intellectual conscience and inspiration, was that of the *Freigeist* or "free spirit," older and wiser heir of the Enlightenment. Nietzsche paid explicit tribute to the ethos of this newly adopted lineage in his dedication of the first edition of *Human, All Too Human* to Voltaire, Enlightenment thinker par excellence, who had died exactly a century earlier, and whose spirit he now embraced.

Human was Nietzsche's second actual book. (What is now another post-*Birth* book, which he published as such prior to *Human*, consists of four monographs from 1874 to 1876 that he later put together and published under the title *Unzeitgemässe Betrachtungen* [*Unfashionable Reflections*].) It was as far removed as anything could be from the kind of book professors of classical languages and literatures—which he still was at the time of its first appearance in 1878—were supposed to write. It was also something entirely different from anything Nietzsche had written previously.

It further was nothing like a conventional philosophical essay or treatise. (That is hardly surprising; for he had had no formal academic philosophical education and training.) As initially published, it consisted of nine titled groupings of 638 sections or "aphorisms" (as they have come to be called)—that is, brief quips and observations and short reflections—ranging from one or two sentences to a full page or two, of a relatively self-contained nature. This style was a radically new one for Nietzsche, reminiscent of the writings of such earlier observers of the human scene as Montaigne and La Rochefoucauld. He had long greatly admired their manner of thought and expression, and found himself drawn to emulate them, even if adapting rather than simply adopting their aphoristic style, in his search for a voice that lent itself both to his own changing temperament and circumstances and to the decidedly unphilological tasks toward which he was turning.

It would be unwarranted to assume that Nietzsche's recourse to an aphoristic style is indicative of the absence of any underlying cohesiveness and coherence of thought and intention here and subsequently. So he himself remarked, in *Human's* second installment, very much to this point (and no doubt to make it clearly): "*Against the Shortsighted.*—Do you think that something must be mere patchwork [*es müsse Stückwerk sein*] because one gives it to you (and has to give it to you) in pieces [*weil man es euch in Stücken gibt (und geben muss)*]?" (*HH* II:I:128).[4] His parenthetical "(and has to give it to you)" presumably is a frank admission that his severe chronic health problems made it impossible for him to think and write in a sustained fashion.

The publication of *Human* completed Nietzsche's estrangement from his erstwhile scholarly and academic profession, from which he officially retired shortly thereafter. It also completed his much more painful estrangement from Wagner, whose devoted admirer, champion, and intimate younger friend Nietzsche had been. Nietzsche himself claimed to have begun writing the book in reaction to the first Bayreuth production of Wagner's *Ring* cycle, the entire social spectacle of which appalled him, the cycle's extraordinary operatic qualities notwithstanding. And although he in fact would appear to have begun work on *Human* some months earlier, in the spring of 1876, it was readied for publication during a period in which his formerly close relationship to Wagner had become severely strained. Nietzsche actually was quite sure that Wagner would loathe the book, and its dedication to Voltaire was undoubtedly a very deliberate gesture of defiance and independence in Wagner's direction.

Remarkable as *Human* is, little notice was taken of it during Nietzsche's lifetime, to his dismay. Of the one thousand copies in the first printing of its original version, only 120 were sold in the first year.[5] And more than half remained unsold as late as 1886, when Nietzsche reacquired them and repackaged them with a new introduction as the first volume of the two-volume second edition. The supplement he published in 1879 under the subtitle *Assorted Opinions and Maxims* sold even more poorly: of the thousand copies printed, only a third had been sold by 1886. The second supplement, to which Nietzsche gave the title *The Wanderer and His Shadow* and also published separately another year later (1880), fared even worse: fewer than two hundred of its initially printed thousand copies had been sold by 1886. The two-volume second edition combining them that Nietzsche brought out that year involved no new printing, was a largely invisible event at the time, and generated few new sales.

There was no new printing of that new version—*Human, All Too Human* as we now know it—until 1893 (four years after Nietzsche's collapse), when a thousand copies were printed. And its sales remained slow even after others of his works began to receive more attention. It attained greater circulation and availability as part of the editions of his collected works that began to appear in the years after his death; but it was long eclipsed by *Birth* before it and by *Zarathustra* (1883–85) and its sequels after it, both in Europe and in the English-speaking world. The same is true of the other two works in Nietzsche's "free spirit" series: *Daybreak* (1881) and the 1882 version of *Die fröhliche Wissenschaft* [*Joyful Inquiry*, aka *The Gay Science*]. The appreciative readers he so hoped for were long in coming. It is small wonder that, when he resumed prose writing and publication after *Zarathustra*, beginning with *Beyond* (1886), he began raising his voice.

III

It had been Nietzsche's discovery of Schopenhauer's *The World as Will and Representation* (while browsing in a bookstore in 1865) that had introduced him—and began to seduce him—to Schopenhauer's kind of philosophy.[6] His spiritual seduction by Wagner three years later influenced him even more profoundly. The spell cast upon him by the two of them together is very apparent, both in his thinking and enthusiasms in *Birth* and in the fact that he ventured to write and publish such a book. Nietzsche's father had died when he was a young child; and he in effect adopted Schopenhauer as his intellectual godfather, and Wagner as his emotional and spiritual father figure. It was for good reason that it occurred to him to write, in *Human*: "Correcting Nature.—If one does not have a good father one should furnish oneself with one" (*HH* I:381). Yet by the time he wrote these words he was well beyond this point, attempting rather to *liberate himself from* the surrogate fathers with whom he had furnished himself.

   In his discussion in *Ecce Homo* of the "crisis" of which *Human* was the "monument," however, Nietzsche went on to say of it (in the passage cited at the outset): "Here I freed myself [*mich freigemacht*] from what in my nature did not belong to me." He had given *Human* the subtitle *A Book for* Free *Spirits* [freie *Geister*]; and he went on to characterize the "free spirit" in similar language: as "a spirit that has *become free* [ein freigewordner *Geist*] that has again taken possession of itself" (*EH* "Books," *HH*:1; see chapter 10 below). Among the things he clearly had in mind were his attachments to Schopenhauer and Wagner, who had been at the center of his intellectual life for the previous decade. They had been the subjects of his last two major publications prior to *Human*: the Schopenhauer essay (1874) and *Richard Wagner in Bayreuth* (1876)—in which he had lavished praise upon them even while privately beginning to distance himself from them.

At the time of *Human* Nietzsche was certainly not yet the philosopher he was to become. The author of that book, moreover, was indeed a kind of psychologist, both under development and at work, inventing a kind of psychologizing for which he found a wealth of applications all around him—socially, culturally, behaviorally, intellectually, even philosophically. And he further was simultaneously—and, for the first time in print, explicitly—inventing himself as a new kind of philosopher, capable of employing that sort of psychological analysis to fascinating and important philosophical effect.

The gulf that separates *Human* from Nietzsche's previous writings is wide. The enthusiasms, aspirations, and assumptions that so strikingly pervade and animate his earlier publications are no longer in evidence. It is a much more sober and analytical, colder and clearer thinker who is at work here. Its author was still hopeful of finding both a diagnosis and a cure to what ails our culture and threatens its future—and a counter to Schopenhauer's life-denigrating pessimism as well. Yet he was as disillusioned now with Wagner as he earlier had been with traditional religious consolations and their philosophical cousins.

Nietzsche had become convinced that only something like a continuation and radicalization of Enlightenment thinking, getting to the bottom of things and ruthlessly exposing all false hopes and dangerous palliatives, can show the way at least to the possibility of a future worth having and a life worth living. Nietzsche's dedication of the first edition of the work to Voltaire, the French thinker who was the Enlightenment's leading light, was more than a slap at Wagner (although it surely was that). It also was the announcement of a major intellectual reorientation, placing him squarely in the tradition of Enlightenment thought and effort, shorn of its optimistic new faith in rationality.

For the Nietzsche of *Human,* nothing is beyond criticism—and there is a strong suspicion that (as he would later put it) all "idols" of our reverence will turn out to be hollow and all too human when subjected to critical scrutiny. The new psychological tools he was developing are brought to bear upon them in it, with results that amply support this suspicion. But there is more than this to the outlook and way of thinking that he is devising and putting into practice here. In his early (1873) manuscript fragment *On Truth and Lies in a Nonmoral Sense*, Nietzsche sketches a fundamentally and severely naturalistic picture of our general human condition, in a world over which no benevolent deity reigns, and in which no beneficent rationality is at work. We are depicted as finding ourselves to be alone and adrift in a godless universe, a mere cosmic accident and fleeting incident, ill-equipped either to comprehend what is going on or to do much about it; and we are deluding ourselves if we think otherwise—although we seem almost irresistibly drawn to do so. Can we live without such illusions?

Nietzsche was at first inclined to doubt it—as one sees in *Birth*, written the year before. By the time of *Human*, however, he seems to have resolved to try. The power of myths and illusions to sustain anyone possessed of an uncompromising intellectual conscience is undermined when one sees through them; and so one may have little other choice—if (as for Nietzsche) a Kierkegaardian "leap of faith" is out of the question, and a Schopenhauerian negation of life is repellent. *Human* is a work of cold passion, in which nothing sunnier is assumed about our human nature and condition than the picture sketched in *Truth*, and in which everything in human life that might seem to be of loftier origins is called before the tribunal of scrutiny, with humbling results. Disillusioning critique is its first order of business.

Yet the spirit of the investigations Nietzsche undertakes in *Human* is profoundly and pervasively affirmative. The passion that drove them was not only that of an intellectual integrity that would tolerate no nonsense or groundless wishful thinking, but also of an anxious but hopeful search for enough that can be made of this life in this world to sustain ourselves despite all. To call this "secular humanism" would be to sell it short; for while Nietzsche's outlook is radically secular, he is far from taking humanity—either in general or as embodied in each and every one of us—to be the locus of intrinsic, unconditioned, and unconditional meaning and value. But it is a kind of tough-minded and yet doggedly affirmative naturalistic outlook, attentive to the humanly possible and meaningful as well as mindful of all that is creaturely and all too human in and about our humanity.

In short: for the Nietzsche of *Human*, if we are to make something worthwhile of life in the absence of anything supernatural to rely upon or appeal to, we must take a good hard look at ourselves. And this, for him, means many things. It means looking at ourselves in the light of everything we can learn about the world and ourselves from the natural sciences—most emphatically including evolutionary biology, physiology, and even medical science. It also means looking at ourselves in the light of everything we can learn about human life from history, the social sciences, and the study of arts, religions, languages, literatures, mores, and other features of various cultures. It further means attending closely to human conduct on different levels of human interaction, to the relation between what people say and seem to think about themselves and what they do, to their reactions in different sorts of situations, and to everything else about them that affords clues to what makes them tick.

All of this, and more, is what Nietzsche is up to in *Human*. He is at once developing and employing the various perspectival techniques that seem to him to be relevant to the understanding of what we have come to be and what we have it in us to become. This involves gathering materials for a reinterpretation and reassessment of human life, making tentative efforts along those lines, and then trying them out on other human phenomena—both to put them to the test and to see what further light can be shed by doing so. They are offered for our consideration tentatively rather than dogmatically. Each aphorism is a kind of experiment, as are the lines of thought that some series of aphorisms try out and explore. I will be examining one of the most notable parts of its first volume in the second half of this chapter, as an illuminating and important instance of what Nietzsche is doing here, and of how he is proposing to do it.

The multiperspectival and multidimensional manner of proceeding we see in action here, which Nietzsche employed with increasing dexterity and ingenuity throughout the remainder of his productive life, finds its first extended trials and applications in this work. The results are uneven, as one might expect—and indeed as is always the case in Nietzsche's writings (or, for that matter, in any such complex and adventuresome analytical, diagnostic, and interpretive enterprise). Among the hundreds of aphorisms in this work, distinguishing between genuine insights, on the one hand, and personal preferences, overgeneralizations, irresistible puns and quips, and (yes, sometimes all-too-human) prejudices, on the other, is not easy.

But its author knows that even an intellectual conscience as alert and vigorous as his does not suffice to do this in advance—for which reason kindred free-spirited readers and intellectual companions are needed. And by precept and example Nietzsche invites us to subject *him* to the same sort of scrutiny to which he subjects others. He only asks that one be prepared to have one's very objections subjected in turn to the same searching critical assessment— for they, too, may be problematic.

IV

Nietzsche himself looked back on *Human* twice in print. The final time was in *Ecce Homo*, in 1888, in the course of a review of all of his main publications, with the characteristically immodest heading "Why I Write Such Good Books." The occasion of his first subsequent retrospective—the 1886 reissuing of all three installments together—may itself have had its all-too-human motivations (not the least of which was Nietzsche's hope that, by repackaging them with new prefaces, he might be able to sell more of them and attract more attention to them). Nonetheless, the two new prefaces he wrote on that occasion are of no little interest; and it is important for readers to bear in mind that they were written long after the material they precede—eight years after the first volume, and six and seven years after the two parts of the second volume. Each deserves close reading, both before and after one has made one's way through the maze of the 1,400 aphorisms.

In the preface to the 1878 first volume of *Human*, written in 1886 (on the occasion of his republication of it), Nietzsche sees himself at the time of the first volume as already burdened with the large and heavy questions that impelled him toward philosophy. He also sees himself as having been struggling to achieve the intellectual and spiritual freedom and resources needed to deal with them, both of which he feels he had lacked in sufficient measure previously. He further describes himself as having been in a precarious state of health, both physically and intellectually, slowly convalescing from the maladies of both sorts that had threatened to engulf him.

The same themes are sounded again in that two-part second volume's added (also in 1886) preface; and there he makes it even clearer what the chief dangers were to which he had to develop resistance and learn to overcome. He refers to these writings as "a continuation and redoubling of a spiritual cure, namely of the *anti-romantic* self-treatment that my still healthy instinct had itself discovered and prescribed for me against a temporary attack of the most dangerous form of romanticism," and as the expressions of a "courageous pessimism" that is the "antithesis of all romantic mendacity" (*HH* II:I:P:2).

As Nietzsche further observes in this preface, his determination to resist and reject all such temptations (which for him could be summed up in a single name: *Wagner*) was still immature here, and was not yet "that *mature* freedom of spirit which is equally self-mastery and discipline of the heart and permits access to many and contradictory modes of thought," and which he evidently feels he subsequently had come to attain (*HH* I:P:4). But he takes himself in *Human* as having been on the way to it. And it should be noted both that he gives this interpretation to the direction and outcome of his own intellectual development, and what he takes to be fundamental to it: the repudiation of "all romantic mendacity," and its replacement by the cultivation of the intellectual conscience and analytical, critical, and interpretive abilities of the "free spirit" he was at once promoting and attempting to become.

Nietzsche thus saw himself here as having turned away from the Wagnerian-Schopenhauerian romanticism of *Birth* (of which he was explicitly critical along these very lines, in a new preface to that work that he also wrote in 1886, entitled "Attempt at a Self-Criticism"). In doing so, and partly as a way of doing so, he had turned with all the self-discipline and intellect he could muster in an analytical direction, replacing art with *Wissenschaft*—cognitive endeavor, including the sciences—as his new paradigm of high spirituality. Thus, in the preface to the second volume, he refers to the various installments of *Human* as "precepts of health that may be recommended to the more spiritual natures of the generation just coming up as a *disciplina voluntatis* [discipline of the will]" (*HH* II:II:P:2). (It is a discipline as much needed today as it was needed by Nietzsche himself and by "the generation just coming up" in his own time that he thought of himself as addressing.)

This in part answers the question of *Human*'s intended audience. Nietzsche did not think of himself, either at this time or subsequently, as writing primarily for academic philosophers, or for students in philosophy courses. He clearly was moving in what he conceived to be a philosophical direction; but he was writing first and foremost for inquiring and adventuresome minds of sufficient sophistication to keep pace with him, whoever and wherever they may be—not only in academia but also among the intelligent reading public. He hoped in particular to be able to reach the better minds of the younger generation, who might be more receptive than their elders (their academic-philosophical professors among them) to challenges to preconceived ideas and assumed values. He undoubtedly had hopes of having the sort of wider impact Voltaire and other firebrands of the Enlightenment had had a century earlier.

For a time, Nietzsche considered publishing *Human* anonymously or under a pseudonym.[7] This book may not seem to us today to be scandalously radical, however provocative it may be on some topics. At the time, however, Nietzsche rightly feared that it would be deeply offensive to many of its readers—not in the ways *Birth* had been to his fellow philologists, but in an almost opposite way. Now it was those who had been enamored of Nietzsche the romantic who were offended, by his abandonment of romanticism in favor of an unsentimental, cold-blooded, and science-aligned "historical" naturalism—for which he sought the widest possible audience.

Beyond the circle of those who already knew of him, however, Nietzsche need not have worried about the scandalousness of his new venture—for, to his dismay, no one else paid the slightest attention. Even today, few recognize it as the intellectually and spiritually severe and adventuresome gold mine it is, not only as an excellent way of becoming acquainted with his initial philosophical thinking, but also for its wealth of ideas and insights.

V

In his 1886 preface to the first volume, Nietzsche observes that although he may not have realized it at the time, he was on the way to realizing that it was the problem of "rank-ordering"—of values and their revaluation and ordering—"of which we may say it is *our* problem." And he had already come to understand that, to position ourselves to address such large issues, we must do more than simply become "free spirits." "We free spirits" [*wir freien Geister*] first have to become, as he puts it, "adventurers and circumnavigators of that inner world called 'human' [*jener inneren Welt, die 'Mensch' heisst*], as surveyors of that 'higher' and 'some above others' that is likewise called 'human' [*jedes 'Höher' und 'Übereinander' das gleichfalls 'Mensch' heisst*]—penetrating everywhere, almost [!] without fear, disdaining nothing, losing nothing, asking everything, cleansing everything of what is chance and accident in it and as it were thoroughly sifting it" (*HH* I:P:7).

That is a fair characterization of what Nietzsche is advocating and attempting to do in *Human*; and it is in *that* sense that the term "psychological" applies to his task and way of going about it. Philosophy for him revolves around the exploration of *things human*, and is first and foremost the attempt to comprehend them—even if that comprehension is not an end in itself. It prepares the way for the further comprehension of the whole complex matter of *value*, as it relates to issues of quality and worth in and about human life, in the service of its enhancement.

In *Human* Nietzsche took (and in his prefaces saw himself as taking) major steps in that direction. He had yet to learn to temper his new enthusiasm for the natural sciences (expressed in the first aphorism of the work, *HH* I:1), and to wed it with his equal enthusiasm for what he calls "*historical* [*historische*] philosophizing" (expressed in the very next aphorism, *HH* I:2). For that kind of culturally attuned and sophisticated developmental thinking is needed to be able to revisit and draw upon the perspectives relating to the arts and culture he had known so well without becoming captive once again to them; to supplement both with yet others; and to develop the ability to make larger interpretive sense of our humanity in the light of this multiplicity of perspectives upon it. But he was on his way.

Many readers—and interpreters—make the mistake of regarding these "free spirit" works as a mere interlude between the early (1872) *Birth of Tragedy* and *Zarathustra* more than a decade later (1883), and of reading them (if at all) from the perspective of his later writings, in relation to which they are generally found to pale by comparison, both rhetorically and philosophically. But it would make more sense to view Nietzsche's later writings in the perspective of his "free spirit" works, taking *Human* as one's point of departure (as it was for him), and regarding *Zarathustra* as an interlude between the last of those works (the first 1882 version of *Joyful Inquiry*) and the resumption of Nietzsche's prose writing, beginning with *Beyond* (1886) and the new fifth Book of *Inquiry* he published a year later. The continuities between them are strong, even though Nietzsche's arsenal of perspectives grew, his philosophical sophistication increased, his rhetoric sharpened (and heated up), and his intellectual pendulum swung back from its pre-*Zarathustra* esteem of science, in the direction of his deepening artistic and cultural concerns and sensibility.

This even applies to the organization of *Human* and the two later works that are not devoted to specific topics or figures: namely, *Beyond* and *Twilight*. Like the latter two works, the first volume of *Human* does have an organization, in the form of its division into parts with headings. It can hardly be a sheer coincidence that all three have the same number of major parts—nine— plus an epilogue. And there is a striking similarity among the headings as well. Each starts out with sections on topics relating to philosophers and philosophy; each has a section relating to morality, and another to religious and metaphysical matters; each has a section on social and political matters, and another on cultural and intellectual topics; and each, at some point, contains a collection of one-liners on a variety of sensitive topics guaranteed to offend almost everyone.

To be sure, the parallels are not exact; but they are close enough to warrant the suggestion of a continuity for Nietzsche in the kind of philosophy they represent—and in content there are not only significant differences but also remarkable similarities. One might well ask oneself in what ways Nietzsche's thinking *changed* on these matters from his initial discussions of them in *Human* to those on the same topics in *Beyond* and *Twilight*, what his reasons may have been (if he does not make them explicit)—and whether the changes were invariably for the better.

VI

Nietzsche did not supply the two added installments of what is now the second volume of *Human* with the same sorts of headings when he brought them all together in 1886 or indeed with any such part headings at all. Most of the aphorisms in them can easily be assigned to one or another of the part headings Nietzsche uses in the first volume, however, for they chiefly range over and fall under the same general topics. An examination of the list of these topics makes it clear both that *Human* is far from being as formless as it is often taken to be, and also that Nietzsche's interests include but are not restricted to issues that are normally deemed "philosophical."

The first part (appropriately enough), "Of First and Last Things," deals with metaphysical thinking—but in a curiously detached sort of way, more as a phenomenon to be understood than a set of arguments to be engaged head on. Nietzsche takes the same approach to morality in the second part ("On the History of Moral Sentiments [*Empfindungen*]"—Nietzsche's first foray into what he came to call the "genealogy of moralities"); to religion in the third ("The Religious Life"); and to art in the fourth ("From the Souls of Artists and Writers"). In each case he is proposing that we make the experiment of looking at these seemingly sublime things naturalistically, as mundanely originating *human* phenomena, and of asking what is going on when such things occur in human life—shifting the presumption from that of their sublimity to the suspicion that their appearance of sublimity may well be deceiving and undeserved.

In the next four parts Nietzsche turns his attention to the domain of cultural, social, and interpersonal relationships and types. There is more to "culture" for him than art and literature; and he attempts to bring it into focus in the fifth part ("Signs of Higher and Lower Culture"). Social institutions and relationships are the logical next stop, in the sixth part ("Man in Society"), with family matters coming next ("Woman and Child"), followed by political life ("A Glance at the State"). If in the first four sections he surveys things that claim some sort of transcendent significance, of the kind Hegel sought to express in his characterization of their domain as that of "absolute spirituality," here Nietzsche surveys those things that flesh out what Hegel had called "the life of a people" on the level of its "objective spirituality."

These, too, are among the chief sorts of things in terms of which our humanity and human meaning and worth are commonly conceived. If one asks what it is that sets us apart from and above other creatures whose existence is merely animal, and is not permitted to give a quick religious or metaphysical answer appealing to transcendent principles and powers, this is a fair inventory of possible answers. That would seem to be the larger (and genuinely if unconventionally philosophical) point of these collections of reflections, many of which might not appear to have any philosophical significance whatsoever.

In the final part of the first volume, Nietzsche turns to what he considers to be left after one has considered all of these other dimensions of human life: what we are or can be on our own, as individuals, within or by ourselves ("Man Alone with Himself"). Later he would add another item to the first four on the list, belonging with them, but not yet as problematical in his eyes as he subsequently recognized it to be: *scientific thinking*, of the very sort he had become so enamored of and (nominally) reliant upon here, at least as a kind of model. Like the glasses with which one may be provided to deal with vision problems, and to which one may become so accustomed that one ceases to be aware of them, this sort of thinking can come to be taken for granted beyond the point to which uncritical reliance upon it is warranted.

To his credit, Nietzsche was far quicker than most to become sensitive to the limitations of ways of thinking to which he was attracted—and then, hav-

ing done so, to get past his disappointment with them, and attempt to ascertain the best uses that might still be made of them, their limitations notwithstanding. In *Human*, however, his romance with the sciences was still young, and this process had yet to run its course.

Human is proclaimed in its subtitle to be *A Book for Free Spirits*. Three years after the publication of its first installment, when Nietzsche published the first version of *Inquiry*, he had the following printed on its back cover: "This book concludes a series of writings by FRIEDRICH NIETZSCHE whose common goal it is to erect *a new image and ideal of the free spirit* [*deren gemeinsames Ziel ist, ein neues Bild und Ideal des Freigeistes aufzustellen*]." He then went on to list *Human* and its supplements, its 1881 sequel (*Daybreak*), and *Inquiry* itself as that "series of writings."[8]

Nietzschean "free spirits" are not necessarily philosophers; but Nietzschean philosophers must (among other things) have become *his* kind of free spirit. Voltaire,[9] for Nietzsche, was an exemplary "free spirit," as the original dedication of *Human* indicates: "To Voltaire's memory, in commemoration of the day of his death, 30 May 1788." The example of Voltaire's free-spiritedness undoubtedly helped Nietzsche the erstwhile devoted disciple of Wagner to come to realize and understand something he badly needed to learn, and attain: what it means, and requires, to be a truly "free spirit." In chapter 10 I discuss Nietzsche's developing conception of the "free spirit" and free-spiritedness, in *Human* and subsequently.

VII

But what is it actually like to engage in this new kind of "philosophizing"? To convey a sense of it, I shall now take a close and extended look at one of the nine parts of the initial version of this inaugural work: part 5, "*Anzeichen höherer und niederer Cultur.*"[10] I have chosen it for this purpose because I consider it an excellent example of what the Nietzsche of *Human* does in this work, and of how he does it—and so of his kind of philosophy at this juncture. This fifth part of the book is central to it, both literally (it is both preceded and followed by four other parts) and substantively. Its title may be translated as "Signs of Higher and Lower Culture." What Nietzsche means by that, however, remains to be seen. It also is of considerable interest because he here broaches and attempts for the first time to come to grips with one of the ideas with which he continued to be preoccupied for the rest of his productive life: the idea of the human reality and possibility of various sorts of "higher" humanity.

Before proceeding with a reading of the fifth part, several things relating

to *Human's* first part warrant comment, because they set the stage for part 5 in ways that are significant. The importance of the first two sections of part 1 for the understanding of the project of the book as a whole—and indeed of much of Nietzsche's subsequent thinking and philosophical endeavor—can hardly be overestimated. The book was first published with no preface or introduction whatsoever. What now appears as its "preface" was added only in 1886 (to an expanded second edition, which incorporated two shorter sequels under the same original title). These first two substantial sections (*HH* I:1 and 2), in effect, *are* its "introduction"—and are as much of an introduction as Nietzsche supposed the book to need, either in 1878 or in 1886. We should recall them when we turn our attention from the first four parts to part 5, and to what Nietzsche does and says there.

In the first section, Nietzsche begins the book by calling for a new kind of philosophy, that is to be "historical" [*historisch*] (rather than "metaphysical") and allied with "natural science" [*Naturwissenschaft*], from which it henceforth is very definitely "no longer to be separated" [*gar nicht mehr getrennt*] (*HH* I:1). The fact that he calls it "historical"—rather than, for example, "natural-scientific"—would seem to suggest that this alliance is to be understood as something other than either restriction or subordination (let alone absorption), but remains to be clarified. It therefore further remains to be seen whether or in what sense the *historische Philosophie* of which he speaks is to be conceived as "naturalistic" in character—and, for that matter, how it is to be *historisch*.

Nietzsche answers that second question immediately, in the very next section. There he asserts that what is needed from now on is the recognition that "*everything* has *become*" [Alles *ist geworden*]; that "there are no eternal facts" [es gibt keine ewigen Tatsachen], and therefore also "no absolute truths" [*keine absoluten Wahrheiten*] (*HH* I:2). Therefore human reality and everything human—our cognitive abilities [*Erkenntnisvermögen*] included, along with the farthest reaches of our human mentality and all of human culture and spirituality—must be reconsidered and reassessed. And this is to be done in a spirit of "modesty" [*Bescheidung*], befitting its merely "historical" (and "human-historical" at that, rather than metaphysical) status and character, and taking its origins and circumstances into account. For they are one and all *not* to be thought of as divinely bestowed from on high, but rather are mundanely and contingently emergent *human* phenomena, that have *geworden* or "come to be" what they are in the course of human events.

Further: as human phenomena, with human origins rather than any sort of supra-human pedigree, it must be not only suspected but expected that, in both their origins and their development—and so quite possibly, in vari-

ous respects, in their current forms as well—they have been and may remain *merely human* [*menschlich*] (and perhaps even *all-too*-human) phenomena, even if they also may have come to be something more and even quite different than they were in the first place. If Nietzsche is to be considered not only a reinterpreter of all things human but a "naturalistic" one, here and subsequently, this is the heart—and perhaps also the full modest extent—of his rather open-endedly developmental *kind* of philosophical "naturalism." (That is the topic of chapter 11.)

VIII

Working all of this out, and considering further issues this raises, is precisely what Nietzsche proceeds to begin to do in the rest of *Human*'s part 1 (in which old-style "metaphysical philosophy" is subjected to this sort of deflating treatment). It is what he continues to do in the parts of the original version of *Human* that immediately follow it—in which morality, religion, and art are dealt with in turn, exemplifying what he means by "historical philosophizing." And it is what he goes on to do in part 5 as well—but in ways that are rather different and have a more constructive intent than do these previous parts.

Part 5 might be thought of as an anticipation or initiation and instance of the sort of "naturalizing" reinterpretation and reassessment of human reality that Nietzsche (again) called for in *Joyful Inquiry*, four years later, after announcing the "death of God" and the task it entails of the "de-deification" [*Entgöttlichung*] of "nature." There he characterizes it by the phrase "naturalizing ourselves"—or, more literally, "naturalizing us human beings" [*uns Menschen zu* vernatürlichen] (*JI* 109). And in part 5 the dimension of human reality that is his specific topic is human *Cultur*.

But this, for Nietzsche, is by no means to say that his topics in the first four parts—philosophy, morality, religion, and art—are one and all *undeserving* of a human future in any way, shape, or form. It is rather to say that it is now an open question what humanly possible phenomena of these general sorts (if any) *are* deserving of such a future, and what that future might best be. And it is with these issues already having been addressed in the first four parts that he turns to the rather different topic of "higher and lower" [*höhere und niedere*] *Cultur*—a topic that can no longer be deemed to be settled simply by reference to the aforementioned and traditionally revered human-spiritual possibilities in their familiar forms.

Hegel had conceptualized these phenomena in terms of *Geist* [spirituality], of which these kinds of experience and activity, in their most refined forms, were the "highest" in significance.[11] For Nietzsche this issue had to be posed

anew, in terms of human reality and *Cultur*. Yet he, too, avails himself rather freely of the language of *Geist* in doing so—shorn of its Hegelian pretensions, but serving to mark out the dimensions of human reality that transcend the merely natural most fully and significantly—in his case, by way of its mundanely occurring but nonetheless sometimes substantially transformative development.

Finally, it is also helpful (and important), as one reads part 5, to recall what Nietzsche has to say about its announced topic—*Cultur*, *höher* and otherwise—in *Human*'s first part. It is mentioned strikingly in the very first sentence of the third section: "It is the sign of a higher *Cultur* [*Es ist das Merkmal einer höheren Cultur*] to esteem more highly the little modest truths [*die kleinen unscheinbaren Wahrheiten*] that have been discovered by way of strict methods than the delighting and dazzling errors deriving from metaphysical and artistic ages and people" (*HH* I:3). Here Nietzsche is using the term *Cultur* in a culturally neutral way, to refer to a more or less highly developed, refined, and "cultivated" level of intellectual sophistication. In a number of the aphorisms that follow (such as *HH* I:23–24), he reverts to using *Cultur* in its more conventional cultural-anthropological sense. But in its next and last significant appearance in part 1, it is perhaps to be understood in *both* senses. And what he says there is of the utmost importance for the understanding of part 5, as well as of such later works as *Beyond* (part 9 in particular) and *Genealogy*. Supposing that the qualitative enhancement of human life is bound up with that of human culture, he observes that their flourishing and development may well make it "not at all desirable" [*durchaus nicht wünschenswert*] that human beings should "all act the same" [*gleich handeln*]. And he then goes on to suggest that "the tremendous task" [*die ungeheure Aufgabe*] of "the great thinkers" [*der grossen Geister*] of the years to come will be to attain a general "comprehension of the prerequisites [*Kenntnis der Bedingungen*] of *Cultur*" (*HH* I:25).

IX

Nietzsche's main task in *Human*'s part 5 is not (except perhaps derivatively) the rank-ordering or qualitative assessment of the "cultures" of various *Völker* ("peoples," societies, nationalities), or of various "subcultures" and *Lebensformen* ("forms of life") that have come to exist socially within them. It rather is to show how he proposes to think, in his new-philosophical way, about different sorts and levels of emergent human-spiritual development—or, briefly put, *spirituality*. And the locus of this human phenomenon of *Cultur* is twofold: in the mentalities and sensibilities of human beings who exhibit them, and also in the social forms of life ("cultures") associated with them that en-

gender and foster them; for they are what make those mentalities and sensibilities humanly possible. This involves an awareness of and attention to something that, in this new way of thinking, replaces the idea of the origin and association of that spirituality in some sort of supra-mundane reality: namely, the recognition (and insistence) that these are *human phenomena*, that are realizable and exist only in historically developed sociocultural contexts conducive to them, for creatures such as we.

So, in the very first section of part 5 (*HH* I:224), Nietzsche makes it clear that what he is interested in here is *"spiritual advancement"* [geistige Fortschreiten] [his emphasis], or humanly attainable and more or less "advanced" [*fortgeschrittene*] forms of *Geist* or *Geistigkeit* (spirituality), understood in his fully "de-deified" and "naturalizing" way. And what he is proposing and attempting to develop here is a manner of analyzing and interpreting that adheres to the *guiding ideas* of the mundane original character of human reality (as one sort of living creature among others), and the mundane character of its differentiations and mutations, as human life came to have social and cultural as well as physical and biological contours.

In short: Nietzsche's focus here is not upon the existence of various forms and types of *Cultur* that have become humanly possible—their origins, their development and transformations, their "uses and disadvantages" (in the language of his *History* essay[12])—but rather upon what their enhancement and superiority among them involves and requires. But that consideration is undertaken and pursued with an important presupposition: *Cultur*, for Nietzsche, must be recognized to be a cluster or array of human possibilities that exists in a multiplicity of historically arising and emerging forms—and so, both humanly and individually, it exists only as *human* phenomena that have "become," having entirely human biological and social origins and developmental genealogies.

Further: Nietzsche makes it clear from the outset, and in the very title of part 5, that his abandonment of religious and metaphysical ways of thinking, in favor of his new historical-developmental and science-friendly kind of philosophical thinking, by no means requires the abandonment of all evaluative assessment. Types of human spirituality and *Cultur* differ; and they *can* be thought of as being (simply) *different*. But for Nietzsche they also *can* legitimately be thought of—new-philosophically—as being either "higher" or "lower" in relation to others, as he himself wishes to do and does here (and does again and again subsequently). He can and does make evaluative assessments—but of a different sort from those who do so in a manner that is religiously or morally grounded and motivated.

This is an important point. *Human's* opening aphorisms make clear that the post-religious and post-metaphysical, naturalizing and developmental *re-thinking of human reality* is at the center of Nietzsche's philosophical interests and program from the outset. And this central fifth part of the book shows that the same is true of the associated issue of what becomes of the ideas of human worth and human quality—and the qualitative superiority of some sorts of human possibility to others—in this dawning new philosophical era. (Here, importantly, the locus of that worth and quality is neither human life as such nor the human individual as such nor humanity as such, but rather some human *possibilities* and their realization.)

This part makes equally clear that for this Nietzsche it is to the emergent dimension of human reality he here calls *Cultur* that one needs to look, post-religiously and post-metaphysically, to make new sense of the qualitative dif-ferentiation of "higher" and "lower" versions of human reality. When he sub-sequently distinguishes between and contrasts "higher *Menschen*" and others, and speculates about their biological and physiological differences, it is im-portant to remember that, again from the outset, it was differences in their ex-pressions in human life at the level of what he calls *Cultur* with which he was most centrally concerned.

Further: there are two basic issues Nietzsche wants to pursue in this dis-cussion of "higher" and "lower" types of *Cultur* (and *Menschheit*). One is the issue of what he takes to be *Anzeichen* (signs or indications) that are indica-tive of their being either "higher" or "lower" types of human spirituality. And the other is that of what the human conditions of the possibility or likelihood of their human *realization* are, and what is conducive or detrimental to their realization. In the course of part 5, Nietzsche provides many examples of the sorts of conditions he considers to be developmentally relevant to the kinds of human phenomena he deems deserving of attention in this connection.

X

Human's part 5 is of particular importance because it shows, very clearly and tellingly, the kinds of questions and issues Nietzsche has in mind for which he believes the new-philosophical project he calls "historical philosophizing" (and later called "naturalizing") is needed, and illustrates the kinds of think-ing he takes them to call for. They are an interesting array of human phenom-ena, the reality—and even the significance—of which he does not challenge, but which may well warrant reconsideration in the light of the necessity of accounting for their emergence by nothing loftier than serendipitous accident. As Nietzsche puts it here, "when one gives up the belief in a God and his care," that is the end of all divine plans and teleological thinking, and of all miraculous thinking and explanation as well. "Miracles then are nevermore to be found" (*HH* I:242).

So, for Nietzsche, what there is of "higher" humanity and spirituality in this world—and for him there is a good deal of it—can only have originated in what was at first devoid of it. Nothing remains for its origins but pre-human, sub-human, merely human, and all-too-human human interactions and practices—emerging out of them in ways themselves initially fortuitous or even pernicious. But what sorts of things? Out of what sorts of things? And how could that have come about? These are the kinds of questions Nietzsche is setting for himself, and to which he begins to try to develop plausible answers. And it is of considerable interest to observe what the phenomena are that he here selects, as deserving of recognition, attention, reflection, appreciation, and even further cultivation.

Nietzsche's strategy here, as so often elsewhere and subsequently, is to try to envision a process or dynamic that presupposes nothing problematic, is not implausible as *the sort of thing* that could have happened—*and* suffices to make sense as the idea of a mundane happenstance initiating a new and different sort of dynamic. It is perhaps only retrospectively, and from a standpoint or perspective that is an outcome of a succession of such changes, that such change can and does come to be deemed to represent a kind of advancement or qualitative enhancement. At this early point in his philosophical development, however, Nietzsche had not become as sensitive to questions of that sort as he subsequently became. His question here takes it to be the case that certain traits exist and are estimable, and that their emergence and development are examples of "spiritual advancement," and then asks: how could their emergence and development have come about in a world that is not disposed in their favor, with no supernatural assistance?

Nietzsche's first such suggestion in part 5 is summed up in the heading of its first section: "*Veredelung durch Entartung*"—"Ennobling through Degeneration" (*HH* I:224). Here he addresses himself to the fundamental anthropological question of how the very phenomenon of *Veredelung*, or ennobling—which he glosses as "spiritual advancement" [*geistige Fortschreiten*] and "furtherance" [*Fortbilden*]—became humanly possible, in the absence of any supra-mundane agency or metaphysical impetus. He takes it for granted that such qualitative advancement *occurs*. His question is *how it could have* occurred and *may have* occurred merely in the course of human (and even all-too-human) events, and in the absence of any sort of developmental imperative in that direction, either external or internal.

Nietzsche's thought here is that a certain sort of degeneration [*Entartung*], at a certain juncture in a society's history, can open the way for a creative departure from an existing imperative. That, for him here, is only a part of the story of how some sort of *Veredelung* or ennobling transfiguration could—and may have—come about, even in the instance of the phenomenon he goes on to consider: that of what he calls *Freigeist*, "free spirit" (*HH* I:225). But it illustrates what is going to be one of his recurring themes: seemingly harmful or all-too-human tendencies, combining in certain ways and circumstances, can turn out to have transformative consequences.

XI

Nietzsche then turns to the idea and human possibility of the *Freigeist* phenomenon, and its contrast with the sort of spirit and spirituality that is in thrall to whatever the existing traditional cultural order may be. And it is important to bear in mind that, for him here and subsequently, what the term *Freigeist* designates first and foremost is not an individual or type of individual, but rather a type of *sensibility*—variously describable as "freedom of spirit" or "free-spiritedness"—which some human beings may come to have or attain, and which may be fostered and cultivated in some human communities and cultures while being discouraged and hindered in others.

In this first portion of part 5, Nietzsche's focus is upon what it is for thinking to be "free" [*frei*] as opposed to being *gebunden*—by which he means liberated from rather than "bound" [*gebunden*] by and in thrall to the "traditional" [*Herkömmlichen*]. "Free-spiritedness" is characterized and animated by a desire and daring to "think differently" and unconventionally (*HH* I:225). That is a paradigm instance, for Nietzsche here, of a contrasting pair of *Anzeichen* [indications] of "higher" and "lower" sensibilities, spirituality, and *Cultur*. His expression for the much more common latter human type is the "*gebundene* [bound or constricted] *Geist*" phenomenon. The "bound" type of human spirituality is said to greatly surpass the "free" type in terms of one sort of "strength"—that of commitment and steadfastness; but it is one of Nietzsche's concerns to illuminate the very different and very important sort of "strength" that the *Freigeist* phenomenon both requires and cultivates.

Nietzsche links this contrast to one of the differences he highlights between the two sorts of *Geist*: the *gebundene Geist* is guided unreflectively by some set of rules, principles, and values it has absorbed from the tradition to which it has become habituated, and which for it is a matter of unquestioning faith. The *Freigeist*, on the other hand, is suspicious of any such faith, operates by way of reasons [*Gründe*], and will settle for nothing less in both thought and action. It also is said to be a mark of a higher sort of *Cultur* that one would not be simply the sort of person one would expect someone to be "on the basis of his heritage, surroundings, social class and office, or on the basis of the prevailing character of the time" (*HH* I:225).

However, this contrast is immediately conjoined, in this very section, with a different contrast: that of being endowed with or devoid of the "properties and sharpness" [*Güte und Schärfe*] of what Nietzsche himself calls "*Intellect.*" And he concludes this section by adding something further to the portrait of "free-spirited" sensibility he is sketching here, saying that for such a person it is "usual" [*gewöhnlich*] to proceed with "the spirit of truth-seeking [*der Geist der Wahrheitsforschung*] at his side." By this he means: "He gives *reasons*, the other *beliefs*" [*er fordert* Gründe, *die Anderen* Glauben] (*HH* I:225; emphasis added). This emphasis on proceeding on the basis of "reasons"—rather than on the basis of "beliefs," and therefore "without reasons" [*ohne Gründe*]—is the theme of the next two sections as well (*HH* I:226, 227). Nietzsche's conception of "free-spirited" thinking is thus that it is characterized not only by being *independently minded*, but also *truth-minded*.

This is only the beginning of Nietzsche's exploration here of forms of "higher" (and "lower") *Cultur* and spirituality, and of their human-historical genealogies. But the portrait of what it means to be a human being or a human society of "higher" rather than "lower" *Cultur* that he proceeds to present in this part of the book is basically an amplification and elaboration of this initial sketch. Independent thinking and highly developed intellect are central traits of the sort of higher humanity and spirituality the Nietzsche of *Human* has in mind here, and calls *Freigeist*. Religion has no place in it, other than as a (lower and less advanced) form of spirituality that contrasts with it, and must be transcended and left behind. The same is true, for him, of the conventional forms of morality and ethicality that he discusses in part 3 of *Human*, which he deems to be "all-too-human," stunting, and even pathological forms of spirituality.

By the time of *Human*, Nietzsche also had come to have serious second thoughts and reservations about the arts (music included) and the sorts of spirituality they both express and promote, no longer idolizing them (as he had earlier, in *Birth* in particular). In fact, the Nietzsche of *Human* now considers them, too, to be not only problematic but actually inferior to those he associates with the mentality of the "unbound" and independently thinking and intellectually astute *Freigeist*. (In the course of his *Freigeist* series, however, and by the time of *Inquiry*, he came to a different conclusion with respect to these last two [normative and artistic] forms of spirituality, within the context of a more comprehensive conception of both higher humanity and his "philosophy of the future" that incorporated elements of each of them.)

XII

The topic of the next five sections (beginning with *HH* I:255) is "genius" [*Genius*]. By this term Nietzsche would seem to have in mind something like the highest sort of energized mentality directed toward "spiritual goals" [*geistige Ziele*] (*HH* I:234). And that, for this Nietzsche, makes it is almost self-evidently a mark and phenomenon of the highest sort of *Cultur*. He takes the phenomenon of genius as a genuine human possibility and reality; and his reflections and speculations about how it might have become so, through an interplay of circumstances having nothing divine or admirable about them, are an excellent as well as interesting example of his early new-philosophical "historical" and "naturalizing" thinking in action. His main question here is not why it is so admirable, but rather how this phenomenon might have become humanly possible and individually manifested.

The phrase "spiritual goals" is rather general, and could be used to subsume creative as well as intellectual endeavors and expressions. And, particularly since the earlier Nietzsche's paradigm exemplar of genius had been Wagner, one might have expected musical (and more generally artistic and literary) "genius" to be at least a cluster of forms and instances of what he has in mind here. But the language he uses—such as "great intellect" [*grosse Intellect*] and "highest intelligence" [*höchste Intelligenz*], for example (*HH* I:235)—suggests that he is here conceiving of "genius" primarily intellectually, and even cognitively.

Indeed, as Nietzsche proceeds, it becomes clear and increasingly explicit that it is *wissenschaftlich* thinking and the *wissenschaftlich* pursuit of knowledge that have become paradigmatic for the Nietzsche of *Human* among the "spiritual goals" that are the concerns of genius. And by *wissenschaftlich*, it must be remembered, he means the kinds of thinking and inquiry characteristic of the developed cognitive disciplines generally (inclusive of but not exclusively limited to the natural sciences). He does say that "strong energy" [*starke Energie*] is "the fundament [*der Erdboden*], out of which great intellect and the powerful individual [*mächtige Individuum*] in general grows" (*HH* I:235). It is clear, however, that he here deems intellectual endeavor of a *wissenschaftlich* sort to be the highest sort of spirituality, to be the domain of a higher sort of *Genius*, and to be the aspiration of a higher *Cultur*, than any other ways in which a "powerful individual" might find self-expression.

In the next sections (*HH* I:236–40), Nietzsche offers a number of reflections on ways in which various sorts and instances of *Cultur* and spirituality can and do evolve and differ, and on both the inevitability and the desirability of such differences. So, for example, he suggests that they may be characterized by different temperaments, and different traits akin to those observable in different stages of life (*HH* I:236). But one point that comes through very clearly in these sections is that already for the Nietzsche of *Human*, the kinds of human phenomena that flesh out human reality at any given time and place are social, cultural, and historical through and through, even if they may have other dimensions as well.

XIII

In the following ten sections (*HH* I:241–50), Nietzsche offers some remarkable reflections toward a "philosophy of culture" in the more usual sense of the term "culture" (which is to say: human cultures, in all of their diversity). Here he makes it clear that, for him, culture (broadly conceived) is the locus of all there is in and about human reality that makes it more than just another piece of nature and type of animal life; and that culture therefore is the only possible venue for any sort of qualitative advancement and enhancement of human life and "higher" humanity there can be.

But he also makes it clear that he regards this dimension of human reality as deeply and perhaps inescapably and insolubly problematic. For everything cultural is ephemeral, has no reality apart from its human embodiments, has "become" (along with everything else), and has human origins and undergirdings, which are neither divine nor otherwise sublime (*HH* I:245). We must recognize—and must learn to live with and accept the recognition—that there is much about it and its origins and history that reflects impulses that are as primitive as they are powerful, and much that is not only mundane but often *allzumenschlich* (*HH* I:247).

This is a significant part of what Nietzsche calls "the problem of culture" [*das Problem der Cultur*] (*HH* I:249). The origins of culture in general, he contends, turn out to be disconcerting when they are laid bare (*HH* I:246). So he writes: "*Cultur* originates like a bell, inside a mold [*Mantel*] of coarser, meaner stuff [*gröberem, gemeinerem Stoffe*]: untruth, violence, unrestrained expansiveness of particular egos, of particular peoples [*Unwahrheit, Gewaltsamkeit, unbegränzte Ausdehnung aller einselnen Ich's, aller einselnen Völker*], have been this mold" (*HH* I:245). In short: *Cultur*, for Nietzsche, is all we've got, beyond our animality, and so everything depends upon what is made of it; but he wants us to have no illusions about it and its origins.

One of the most tempting of these illusions, he observes (*HH* I:238), is what he calls the "metaphysical" idea that "becoming" *is itself divine*, filling the

void left by the demise of the God-idea; and that *Cultur* is its crowning realization and vehicle—a kind of "evolving divinity" [*werdenden Gott*]. Fortified
by that conviction, one can still affirm—even in the absence of a transcendent
Deity—that "everything is not mere blind mechanism, a meaningless and pur-
poseless interplay of forces [*sinn- und zweckloses Durcheinander-spielen von
Kräften*]." This, to the Nietzsche of *Human*, is a mere (and illusory) "consolation" [*Trost*]—the appeal of which, however, he finds understandable enough
to say: "one ought not to get annoyed at it, however erroneous [*irrtümlich*] it
may be." But it is a temptation to be resisted nonetheless, by the intellectually
conscientious.

This predicament deepens "the problem of culture." Culture is the locus
and only source of meaning and meaningfulness there is—and yet, we now
realize, it is only human, and is contingent in its content. It has no substantive
anchor either within or transcending the larger reality of which we are a part.
It must be recognized to be ultimately meaningless outside of the context of
human life, within which it has come to be needed. It is but an ever-changing
stream of humanly engendered, linguistically articulated and borne *Lebensformen* [forms of life] that flows on, as they come to be and pass away (*HH*
I:248). So it is with "manners" [*Manieren*] (*HH* I:250)—and presumably also
with *Sitten* (customs) more generally, and all cultural traditions as well.

And there is yet another part of the "problem of culture," on a very different level, that Nietzsche mentions here: the heaviness of "the sum of feelings,
knowings, experiences [*die Summe der Empfindungen, Kenntnisse, Erfahrun-
gen*], in short, the whole burden [*Last*] of *Cultur*," that increases as a culture
becomes richer—from which some sort of relief must be found, if it is not to
become unbearable and self-destructive. As he goes on to suggest, this would
seem to be a problem that Nietzsche associates primarily with cultures like
our own, in which the human emotions and imagination have long been pro-
fusely creative.

So while Nietzsche later came to think that *Wissenschaft* can all too easily become a part of this problem, he here sees the "spirit of *Wissenschaft*"
as a source or form of the needed relief—an antidote to the obsessions that
such traditions instill and enflame. For that *wissenschaftlich* spirit serves to
make the thinker "somewhat colder and more skeptical" [*etwas kälter und
skeptischer*], and "cools the ardor of belief [*den Glutstrom des Glaubens*]"
(*HH* I:244). And with this observation Nietzsche sounds a new theme: that
the healthiest and highest sort of "higher culture" is one in which both artistic and *wissenschaftlich*—creative and cognitive—capacities are active, highly
developed, and partnered. (This is a point to which I will return shortly.)

XIV

In the sections that follow (beginning with *HH* I:251), Nietzsche elaborates his inventory of traits and forms of spirituality and mentality that he regards as "higher," or as *Anzeichen* of such "higher" types of *Geist* and *Cultur*, in some surprising ways. He began with the idea of *Freigeist*, which for him conjoined enlightenment (in relation to superstition and illusion) with independent-mindedness, and supplemented these qualities with intellectuality, rationality, and truth-mindedness, complemented yet again by creativity and the sort of genius it differently requires. And his task was not only to identify these traits but to inquire into the developmental conditions of their human possibility, in the absence of anything beyond the initially human and all-too-human qualities and conditions of primordial humanity.

Beginning in *HH* I:251, however, Nietzsche abruptly shifts his attention to the emergence of the kind of thinking and knowing that has culminated in *Wissenschaft* as an activity, and in the emergence in human life of a "knowing drive" [*erkennende Trieb*] (*HH* I:254) or "desire to know" [*Lust am Erkennen*] (*HH* I:252). The question of their human origins—in a creature and a world to which they were fundamentally quite alien—had been on Nietzsche's mind since the time of his early *Truth* essay fragment, and continued to be throughout his philosophical life. But their story, as he surmises it, was and remains a very different one from much else in the domain of *Cultur*, both "higher" and "lower."

Both modes of human spirituality, regarded in a naturalizing way, have human-historical genealogies, setting the stage for further developments to which each contribute. The resemblance to the basic thesis of *Birth* is neither coincidental nor surprising. But there is a change: now it is "the spirit of *Wissenschaft*" that is suggested to be the heir of the Apollinian form of spirituality, and it is the kind of sophistication, discernment, and attitude associated with it that Nietzsche clearly favors over latter-day versions of its Dionysian companion.[13]

That is a theme that figures strongly and significantly in the last dozen sections of part 5. Differently surprising is the quick catalog Nietzsche provides in the intervening set of sections preceding them (beginning with *HH* I:265) of other things that he clearly considers to contribute to the attainment of a level of *Cultur* that he deems "higher." In *HH* I:264 he distinguishes between those who are "gifted" [*begabte*] in the sense of being "spirit-rich" [*Geistreiche*] but are not *wissenschaftlich*, and those who are "gifted" in the opposite way (*die wissenschaftlichen Naturen*, the scientifically inclined). The latter, he says, have attained a kind of sophistication and intellectual conscience that puts a brake on enthusiasm for "that which glitters, shines, and excites," and know that "the gift of being able to have all sorts of ideas must be held in check [*gezügelt*] by the most rigorous spirit of *Wissenschaft*" (*HH* I:264). Both are forms or types of higher spirituality and mentality, for Nietzsche; but by themselves each leaves something very important to be desired: namely, their counterpart. The highest form of spirituality and *Cultur* is that in which both capacities are strongly present, highly developed, and deeply combined.

XV

In the sections that follow (beginning with *HH* I:265), Nietzsche elaborates upon a cluster of traits—more "signs of a higher *Cultur*"—that he associates with the attainment and expression of the *wissenschaftlich* side of this higher sensibility, and that are unattainable in the absence of the right sort of "school" and schooling. The first and foremost among them is the capacity for "rigorous thinking, careful judging, and sound reasoning" [*strenges Denken, vorsichtiges Urteilen, consequentes Schliessen*] (*HH* I:265). The next is the capacity for "abstraction"—a kind of "higher gymnastics for the head," through which the ability to cope and operate with "concepts, technical expressions, methods, and allusions [*Begriffe, Kunstausdrücke, Methoden, Anspielungen*] in the abstract language appropriate to them [*in ihrer Sprache*]" is acquired, supplementing the outpourings of creative imagination (*HH* I:266). And to this list Nietzsche goes on to add the different sort of sophistication that is cultivated by "learning many languages" (*HH* I:267).

Nietzsche concludes this inventory of phenomena he deems characteristic—or perhaps definitive—of higher spirituality and *Cultur* by identifying two abilities that go to the very heart of his own two kinds of thinking: "the art of *reading*" [*die Kunst, zu lesen*], cultivated by philology and the training it provides in rigorous interpretation (*HH* I:270), and "the art of *inferring*" [*die Kunst, zu schliessen*], or sound *reasoning*, cultivated by the explanatory disciplines [*Wissenschaften*] (the *Naturwissenschaften* in particular), and the training they provide in rigorous and careful reasoning and conclusion-drawing. Both, for Nietzsche—the interpretive (linguistic and historical) and the explanatory disciplines—are *Wissenschaften*, of different but complementary sorts; and both contribute to the "spirit of *Wissenschaft*" (cognitive inquiry) that they collectively foster, nurture, and develop (*HH* I:271).

That spirit, he goes on to contend, leads one *away* from art—which he here relegates to the status of a kind of transitional refuge from religion for those who have outgrown the latter but are not yet ready for more. It leads one instead toward "natural science and history, and so to the most rigorous methods of knowing [*und namentlich zu den strengsten Methoden des Erkennens*]" (*HH* I:272, 224–25).

For the Nietzsche of *Inquiry* and subsequent writings, both of these abilities figure significantly in his eventual kind of philosophy. There creative and artistic powers receive comparable emphasis, and "value creation" is accorded central importance. Here, on the other hand, in the "new philosophy" the Nietzsche of *Human* is championing, art (and presumably anything of the sort, such as music and literature) "acquires an ever milder and lesser significance" [*eine immer mildere und anspruchslosere Bedeutung zufällt*] compared to the spirit of *Wissenschaft*—and in what Nietzsche calls the "annals of individual *Cultur*" [*Jahresringe der individuellen Cultur*] as well (*HH* I:272).

Yet just a few sections later he suggests that the *highest* level of *Cultur* is attained when—and perhaps only when—these "two different powers" [*zwei heterogene Mächte*] are *both* powerfully developed and active, and are brought into a kind of harmonized and fruitful concord (*HH* I:276). He employs the metaphor of a "dance": "High *Cultur*"—at its finest?—"will be akin to an amazing dance [*einem kühnen Tanze*]." Perhaps meaning: a dance in which now the one and now the other takes the lead, responding to as well as differing from the other (*HH* I:278). And a few sections later Nietzsche goes further, envisioning something even more complex: a "*höheren* vielsaitigeren" [higher, *many-sided*] *Cultur*, in which other powers and impulses are brought into play and are incorporated into the dance (*HH* I:281).

XVI

In the end, however, the Nietzsche of *Human* rather surprisingly accords the highest rank—among levels of *Cultur* of humanity and sensibility in both a society and a human being—to a quite different kind of spirituality he envisions. He introduces it by way of the classical expression *vita contemplativa*—the "contemplative life," which rises above involvement in all things human, reflects upon them, and endeavors to comprehend them. In one section, anticipating an idea he expands upon in *Beyond*, he envisions a rather remarkable *active* role for this contemplative spirit: "it has the completely different and higher task of commanding the entire army of *wissenschaftlichen* and scholarly *Menschen*, from a solitary standpoint, showing them the ways and goals of *Cultur* [*ihnen die Wege und Ziele der Cultur zu zeigen*]" (*HH* I:282). In short: it provides *direction*—presumably in the selection and pursuit of those "goals of *Cultur*." In the remaining sections of part 5, however, Nietzsche's theme is that of a spirituality for which lofty contemplation is an end in itself, and the highest of all ends humanly attainable and even imaginable.

Thus the philosophically aspiring author of *Human* characterizes this highest of human-spiritual standpoints as that of both a supremely enlightened, sophisticated, and discerning thinker devoted to the *comprehension* of life, and a *censor vitae* [judge of life]. Science-friendliness notwithstanding, such a thinker "would be free in his judgments concerning life" [*frei in seinem Urteile über das Leben werden will*], beyond all hate and love of things particular—differently disposed at times ("sometimes summery, sometimes autumnally minded"; *bald sommerlich, bald herbstlich gensinnt*) (*HH* I:287), but to no worldly end or purpose. "His will, that is to say, desires nothing more programmatically than knowing and the means thereto [*will Nichts angelentlicher, als Erkennen und das Mittel dazu*]" (*HH* I:288).

This Nietzsche describes that sort of supremely "free-spirited" [*Freigesinnte*] one who "lives for knowledge alone" [*der Erkenntnis allein lebende Mensch*], and proposes it as a new model of "refined heroism" [*verfeinerten Heroismus*] of the highest order (*HH* I:291). And he concludes *Human*'s part 5 with a lengthy peroration that gives eloquent expression to the outlook and wisdom he believes himself to have attained. It is clearly intended to stand as the capstone of the conception of higher spirituality and *Cultur* that he has been developing here. And it is one that he believes to be a real as well as admirable human possibility, our mundane and *allzumenschlich* origins notwithstanding, and despite the absence of anything beyond ourselves and our mundane conditions to assist us.

Nietzsche goes so far as to say, in this concluding section, that in this way "your own life will acquire the value of an instrument and means of knowledge [*eines Werkzeuges und Mittels zur Erkenntnis*]." And further, bringing the discussion back to *Cultur*: "This goal is yourself to become a necessary chain of rings of culture [*eine notwendige Kette von Cultur-Ringen zu werden*], and from this necessity to derive [*schliessen*] the necessity in the course of *Cultur* in general [*im Gange der allgemeinen Cultur*]" (*HH* I:292). Science, in the end, is simply a part of it. Nietzsche's self-assurance in this conclusion (short-lived as it turned out to be) is evident in the sentence with which this final section begins: "Und damit vorwärts auf der Bahn der Weisheit, guten Schrittes, guten Vertrauens!" [And so—forward on the path of wisdom, in good stride and good confidence!] (*HH* I:292).

This final section is also Nietzsche's first explicit and elaborated version of the "idea and ideal" of an attainable and admirable "higher humanity," within the bounds of his post-religious and post-metaphysical "naturalizing" new philosophy, that he announced four years later (on the back cover of the first edition of *Inquiry*) was the "common goal" of his *Freigeist* series. That "idea and ideal" turned out to be a "work in progress" that evolved and changed markedly in the years that followed. But this part of *Human* was Nietzsche's point of departure in its development, with his *Freigeist* concept featured prominently. For the Nietzsche of *Human*, the concluding sentence of part 5 encapsulates *Cultur* and humanity at their "highest," and represents the epitome of "freedom of spirit."

I shall conclude this discussion of this Nietzsche, however, on a different note. My suggestion is that much of what Nietzsche does and says in it—and subsequently, even after he changed his mind about where "the path of wisdom" leads—relates to thoughts expressed in an aphorism he placed in this part's center. In it he sounds what became another of his recurring themes—that of "becoming who or what you (potentially) are"—which he had earlier espoused in *Schopenhauer as Educator*, and which eventually supplanted that contemplative one. Here it is, in its entirety:

> Begabung.—*In einer so hoch entwickelten Menschheit, wie die jetzige ist, bekommt von Natur Jeder den Zugang zu vielen Talenten mit. Jeder hat* angeborenes Talent, *aber nur Wenigen ist der Grad von Zähigkeit, Ausdauer, Energie angeboren und anerzogen, so dass er wirklich ein Talent wird, also* wird, was er ist, *das heisst: es in Werken und Handlungen entladet.*

> Giftedness.—In a humanity as highly developed as ours is now, nature endows everyone with the possibility of [literally, "access to"] many talents. Everyone has *innate talent*, but only few possess the degree of innate and acquired toughness, endurance, and energy to *actually become* a talented one—and thus, to become *what he is*: that is, manifest it [literally, "unload it"] in works and actions. (*HH* I:263)

Addendum: The Nietzsche of *Daybreak*

The Nietzsche of the 1878 version of *Human* wrote and published two supplements during the next two years that became its second volume; but there is little in them that is of any substantial relevance and significance for the understanding of his developing kind of philosophy. Apart from some musings on morality, and a fair number of interesting reflections on art and music, he seems to have taken a kind of holiday philosophically—at least in print. But substantial portions both of what is now the first volume of *Human* and Nietzsche's next book, *Daybreak*, are also devoted to many and diverse matters that are equally far removed from his explicit philosophical interests and concerns. And this does relate to his kind of philosophy, in several respects.

Nietzsche was a remarkably avid, wide-ranging, and astute observer of the human scene, in all of its social, cultural, artistic, musical, literary, psychological, intellectual, personal, and interpersonal dimensions. That gave his thinking about human reality a great richness that he could and did draw upon; and it should be recalled when considering what to make of points he makes and positions he takes. Moreover, his philosophical and other concerns and interests were never far from each other in his life, and therefore in his mind and thinking—and so also in his book planning and writing. They seemed to feed off of and into each other, rather than being pursued with completely different and separated mind-sets. That is certainly the case with respect to his ideas concerning the generally human, the all-too-human, and the exceptionally human in *Human*. Nietzsche's kind of philosophy developed as a part of an intellectual panoply that seems always to have been in motion. And that shows and says something important about the kind of philosopher he was both inclined to be and able to be.

These observations apply to *Daybreak* as well. But in this least-well-known of Nietzsche's books, he resumed the mix of philosophical and more broadly human reflections that had characterized *Human* two years previously, in much the same spirit—as he would continue to do in *Joyful Inquiry* in the following year. That is not surprising, in view of the fact that these books together make up what he conceived to be his developing "free spirit" series, in which subsequent works were at first thought of as continuations of the same multifaceted project.

What sets *Daybreak* apart from *Human* is not a significant change in his kind of philosophy, but rather the evolution of his thinking on some philosophical issues, its extension into some areas that he had not previously been thinking about, and his remarkably increasing philosophical sophistication. That is why I have not given it a chapter of its own. In this addendum I will take brief note of some of what I consider to be the most important and interesting examples.

Nietzsche gave *Human* the full title he did because the general aim of the book was a sobering one: to take the idea of humanity as something supra-natural, uniquely akin to the divine, off of the lofty pedestal accorded it in traditional religious and philosophical thought. And then to begin its much more modest (and so deflating) reinterpretation, as a piece of nature with entirely mundane beginnings that has "become" what it is—and in which the all-too-human is much more prevalent than the admirable.

Nietzsche contrastingly gave *Daybreak* [*Morgenröte*; literally, "morning red-ness" or "rosy morn"] that very different and more upbeat sort of title to con-vey the idea that, while disillusionment is still the order of the day, that is only a necessary step on the way to the dawning of a new day that holds the promise of becoming a much brighter one for humanity than the one we know. And as its subtitle—*Thoughts on the Prejudices of Morality*—suggests, one of the kinds of obstacles that have to be cleared away is "prejudices" he associates with morality as we know it, as well as religion as we have known it.

So the first of the five "Books" (as Nietzsche calls its parts) of which *Day-break* consists concludes with a short series of sections having to do with what Nietzsche calls "the *euthanasia* of Christianity" (*D* 92) and the strategy he favors for dealing decisively with the God-idea—namely, of simply *deflating it*, by way of its "historical disposal" [*Wiederlegung*, "riddance"]. (That is: to *subvert*—rather than trying to *disprove*—the idea of the "existence of God.") He calls it a "historical" strategy because it undertakes to show "how the be-lief that there is a God could *arise* and how this belief acquired its weight and importance." And Nietzsche thinks that should be sufficient to deprive it of credibility, and so dispose of it (*D* 95).

He in effect adopts the same sort of strategy for dealing with the "preju-dices" and presuppositions of modern-day "morality." By exposing them and subjecting them to various sorts of analysis (historical, psychological, moti-vational, and the like), he intends to subvert them as well. But the first sort of morality he subjects to this sort of treatment is a different one. He calls it the "*Sittlichkeit der Sitte*"—often translated as "the morality of mores" but perhaps best rendered as the "ethicality of custom"; and he discusses it at length (*D* 9–19). It consists entirely in "obedience to customs," which are "*traditional* ways of behaving and evaluating" (*D* 9).

Nietzsche contends that this sort of morality once—and for a very long time—was ubiquitous in human life. He also accords enormous importance to it in the shaping of our humanity. So he speaks of "those tremendous eras of '*Sittlichkeit der Sitte*' which precede 'world history' as the *actual and deci-sive eras of history which determined the character of mankind* [*Menschheit*]" (*D* 18). And that is because he believes that our domestication—our transfor-mation from our original pre-social animality into creatures adapted to the re-quirements of social existence—was accomplished under the pressure of the need for us to become creatures responsive to the "authority of custom."[14]

This is a theme that Nietzsche had sounded in the very last section of his previous monograph (which became the second half of the second volume of *Human*), *The Wanderer and His Shadow* (*HH* II:II:350). And it is not only this type of morality that he believes can influence and have influenced the shaping of our human constitution. There is another example of this emerging feature of his philosophical thinking in this Book of *Daybreak*, in a section bearing the heading "*Drives Transformed by Moral Judgments*," when those "moral judgments" have been internalized (*D* 38).

In one of the sections of this Book dealing with this subject (*D* 28), Nietzsche brings in a term that he subsequently made much use of (in noun form): *übermenschlich*—perhaps best translated as "supra-human," in the sense of "transcending" either the humanly typical, the humanly exceptional, or the humanly possible. Needless to say, it matters a good deal which of these he means. Here he would seem to mean the first of these ways. He uses the term in the context of a discussion of the transformability and qualitative enhancement of our affective nature and "passions"; and he uses it to convey the idea of a trait that certainly contrasts with both *allzumenschlich* [all-too-human] and *untermenschlich* [sub-human] versions of that trait, and contrasts with the typically human version of it as well.

More specifically: Nietzsche seems to have in mind the enhancing transformation of an ordinary human (*menschlich*) "passion" [*Leidenschaft*] into a transfigured (and so *übermenschlich*) passion as a real human possibility, rather than just an ideal. He (interestingly and importantly) associates the realization of this possibility with "institutions and customs" that cultivate "belief" in the real possibility of the enhanced form of the passion, and establish practices that enable it to *come true*. And it is noteworthy that he says, of such a process, that it is humankind "elevating" [*hebend*]. This would seem to anticipate his subsequent idea of the "enhancement" of human life that the *Übermensch* was to represent. And I would suggest that, when he came to make much of the *Übermensch* idea shortly thereafter (in *Thus Spoke Zarathustra*), this understanding of it was quite probably his point of departure.

Another set of sections in Book 1 (*D* 41–45) also warrants comment. It begins by picking up on the idea of the "contemplative life" [*vita contemplativa*] that Nietzsche not only had discussed but also lauded in *Human*, as has been seen. Here he includes himself among those who choose and live such a life ("*wir als Menschen der vita contemplativa*"), discusses the human origination of such types, and proceeds to write at length about "the many forces that now have to come together in the thinker," to turn such human beings into those who realize that human possibility (*D* 43). (This is a topic to which Nietzsche repeatedly returns subsequently.) And he then concludes with a rather surprisingly powerful reflection on "the idea of *self-sacrificing humanity*," that would make "the knowledge of truth [. . .] the one tremendous goal commensurate with such a sacrifice, because for this goal no sacrifice is too great" (*D* 45).

This, too, is a topic to which he returns—in this very work, in Book 5, in a section bearing the title "The New Passion." There he writes: "Knowledge has in us been transformed into a passion which shrinks at no sacrifice and at bottom fears nothing but its own extinction" (*D* 429).

Yet these pronouncements are made in a work—*Daybreak*—in which Nietzsche also makes one of his strongest statements in print about the seeming human impossibility of knowledge—in Book 2, section 117 ("In Prison"). In this seeming update and reaffirmation of the upshot of his reflections on this topic in the early manuscript fragment *On Truth and Lies*, he writes: "The habits of our senses have woven us into lies and deception of sensation: these again are the basis of all our judgments and 'knowledge'—there is absolutely no escape, no backway or bypath into the *real world*!" And he memorably concludes: "We sit within our net, we spiders, and whatever we may catch in it, we can catch nothing at all except that which allows itself to be caught in precisely *our* net" (*D* 117).

This is a view of the matter to which Nietzsche was again drawn the next year, in *Joyful Inquiry*. But by then, as I read him, he was beginning to see our situation and prospects as human "knowers" in a somewhat different and more positive light, offering the prospect of a kind of way out of the apparently hopeless bind to which he here gives expression (as shall be seen in the following chapter). The question with which he leaves us (and perhaps himself) here, however, is whether knowledge of "that which allows itself to be caught in [. . .] our net" can possibly satisfy "the new passion" of which he speaks in the two passages cited above.

Book 2 consists almost entirely of such philosophical reflections. Most of its sections are extended discussions, and are aphorisms only in the sense that they are not broken into paragraphs. The most significant and sustained of them is a set of sections having to do with morality, and different ways of thinking about it (*D* 102–8). Section 103 is something that ought to be required reading for anyone interested in "Nietzsche on morality." Here he elaborates on what he calls "*my* point of view"—namely: "deny that moral judgments are based on truths," but "admit that they are really motives of action" (*D* 103). (Here he is definitely talking about *Moralität*, not about the *Sittlichkeit* of custom and other such norms.) And then he goes on to reflect in interesting ways on some of the issues that must be dealt with if one opts for a morality that takes as a goal "the preservation and advancement of mankind" (*D* 106), or if one commits to "the 'happiness and welfare of mankind'" as one's basic principle (*D* 108). He himself is often supposed to favor something like the former principle as the basis of his own recommended "positive morality"—and then frequently derided for not recognizing the very kinds of issues he here points out need facing. He in fact shows here that he gave them serious consideration quite early on.

This somewhat extended discussion is followed by a number of other stand-alone sections of considerable length, and of comparable significance and philosophical sophistication, on a remarkable range of issues, most of which Nietzsche had not previously (in *Human*) addressed. They include one with the heading "On the Natural History of Rights and Duties" (*D* 112). In it he reflects on the question: "Our duties—are the rights of others over us. How have they acquired such rights?" And in the course of his answer he contends that "rights originate [as] recognized and guaranteed degrees of power," and observes that "if power relationships undergo any material alteration, rights disappear and new ones are created."

Nietzsche then turns to a very different sort of question: how to understand the phenomenon—obviously important for him—of "the striving for distinction" (*D* 113). And he not surprisingly contends (with respect to its origin at any rate): "The striving for distinction is the striving for domination over someone, even though it be a very indirect domination and only felt or even dreamed." Two sections later (*D* 115) his topic is "the so-called ego"; and he begins with a complaint that subsequently became a frequent refrain: "Language and the prejudices upon which language is based are a manifold hindrance to us when we want to explain inner processes and drives." Here his point is that we are led by language's ineptitude to mistake "*our opinion of ourself*" for our "ego" or actual self—whereas: "*We are none of us* that which we appear to be [to ourselves] in accordance with the states for which alone we have consciousness and words."

Nietzsche continues that line of reflection in the following section, "The Unknown World of the 'Subject'" (*D* 116), in which he writes: "The primeval delusion still lives on that one knows, and knows quite precisely in every case, *how human action is brought about.*" The truth of the matter, he argues, is quite the opposite: "Actions are *never* what they appear to us to be!" The very next section is the reflection bearing the heading "In Prison" (*D* 117), discussed above. That is followed by an extended discussion of "experience and invention" (*D* 119). And so it goes for another thirty sections, to the end of Book 2. It is an impressive display of the kind (and diversity) of philosophical thinking of which he had come to be capable at this point, on a set of issues that would be readily recognizable by a good analytic philosopher, and dealt with in a way that could have engaged the attention and interest of a Hume or a Mill.

The three further Books of *Daybreak* that follow each have their philosophical moments, but are devoted for the most part to reflections on a wide range of human phenomena that are of little direct philosophical interest, but attracted the attention and interest of Nietzsche the observer of the "all-too-human," Nietzsche the psychologist of human peculiarities and pathologies, and Nietzsche the cultural, social, and political critic and analyst.

But recall my opening remarks concerning the wealth of his interests, which were by no means exclusively and narrowly philosophical. His passion for knowledge of things human, human reality, and the human world was vast— and it was a passion that was by no means quenched by the message of the "In Prison" reflection (*D* 117), as *D* 45 and *D* 429 both show. For this Nietzsche— and, I would say, for the Nietzsche he was coming to be philosophically—what we *can* have and know and do mattered more than what we can't. And so it comes as no surprise that he ended this second-longest of his works (surpassed only by *Human*) on an exuberantly positive note, with a last section titled "We Aeronauts [*Luft-Schifffahrer* (!)] of the Spirit!" (*D* 575). Nor is it any surprise that he concludes it with the following thought (even though followed by a final large question mark), pertaining to "all those brave birds that fly out into the distance": "All our great teachers and predecessors have at last come to a stop [. . .]. But what does that matter to you and me! *Other birds will fly farther!*"

The Nietzsche of *Joyful Inquiry* I–IV (*The Gay Science*)

DIE FRÖHLICHE WISSENSCHAFT ("LA GAYA SCIENZA")

This book concludes a series of writings by FRIEDRICH NIETZSCHE, whose common goal it is to erect *a new image and ideal of the free spirit*. To this series belong:
> *Human, All Too Human. With a Supplement.*
> *The Wanderer and His Shadow*
> *Daybreak: Thoughts about the Prejudices of Morality*
> *Joyful Inquiry*
>> Nietzsche's Advertisement on the Back Cover
>> of the 1882 Version[1]

New struggles [. . .]. God is dead [. . .]. And we—we still have to vanquish his shadow too!
> *Joyful Inquiry*, 108

When will all these shadows of God cease to darken our minds? When will we have completely de-deified nature? When may we *Menschen* begin to *naturalize* ourselves in terms of a pure, newly discovered, newly redeemed nature? [*Wann werden wir die Natur ganz entgöttlicht haben! Wann werden wir anfangen dürfen, uns Menschen mit der reinen, neu gefundenen, neu erlösten Natur zu vernatürlichen!*]
> *Joyful Inquiry*, 109

The dear human beast seems to lose its good mood [*gute Laune*] when it thinks well [*gut denkt*]; it becomes "serious [*ernst*]"! And "where laughter and joyfulness [*Fröhlichkeit*] are to be found, thinking gets nowhere [*taugt Nichts*]"—that is the prejudice of this serious beast against all "*fröhliche Wissenschaft*." Well then, let us show that's a [mere] prejudice!
> *Joyful Inquiry*, 327

The first (1878) version of *Human, All Too Human* was written and published while Nietzsche was still a professor at the Swiss University of Basel, in a discipline (classical philology) and an academic and cultural environment to which he had become ill suited, and from which he was attempting to distance himself. The first (1882) version of his next book, *Die fröhliche Wissenschaft*, was written and published when he had emancipated himself from all of that, and while retaining an attachment to the Swiss Alps, had been driven by his need for a warmer climate to discover the French and Italian coasts of the Mediterranean. It was a much more congenial environment for him in every respect, and became his new spiritual world, in which his spirits revived, even as his health problems continued to afflict him.

Nietzsche also became acquainted with an "Enlightenment" tradition earlier than that of Voltaire and his eighteenth-century French intellectual kindred spirits: that of the twelfth-century southern French troubadours, who had briefly flourished in the same part of the Mediterranean world in which he found himself to be newly at home, before they were extinguished by the plague and the Catholic establishment's Albigensian Crusade. The troubadours began as relatively free-spirited poet-musicians, whose secular art and craft came as a breath of fresh air.

In Nietzsche's rather idealized picture of them, the troubadours were kindred spirits—musically and poetically creative and intellectually emancipated secular humanists, unfettered by oppressive forms of religious and moral dogma and doctrine. (And, amazingly, they sprang up and flourished in the very heart of the Christian Middle Ages, centuries before the Renaissance!) They had come to have an art and craft of cultivating the most valuable sort of knowledge— that of how, aided by music and poetry, to joyfully laugh, love, and live. That came to be called their *gai saber* (in the Italian of the time). Nietzsche inserted a version of it, *la gaya scienza*, in the second edition of *Die fröhliche Wissenschaft*, on its title page, in quotation marks and parentheses, making it something like an epigram or subtitle. It is possible that he had known of it earlier, and was using his rendering of the idea in the German of his own time when he gave this book that title. In any event, that is the title that he gave it, and that I am rendering as *Joyful Inquiry*.[2]

This book was Nietzsche's inauguration of his attempt to move beyond what he had done in *Human*, and pursue the kind or kinds of life-liberating and life enhancing endeavor that this takes, and so make common cause with them— with the provision that, for someone like him (even if not for all), intellectual integrity and attaining as much comprehension of human reality and our world as is humanly possible are parts of the mix. One might say that what he wanted to be, at this point, was a kind of troubadour of philosophy. And his kind of philosophy, again at this point, is this kind of philosophy.

Joyful Inquiry[3] is a crucially important text for the understanding of Nietzsche's philosophical enterprise and thinking. Its initial 1882 four-"Book" (four-part) version was the last thing he published prior to *Thus Spoke Zarathustra*, and was presented as the culmination of his "free spirit" series that began with *Human, All Too Human* (1878).[4] The next prose expression and display of his kind of philosophy that he published was *Beyond Good and Evil* (1886) four years later. (That book will be the subject of chapter 5.) And the next one was, rather surprisingly, a resumption of this very work—a fifth "Book," added to a reissue of the original four Books, in 1887. In this chapter I will focus on the Nietzsche of 1882 in the initial version of the work—Nietzsche's kind of philosophy prior to *Zarathustra*, philosophy as free-spirited and *fröhliche* [joyful] *Wissenschaft*. (I shall, however, say something about that later, very important fifth Book subsequently, in an addendum to chapter 5.[5])

As the last passage cited at the outset makes clear, that kind of philosophy is a kind of thinking that, despite the seriousness of its concerns, is also meant to have something lighthearted about it. That is intended to be in marked contrast to most traditional philosophical writing, and in vivid contrast to the grim pessimism of Schopenhauer, ever on Nietzsche's mind as both "educator" and provocation.[6] In that respect it also differs, at least in tone, from the increasingly polemical works of Nietzsche's own that followed *Beyond* and the fifth Book of *Inquiry*. (There are certainly parts of *Genealogy*, his next book and last prior to those of 1888,[7] that live up to its subtitle: *A Polemic*.)

Between the 1880 monograph *The Wanderer and His Shadow* (*Der Wanderer und sein Schatten* [*Wanderer* or *WS*], which became the final part of *Human*) and the appearance of *Inquiry*, Nietzsche had published another very substantial five-part (or "Book") volume of aphorisms that he titled *Morgenröte*—variously translated as *Daybreak*, *Dawn*, and *Dawn of Day* (1881). He gave it the subtitle *Thoughts about the Prejudices of Morality*. "With this book," Nietzsche later wrote of it (in *Ecce Homo*), "my campaign against morality begins." But in many respects it was a transitional link between *Human*—and more specifically, *Wanderer*—and *Inquiry*. I shall, however, give it at least some of the attention it deserves in the addendum to this chapter.

Two notable things about these transitional works are Nietzsche's quite evident increasing philosophical sophistication, and his increasing hostility to the kind of morality that *Beyond* is intended to take us "beyond" and *Genealogy* is intended to subvert. But perhaps the most significant change is the disappearance of any trace of the surprising embrace of the rather Stoical disposition of contemplative serenity as the highest attainable form of humanity with which he had concluded part 5 of the first volume and version of *Human*.

Nietzsche actually initially conceived of what became the first three Books of *Inquiry* as a continuation of *Daybreak*—as its sixth, seventh, and eighth Books—with two more planned; but he subsequently decided to make them a separate volume and work in their own right. He published them as the first three Books of *Die fröhliche Wissenschaft* upon his completion of a fourth Book in 1882. So the fifth Book that Nietzsche added in 1887 was not just an afterthought. It was the tenth and last Book of that original plan, thereby in a sense completing it, with five of the Books in each of two works—*Daybreak* and *Inquiry*.[8]

It is difficult, of course, to be sure of what relationship there was between the originally planned tenth Book and the one that he finally did compose and add to the first four-Book version of *Inquiry* five years later, a year after *Beyond*. This does speak, however, in favor of the idea that there is some sort of continuity (if not unity) between what might be thought of as Nietzsche's larger post-*Human* philosophical "project" that began with *Daybreak* and was still intact at least as late as the fifth Book of *Inquiry*, notwithstanding the "interruptions" of *Zarathustra* and *Beyond* (and its sequel, *Genealogy*).

Nietzsche's decision to give these five post-*Daybreak* "Books" a separate identity was quite appropriate, however, not only because *Daybreak* was already quite long, but also because the Books that became *Inquiry* marked the launching of a more specific campaign within that larger project. It had been present in a general sort of way all along, from the very beginning of *Human* onward; but it had not previously emerged and been singled out clearly and distinctly as one of his major concerns. Begun implicitly with *Inquiry*'s first Book, Nietzsche announced this campaign with some fanfare at the outset of its third Book. I refer to Nietzsche's call in its second section for a "naturalizing" reinterpretation of human reality (*JI* 109).

This makes the third Book of *Inquiry* a text of considerable importance— not least owing to its bearing upon the issue of Nietzsche and "naturalism." Indeed, there may be no other text in which Nietzsche so clearly, explicitly, and unambiguously associates himself with the idea of a "naturalizing" reinterpretation of human reality. He does so in a very prominent place and way. Immediately after proclaiming that "God is dead" (*JI* 108), he proceeds to a long and striking discussion (in the next section) of "the world" as it must now be seen and reckoned with, in all of its discomforting godlessness. And in its concluding sentence he makes plain what he deems our immediate challenge (as philosophers) to be: to reinterpret our human reality correspondingly, as a piece of that larger mundane reality—and more specifically "to begin to *naturalize* [*vernatürlichen*] ourselves [*uns Menschen*] in terms of a pure, newly discovered, newly redeemed nature" (*JI* 109). (This is a passage I have already taken notice of, and which I will often have reason to mention again in subsequent chapters and contexts.)

This challenge is made all the more formidable, for Nietzsche, by the realization that our understanding of this "nature" of which we are a part must be not only "de-deified" but also (and perhaps consequently) "de-moralized"— that is, purged of the pervasive and distorting influences of the kindred anti-natural morality of "good and evil" against which he had launched his other campaign in *Daybreak* the year before. Moralities are real enough as human phenomena; but *as* human phenomena, our understanding of them, too, must be *vernatürlicht*, and they likewise (like religions) must be reassessed as the "naturalized" human phenomena they are. Thus the task of de-deified self-reinterpretation is not the only challenge that awaits us; for this assessment—which Nietzsche was to come to call a "revaluation of values" (informed and assisted by an investigation of their "genealogy")—lies beyond it.

And beyond that undertaking, for him, lies yet another task, of a kind very different from that of his *fröhliche Wissenschaft*, to which he was already turning his attention. Nietzsche was to come to call this further sort of challenge that of "value creation"; and this challenge is arguably the underlying issue of his next work, *Thus Spoke Zarathustra*, the opening lines of which are the final section of the 1882 version of *Inquiry*. This suggests that, different as these two works and projects may seem (and be), he also considered them to be linked, and wanted them to be so regarded—perhaps with *Inquiry* serving as a *preparation* of some sort for the project of *Zarathustra*, as Nietzsche then conceived of it.

Two other points of a very different, biographical nature are worth bearing in mind, as one reflects upon *Inquiry* and its author. One is that the year in which it was written was an extraordinarily stressful and difficult one for Nietzsche. This makes the *Fröhlichkeit* he not only proclaims to be the spirit of his *Wissenschaft* in *Inquiry*, but also displays repeatedly in the quips and wit that enliven it, quite remarkable. His general condition and circumstances were hardly conducive to a *fröhlich* state of mind.

Moreover, the word *written* here is something of a misnomer, because Nietzsche's eyesight problems had become so severe that he literally could hardly read, let alone write. He therefore had to compose ("write") mainly by dictation, and had to have his own notes and drafts read to him as he worked on the book. Much of the time he was in seriously poor health in other respects as well, as the opening of Book 4 reflects. The year 1882 was also the year of his five-month infatuation with Lou Salomé (the only woman he ever cared deeply about in a romantic way) and of her devastating rejection of him. And the impact of that episode left the rest of his personal life—his relations with those closest to him—a shambles as well.[9] So the *Fröhlichkeit* of this work was no mean achievement; and Nietzsche's insistence upon the need for and importance of it may have had a very personal inspiration.

The second of these two points relates to a different sort of stress. By 1882 Nietzsche's relationship with his publisher was becoming increasingly fraught, and was on the way to its final rupture a few years later. And worse still, it had become apparent to both of them that the books of his "free spirit" series were publishing failures, both in their sales (which were minuscule) and in their reception (which was virtually nonexistent). None of Nietzsche's earlier books after *Birth* had sold more than a few hundred copies; and no one seemed to be paying attention, which dismayed him greatly. That gave his writing of *Inquiry* a special urgency and—as his announcement cited at the outset shows—a sense of finality. Unfortunately, it suffered the same fate in terms of sales and reception as had the earlier "free spirit" series works. It is fortunate that he persisted with it; for it turned out to be one of his finest works, not only developmentally but for what it was and is in its own right.[10]

I

While Nietzsche reserved his announcement of the general project of *Inquiry* for the opening of its third Book, it was underway from the outset. Book 1 opens with a clear indication of it—as *Human* had four years before, but this time with more specificity. The reader is immediately put on notice that, for Nietzsche, *human* reality is first and foremost to be understood to be that of a particular biological species. And the most fundamental imperative of this species is asserted (naturalistically) to be that of its own survival, not as individual creatures but as a type—"the preservation of the human species" [*Erhaltung der menschlichen Gattung*].

Nietzsche would appear to be suggesting that this perspective—the perspective of "life" and of forms and types of "life"—is to be his point of departure for the refinement of our further reinterpretation of ourselves as *Menschen*. And he suggests that it follows that, biologically speaking, "the species is everything, the particular is nothing [*Einer ist immer Keiner*]." Where the basic purposes or dynamics of "life" are concerned, "the amazing economy of the preservation of the species" is a game that has nothing to do with morality, or anything like it (*JI* 1).

This theme is sounded repeatedly in the course of Book 1. Our origin can have been nothing more or loftier than what "life" is at the level of biological reality and nascent organic types; and the phenomenon of "life" is far from having begun and developed in a "moral" manner (*JI* 26). The basic question is what preserves various species and serves their development and advancement in the contest among them (*JI* 4). The problem of what to make of "consciousness" in such a world must therefore be understood to be the problem of the particular sort of "development of the organic" it represents; and of how something like the "knowing" we are capable of could have acquired the requisite sort of embodiment and expression in the life of such a creature (*JI* 11).

Yet interwoven among such observations are reflections of other, very different sorts, serving to make the point that such truths as these are not the *whole* truth about human reality, and that somehow a great many phenomena that are far removed from "life" so understood have come to be humanly possible and real. So, immediately following the sobering first section of Book 1 just mentioned, Nietzsche turns to the topic of "intellectual conscience," as a human possibility that is rare but possible, and of great importance. And that is followed by the first of several sections in this Book that explore the possibility of "higher" or "noble" qualities that contrast with others of a lower or more common nature, and of the sorts of difference these contrasts involve (*JI* 3, 9, 10, 55). Others follow in which such significant, more than merely biological human phenomena are discussed as the need for the compulsion of "unconditional duties" (*JI* 5), the study of "moral matters" (*JI* 7), different human ends that *Wissenschaft* can serve (*JI* 12), different forms of love (*JI* 14), how things can come to be valued (*JI* 21), and more.

The larger point Nietzsche is making here is that the kind of reinterpretation of human reality he is calling for and engaging in is one that is as mindful of these sorts of phenomena that have emerged and developed in the course of human events as it is of the first set of considerations he advances, beginning with that very first section. And by way of both his *sampling* of these various sorts of emergent (and clearly by no means merely biological) human phenomena and his *treatment* of them, Nietzsche is providing examples in advance of what is involved in the "naturalizing" of our understanding of *uns Menschen*— and of human phenomena he calls for at the outset of the third Book of *Inquiry*.

One of the best examples of such a phenomenon, for Nietzsche, is that of *Wissenschaft* itself—that is, of the various sorts of cognitive inquiry of which we have become capable, ranging from the natural sciences to the disciplines that concern themselves with historical, social, linguistic, and other such phenomena. Others include the further forms of interpretive psychological, genealogical, and philosophical inquiry in which he himself engages. Such inquiry may serve multiple human purposes and needs (*JI* 12), and may have its own genealogy and "chemistry" of ingredients, none of which by themselves have any cognitive worth (as Nietzsche goes on to suggest in the Books that follow, e.g., *JI* 333). And, as he observes in *JI* 37, its development may have even been promoted by various "errors." But none of that means, for him, that *Wissenschaft* is not really *Wissenschaft*, or does not actually exist (as a variety of forms of human intellectual endeavor that yield a variety of forms of comprehension). Indeed, in Book 4, he even goes so far as to observe that it has become humanly possible to entertain the idea of valuing such comprehension not simply as a means to various noncognitive ends, but for their own sake, and of conceiving of "life as a means to knowledge" (*JI* 324).

Yet this does not mean that Nietzsche is here abandoning his "naturalizing" project. On the contrary: these reflections are instances of his way of extending that project to this phenomenon and others of an intellectual and cultural nature. They show that and how mundane developmental sense can be made of the emergence and development of something as extraordinary as *Wissenschaft* has become and actually is (even if it is not all that some of its enthusiasts make it out to be, or to be worth).

II

Book 1 ends and Book 2 begins with reflections that are important to the understanding of Nietzsche's thinking and kind of philosophy at this point; and they help to make sense of why he devotes so much of Book 2 to reflections on art and artists. In *JI* 51, to which he gives the heading "*Wahrheitssinn*" ["Sense of Truth"], he signals both that there is a kind of "truth" that is meaningful and important to him, and that its real meaningfulness and importance are limited to human reality and the world of human experience and activity, insofar as it is possible for us to come to know them and discover what can make differences within them. "Things and questions that don't admit of experiment," he says, such as absolutist "forms of skepticism," have no place in his kind of philosophy, any more than do abstract and absolutist forms of realism and rationalism that reserve the ideas of what is real and what is true to something independent of life and experience. This relates to a very important point about Nietzsche's *fröhliche Wissenschaft*: it is intended to be human-reality-centered and human-life-focused, with their comprehension serving the higher end of their enhancement—conceived fundamentally as *living humanly well* and *turning out humanly well*.[11]

In *JI* 54, which bears the heading "The Consciousness of Appearance [*Scheine*]," Nietzsche goes on to reflect upon something he says he has "*discovered* for himself"—something "*Ich habe für mich* entdeckt"—and now claims to be his "knowledge" [*meiner Erkenntnis*]. It is related to the *Wahrheitssinn* just mentioned, and to what he now considers to be the meaninglessness and misguidedness of cutting philosophical thinking loose from that sense for the comprehension and enhancement of the reality that is life as we know it, and do and can live it. As he goes on to explain, it is the insight that, while the whole of our experience might be likened to a kind of "dream," in which "ancient humanity and animality, and indeed the whole prehistory and past of all sentient being" lives on and is reflected (and so has long been regarded as "*mere* appearance"), there is no ultimately real "being or essence of some sort" [*irgend welchem Wesen*] that is *true reality*, and to which the world of such "appearance" can and should be invidiously contrasted.

On the contrary: "Appearance is for me *the effecting and living* itself" [*Schein ist für mich das Wirkende und Lebende selber*]—the very manner in which "doing and living" go on. Here, Nietzsche suggests, the "appearance versus reality" distinction collapses, or ceases to make sense. It would be another sort of mistake to suppose that our version of *das Wirkende und Lebende* is the only one there is or could be. But for the Nietzsche of *Inquiry*, this realization does make *human reality* (in all of the ways we can come to know it), and *human possibility* (in all of the ways we can avail ourselves of it to enhance that reality), the proper foci of philosophy.

In Book 2 Nietzsche picks up where he leaves off in this manner at the end of Book 1, and shows what he takes one further step in this line of thinking to be. In its first section, *JI* 57 ("To the Realists"), he continues his attempt to subvert the "appearance/reality" distinction and prejudice against the former in favor of some imagined "true world of being" transcending or underlying it. If "reality" is conceived in that manner, then for Nietzsche, "There is no 'reality' for us." But, having disposed of that sort of idea and ideal of what is absolutely and ultimately "real," the word and idea become available for other uses, to which they are quite appropriate, subject to certain (rather significant) modifications. And again, for this Nietzsche, human reality and the world as we know and deal with it are cases in point.

So, in Book 2's second section, *JI* 58 ("Only as Creators [*Schaffende*; literally, "makers"]"), Nietzsche makes a number of points. One is that in this reconceptualization of the "real," these realities are and contain many sorts of "things" that *have come to be*. Further: when it comes to human life and experience, "we" have had much to do with what sorts of things have come to be and how they have come to be. And relatedly: in what he elsewhere calls "the world that matters to us," it is often the case that the attained natures of things owe more to "what they are called" [*wie die Dinge heissen*] than what they had come to be prior to or apart from our taking an interest in them and bringing language to bear upon them. The rough-and-ready descriptive and evaluative "names" used to mark them—"almost always something mistaken and arbitrary"—subsequently "slowly grow onto and into" them. What starts as mere name and "appearance" actually "becomes" the thing's *Wesen*—its nature and reality—"and *operates* [*wirkt*, functions] as *Wesen*."

In short: far from being something illusory or *merely* "apparent," such engendered objects of experience thereby *become realities*. "In the long run," Nietzsche concludes, "fashioning [*schaffen*, making or creating] new names and valuations [*Schätzungen*] and probabilities [*Wahrscheinlichkeiten*] suffices to create new 'things' [*neue 'Dinge' zu schaffen*]." In this way human reality and the world as we know it have been and continue to be elaborated into enriched, intertwined realities that, while strikingly different from the elaborated configurations of other forms of life, are *no less real*—for our human purposes—on that account.

Nietzsche's implied contention is that there is no other sort of reality to which it makes any human sense for us to aspire to apprehend, or to embrace as an ideal in relation to which human reality and its world should be assessed and found wanting. And his implied suggestion is that the course of wisdom in the situation in which we thus find ourselves would be to make the most and best of it that we can. He therefore proceeds to devote the rest of Book 2 to observations and words of wisdom relating to living (humanly) well, and to reflections on artistic creation and creativity and to what we owe to them and can be learned from them, as paradigms of the best way (humanly) possible to achieve the end of turning out (humanly) well. That is how Nietzsche chose to prepare the way for Book 3, and his preliminary discussion in it of the kinds of philosophical thinking that he considered to be both appropriate and needful—or at any rate most helpful—in conjunction with this message. (In the fourth and initially concluding Book, these two strands are extended and brought together.)

Before turning to Book 3, we should take notice of *JI* 107 ("Our Ultimate Gratitude to Art")—the concluding section of Book 2. And it is a conclusion of great importance. In it Nietzsche is quite candid about his "passion for knowledge" [*Leidenschaft für Erkenntnis*] and his "sensitive honesty" [*reizbaren Redlichkeit*, "intellectual integrity"]—which, he says, would "lead to nausea and suicide" if it were not countered by *something else*, owing to "the insight into general untruth and mendacity that is now given to us by science." By that, he says, he means "the insight into delusion and error as a condition of cognitive and sensate existence."

Nietzsche's theme here is reminiscent of *The Birth of Tragedy*; but his point is significantly different—despite the fact that he quotes what is perhaps the most famous line in that work virtually verbatim: "As an aesthetic phenomenon existence is still *bearable* to us." To this he adds: "and art furnishes us with the eye and hand and above all the good conscience to be *able* to make such a phenomenon of ourselves" (*JI* 107). But his thesis in *Birth* was that the Greeks were saved from those harsh fates (to which their awareness of the "terror and horrors of existence" would have driven them) by the various sorts of "illusions" they conjured up for themselves by their associated arts, and were able to buy into. His problem at that time became how we can avoid suicide-inducing nausea—and can even manage resoundingly to *affirm* existence in this life and world, as his Greeks did—if we not only *lose* our illusions but further *forbid ourselves* any resort to anything else of the kind.

So the problem for Nietzsche has shifted. What he now is concerned about is *not* the "insight" of "Dionysian wisdom" into the true nature of existence and the dreadful plight of all sentient creatures caught up in it. Rather, it is the predicament of a rather special sort of human being: (1) someone who is a *knowledge fetishist*, for whom "the truth, the whole truth, and nothing but the truth" not only *matters*, or even simply *matters most*, but is *all that matters*; someone who also (2) is a *truth purist*, for whom "truth" is conceived in terms of criteria that human thought and experience cannot satisfy; and (3) someone who further takes this to mean, as Nietzsche here writes, that: "delusion and error" [*Wahn und Irrtum*] are inescapable, and indeed are an actual "condition of cognizing and sensate existence" [*Bedingung des erkennenden und empfindenen Daseins*].

In short: what Nietzsche is suggesting here is this: *Wissenschaft*—sophisticated cognitive thinking and knowing—has led us to the "insight" [*Einsicht*] that both sense experience and cognition involve and require forms of "untruth and lying" [*Unwahrheit und Verlogenheit*], owing to the imposition of artificial forms upon or within experience without which neither sensation nor cognition as we know them would not be possible. And that "insight" would seem to have the consequence that truth and knowledge, strictly speaking (that is, conceived in thought/reality correspondence terms), are impossible.

That is the upshot that Nietzsche is saying here would be "utterly unbearable" for the truth-seeker and truth-valuer—were it not for something for which we are indebted to art: namely, a kind of "cult of the untrue." It is said to be a "counterforce" to the "honesty" [*Redlichkeit*] of commitment to the ideal of a kind of truth unsullied by any extraneous admixture. For art is said to have enabled us to develop a "good conscience" for something else, its "untruth" notwithstanding: namely, "aesthetic" phenomena—phenomena that involve the creative transformation of life and experience. It has made possible (and cultivated) a positively "*good* will to appearance" [gute *Willen zum Scheine*]: that is, a positive disposition toward things for which puristically conceived "truth" cannot be claimed, and is not even thought of as relevant, let alone imperative.

But there is more going on here than meets the eye. This story is told from the standpoint *of those whom* Nietzsche has already *left behind*—those who have not yet had the further insights of the previous sections just discussed. The point is that art had already readied "us" for release from the obsessions of both truth purism and knowledge fetishism, as categorical imperatives of intellectually conscionable thought, by making humanly possible the attainment of a different sort of sensibility, and with it a different sense of what is intellectually conscionable—and even estimable. It is a sensibility giving rise to a new sort of satisfaction, from the refinement and development of a sort of transformation of ourselves and our world that is quite independent of practices associated with what Nietzsche later called the "ascetic ideals" of truth purism and knowledge fetishism.

Further: although Nietzsche does not say so here, this is a kind of sea change that helps to prepare the way for a new appreciation of the sorts of reality that not only kinds and works of art but also human life and our world constitute and exemplify—and of the sorts of knowing, meaning, and mattering that are humanly possible as well. And this, for him, is a development of profound importance, both philosophically and humanly.

What Nietzsche says here, at the end of Book 2 in *JI* 107, is by no means his last word with respect to the various matters he mentions and comments upon—as he goes on to make clear in what follows. "Our ultimate gratitude to art" is gratitude for its having shown the way out of the crisis to which knowledge fetishism and truth purism would seem to lead, by its cultivation of a humanly attainable alternative ("aesthetic") sensibility; but that is only half the battle. The other half is to rethink "knowing" and "truth"—and meaning and mattering as well—aided by this new perspective, but moving beyond the seeming dichotomy of ways of thinking that Nietzsche here seems to be suggesting and embracing, to the disparagement of "the passion for knowledge" altogether. As becomes clear, in the course of the next (third) Book, that is by no means what he takes the moral of the story to be.

III

I shall now take a close and extended look at Book 3, because I consider it to be the philosophical heart of *Joyful Inquiry* (as well as the structural centerpiece of the expanded version's five Books). It begins with Nietzsche's first proclamation in print of the "death of God"—the demise of the viability of the God-idea—and his attendant announcement of the necessity of undertaking to confront and deal with the consequences of that idea (and event), and so of vanquishing its "shadow" (*JI* 108). That, Nietzsche is in effect telling us, is what he is going to be undertaking in what follows—which, we soon learn, involves a thoroughgoing *Entgöttlichung* [de-deification] of *Natur*, and a consequent rethinking of all aspects of human thought and life in which shadows of the God-idea may linger. Those tasks are essential to his larger, evolving twofold project of *reinterpretation* and *revaluation*, of which he also offers hints in this work. This third Book is of particular importance in this connection, because it shows what he chose to begin by addressing, and also how he sought to proceed.

At the outset of Book 3, Nietzsche expressly links the task of a "naturalizing" reinterpretation of human reality with his opening points about the demise of the God-idea and the vanquishing of its shadow articulated in the previous section. And he shows and indicates what *he* means by "naturalizing" in the sections that immediately follow. If Nietzsche is to be considered a "naturalistic" thinker, his "naturalism" should be understood along the lines of the kind of "naturalizing" that is on display there. Or at any rate: his "naturalism" must be construed in such a manner that there is room in it for the kinds of things he says and does and evidently thinks in what follows, in this Book in particular.[12]

Nietzsche's mantra "God is dead" [*Gott ist tot*] can be construed very broadly; but it would seem that, in its initial appearance in *JI* 108, it is properly understood precisely as he glosses it when it appears again in the opening sentence of the fifth Book added five years later: "The greatest recent event [*Ereignis*]— that 'God is dead,' that belief in the Christian God has become unworthy of belief [*unglaubwürdig geworden ist*]—is already beginning to cast its first shadow over Europe" (*JI* 343). The "event" to which he refers is the waning of the believ ability of the idea of "the Christian God"—presumably including its religious and philosophical kin, which for him include (or at any rate came to include) a variety of metaphysical absolutes.

It is interesting—and may seem odd—that, in this subsequent invocation of the idea, what is said to cast a problematic "shadow" needing to be reckoned with is not the God-idea itself (as in *JI* 108), but rather the demise of *its being taken seriously*. But that may have been deliberate, as a nice way of making the point that the two shadows are related, and that the "de-deification" process will not be complete until the absence of God itself has ceased to *seem to matter*. Nietzsche's question in the later passage is whether that point has yet really been reached; and his answer would seem to be that it is still too soon to tell— notwithstanding the surprising "cheerfulness" [*Heiterkeit*] of which he goes on to speak.

In the 1887 reappearance of the idea of this death-of-God "event" (*JK* 343), Nietzsche's focus would seem to be upon its consequences for "the whole of our European morality"—even though it soon turns out (in the very next section) that he considers much more than just "morality" to be at stake. In *JI* 108, on the other hand, five years earlier, he would seem to have been thinking primarily of its consequences for our understanding of the world of which we are a part, and of our human reality, both along with it and in relation to it; for it is to these consequences that he immediately turns.

There are few if any passages in Nietzsche's writings that are comparable to the depiction he gives here (in *JI* 109) of what he takes them to be, and the harshness of the aspect of this world when looked at with the sensibility of one accustomed to viewing it through the lenses of the God-idea. (It also is of no little interest that Nietzsche seems prepared here to consider himself in a position to be quite sure of the way the world actually *is* and *is not*, at least at this broad level of consideration. This is a Nietzsche who considers it possible as well as important to grasp and "tell it like it is"—and who supposes that it makes sense to speak of there *being* some way "the world" actually is that is ascertainable.)

And yet Nietzsche takes this occasion to give another kind of signal, at the very end of the section, where he quite surprisingly does what seems to be an about-face, and refers to this same world almost glowingly. When our reinterpretation and reassessment of it has truly been "*ganz entgöttlicht*" [completely de-deified], and the shadow of the God-idea has been completely eliminated, he suggests that we will be able to reinterpret our human reality in terms of a world that will then be for us a "*reinen, neu gefundenen, neu erlösten Natur*" [pure, newly discovered, newly redeemed nature].

What is most striking about this characterization is Nietzsche's reference to this "pure, newly discovered" nature as also newly "redeemed." Its de-deification is to be its "redemption"—its redemption from the language that makes his characterization of this world in *JI* 109 prior to this sentence seem so harsh and dismaying. But for that transformation to be accomplished, a new *sensibility*[13] will be needed as well—of the sort that Nietzsche envisions in the penultimate section (*JI* 341) of the fourth and final Book of the first version of *Inquiry* that features his parable of the "demon" and the "eternal recurrence" idea. (This is a point to which I will return.)

I thus mean to suggest that there is an arc in the structure of this 1882 four-Book work that connects the beginning of its third Book with the conclusion of that fourth Book—and so with the project of *Also Sprach Zarathustra*[14] on which he was already working. (And, I would add, with the continuation of the project of this work in the fifth Book that was subsequently added to it.) These are matters I shall not pursue here; but I mention them because I believe that they contribute to the understanding of the third Book (as well as of these other efforts), and of the moment it represents in the development and course of Nietzsche's thinking.

Having broached the idea of a "naturalizing" reinterpretation of human reality at the conclusion of *JI* 109, Nietzsche makes it clear that his answer to the question of "*Wann werden wir anfangen dürfen*" [when will we be permitted to begin] to undertake this task is: *here and now*, in this very Book. That is precisely what he immediately proceeds to do, in the set of sections that follows. He was by no means doing so for the first time here, however; for he had long been given to reflection on how various human phenomena originated.

That was what he was already doing in *The Birth of Tragedy* (as its very title indicates), a decade earlier, and in the contemporaneous essay manuscript fragment *On Truth and Lies*. It is what he was doing even more self-consciously and programmatically in *Human*, calling at its outset for "historical philosophizing" in the consideration of human reality and all things human, because *"der Mensch* has become," and indeed *"everything* has become" (*HH* I:1–2). That is what he does again here. And he begins with the very thing he was talking about in that early section of *Human*: our cognitive abilities. There his point had been that not only *der Mensch* but "also the ability to know [*das Erkenntnisvermögen*] has become." And here his topic is the "Origin of Knowledge" ["*Ursprung der Erkenntnis*"] (*JI* 110).

IV

Nietzsche begins with a little speculative fable (reminiscent of the opening of *Truth*) about how "knowing" could have gotten going, among creatures who started out as just a peculiar sort of animal that had developed language and the ability to produce and use propositions. These propositions [*Sätze*], he supposes, initially were "nothing but errors" [*Nichts als Irrtümer*]; but some of those "errors" may have turned out to be "useful and species-preserving" [*nützlich und arterhaltend*]. Nietzsche spins the tale out at some length. In it, his primary explanatory concepts are *"applicability to* life" (propositions that are *"auf das Leben* anwendbar [applicable to it]") and *"utility for* life" (having greater or lesser, positive or negative "*Nutzen* [uses] *für das Leben*"). His only further supposition is that a kind of play impulse [*Spieltrieb*] could have arisen and entered in, seizing upon and developing other *Sätze* that were neither useful nor harmful, in a context that had social and psychological dimensions (since both language and social interactions were involved).

This fable is a story of human circumstances of an entirely *mundane* character (that is, of an entirely this-worldly, pedestrian, practical, social, psychological, and interpersonal nature), fortuitously combining to make the beginnings and development of what has come to be known as *Erkenntnis* [knowledge] humanly possible. In this way "knowledge became a piece of life itself [*einem Stück Leben selber*]," capable of *opposing* "those ancient fundamental errors [*uralten Grundirrtümer*]": "both as life, both as powers, both in the same *Menschen*" (*JI* 110). The humanly mundane is no longer simply "natural," proceeding in accordance with the determinations of the *merely* natural; but it is a kind of modification and extension of the natural, in the transformed and transforming circumstances of human-language-mediated social and cultural life. It was the humanly mundane that Nietzsche had been exploring in *Human*;

and it is to this mundane extension of the natural that he looks again here, to suggest how the "origin of *Erkenntnis*" may be naturalizingly accounted for and understood.

The story Nietzsche tells of course is entirely speculative; but his point would seem to be that *something like* this can plausibly be supposed to have happened, as an entirely (but transformingly) mundane development in the lives of creatures whose pedigree was exclusively that of a piece of nature. Indeed, it *must* have happened in *something like* this way, if that is all we originally were, in view of the fact that there *have come to be* "thinkers," in whom *Erkenntnis* and *Wissenschaft* as we know them have become realities, and the grand "experiment" is occurring of finding out "to what extent truth is capable of embodiment" [*inwieweit verträgt die Wahrheit die Einverleibung*].

Pursuing such conjectures, with a view to seeing whether (and showing that) human phenomena as seemingly remote from natural phenomena as *Erkenntnis* (and others that he goes on to consider) *can* plausibly be accounted for in this manner, is precisely at least one of the sorts of thinking Nietzsche meant by "naturalizing" our understanding of our human reality in the previous section. (Likewise his talk of "translating [it] back into nature" [*zurück-übersetzen in die Natur*] in *Beyond*, BGE 230, four years later.)

Showing in this way that nothing more than such developmental accounts is *needed to make sense of* human capacities that might seem to be the hardest cases for the "naturalizing" program proposed in *Inquiry* (*JI* 109) is no knockdown argument; but it is a significant part of Nietzsche's way of *making a case* for this program. For doing so reinforces the guiding idea that all such phenomena are to be regarded as human phenomena that have originated in the course of entirely mundane human events, however impressive they may have become. The strategy here is to shift the "burden of proof" to those who would suppose otherwise, to come up with examples of phenomena that cannot plausibly be so accounted for. It is a further part of Nietzsche's strategy to attempt to preempt such countermoves by undertaking to anticipate what might appear to be the most promising possible counterexamples and show that they can be handled in this manner, while also taking the opportunity to flesh out the "naturalizing" reinterpretation of human reality that is being advocated and defended.

This, I suggest, is how best to understand Nietzsche's "naturalizing" and his kind of "naturalism," as we encounter it in the sections that follow *JI* 109. It pertains to the emergence and development in human life of capacities—such as what he had earlier called our "cognitive ability" (*HH* I:2)—and ways of thinking, sorts of experience and forms of activity that may seem to set human reality entirely apart from the world in which we find ourselves. They *do* differ markedly from what goes on at the level of the merely natural in ourselves as well as the entire existence of other life forms in this world; but that is because they have *come to do so* by way of nothing more grand than mundane developments in the course of human events.

This "naturalizing" endeavor thus proceeds by way of Nietzsche's attempt to show that it is possible to account for (and thereby make sense of, and do some justice to) the emergence and remarkable development of these human phenomena, and of that difference, *without* appealing to anything beyond the "natural" or life in "this world." The "natural," however, is to be understood to include not only the physical and biological dimensions of organic life on this earth, but also the mundane dimensions of human life that have developed out of and beyond them. As we shall see, this "naturalizing" mode of reinterpretation also provides Nietzsche with opportunities to take certain of these human phenomena down from their lofty pedestals, to the extent that their reverence is rendered problematic if they cannot be vindicated by considerations rendering the question of their origins irrelevant.

V

In the next three sections (*JI* 111–13), Nietzsche touches on related topics in a similar way, and to similar effect. Their topics are not exactly what they might seem to be: logic, causal explanation, and science. Nietzsche reframes them as three rather rarefied sorts of *thinking*—logical, causal, and scientific—considered as *human phenomena*, and with the question of how they might have arisen and developed in human life. And in each case, his intent is clearly to problematize them, even while acknowledging how remarkable each of them is.

In the case of the third of them, for example, Nietzsche begins by remarking: "So much had to come together for a *wissenschaftlich* kind of thinking to arise" (*JI* 113). He then suggests what some of them may or must have been— and they are all "powers" [*Kräfte*] and "drives" [*Triebe*] that themselves would seem in and of themselves to have nothing to do with comprehension. But they were available as dispositional resources in the mundane tool kit of pre-scientific human beings that serendipitously could under the right circumstances be pressed into service to constructive effect.

Nietzsche's primary concern here is not to question the idea that scientific thinking can and does make possible the attainment of a variety of impressive sorts of comprehension. Rather, it is to make two points: first, that "naturalizing" sense can be made of the emergence and development of this remarkable sort of thinking that is capable of things far greater than and different from what one might have expected of any or even the sum of its parts. But second:

the modesty and even motleyness of this array of elements should lead one to realize that such thinking is not to be trusted uncritically and relied upon exclusively.

To these points Nietzsche adds a tantalizing third. He envisions the development of a further—and "higher"—kind of activity in which "artistic powers and the practical wisdom of life [*die practische Weisheit des Lebens*]" will be joined with "*wissenschaftlichen* thinking," in an "organic" (rather than merely supplementary) way, surpassing each and all of these and other related activities (presumably including philosophy) as we now know them. This sounds very much like a recipe for something other than an enhanced sort of physics or biology: namely, the kind of philosophical *Wissenschaft* to which Nietzsche himself aspired. That kind of philosophy is indeed—among other things—to be scientifically sophisticated and attuned (in the spirit of *Human* I:1). That is a theme he had by no means abandoned at this point, and which he sounded again in this very work—most vividly in the following Book, in *JI* 335 ("Here's to Physics!"). But what he adds to such sophistication here is important, and separates such thinking from that which is characteristic of the various special *Wissenschaften*—natural, mathematical, linguistic, social, and historical. I shall return below to these additions.

Nietzsche offers a further reflection on *Wissenschaft* in *JI* 123, just ten sections later, that warrants comment in this connection. Its heading derives from its concluding sentence: "It is something new in history, that knowledge wants to be more than a means [*die Erkenntnis mehr sein will als ein Mittel*]"—which is to say, an end in itself, to be pursued for its own sake. Nietzsche begins the section by observing that *Erkenntnis* has become a "new passion" [*Leidenschaft*]—somewhat akin (he does not say but does not need to say) to the "religious feeling" he has just been discussing (*JI* 122)—although he observes that *Wissenschaft* certainly can be pursued *without* the "passion" that endows its pursuit with this higher order of significance.

It may seem that, in noticing and mentioning the emergence of this new phenomenon, expressed in the idea and ideal of "knowledge for its own sake," Nietzsche is doing so approvingly. While it is clear that he finds it *interesting*, however, he stops well short of its unqualified endorsement here. So he refers to it rather offhandedly as "this unconditional *Hang und Drang*"—a somewhat belittling phrase that means something like a "hankering and compulsion," that leaves entirely open the question of what is to be made of it, particularly if it becomes an obsession.

But Nietzsche quite certainly is inviting us here to consider whether it might not be better, all things considered, for *Wissenschaft* to be pursued, and *Erkenntnis* sought and valued, as more than a mere means, but conjoined with and supplemented by other sorts of endeavor (for example, of an artistic nature), rather than by itself alone. He could well have been thinking of the alternative of a pursuit of *Wissenschaft* within the context of (or in conjunction with) the higher-order sort of activity envisioned at the end of *JI* 113, the other elements of which might help to keep this "passion for knowing" from becoming an obsession—and so another (and possibly deadlier) of that section's "poisons," as the latest host for the ascetic ideal (*GM* III:25). In the fourth Book, however, we do find him giving it a strong endorsement, as shall be noted in due course (*JI* 324).

VI

Returning now to the subsequent sections of the third Book: *JI* 115 is of particular interest and importance for the understanding of Nietzsche's "naturalizing" reinterpretation of human reality and its development. Its suggestion is that much of what "humanity, humanness and 'human worth'" [*Humanität, Menschlichkeit und "Menschenwürde"*] have come to involve is owing to the developmental influence of four "errors" in our ancestors' understanding and estimation of themselves and their values. "*Der Mensch* has been educated [*erzogen*] through his errors [*Irrtümer*]"—brought up and raised by them, shaped by them, developed by them, in ways that have had a significant impact upon the contours of our human reality, their erroneousness notwithstanding (*JI* 115). This is another example of the kind of thing Nietzsche calls "naturalizing" our understanding of ourselves as human beings; for it is an example of seeing how significant aspects of our human reality could have originated and developed owing to influences of an entirely mundane nature—which, for him, is what such erroneous ideas are, even though they are at some remove from the merely natural.

The same applies to what Nietzsche discusses next, as he turns his naturalizing attention briefly but incisively to yet another of the purported jewels in humanity's crown: "morality" [*die Moral*]. Here his suggestion is that, different as "various moralities" [*verschiedene Moralen*] may be, they fundamentally are but different versions of a very human phenomenon through which "the individual" [*der Einzelne*] is "taught to be [*angeleitet*] a function of the herd," giving rise to a kind of "herd instinct" [*Herden-Instinct*] (*JI* 116) and "*herd* conscience" (*JI* 117) that he goes on—rather disparagingly—to discuss.

That sort of morality, for Nietzsche, is a very variable social phenomenon, involving "valuations and rankings" [*Schätzungen und Rangordnungen*] that are "always the expression of the needs [*Bedürfnisse*] of a community [*Gemeinde*]"—all of which elements are instances of mundane outgrowths of the merely natural, even though they have come to be far removed from the merely natural in both form and function. The associated sorts of "instinct" and "conscience" are suggested to be but social-psychological phenomena of an equally mundane nature, the lofty pretenses made on their behalf notwithstanding. What Nietzsche is offering here is a sketch of a "naturalizing" reinterpretation of the character and status of this entire array of moral phenomena—and of that part of human reality to which they have given rise, and which they involve. He pursues the same strategy in the following several sections (*JI* 118, 119).

The topic changes markedly in the next section, "Health of the Soul" ["*Gesundheit der Seele*"] (*JI* 120). It offers another window onto Nietzsche's "naturalizing" project. The ideas of "soul," "body," and their "health," along with the classical moral idea of "virtue" [*Tugend*] conceived in terms of the soul and its health, are at once problematized and pluralized, to take account of the mundane specificity and variability of the human reality to which they apply—which, however, only make the whole topic more interesting. Nietzsche's way of naturalizing it draws attention to the need for an account of human reality that is sensitive to the complexity and developmental diversifiability of what it has become.

In the two following sections, Nietzsche suggests the appropriateness of skepticism with respect to the reliability of any inferences one might be tempted to make with respect both to basic concepts we feel we could not dispense with in our attempts to make thought and action manageable in the world in which we find ourselves (*JI* 121), and to moral models and religious ideas that once were deemed compelling. This sets the stage for a new kind of uneasiness that is acknowledged in *JI* 124 to be an understandable reaction to the dawning recognition that there is no solid ground under our feet—"*kein 'Land' mehr!*"—of any kind that might serve as some sort of firm foundation, in the absence of the foundation God was long thought to provide.

This for Nietzsche is a consequence of the "naturalizing" reinterpretation not only of our own human reality but of everything to which we have any access, the experience of which must be recognized to be a human phenomenon of some sort that is therefore subject to the same reinterpretation requirement, rendering its authoritativeness problematic. It always was problematic, but is only now coming to be *recognized* to be so. Thus we are realizing that we are adrift on a boundless sea, "in the horizon of the infinite" [*im Horizont des Unendlichen*] (*JI* 124).

Nietzsche's task here now becomes that of trying to position himself to address the large question with which *JI* 124 leaves him—and us: How, being thus "at sea," are we now to *think*—and to *live*? Along the way, he reflects from time to time—as he continued to do subsequently—on the question of what sorts of *Erkenntnis* and comprehension remain (or turn out to be) *humanly possible*, these skeptical reservations and problematizing considerations notwithstanding. For he quite evidently considers philosophical reflection and inquiry—of the sorts in which he is here engaged, for example—to remain not only possible but worth pursuing, and to be no mere exercise in futility. His *fröhliche Wissenschaft* is to contribute both to *thinking well* and to *living well*.

But Nietzsche knows that the adjustment will not be an easy one—owing in no small measure to our addiction to the God-idea. That addiction, generalized into the need and craving for absolutes of some sort (even if not with all of the attributes of "the Christian God"), and the difficulty of recovering from being thus addicted, are among the effects of that idea's long and lingering shadow. Hence the famous "Madman" ["*Der tolle Mensch*"] section (*JI* 125) that immediately follows the "Horizon of the Infinite" section. The plug of the life-support system on which "we" (speaking generally) have come to depend has been pulled—and it is "we" (in some sense) who have pulled it, without realizing just how disorienting and traumatic the results could be. Of course it was also "we" who constructed it and connected ourselves to it in the first place; but that does not diminish the magnitude of the sense of both need and loss that the "madman" expresses.

Understandable though the anguish of the *tolle Mensch* may be, however, it clearly is something for Nietzsche that we must anticipate, understand, be prepared for—and get over. Withdrawal from addiction is seldom easy or pretty—yet if it can be accomplished, life on the far side of it can be not only possible but better. And that is surely Nietzsche's hope and expectation in this case—as the possibility and attainability of the completely different sensibility of the very next section presumably is intended to convey. The distress of the *tolle Mensch* is made abruptly to seem to be much ado about nothing. "Mystical explanations" [*mystische Erklärungen*], and so also the ideas and beliefs that are required to give them any plausibility, are *not* "deep" at all, and indeed are "not even superficial." Such thinking, for Nietzsche, far from even being coherent, is simply nonsense (*JI* 126).

VII

In this way Nietzsche undertakes to change the discourse about religion, and turn it from a kind of thinking the content of which can and should be taken seriously as a divinely inspired *explanans* (something that explains) into a very human *explanandum* (something to be explained). It warrants being taken seriously only symptomatically, and being dealt with as a phenomenon (or cluster of human phenomena) that may be presumed to have the same general type of explanation (or multiple explanations) that other such phenomena do. And a part of this strategy is to place it in the larger context of what Nietzsche had called "the religious life" in *Human*, or what he would call the phenomenon of "religiousness" [*das religiöse Wesen*] in *Beyond*. He thus treats religion as he treats morality, here as in both of these other works (and in *Dawn* and *Genealogy* as well): as a real and significant but problematic human phenomenon.[15]

Nietzsche's approach to both religion and morality in *Inquiry* is reflected in the titles he gives to the sections on moral phenomena in these other two works—"On the History of Moral Feelings" ["*Zur Geschichte der moralischen Empfindungen*"] and "On the Natural History of Morality" ["*Zur Naturgeschichte der Moral*"]—and in the similar title of *Beyond*'s sequel, *On the Genealogy of Morality* [*Zur Genealogie der Moral*].[16] He proceeds in all of them as though it can be taken for granted that the varieties of morality and moral phenomena with which we find ourselves confronted in human life and history are *human phenomena*. And further: That all such phenomena have originated and developed in the course of human events, and warrant construal and treatment as pieces of life having entirely mundane—even if also more than merely biological—"natural histories," in which social circumstances, cultural developments, psychological factors, and interpersonal dynamics have loomed large. He does the same with the varieties of religion and religious phenomena (religious thinking among them) that he identifies and considers in them, and in this Book, in the sections that follow *JI* 126 (through 151). He even does them the indignity of associating them with various (other) "narcotics" (*JI* 145, 147).

This treatment might be thought of as Nietzsche's "naturalizing" neutralization or subversion of the claims of religiousness to deserve to be regarded with respect and reference and given the benefit of the doubt, rather than as another of the families of cultural and social-psychological phenomena that have figured significantly in the genealogy of human reality. It has had powerful effects; but the kind of thinking associated with it is no serious rival to his philosophical orientation. So he concludes this part of the third Book by summarily dismissing the "Apprehension [*Annahme*] of an 'other world'" that has long been so central to it as nothing more than "a *mistake* [*Irrtüm*] in the interpretation of certain natural processes [*Naturvorgänge*], a failure [*Verlegenheit*, embarrassment] of the intellect" (*JI* 151).

In the course of his remarks, Nietzsche makes a particularly interesting suggestion that clearly shows that he by no means considers all types of religiousness to be of the same character, and also illustrates how significantly different he considers their human-developmental influences to have been once they got going (their mundane origins and the erroneousness and fictitiousness of their conceptual schemes notwithstanding). He credits "polytheism" (belief in multiple gods) with having played a major role in the emergence and development of the human possibility of creative differentiation, not only at the cultural level, but ultimately even at the individual level, making it possible for individuals "to establish their ideal, and to derive from it their own law, their joys, and their rights [*sein Gesetz, seine Freuden und seine Rechte*]."

Nietzsche takes this to have been important. It was developmentally necessary to give a good conscience to resistance to both the oppressive monolithic ideal of monotheism and the norms and imperatives associated with it—such as "the central law of all morality," that for human beings "there is only one norm [*Norm*]: *the* human [der *Mensch*]," prescriptive for all. "The wonderful art and power to create gods—polytheism—was the medium in which this drive [to establish something as an ideal] expressed itself, and in which it then purified, perfected and ennobled itself." Polytheism legitimized the idea of "a *plurality of norms*" [*eine* Mehrzahl von Normen] (*JI* 143).

Nietzsche goes on in this section to lament the triumph of monotheism, the "rigid consequence of the doctrine of one normative human type [*von Einem Normalmensch*]," which he regards as "perhaps the greatest danger to humanity hitherto: it faced the threat of its premature stagnation [*vorzeitige Stillstand*]." And he concludes it with the thought that polytheism helped to create the conditions of the possibility of the very sort of diversified higher spirituality that was and remains needed for humanity to regain its bearings: "In polytheism the free-spiriting and many-spiriting [*Freigeisterei und Vielgeisterei*] of man was foreshadowed [*vorgebildet*]: the power to create new and distinctive eyes for ourselves [*neue und eigene Augen zu schaffen*]," contributing significantly to our unique liberation—"alone among all animals"—from the bondage of "eternal [that is, fixed and unchangeable] horizons and perspectives" (*JI* 143). This is directly relevant to the challenge posed in *JI* 124.

Nietzsche thus shows himself here—neither for the first nor the last time—to be as positively disposed to one sort of (commonly ridiculed) religiousness as he is negatively disposed to its more familiar and generally highly regarded (Christian) counterpart. In both instances, he is so disposed for reasons relating to what he takes to be the very different ways in which they affect human possibilities, opening up and fostering some, hindering and discouraging others. That, for him, is how such human phenomena are most appropriately assessed: in terms of their "value for life" and significance in relation to its enhancement. And, on a different level of consideration, that is one of the ways in which such transformations of our human reality have come about in the course of entirely human events.

This is an important point. Both sorts of religiousness are excellent examples of phenomena that Nietzsche considers to have made a real difference
in how human beings have turned out that is at once far removed from the
"merely natural" and one of the very kinds of considerations that his "naturalizing" of our understanding of human reality involves. For these forms
of religiousness have their "natural"—which is to say, mundane—histories
and genealogies, as do the sensibilities and forms of life of the human beings
they affect. As sublime as their associated forms of experience and activity and
artistic and literary expressions may be, they are nonetheless anchored in the
mundane—itself a manifold of developments of the originally merely natural—
of which they are further transformations.

Inquiry 143 is thus a case study of what it means for Nietzsche to pursue
the "naturalizing" project announced at this Book's outset. And the kind of
"naturalism" it reflects—Nietzsche's kind of "naturalism," at this juncture at
any rate—must be construed in such a way that it has room in it for the human phenomena and possibilities he discusses here and elsewhere. Among
them is what he calls an impulse or drive to have "ideals of one's own" [*Trieb
zum eigenen Ideale*], that he supposes to have been "originally a crude and un-
distinguished impulse, related to those of willfulness, stubbornness, and envy
[*verwandt dem Eigensinn, dem Ungehorsame und dem Neide*]," but to have un-
dergone major development and transformation. It eventually could and did
enter into and find sublimated expression in the transfigured and transfiguring cultural activity of "creating gods" [*Götter zu schaffen*], through which it
was then further "refined, perfected and ennobled."

It is in this context that Nietzsche makes use of an expression that was to
loom large in *Zarathustra* a year later. "The invention [*Erfindung*] of gods,
heroes, and *Übermenschen* [NB!] of all sorts [. . .] was the invaluable preparation for the justification of the self-centeredness and self-assertiveness [*Selbstsucht und Selbstherrlichkeit*] of the individual." For, he explains, "The freedom
that was attributed to gods in relation to other gods" was something that subsequently could be claimed by and "accorded to oneself in relation to laws,
customs, and neighbors [*Gesetze und Sitten und Nachbarn*]." And here "*Übermenschen* of all sorts" [*aller Art*] quite clearly is both a pluralistic idea and one
that simply refers to the conceivability of significant sorts of exceptionality to
the human rule.

In short: Nietzsche's two larger points here are that, first, this diversely creative and expressive capacity, suppressed though it has been by the long dominance of (Christian) monolithic monotheism, nonetheless remains accessible
as a human-spiritual possibility. And, second, it is one that has prepared the
way for that original rudimentary impulse to be expressed and realized as it

never could have been originally: as the emergent human possibility of the self-directed, self-creative, and self-expressive "individual" [*der Einzelne*] evoked in the section's opening sentence, cited above (*JI* 143).

In an earlier section Nietzsche permits himself the jibe, "Now it is no longer our reasons [*Gründe*] but our taste [*Geschmack*] that is decisive against Christianity" (*JI* 132). However, as he shows in the section under consideration (not to mention in *Der Antichrist*, some years later), it would have been more accurate if he had said: "Now it is no longer *only* our reasons." He seems to have been thinking here of his "reasons" for considering the idea of "an 'other world'" [*einer "anderen Welt"*] to be "an error," and the God-idea to be "a mistake." Yet his conviction and argument that monotheisms in general (and Christianity in particular) are detrimental to the health and enhancement of human life is also a "reason" for him, and the most decisive one at that—even if it is a reason of a different sort.

Nietzsche's reference to "our taste" does gesture in that direction. But it understates what he takes the real force and significance of that consideration to be. It is a great oversimplification to suggest—as he seems to be doing here—that any consideration that is not a "reason" *of the sort* one might have for considering a belief to be "a failure of the intellect" can only be a (mere) matter of one's "taste." (Nietzsche often oversimplifies in this manner for the sake of being able to make a nice quip that has a point.)

VIII

Having dealt with religious thinking and dismissed it as any sort of serious rival, Nietzsche concludes this very substantial portion of the third Book of *Inquiry* with two reflections, the first of which he entitles "The Greatest Change [*Veränderung*]." Its theme is that, with the "death" not only of the God-idea but also of the various forms of religiousness that previously (and variously) illuminated and humanized our sense of our world and ourselves, we find ourselves newly challenged. Our situation is different from that of a transition from one sort of religious sensibility to another. We now find ourselves having to learn to get along without *anything of the sort*—anything like a transcendent source of illumination, consolation, and warmth.

A thoroughly de-deified and naturalized world would seem to be not only a disenchanted one, but also a darkened and colder one. "We have given things new colors, and go on painting them," Nietzsche writes, perhaps with the *Wissenschaften* and the arts in mind; but he confesses to the sense that our efforts seem rather feeble when compared to "that old expert [*Meisterin*]" at this sort

of thing—namely, "ancient humanity" (*JI* 152). But we can no longer avail ourselves of their palates and options, which are no longer live ones for us. Now
the real reckoning with "the death of God" must begin.

In short: where do we go from here? That is what Nietzsche asks in the
second of these two sections, which he titles "*Homo poeta*" (*JI* 153). Echoing
the "Madman" section, he writes (putting his words in quotation marks, perhaps again in the spirit of that section) that the situation would seem to be an
impossible one, and a tragic one at that; for it would seem that nothing short
of "a god" [*ein Gott*] will suffice—and yet nothing transcendent of morality
and religiousness remains. "I myself have now, in the fourth act [operatically
speaking], done in all gods [*alle Götter umgebracht*]—out of morality [*aus
Moralität*]!" (That is: out of a sense of obligation to be honest and truthful.)

So Nietzsche wonders about the possibility of an appropriately "tragic resolution [*Lösung*]"—or, alternately (and perhaps more interestingly), "a comic
resolution"! He concludes the initial version of *Inquiry*, at the end of the fourth
Book, by citing the opening of *Zarathustra*, giving it the heading "The Tragedy Begins" ["*Incipit tragoedia*"]—seemingly opting for the former. If so, it is
"tragedy" of an unusual sort—neither Greek, nor Shakespearean, nor Wagnerian, but rather (so to speak) Zarathustrian; although it is not easy to parse
Nietzsche's *Zarathustra* as tragic, in any sense at all, notwithstanding his apparent invitation to us to do so.

But be that as it may—what is to be made of the rest of the third Book?
The remainder of it, from *Inquiry* 154 onward, might be thought of as having
two parts. Both are aphoristic, with few sections running to more than a half
dozen lines, and many of them single-sentence quips and observations. The
first part—all but the set of a dozen questions and answers with which the Book
concludes—is reminiscent of *Human* in style, tone, and content. It deals with
many different facets of "the human"—from the all-too-human to the typically
human, to both the pathologically human and the exceptionally human in some
of its many different developments and manifestations.

A few of these aphorisms are also of interest for their bearing on various
aspects of Nietzsche's developing philosophical thinking. One of them, often
cited as though it were his last word on the subject, is an aphorism bearing
the heading "Final Skepticism" ["*Letzte Skepsis*"], in which he asserts that "man's
truths" [*die Wahrheiten des Menschen*] are "ultimately" [*zuletzt*] actually simply
"man's *irrefutable* [*unwiderlegbaren*] errors" (*JI* 265). It is far from clear, however, that he means this assertion to apply not only to ideas that are commonly
taken for granted or are indispensable to our thinking and reasoning in various contexts, but also to *all* forms, kinds, and instances of "truth" and "truths"

in all domains of discourse in human life, ranging from ordinary-life contexts to the many special contexts—for example, legal, historical, mathematical, medical, and scientific—in which there are established truth-conditions.

It also is far from clear that Nietzsche also means this characterization to apply to everything even he and his kind of philosopher might come up with in their reinterpretations and revaluations; for that verdict then would apply to this proposition itself, which would be nonsensical—which it is quite obviously not meant to be. Moreover, this aphorism is preceded by another, only a few pages prior, in which he shows himself to be one who well "knows" [kennt]—as he himself does—"the passion of the knower [Erkennenden]" (JI 249), problematic though he may consider that "passion" to be (as has been noted above).

What I take Nietzsche to have in mind in the passage just cited (from JI 265)—as he sometimes makes explicit on other occasions in which he says such things—is a special class of supposedly privileged and fundamental purported "truths": namely, the principles basic to logical and scientific reasoning, such as those of "(non)contradiction" and of "sufficient reason" or causality— the "human" (and problematic) character of which he frequently insists upon. But he also makes much of the very real human possibility of various forms of knowing and knowledge, not only elsewhere but in this very work and Book.

So, for example, shortly before this aphorism, Nietzsche had made the interesting suggestion that it is desirable for "the refinement and rigor of mathematics" to be introduced into "all Wissenschaften" (cognitive disciplines), not in the belief "that in this way will be able to know all things," but rather because mathematics is "merely the means of the general and ultimate knowledge of man" [nur das Mittel der allgemeinen und letzten Menschenkenntnis] (JI 246). And Menschenkenntnis—which can and does for Nietzsche mean both "knowledge of man" and "human knowledge"—is the very sort of comprehension that he cares most about, and has in view throughout this work. So also, earlier in this set of sections, he had written of the need for "the Germans" to get over their "moralistic prejudices against the worth of knowledge" (JI 178).

In short: the Skepsis of which Nietzsche speaks in JI 265 is not a global and total one.[17] The Nietzsche we encounter in this third Book of Inquiry shows himself to be a committed philosophical Wissenschaftler (inquirer) convinced of the possibility—and "worth," as JI 178 implies—of attempting to comprehend and coming better to comprehend at least some things, relating to our human reality in particular. Indeed, this set of sections contains a good many examples of what he would seem to regard as cases in point.

A sampling of at least a part of what he means by Menschenkenntnis, I suggest, is precisely what this last part of this Book is intended to provide. This would make good sense of the presence and placement of its many aphorisms here, which differ so considerably in character from those that precede them. Indeed, I take them to illustrate what Nietzsche was talking about in *JI* 113, in speaking of "practical wisdom" *des Lebens*—which can and I believe does here mean both "of life" and "concerning life"—as one of the important ingredients in the mix of the higher-order kind of thinking he there envisions, along with *wissenschaftlich* sophistication and "artistic powers" [*künstlerischen Kräfte*]. That sort of "practical wisdom" is something for which these other qualities do not suffice, and by which they need to be complemented if justice is to be done to human reality in its new-philosophical naturalizing reinterpretation.

I would suggest that Nietzsche is here indicating something about his own thinking: namely, that he wanted it to have this third dimension (which has been on display from *Human* onward), as well as the other two. It had the first of them, at least in aspiration and purport; and the second was soon to be demonstrated (by the impending literary-philosophical creation *Thus Spoke Zarathustra*, that the first edition of *Inquiry* introduces at its conclusion). This part of the third Book might be thought of as a component of Nietzsche's own audition (as it were) for the multifaceted role of the kind of new, higher-order thinker he envisions and describes in *JI* 113—the filling of which role thus may not for him have been as distant a prospect as he appears to be suggesting.

IX

The second short set of aphorisms (*JI* 268–75), with which the third Book concludes, has the form of a kind of catechism. In this series of questions and answers, Nietzsche puts a number of his cards on the table in vivid form, to convey something of the character of the kind of philosophical thinking to which he was committed and aspiring at this juncture. It is a kind of thinking that he considers not only to be compatible with the de-deifying and naturalizing program he heralds at the Book's outset, but also to be called for by it, in order to move constructively beyond it—as one moves on to the question of where we go from here, humanly as well as interpretively.

In these concluding aphorisms, Nietzsche touches on matters relating to the ideas of a "higher" and "healthier" humanity, and so of its enhancement. He does so very cryptically, yet revealingly, making it clear that it is considerations such as these for which all that has preceded these *Sätze* (propositions) has been preparing the way. They also are indicative of aspects of the new sort of *sensibility* that he goes on to introduce in both the next (fourth) Book of *Inquiry* and the very different work that followed it, and that is the subject of the next chapter: his *Zarathustra*.

These rather hortatory concluding aphorisms may be read at least in part as further expressions of "the practical wisdom of life" that has been on display in this last part of the Book prior to them, offered here to show that such "wisdom" is not limited to the recognition and exploration of the "all-too-human" character of so much of the human. But there is more to them than that. Nietzsche here chooses to conclude with some words of wisdom with respect to human possibilities that may be exceptional but are also to be discerned and taken seriously. These last aphorisms, for him, are deserving of being his "last words" here, particularly after the sobering series of reflections with which the Book began and proceeded. These aphorisms suggest where and how enlightened (and disillusioned) free spirits might go from here, both philosophically and humanly, beyond the "death of God," the de-deifying of nature, and the naturalizing of human reality.

In *JI* 268, with which this little catechism begins, Nietzsche envisions a new, possible, and admirable sort of tragic "heroism" of the spirit in which highest hopes are dared and pursued, undaunted by the recognition of the highest suffering they invite. In *JI* 269 he expresses belief in the necessity—and therefore the possibility—of a revaluation (*Umwertung*, as he was soon to call it) of values that is no mere *de*-valuation or Ent-*wertung*: "that the weights of all things must be newly determined [*neu bestimmt*]." And in *JI* 270 he embraces the idea of a new, post-religious and post-moral form of "conscience," with a new kind of call (exhortation or appeal), which he famously formulated in variations of his wording here: "*Du sollst der werden, der du bist*" [Thou shalt become who you are].

I shall not discuss here the meaning of this call, which warrants careful consideration; but it very evidently connects with his own parsing of this very idea toward the end of the next and final (fourth) Book of this work's first version: "We, however, want to become those we are—the new, the unique, the incomparable, the self-legislators, the self-creators!" [*Wir aber wollen Die werden, die wir sind,—die Neuen, die Einmaligen, die Unvergleichbaren, die Sich-selber-Gesetzgebenden, die Sich-selber-Schaffenden!*] (*JI* 335). This, for the Nietzsche we encounter here, is clearly a real and meaningful—if also difficult and precarious—human possibility.

In the next aphorism, Nietzsche points to what—for him, at any rate—seems to be at least one of the dangers to the realization of this possibility, which Schopenhauer had actually championed, and had made all too seductively attractive: "your greatest dangers" are said to lie in "pitying" [*Mitleiden*] (*JI* 271). He presumably has in mind both pity (in various ways) for others and pity for oneself. He could also have in mind what he had Zarathustra refer to, three years later, as his own "final sin" [*letzte Sünde*], just before the ringing conclusion of the fourth part of that work made possible by its overcoming: the "sin" of "pitying" the "higher" types of human beings ("*höheren Menschen*")—not only because even they remain not only human and all-too-human, but also because they are ever at risk.[18] So, coming just after *JI* 268, this aphorism stands as a warning against allowing the "highest suffering" [*höchste Leide*] that their kind of heroism dares to risk, in conjunction with their "highest hopes" (so easily and often dashed), to give rise to a paralyzing pity (and self-pity) that would pose a deeper danger than any such "suffering" itself to the kind of life and its enhancement that he is envisioning.

The theme of such a hope is sounded again in the next aphorism, in which what Nietzsche says he loves "in others" is: "my hopes" (*JI* 272). And as a counterpoint to the aphorism about the danger to his hopes posed by the seductiveness of that sort of pity that is self-pity, Nietzsche had just made the point (a few aphorisms previously) that "those who have greatness" [*wer Grösse hat*] must have the capacity for a kind of "cruelty" [*Grausamkeit*] strong enough to override the tendency to pity. And what he has in mind is the capacity to be "hard" (as he likes to say), not in the first instance heedlessly toward others, but rather on themselves, and even "against their own virtues"—although also against what he rather vaguely (and perhaps worrisomely) calls "considerations of secondary importance" [*Erwägungen zweiten Ranges*] (*JI* 266).

Nietzsche concludes this series of questions and answers (and this Book) on a seemingly surprising note, with three aphorisms on the topic of shame [*Scham*]. In *JI* 273, in response to the question "Whom do you call bad?" [*Wen nennst du schlecht?*] he answers: "Those who always want to shame" [*Den, der immer beschämen will*]—thereby seemingly suggesting the *inculcation* of the feeling of shame to be at the top of his list of reprehensible things people can do to others. In the next aphorism, he says that what is most humane (*das Menschlichste*) is "shame sparing" [*Scham ersparen*]—refraining from cultivating the sense of shame and prompting feelings of shame in others, even when doing so might be tempting (*JI* 274). And in the final aphorism, he carries the theme of liberation from shame a final step farther, into oneself: the "seal [final sign] of attained freedom" is said to be: "no longer being ashamed in front of oneself" [*Sich nicht mehr vor sich selber schämen*] (*JI* 275).

What is to be made of this—particularly as a conclusion intended to be taken as culminating? The very fact that Nietzsche devotes not just the final aphorism but the final *three* aphorisms to this theme suggests that he considered it to be a matter of great importance. He also attached importance to liberation from the sway of a variety of other such phenomena, owing to their blighting effect—the senses of guilt and sinfulness among them. At this point, however, it was the sense of shame that he seized upon (in the spirit of *JI* 269, it may be noted), as a salient instance of something he considers to be in serious need of revaluation.

I suggest that he may have done so because he regarded shame as a particularly insidious device that has long been employed to make people feel and think badly of themselves. Here he has in mind, more specifically, everything about themselves relating to *natural* states, functions, and dispositions, from nakedness[19] and lust to assertiveness and competitiveness to curiosity and selfishness. This shows that he considered this tendency to be one of the salient "shadows of God" that we must "vanquish" [*besiegen*].[20] This is a theme to which Nietzsche returned, using similar language, in *Twilight of the Idols* (1888), in which he associates the demise of "the concept 'God'" with what he calls "the great liberation—only thereby is the *innocence* of becoming [*die Unschuld des Werdens*] restored again."[21] That "innocence" (or, more literally, "un-guiltiness") is akin to the condition of being able to be unashamed that he is envisioning here.

The "shame-overcoming" theme of these last aphorisms also anticipates and is suggestive of one of the basic characteristics of the new sort of sensibility Nietzsche has come to understand is needed in the aftermath of the "death of God." This is how Nietzsche was to frame it at the end of the second essay of *Genealogy*, five years later: It is to be made possible by the "great health" of the "*Mensch* of the future [. . .], this Antichristian and Antinihilist [*dieser Antichrist und Antinihilist*], this victor over God and nothingness [*dieser Besieger Gottes und des Nichts*]," who will "redeem us from the previous [ascetic] ideal [*der uns ebenso vom bisherigen Ideal erlösen wird*]" (*GM* II:24).

This post-religious, post-shame-and-guilt-blighted, and also post-nihilistic sensibility would be life-*affirming*, rather than life-*despising* or life-*undermining* (in the manner of shame with respect to the natural). It would be sufficiently attuned to the "newly discovered, newly redeemed nature" and "naturalized" human reality of which Nietzsche speaks in *JI* 109 to be able not only to endure them but to celebrate them in the "yes-saying" affirmative spirit of the opening section of the fourth Book (*JI* 276)[22] and of *JI* 334 ("One Must Learn to Love").

This sensibility is precisely the sort of sensibility that Nietzsche would appear to be attempting to develop and cultivate by way of his very next work and pedagogical masterpiece. *Zarathustra* is many things—one of which, I suggest, is that it is his bildungsroman-style response to the challenge posed by this third Book of *Inquiry* and its last brief aphorisms—along with *JI* 341 ("The Greatest Burden [*Schwergewicht*]"). And that is the challenge of showing that a new (shame-free, entirely this-worldly) sensibility of this sort is humanly possible, and of making it tangible—and even accessible. (This may be at least a part of why Nietzsche attributes such importance to it in *Ecce Homo*.)

In sum: I attach great importance to Book 3 of *Joyful Inquiry* because, as I read it and understand its author, it is here that Nietzsche gets down to the serious business required by its dramatic opening lines. This task—the task of thoroughgoing "naturalizing" reinterpretation, revaluation, and sensibility transformation—is one for which his previous thought and work had prepared him. It is a task that animates *Zarathustra*, its sequel. And it is a task of which all that followed was the continuation.

X

The fourth and last Book of the initial version of this work is as different from the first three Books, in its own way, as the fourth part of *Zarathustra* was to be from the first three of its parts. And it also is a very different sort of Book from the fifth (and final) Book that followed it five years later. It was written after a pause that followed the completion of the third Book, that had ended with a flourish (as the third part of *Zarathustra* was also to do).[23] That ending seemed to bring the work to a kind of conclusion, with no place to go other than back to the further development of ideas already advanced.

But what Nietzsche instead does in the fourth Book of *Inquiry* is to shift gears quite dramatically. Book 4 is quite different in style and content from the first three. What he does in it, for the most part, is *talk about* philosophy for him at that point, in ways serving to illuminate what being his kind of philosopher involves and is like, as a way of thinking life. It is a much more personal and self-reflective collection of aphorisms than the first three Books are (and his previous writings had been)—while at the same time conveying quite simply and directly some of his central philosophical convictions at this juncture, and making some very interesting and important points. I can do no more here than call attention to some of the most notable of them. For the rest, the reader must simply *read* this remarkable fourth Book.

In *Inquiry* 283 (which bears the heading "Preparatory Human Beings"), as he was to do again in *Beyond*, Nietzsche discusses the kind of philosopher that he is calling for and is himself trying to be, preparatory to the "philosophy of the future" he envisions (to "prepare the way for one yet higher"). What he says is needed is "heroism in the search for knowledge," and "courageous human beings" ready, willing, and able to "*wage wars* for the sake of ideas and their consequences." He describes their traits, as he conceives of them, at considerable length, and exclaims that this is not only what the "search for knowledge" requires, but also the key to the highest of human goods attainable: "For believe me: the secret for harvesting from existence the greatest fruitfulness and the greatest enjoyment is—to *live dangerously!*" For that is what one committed

unconditionally to the "search for knowledge" is doing. Nietzsche further explicitly calls (in *JI* 289) for "a new *justice*! And a new watchword [*Losung*]!
And new philosophers!"—who he makes clear are to be beyond the morality
of good and evil: "The moral earth, too, has its antipodes." His "new watchword" for them is: "Embark, philosophers!" Set sail, and get underway!

On a different level, what Nietzsche takes to be needed is a new human
paradigm: "To 'give style' to one's character—a great and rare art!" (*JI* 290).
That is at least part of what he means when he shortly thereafter (in *JI* 335)
speaks of "creating oneself" [*Sich-selber-Schaffend*]. "Here a large mass of second nature has been added; there a piece of original nature has been removed."
Nietzsche explores and pursues this theme at some length in this part of the
Book, concluding with a lesson that he says we "should learn from artists": the
importance of learning how to "make things beautiful, attractive, and desirable for us when they are not." He says of artists: "For them this subtle power
usually comes to an end where art ends and life begins." Whereas, he memorably continues, "we want to be the poets of our life—first of all in the smallest,
most everyday matters" (*JI* 299).

XI

The last twenty aphorisms of this fourth Book are quite remarkable; and what
makes them all the more important is that they are the last things Nietzsche
said in philosophical prose print prior to *Zarathustra*, and prior to his resumption of prose philosophical publication in *Beyond Good and Evil* four years
later. In them he brings together two themes that seem to be at odds with each
other, but that he seems determined to unite. One is the importance (and reality) of knowledge; while the other is its problematic character, in a number
of respects, which would seem to make its importance problematic as well.

In *JI* 324 Nietzsche makes his strongest affirmative statement anywhere with
respect to knowledge: "'*Life as a means to knowledge*'—with this principle in
one's heart one can live not only boldly but even gaily, and laugh gaily too."
And he makes clearer what he meant in his remarks earlier in the Book about
knowledge and the heroism of "waging war" for it: "And knowledge itself: let
it be something else for others [. . .]—For me it is a world of dangers and
victories in which heroic feelings, too, find places to dance and play."

But Nietzsche earlier had made a striking assertion that would seem to have
implications for the status of knowledge—or at any rate, for what it can only
be knowledge *of*: the only world we have access to is "the world that *matters
to us*" [*die Welt*, die den Menschen Etwas angeht], as we encounter and experience it—and that is a world that "we alone [*erst*] have created." Whatever

might have been around in the first place, he writes, "the great visual and acoustic spectacle that is life," and "the whole eternally growing world of valuations, colors, accents perspectives, scales, affirmations, and negations," is something "that had not been there before" (*JI* 301).

As for our knowing itself: that, too, is something that Nietzsche would seem to be calling into question here, in *JI* 333, which bears the heading "*Was heisst erkennen*" ["What Is Called Knowing"]. Nietzsche observes that Spinoza had contrasted knowing [*intelligere*] with "laughing at, lamenting, and detesting," but suggests that knowing actually is something like doing "all three at once" rather than something altogether different, or at any rate a kind of outcome of a process of reconciliation of the three reactive *Triebe* [drives, impulses]. It therefore is not something "essentially opposed" to them, and certainly "nothing divine," but rather "a certain relation" [*ein gewisses Verhalten*] among them, well beneath the surface.

I take the upshot of Nietzsche's juxtaposition of these seemingly conflicting reflections, as this first version of *Joyful Inquiry* nears its end, to be that while there is nothing immaculate about conception, and nothing eternal and immutable to be known, *there are sorts of knowing* that have come to be humanly possible. There also *is much* in and about human reality and its world that they enable us to comprehend. And what they *do* amount to is what should (or at least can) matter—to us, at any rate—more than *what they are not!* And for the Nietzsche we encounter here, it makes good sense to take that knowledge of that reality to be deserving of what he says about the idea of "life as a means to knowledge" in *JI* 324.

This construal of Nietzsche's general stance, at the 1882 conclusion of this work, seems to me to be strongly supported by another of its most important last aphorisms—the lengthy *JI* 335, which bears a heading taken from the salute to "physics" (the natural sciences) with which it ends: "*Hoch die Physik!*" (which is to say: "Here's to physics!"—and, more literally, "Up with physics!" as well). Here he makes a number of very important things very clear. One is that he takes for granted that there is such a thing as "physics" as a human science, from which philosophers can and should learn much about "everything that is lawful and necessary in the world"—and that its comprehension is a humanly possible form of something deserving of the name of "knowledge." Another is that he considers that sort of knowledge to be relevant to the philosophical endeavor to comprehend life and the world—human reality and possibility included.

But yet another thing that comes across here is that there is something other than "physics," and its kind of knowledge, to which Nietzsche accords even greater importance ("*höher noch*" [even higher]): "that which *compels* us to

turn to physics—our *Redlichkeit!*" That is: our *intellectual integrity* (not simply our "honesty," as that word is commonly translated). And there is something further that matters to this Nietzsche, even more than that—for the sake
of which ("to that end") he esteems physics, the knowledge it yields, and the
Redlichkeit that will settle for nothing less. That is: "*becoming those we are* [Die
werden, die wir sind]—the new, the unique, the incomparable, the self-lawgivers
[*Sich-selber-Gesetzgebenden*], the self-creators [*Sich-selber-Schaffenden*]!" (*JI*
335). This is something for which neither the knowledge physics can yield,
nor the commitment to intellectual integrity that is Nietzsche's highest virtue,
will suffice. It requires imaginativeness, creativity, and commitment.

    And for this Nietzsche, this requires something further as well—which is
the topic of the preceding aphorism (*JI* 334), which bears the heading "One
Must Learn to Love [*lieben lernen*]." The importance of loving—and therefore
of the ability to love and of its actualization—is a point Nietzsche had made in
the very first aphorism of this fourth Book, in connection with his concepts
of "seeing as beautiful," *amor fati* [love of fate], and *Ja-sagend* [affirmation; literally, "yes-saying"] (*JI* 276). It is crucial to his ideas of self-overcoming, self-
affirmation, life affirmation, valuation, creating, and meaning endowment—
all of which loom large in *Zarathustra*, on which he was already at work.
Knowing is not the same as *loving*, does not entail it, does not guarantee it, is
no substitute for it, and by itself is not enough. But (and this is the point of
this aphorism) there are kinds of learning that can open and lead the way to
loving, even if they do not suffice for it. Nietzsche here barely scratches the
surface of this topic; but he announces it—and pursues it in the work that
follows.

    In the last two aphorisms of this fourth Book, Nietzsche heralds that work
even more directly, going so far as to preview it in the final one by providing
the reader with its opening narrative. But they are preceded by a remarkable
lengthy declamation bearing the heading "*Die zukünftige 'Menschlichkeit.*'"
And what he envisions here is a kind of refined "future humanity" and sensibility he believes to be humanly possible, and to be (for him at this point)
the "highest" imaginable state of human reality, "the heir of all the nobility of
all past human spirituality [*Geist*]." The result, he writes, would be virtually
divine—"the happiness of a god full of power and love, full of tears and laughter,
a happiness that [. . .] continually bestows its inexhaustible riches" (*JI* 337).

    This would seem to be Nietzsche's updated version of the contemplative
state to which he accorded the highest honors at the conclusion of part 5 of
Human, four years earlier.[24] But he was about to take a further step, in *Zarathustra*; and it was to be in a very different direction. This might be the most
elevated form of *Menschlichkeit* he could imagine at his point But as he re-

vealed in the opening lines of *Zarathustra* presented in the final section of this Book (and the first version of the entire work), his Zarathustra was not content with it. It was yet to be realized; but it represented a distillation of humanity's past, rather than a projection of its possible future.

Zarathustra had gone up into the mountains, where "he enjoyed his spirit and his solitude, and for ten years did not tire of that. But at last his heart changed" (*JI* 342). Henceforth Zarathustra's (and Nietzsche's) concern was to be with the attainment or realization of something beyond the best of *Menschlichkeit* as we know it—namely, *Übermenschlichkeit*, its further enhancement and transformation. But that required Zarathustra to descend (*untergehen*) into the real world of actual humanity, which (*Zarathustra*'s narrator is made to say) meant the beginning of his end and going under (*Untergehen*). Hence the aphorism's heading: "The Tragedy Begins." But that, for Nietzsche the author of *The Birth of Tragedy*, is not to say he should have done otherwise.

Finally, there is the puzzle of *JI* 341, with which Nietzsche concluded the fourth Book of *Joyful Inquiry* prior to that invocation of *Zarathustra*, and gave the heading "*Das grösste Schwergewicht*" (perhaps best rendered as "The Heaviest Weight" or "Greatest Burden"). I consider the question with which he ends this aphorism to be the heart of the matter, and the rest to be a rhetorical device he uses to set it up as forcefully as he could. This question is a kind of *affirmation disposition* test. "How well disposed would you have to become to yourself and to life" [*Wie müsstest du dir selber und dem Leben gut werden*], to be able to embrace them unconditionally and wholeheartedly exactly as they are? Even if you were to be informed (and believe) that everything about them down to the last detail is to be repeated endlessly, with no exit? Nietzsche seems to think that this would require a vastly stronger affirmative disposition than would be required if you were to be convinced that the whole thing (you and everything about you and your life included) were—as it in all probability is—a "once and done" affair.

But be that as it may, the basic question is that of how positively and strongly *you would have to be disposed to be*—without recourse to fantasies and delusions—both to yourself as you are and to life and the world as they are, on the most daunting of scenarios (whatever that might be). Or rather (perhaps): how *differently* (as well as positively and strongly) would you have to be so disposed? And it would seem that Nietzsche is thinking that nothing less will suffice than the very thing he began the fourth Book by announcing as his new watchword: "*Amor fati* [Love of fate]: let that be my love henceforth!" (*JI* 276).

That, for this Nietzsche, is the only thing that would enable one to be well disposed enough to pass the "idea of eternal recurrence" test, and with flying colors. This is the ultimate "learn to love" challenge as well. It is only if one is able to come to "love fate"—for one for whom *amor dei* is no longer available as an answer—and to love it all-inclusively, unconditionally, wholeheartedly, *and in the right sort of way*, that one's response to a "what if" hypothetical of the sort Nietzsche poses here can be the one he envisions: "Never have I heard anything more divine!" (*JI* 339). And that, he came to understand, required the *attainment of attunement*—and so of what he might have called a *Dionysian sensibility*.

The Nietzsche of *Thus Spoke Zarathustra: A Book for All and None*

ALSO SPRACH ZARATHUSTRA: EIN BUCH FÜR ALLE UND KEINE

To educate educators! But the first ones must educate themselves! And for these I write. [*Erzieher erziehn! Aber die ersten müssen sich selbst erziehn! Und für diese schreibe ich.*]
Notebook of Spring–Summer 1875[1]

This work stands altogether apart. Leaving aside the poets: perhaps nothing has ever been done from an equal excess of strength. My concept of the "Dionysian" here becomes a *supreme deed*; measured against that, all the rest of human activity seems poor and relative [. . .]. There is no moment in this revelation of truth that has been anticipated or guessed by even *one* of the greatest.
Ecce Homo, "Books," Z:6

"Behold, I teach you the *Übermensch*. The *Übermensch* is the meaning of the earth. Let your will say: the *Übermensch shall be* the meaning of the earth! I beseech you, my brothers, *remain faithful to the earth*."
Thus Spoke Zarathustra, I:Prologue:3

The word "*Übermensch*," as the designation of a type of the highest *Wohlgeratenheit* [turning out well], as opposed to "modern" *Menschen*, to "good" *Menschen*, to Christians and other nihilists [. . .].
Ecce Homo, "Books," 1

Whatever possessed Nietzsche to write *Thus Spoke Zarathustra*—and to think so highly of it? Heralded by the use of its opening section as the final section of its immediate predecessor (the first version of *Joyful Inquiry*, with which the writing of the first of its parts therefore evidently overlapped), it was utterly unlike anything Nietzsche had published previously; and he never again wrote anything like it. He published nothing else prior to his completion of the composition of its fourth and final part three years later, which he only published and circulated privately. Those three years were years of crisis for him in every respect; and his personal and intellectual investment in a work written under such conditions, over such an extended period, may have had something to do with his later feelings about it.

The fact that *Zarathustra* was as close as Nietzsche ever came to creating something comparable to Wagner's (four-part) operatic *Ring* cycle may also be of some relevance.[2] And his claims for it (in *Ecce Homo*) imply that he took it to have surpassed not only Wagner's greatest accomplishment, but also those of Goethe, Shakespeare, and Dante as well (along with "the greatest" among philosophers—presumably including his "educator" Schopenhauer). Indeed, they imply that he considered it to be in a class by itself in relation to any and all of the rest of his own writings. He regarded it as a work of world-historical significance, to which only the founding works of the world's great religions and cultures might properly be compared—to their detriment.

This may be preposterous; and at least some of what Nietzsche says along these lines may be dismissed as symptomatic of his incipient madness. Yet I believe that he was trying to do something both unusual and important in this strange work, which renders his extravagant estimation of it at least comprehensible, even if not justifiable. But what is it that he was trying to do, and seems to have thought he had done?

What, in short, are we to make of *Zarathustra*, and of the Nietzsche of *Zarathustra*? And what, for that matter, are we to make of the "Zarathustra" we encounter in it? That figure is not merely Nietzsche's mouthpiece or stage name (Nietzsche himself, in exotic but transparent disguise). Nor does this figure stand to Nietzsche as Hamlet does to Shakespeare, Ahab to Melville, or even Faust to Goethe. What, moreover, are we to make of what might be called "Zarathustra's Progress," and of the relation of the Zarathustra of *Zarathustra*'s part four to the Zarathustra of its first three parts? And, for that matter, what of the relation of part four to the previous parts of the work? An adequate answer requires an understanding of the entire enterprise of the work.

There are many related questions on which I hope to shed some light here as well. How are we to understand the relation between the Nietzsche of this work and the Nietzsche(s) of his previous and subsequent philosophical writings? What is to be made of his suggestion in *Ecce Homo* that with this work "the yes-saying part of my task had been solved"? (*EH* "Books," *BGE*:1). And what is the relevance of this work—and of Nietzsche's project in it—to the understanding and undertaking of his attempted reformation and transformation of philosophy, and his kind of philosophy?

It seems to me that one important but seldom noticed key to answers to these questions is to be found in the second of Nietzsche's *Unfashionable Reflections* written nearly a decade earlier: *Schopenhauer as Educator* (1874). In and by means of Zarathustra and *Zarathustra* (both the figure and the work itself), I suggest, Nietzsche sought to provide posterity with something capable of performing the kind of "educating" function he had discussed in that essay, and considered Schopenhauer to have performed for him. This is a special kind of education, requiring a special kind of educator. The early Nietzsche of that essay was convinced that the experience of encountering such an educator is quite essential if one is to attain true self-realization and intellectual maturity. And the Nietzsche of *Zarathustra* was convinced that something similar is necessary if we are to find our way to a new Yes to life that does not depend upon buying into the various forms of illusion he began (in *The Birth of Tragedy*) by thinking were the only means of avoiding Schopenhauerian pessimism and the calamity of a dead-end nihilism.

Much has been written about this remarkable work, and continues to be. And much of it is well worth reading.[3] The interpretation I will be offering in this chapter is a development of the above view; and it is of a rather different sort than most of that commentary. It is not a close reading and interpretation of everything that is said and done in the entire work, and of its dramatic structure. Rather, it is a discussion of what to make of the work as a whole and of its parts, as a project and as it relates to Nietzsche's larger philosophical concerns and to the understanding of his kind of philosophy. Both ways of thinking about it, I believe, are helpful and necessary to the understanding and appreciation of the work. As such, I consider my discussion to be complementary to—rather than in competition with—the kinds of book-length close and comprehensive analysis and interpretation of the work that it has been inspiring for quite some time now, of which Paul Loeb's *The Death of Zarathustra* is a striking, original, and provocative recent example.

Much of what I will be saying is broad-brush, rather than focused on particular passages, speeches, and recountings, and relies on the expectation of familiarity with the work. Recognizing that that expectation is unrealistic in the case of many readers, I have attempted to compensate by providing a brief recounting of the entire work at the end of this chapter (section VIII and following), with the heading "Nietzsche as Educator: A Brief Pedagogical Reading of *Zarathustra*." That telling of the tale is also intended to serve a second purpose, in addition to introducing the work to readers who may be new to it: it is meant to provide textual anchoring of what I say about it along the way, and so to be a part of my case for it. It therefore should be considered a part of this chapter, to be read in conjunction with the rest of it, either before or after reading the rest (or both), as readers may prefer.

I

My account begins a half century before Nietzsche's birth, with one of his kindred spirits: Friedrich Schiller.[4] Schiller was not only one of Germany's greatest literary figures, but also a philosopher and public intellectual. In the mid-1790s he published a series of letters that became a remarkable and widely influential book: his *On the Aesthetic Education [Erziehung] of Man.*[5] Schiller's idea was that "aesthetic education" is the key to the attainment of a richer and more complete humanity than had been attained even by the Greeks—who, however, were seen as showing the way. Through such a cultural "education" (by way of the arts and literature), Schiller contended, the "sensuous" impulses of our natural natures may be transformed, and the cultivation of the "formal" impulses of our rational nature is made possible. And then such an education can perform the further service of overcoming the antagonism between those seemingly opposed aspects of our spirituality, by cultivating a new impulse— a "play" impulse, in which elements of both of these other impulses are brought together and joined. A new and higher (artistic/authentic) nature thereby emerges, with a sensibility attuned to beauty and abilities employed creatively.

In this picture, as well as in Schiller's accompanying critique of the impoverished humanity produced by the operation of the modern world, much that we find in Nietzsche from *The Birth of Tragedy* to *Zarathustra* and beyond is anticipated—or echoed. With Schiller in mind, the Apollinian-Dionysian distinction becomes a variation and deepening of a familiar theme. The employment of the idea of "play" in connection with the culminating stage of spiritual development identified in Zarathustra's very first speech "On the Three Metamorphoses" (when one expects to find something like artistic creativity) becomes readily understandable. The ideas of an enhancement of life and an attainable higher humanity, contrasting with the quality of life that leaves so much to be desired in the modern world and throughout so much of history, become easily recognizable. And even the seemingly odd central thesis of *Birth*, that "it is only as an *aesthetic phenomenon* [*aesthetisches Phänomen*] that existence and the world are eternally *justified* [*gerechtfertigt*]" (*BT* 5 and 24), loses its strangeness.

The same is true of Schiller's idea of "education" (*Erziehung*) as the key to the enhancement of life, and of his equally explicit indication that the kind of education meant has above all to do with the twofold cultivation of an aesthetic sensibility and of artistic-creative powers. Nietzsche does more than merely echo Schiller; he deepens and extends these ideas in ways placing him well beyond Schiller and his early-romantic naivete. But in seeking to understand what Nietzsche is trying to do in *Zarathustra*, one does well to recall his Schillerian inheritance. Nietzsche's project, too, may be characterized as a version of Schiller's idea of the need for a further "aesthetic education" of humanity that might bring about a higher form of humanity—and *Zarathustra* was his greatest contribution to this campaign.

Nietzsche's first great case study of this kind of education and call for a new aesthetic education of humanity was, of course, *The Birth of Tragedy*. He may not have thought of it in precisely these terms at the time; but the central theme of the entire first half of the book is that, thanks to their artists, the Greeks received an extraordinary aesthetic "education"—and underwent an extraordinary sort of transformation—that was the key both to their kind and quality of culture and to their ability to relish life as greatly as they did *despite* their acute awareness of "the terror and horror of existence" (*BT* 3), and *in the absence* of anything like Christian-otherworldly consolation.

More specifically, Nietzsche regarded the Greeks' artists as their "educators" in the most important sense, cultivating their sensibility and transforming both their sense of themselves and their sense of their world in such a way that they were unsurpassed in their life affirmation.[6] The Greeks' tragedians had educated their sensibility and self-consciousness, and had shown the Greeks a way of coming to terms with the harsh realities of life without succumbing to nausea and despair. They were the educators through whose efforts the wondrously affirmative and creative tragic culture of the Greeks achieved extraordinary heights. In *Birth* Nietzsche looked to Wagner to serve as such an *Erzieher* to modern European humanity. Wagner was to be their latter-day European counterpart, through whom a new tragic culture—no less affirmative and creative than that of the Greeks—was to be attained.

It was not long before Nietzsche's enthusiasm for Wagner-as-*Erzieher* began to wane; and he soon (by the time of *Schopenhauer*, two years later) settled upon Schopenhauer as being better suited to that role, at least in his own case. In *Schopenhauer* Wagner still looms large as the unnamed epitome of the "genius" through whom the flourishing of culture that is the locus of higher humanity can occur (if enough of the rest of us will play our supporting roles). But now the true educator—the one through encountering whom we are transformed and impelled in the direction of at once "becoming those we are" and contributing to the enhancement of life—is depicted more as a stimulus than as a leader to be followed or a paradigm to be imitated. Such an educator may be a kind of *exemplar* (also *Exemplar* in Nietzsche's German); but this type of educator is anything but an *instructor*, from whom information is received or rules and procedures are learned. The most important things to be learned have to do more with admirable traits to be emulated and standards to be aspired to than with specific ideas and values to be accepted. So in *Schopenhauer* Nietzsche celebrates Schopenhauer as his "educator" without even discussing any of Schopenhauer's views.

Even in *Schopenhauer*, however, Nietzsche did not suppose that Schopenhauer (through his work) could or should be *everyone's* educator, and was already worrying about where the educator(s) needed—to do for others what Schopenhauer (through his work) had done for him—would come from. "Where are we [. . .] to find our ethical models and celebrities [*unsre sittlichen Vorbilder und Berühmteiten*] among our contemporaries, the visible epitome of all creative morality for our time [*der sichtbare Inbegriff aller schöpferischen Moral in dieser Zeit*]? [. . .] Never have ethical educators [*sittliche Erzieher*] been more needed, and never has it seemed less likely they would be found" (SE 2).[7]

Nietzsche's intended audience here is all those "youthful souls" with the need, the courage, and the ability to heed the call to "become yourself!" [*sei du selbst!*]—understood not self-indulgently, but rather in the sense that "your true nature is not concealed deep within you but immeasurably high above you, or at least above that which you usually take yourself to be" [*dein wahres Wesen liegt nicht tief verborgen in dir, sondern unermesslich hoch über dir oder wenigstens über dem, was du gewöhnlich als dein Ich nimmst*] (SE 1). For their sake, he raises a question and poses a challenge that he subsequently took up himself in a variety of ways: "Who is there, then, amid these changes of our era, to guard and champion *humanity* [*Menschlichkeit*] the inviolable sacred treasure gradually accumulated by the most various races [*Geschlichter*]? Who will set up the *image of man* [das Bild des Menschen] when all men feel in themselves only the self-seeking snake and the currish fear and have declined to the level of the animals or even of automata [*in's Tierische oder gar in das starr Mechanische*]?" (SE 4).

Nietzsche's prototype of the "free spirit" in *Schopenhauer* is what he calls the "Schopenhauerian" type of humanity he goes on to sketch, in distinction not only from the all-too-human type of social-animal humanity he considers to be the human rule, but also from two alternative "images" or paradigms of a more genuine humanity he calls by the names of their most prominent representatives: Rousseau and Goethe. "Rousseauian man" for him represents naturalized humanity, renewed and revitalized through emancipation from the shackles of society and restoration to its basic instincts. "Goethean man" is the image of contemplative humanity, cultivated and sophisticated but detached from active involvement in life. "Schopenhauerian man" combines elements of both and also (for Nietzsche) supersedes both as the image of a "truly active" creative humanity, at once vital and spiritualized, and so most fully and truly human.

The significance of these images for Nietzsche in *Schopenhauer* is that they have the power to liberate, stimulate, and inspire—in short, to *educate* [*erziehen*]. Because of the diverse sorts of human development involved and the shortcomings associated with the first two of them, however, he takes them to differ not only in kind but also in value. Only the one he calls "Schopen-

hauerian" expresses and evokes the promise of an alternative form of humanity healthy and vital enough to be enduringly viable in this world, and sufficiently creative and spiritualized to justify itself—and human life and the world
along with it.

Cultural life—*der Kreis der Kultur* [the sphere of culture] is its domain. Its
fundamental principle [*Grundgedanke*] is said to be "the consummation of
nature" [*die Vollendung der Natur*]. And it is to the celebration and service of
culture—through "the fostering of the production of the philosopher, the artist and the saint within ourselves and beyond ourselves" [*die Erzeugung des
Philosophen, des Künstlers und des Heiligen in uns und ausser uns zu fördern*]
(*SE* 5)—that Nietzsche looks in his response to the challenge he sets for himself when he writes: "The hardest task still remains: to say how a new circle
of duties [*Kreis von Pflichten*] may be devised from this ideal and how one
can proceed towards so extravagant a goal [*einem so überschwänglichen Ziele*]
through practical activity—in short, to demonstrate that this ideal *educates*
[*zu beweisen, dass jenes Ideal* erzieht]. [. . .] Is it possible to bring that incred-
ibly lofty goal so close that it educates us while it draws us aloft [*dass es uns
erzieht, während es uns aufwärts zieht*]?" (*SE* 5).

Nietzsche's answer, of course, is in the affirmative; and it is of no little relevance to observe his elaboration upon it: "We have to be lifted up [*wir müssen
gehoben werden*]—and who are they who lift us [*die, welche uns heben*]? They
are *those true human beings, those who are no longer animal* [jene wahrhaften
Menschen, jene Nicht-mehr-Tiere], the *philosophers, artists and saints*" (*SE* 5).
This is a veritable prescription projecting ahead to the "higher educator" that
we encounter in the pages of *Zarathustra*, about whom there is something of
each of this trinity of exceptions to the human rule.

But *Zarathustra* was still years away, in conception as well as well as ex-
ecution. Meanwhile, Nietzsche could only observe: "The difficulty for human
beings lies in relearning, and setting themselves a new goal [*umzulernen und
ein neues Ziel sich zu stecken*]" (*SE* 6). He was convinced that "the goal of culture is to promote the emergence of *true human beings* [*die Entstehung der
wahren Menschen zu fördern*] and nothing else" (*SE* 6); but at this point he
was clearer about the end than he was about what might be done to advance
its achievement.

II

Nietzsche's concern with the inadequacies of what passed for education (and
education of the highest quality at that) in his own time is reflected in his
severe critiques, most notably in *Schopenhauer*. These critiques have as one

of their recurring themes the contention that existing higher and lower forms of education alike were detrimental to intellectual as well as personal and human development, stultifying the minds and stunting the spirits of those submitting to them through overspecialization and regimentation.

This concern did not fade away in the years that followed. On the contrary, Nietzsche's aphoristic volumes from *Human, All Too Human* to the first version of *Joyful Inquiry* may be regarded as an initial if tentative series of efforts on his part to fill this need himself. As I observed in the previous chapter, he wrote of these works (in that first version of *Inquiry*) that their "common goal is to erect a new image and ideal of the free spirit."[8] Here Nietzsche the heir of Voltaire and the Enlightenment sought by way of this "new image and ideal" to provide a beacon of enlightenment and inspiration. This "free spirit" series constituted a kind of experimental effort to contribute to and promote a different type of "education."

This series itself is educational in several respects. Through the hundreds of aphoristic reflections of which these books consist, Nietzsche was educating himself as well as his readers, working his way toward the kind of philosopher, thinker, and free spirit he himself was becoming, while providing others with assistance in moving in the same direction themselves. And it is no system of *doctrines* that is set out here for the instruction of the reader, nor even a set of arguments advanced with the aim of compelling the reader's agreement. Rather, a variety of intellectual abilities and dispositions are being cultivated, with a view to fostering the emergence of the sort of human being realizing Nietzsche's conception of the "free spirit."

This involves a transformation of the way in which one understands oneself and relates to life and the world, along lines that Nietzsche clearly regarded as desirable. An indication of his underlying motivation is provided in the famous penultimate section of the first version of *Inquiry* in which the idea of the eternal recurrence of every moment and episode of one's life is set forth with the question: "How well disposed would you have to become to yourself and to life [*Wie müsstest du dir selber und dem Leben gut werden*], *to crave* nothing *more fervently* than this ultimate eternal confirmation and seal[9] [*dieser letzten ewigen Bestätigung und Besiegelung*]?" (*JI* 341). An education capable of bringing that about, without sacrificing the intellect, would be an education indeed! And it would be an education involving "learning to love" (*JI* 334), at the highest and most comprehensive of levels.

Having reached this point, however, Nietzsche seems to have concluded that something more was needed than the kind of thing he had been doing in his "free spirit" series of books. One of the limitations of this series is that its extraordinary experiment in consciousness-raising was far stronger critically than it was constructively. The "free spirit" did not itself fill the bill, or suffice for this purpose. In the fourth (and at that time last) Book of *Inquiry*, however, and just prior to its concluding invocation of Zarathustra, a number of themes are sounded that point in the direction of this larger task.

These themes might be thought of as so many variations on a larger theme, of the *artistic transformation of our lives* in ways endowing them with value sufficient to warrant their affirmation. Learning to "'give style' to one's character" (*JI* 299); learning to "live not only boldly but even gaily, and laugh gaily, too" by learning to savor such forms of "war and victory" as life affords—the pursuit of knowledge among them (*JI* 324); learning to love—for "love, too, has to be learned" (*JI* 334); wanting and learning "to become those we are, human beings [. . .] who give themselves laws, who create themselves" (*JI* 335); and learning to become capable of dealing with "the greatest weight," existence conceived through the lens of the idea of "eternal recurrence" (*JI* 341)—these are some of the variations on this theme with which this prelude to *Zarathustra* resounds. It was left to *Zarathustra*, however, to take up the challenge of this life-enhancing aesthetic education itself.

III

Nietzsche had begun, in the early 1870s, by thinking (or hoping) that someone—the Greeks, Wagner, Schopenhauer—could be found to serve as exemplars, mentors, and educators for those like himself for whom neither reason nor revelation would suffice. Ten years later he had become disillusioned with all of those he formerly had revered. He had come to be convinced that not only traditional modes of philosophical and religious thought but also the available alternatives—both ancient and modern (including the natural sciences and historical scholarship)—all fall radically short of educating our aspirations and valuations in a manner conducive to human flourishing in a postmodern world in which all gods have died. Indeed, he had come to see them not only as "all too human" and inadequate but as positively *detrimental* to that flourishing, having effects that bode ill rather than well for the future, and requiring something serving as both an antidote and an alternative. The kind of galvanizing educator that was needed was (he felt) nowhere to be found; and while his efforts to promote a "new image and ideal of the free spirit" might be necessary steps in the right direction, they were far from sufficient.

What more could Nietzsche do? He could create and write *Thus Spoke Zarathustra*. Zarathustra and *Zarathustra*, I am suggesting, were conceived to meet this need, "for all and none" (its subtitle): for none, if none were ready for the encounter, but for all who might (come to) be up to it. A work capable of making such a difference on such a scale would indeed be a great gift to humanity, particularly if nothing remotely comparable were anywhere else to be found. In this light, Nietzsche's subsequent extravagant estimation of the work becomes at least comprehensible. It was to be no mere work of literature, scholarship, or philosophy, but rather a unique educational instrument capable of making a real and great difference in human life.

In *Zarathustra* Nietzsche undertook to meet the challenge of Schopenhauer head on—not the "Schopenhauer" of *Schopenhauer* (who was an idealized version of Nietzsche himself), but the actual Schopenhauer whose radical pessimism led him to champion the negation of life, and whom Nietzsche took to foreshadow the advent of nihilism. How can one *affirm* life—and not merely endure it but *relish* it—if Schopenhauer was fundamentally right about the conditions of existence in this world (and the absence of any other, or any redeeming God beyond it), and if one refuses to sacrifice honesty and truthfulness?

Zarathustra is predicated upon the conviction that radical "dis-illusionment," uncompromising truthfulness, *and* unqualified life affirmation are all humanly possible together, even under these circumstances. But Nietzsche's message in it also proceeds from the recognition that this human possibility is not easily realized, and in fact requires the attainment of a new *sensibility*, through an educational development that has free-spirited enlightenment as but its point of departure. To come to be capable of confronting what Nietzsche in *Ecce Homo* refers to as "the fundamental conception of this work, the idea of eternal recurrence, this highest formula of affirmation that is at all attainable" (*EH* "Books," *Z*:1) with exhilaration rather than horror and despair, even the Zarathustra of the first parts of the work must undergo a major transformation. And Nietzsche shows us his education in a way that is designed to help effect ours as well, in the same direction and to the same ultimate effect.

But who—or what—is the educator here? That educator is neither the Zarathustra we encounter in the book nor even Nietzsche himself at the outset, for both themselves had much to learn. The real educator, I suggest, is *the work itself*—not completely in the two parts published in 1883, but in the whole of it. What Nietzsche wrought in this work is the means of a remarkable possible educational experience and transformation that may reach into and affect the fundamental character of our humanity. It might be thought of as a kind of philosophical bildungsroman, akin perhaps both to Goethe's *Faust* and to Hegel's *Phenomenology*, but more radical than either of them. It is to the entire work *Thus Spoke Zarathustra*—rather than simply to the figure and proclamations of "Zarathustra"—that Nietzsche would above all have us respond. Zarathustra, too, has to be educated; and it is his education, as well as what he says and various other things about him, that is meant to serve ours.

IV

The Nietzschean educator is closer to the Socratic "midwife," and perhaps closer still to something like a *catalyst* of change and transformation. The basic concern of his desired kind of education is not simply to increase our knowledge of the world as it merely is, or even of ourselves as we already are. Those kinds of knowledge—of which Nietzsche had acquired and conveyed a great deal in his "free spirit" series—are at most only points of departure. What matters more to him is to raise our sights and awaken us to possibilities we will have to reach out and exert ourselves to realize.

The object of such education is to "draw us out," as the terms *erziehen* [*er-ziehen*, "draw out"] and *educate* [*e-duce*, "lead out"] both fundamentally mean. Nietzsche would draw us out, beyond what we and the world already are, toward what we have it in us to become, and what we might make of ourselves and our world. And for him in *Zarathustra*, as in *Schopenhauer*, that calls for creativity rather than mere receptivity. Its general arena, beyond the empty abstractions and false dichotomies of the mental and the physical, the subjective and the objective, and the individual and the social, is the sphere of cultural life—Zarathustra's wilderness proclivities notwithstanding.

Zarathustra is not only the presentation of an educator who attempts to educate by free-spirited and wholesomely naturalistic enlightenment and counsel, doing a good deal of vivid debunking and reinterpreting and revaluing along the way—even though that *is* some of what we find, particularly in the first part (written more than two years before its final, fourth part). It is also the presentation of the educator's education, and further the vehicle and record of its author's education—and beyond that, the occasion and means of our own possible education; and it is at these levels that the work does its real work, and serves to perform its larger and deeper educative function.

Zarathustra thus is not only Nietzsche's answer to the New Testament, but also his version of *Pilgrim's Progress*; and it is the whole multilevel phenomenon by which we are to be educated in the sense of *Erziehung*, being drawn out and up, toward "becoming those we are" (as he had put it in *JI* 335). Zarathustra's speeches and reflections are part of it; but his transformations matter more, and the transfiguration of the picture of humanity to which all that transpires in the work contributes matters most of all. We are not taught what everyone ought to think and how everyone ought to live; but we are shown the prospect of a possible humanity and the way toward a manner of life that Nietzsche believes can sustain us beyond all disillusionment.

As it is pursued in *Zarathustra*, Nietzsche's educational endeavor at once reflects and transcends the kinds of educating that had previously figured importantly in his thinking—in *Birth*, in *Schopenhauer*, and in the "free spirit" series. But it continues to undergo development in the course of the four parts of the work, in each of which something crucial is added, without which the kind of humanity attained would be seriously lacking. The successive trans- formations of sensibility that are explored supersede rather than negate pre- viously attained forms; but the subsequent transformations are important.

The sensibility of part one is still basically that of the Nietzschean "free spirit"; and it is still some distance from that which is barely envisioned in the penultimate section of *Inquiry* in which the idea of the "eternal recurrence" is invoked to assess one's disposition to oneself and to life (*JI* 341). In a large sense, the task of *Zarathustra* may be said to consist in the educational project of inculcating and cultivating a *sensibility*[10] capable of passing this "recurrence test"—and so of affirming life under what Nietzsche considers to be the most daunting of possible descriptions.

The basic educational function to be performed by these many speeches— elaborating upon the ideas of "faithfulness to the earth" and of the *Übermensch* as the "meaning of the earth"—does not reduce to conveying the specific points advanced in the various speeches. Rather, I suggest, it consists in their use to give one a feeling for a genuine alternative to what Nietzsche elsewhere calls the "Christian-moral" scheme of the interpretation and evaluation that we have come to take largely for granted—and that he believes is bound to collapse in the aftermath of "the death of God." What might it mean to achieve a reori- entation of the way in which we think about ourselves that would make this life in this world the locus of meaning and value, and that would link them to considerations of differential quality of life and possible enhancements of life?

Nietzsche retains the rubric of "tragedy" in connection with this new sensi- bility (Zarathustra is introduced in *JI* 342 under the heading "*Incipit tragoedia*" ["The Tragedy Begins"]).[11] He departs markedly and very significantly from the standpoint of *Birth*, however, in rejecting recourse to *illusion* as the key to life affirmation. He makes much of this point in subsequent remarks about the fig- ure of Zarathustra. Life affirmation may require *more* than "truthfulness"; but the kind of life affirmation Nietzsche associates with Zarathustra also requires nothing less. For nothing short of uncompromising truthfulness is immune to the threat of disillusionment in the aftermath of the severest critical scrutiny. Nietzsche does insist upon the importance of learning to appreciate and esteem surfaces, appearances, creations, and even fictions as a part of the new sensi- bility he envisions; but in this sensibility such appreciation and esteeming are conjoined with truthfulness and honesty rather than indulged at their expense. So, in *Ecce Homo*, Nietzsche makes much of the point that "Zarathustra is more truthful than any other thinker" and "posits truthfulness as the highest virtue" (*EH* "Destiny," 3).

But that is not the whole story, as Nietzsche makes clear in going on to state "what Zarathustra wants" in the following striking passage, which was nearly (and might well have been) his last word: "This type of *Mensch* that he conceives, conceives reality *as it is* [*diese Art Mensch, die er concipirt, concipirt die Realität, wie sie ist*], being strong enough to do so; this type is not estranged or removed from reality, it is *it itself*, it exemplifies all that is terrible and questionable in it—*only in that way can man attain greatness* [damit erst kann der Mensch Grösse haben]" (*EH* "Destiny," 5). Truthfulness may be the "highest virtue"; but what Nietzsche here calls "greatness" is the highest goal. And much of *Zarathustra* has to do with the cultivation of a new sensibility appropriate to this revalued valuation of human life and possibility.[12]

The educational task of the first part of *Zarathustra* may thus be said to be that of confronting the "death of God" and rising to the challenge Nietzsche had sketched in *Inquiry* a year earlier: "God is dead; [. . .] and we—we still have to vanquish his shadow too" (*JI* 108). And that will not be accomplished until, among other things, "we have completely de-deified nature [*die Natur ganz entgöttlicht haben*]," and we "*naturalize*" [vernatürlichen] our understanding of ourselves in terms of "a pure, newly discovered, newly redeemed nature" (*JI* 109). Not to mention dealing with the consequences of this "greatest recent event" for "the whole of European morality," and everything else that "was built upon this faith, propped up by it, grown up into it" (*JI* 343). This is a kind of crisis Nietzsche had already been addressing in his "free spirit" series; but here he gives life to his belief in the possibility of an alternative to the "nihilistic rebound" from the death of God.

V

The lesson Nietzsche had learned from the Greeks, and the lesson of *Birth*, has to do with the role the arts—and tragic art in particular—can play in effecting a transformation of our consciousness in such a way that not only our experience but our lives and the very aspect of existence are transformed, enabling us (through various sorts of distraction and illusion) to take the harsh realities of life in better stride than we otherwise could. And he had further learned from them that tragic art surpassed the other art forms, in its ability to do so even in the face of the most tragic of human situations. He may have given up on Wagner in this respect; but he did not abandon the very idea of what in *Birth* he had called the "justification" of "existence and the world" as an "aesthetic phenomenon." *Zarathustra* was to truly accomplish what Wagner had counterfeited, and so succeed where he had failed—in achieving a rebirth of tragedy ("*Incipit tragoedia*"), as a sensibility attuned to our finitude and yet infused with a fundamentally Dionysian affirmative spirit.

The educational task of *Zarathustra* is to assist those capable of doing so to attain this sensibility, and the associated forms of aspiration and valuation. Hence the "greatest weight" and recurrence test; for this is the education called for by Nietzsche's question, "How well disposed would you have to become to yourself and to life to crave nothing more fervently than this ultimate eternal confirmation and seal?" (*JI* 341). Hence also Nietzsche's characterization in *Ecce Homo* of "what Zarathustra wants" (*EH* "Destiny," 5, cited above).

This kind of education may be conceived as Nietzsche's version of what in an earlier time had been called the cultivation of an "aesthetic sensibility"; and the need for it had already been intimated in *Birth* in his contention that "it is only as an aesthetic phenomenon" that life and the world can ultimately be esteemed, loved, and affirmed. It further may be regarded as an attempt to understand and work out the implications of his conviction that we must learn to sustain and nourish ourselves by means of the kind of thing to which Nietzsche alludes in the section of *Inquiry* on "Our Ultimate Gratitude to Art," in which he has in mind "art as the *good* will to appearance [*als den* guten *Willen zum Scheine*]," and writes: "As an aesthetic phenomenon existence is still *bearable* for us [*Als ästhetisches Phänomen ist uns das Dasein immer noch* erträglich], and art furnishes us with eyes and hands and above all the good conscience to be *able* to make ourselves into such a phenomenon [*uns selber ein solches Phänomen machen zu* können]" (*JI* 107).

Nietzsche recognizes we may well need an education of the right sort to come to appreciate and find this not only a sufficient but also an invigorating diet. If we are to come to be able to relish life on the only terms it offers without the veils of illusion the Nietzsche of *Birth* had deemed indispensable, we must learn not only to accept but also to love and cherish it under some possible interpretation or attainable configuration.

It is the educational task of *Zarathustra* to enable us to do so. To this end, like the tragic literature and culture whose earlier birth and demise Nietzsche had contemplated in *Birth*, it must provide us with a way of facing and coming to terms with what he then had called "the terror and horror of existence" (*BT* 3) under the worst and bleakest of descriptions without being devastated by the encounter. It needs to help us develop a way of emerging from this encounter in an open-eyed but nonetheless exhilarated and affirmative manner. Indeed, it is of the utmost importance for Nietzsche in *Zarathustra* (and thereafter) that one get beyond all naivete and disillusionment, and leave behind *both* all optimistic illusions, idealistic fantasies, and the foolish belief in the sufficiency of fine sentiments and lofty principles, *and* all self-pity and despair.

This project by no means reduces to the inculcation of the secular-humanist maxims and principles one so often finds coming out of Zarathustra's mouth, especially in the first two parts of the work. Nietzsche may subscribe to the latter as far as they go; but one of the most important points of the work, brought out by Zarathustra's own transformation and abandonment of that mode of discourse, is that the "free spirit" mentality they express is far from sufficient as a way of thinking by which one might live. I see no reason to think Nietzsche does not mean us to take seriously the counsel Zarathustra offers in the first parts of the work. Quite clearly, however, he does at least mean to suggest that such rhetoric needs supplementing, not only by means of additional principles but also by way of a fundamentally altered *sensibility*. For by itself and as it stands, this free-spirited enlightenment is incapable of carrying the day and sufficing to get one through the "dark night of the soul" by which Zarathustra himself is subsequently—if only temporarily—overwhelmed.

Otherwise put: the enlightened humanistic outlook expressed in Zarathustra's early speeches and on a number of occasions thereafter is all very well and good as far as it goes; and it would be a most welcome thing if it could be much more widely attained. But Nietzsche did not stop there, and has Zarathustra venture further. The attainment of this outlook is only a step in the right direction, and must be followed by others Nietzsche uses Zarathustra and *Zarathustra* to enable us to see—and to try to prompt us to take. These steps lead from the sunny Apollinian heights Zarathustra loves and evokes at the outset (in the first part) through the depressing all-too-human swamps into which he descends (in the second)—and into the dark Dionysian depths underlying all of human existence, which give way to the strange and problematic brightness that is the other face of Dionysian reality (in the third). And at length (in the fourth part) we are brought back into a human world in which we can recognize ourselves again—but with a difference.

VI

This last part of the journey and educational process is absolutely essential, in my view; and for me this endows the fourth (and final) part of the work—only privately printed and not circulated until well after Nietzsche's collapse—with a significance that is seldom appreciated. The outlook attained, both by Nietzsche at the time he wrote the first part (1883) and by the Zarathustra it features, is only the beginning; and its insufficiency is brought home (in the second part, written within the year). Another crisis looms that the resources of aesthetic-naturalistic enlightenment are not adequate to meet. Zarathustra and his wisdom have to "ripen" further before he can either comprehend it or meet it. The crisis reaches a climax in the third part—the last part Nietzsche published publicly, written a year later (1884)—in which that "ripening" proceeds far enough that Zarathustra has the resources to be capable of coming through it with a more profound wisdom rooted in what might be called an aesthetically transfigured "ecstatic naturalism."[13]

That climax is followed by another, however, or rather by a kind of anticlimax. The educator's education, and ours, is far from complete at the end of the third part. A great gulf has opened up between the soaring height to which it rises at its end and the solid (or at any rate mundane) ground of daily life and human reality. A Monday-morning Dionysianism may not be a human (or even a conceptual) possibility; but in the fourth part (written in 1885) we find that there is a way of bringing it all down to earth that is not entirely a descent from the sublime into the ridiculous. The all-too-human remains, and indeed is very much in evidence in the bizarre array of specimens of "higher humanity" Zarathustra collects; but by the end one can begin to understand what it actually can mean to go on—without illusions and false hopes, yet undeterred by the circumstances that might inspire pity and do warrant talk of tragedy, and sustained by a life-sized reaffirmation of life as the very ambiguous thing it is.

It is particularly important, in this connection, to recognize that Nietzsche employs both the figure of Zarathustra and such notions as the *Übermensch* and "Eternal Recurrence" as devices in the context of his educational project of transforming our sensibility, rather than literalistically. In the language of *Birth*, the image of the *Übermensch* represents his version of the Apollinian moment in this process, while the notion of eternal recurrence represents the Dionysian—and neither, by itself, is enough.

The *Übermensch* may be regarded as an image introduced and employed to provide the (re)education of our aspirations and our thinking about the enhancement of life with a kind of compass, enabling us to gain a sense of direction even if not a clear description of our goal (which would be impossible). Its upshot for our lives is the notion of attained and attainable, naturalistically originating but enhanced "higher humanity." (The relation of these two images may usefully be conceived as somewhat analogous to the relation between the Greeks' Olympian deities and their heroes.) The notion of eternal recurrence, on the other hand, is the idea Nietzsche appropriates from ancient resources and employs in a central way in connection with a larger and more fundamental transformation of our sensibility, as the touchstone of the transformation of our basic disposition toward ourselves and our lives and world. Translated into its upshot, it becomes Nietzsche's conception of the affirmation of life, with *amor fati* (the love of fate) as its insignia.

If there is any such counterpart figure to the third (tragic) moment in *Birth* in which these other two moments come together and are *aufgehoben* (that is, at once negated, preserved, and transformed), I would suggest that it can only be the figure of Zarathustra himself. And by this I do not mean simply the Zarathustra we encounter in the first part, but rather the Zarathustra who begins as a well-meaning enlightened humanist, and winds up far wiser and more deeply human at the end of the work.

The upshot for us and our lives, in this case, is the newly and more truly human "future humanity" Nietzsche had recently envisioned and described (*JI* 337), possessed of what he went on (a year after completing the fourth part of *Zarathustra*) to call the "great health" (*JI* 381).[14] Here one would be neither preoccupied with the dream of the *Übermensch* nor obsessed with the vision of eternal recurrence, but rather concerned to get on with one's life and work (in the spirit of Zarathustra's parting lines), as the only meaningful way of "becoming who one is": "My suffering and my pity for suffering—what does it matter? Do I pursue *happiness*? I pursue my *work*! [*Trachte ich denn nach* Glücke? *Ich trachte nach meinem* Werke!]" (*Z* IV:20).

At this point mythic imagery gives way to actual human life as it must and can be lived—but now finding or working out one's own way ("This is my way; where is yours?"), in a spirit of transformed aspiration and sensibility. Neither the "meaning of the earth" associated with the image of the *Übermensch* nor the "affirmation" and *amor fati* associated with eternal recurrence remain the talk of the town, or become the elements of a new creed and catechism; for their work is done when they have supplemented the "free spirit" and seen the latter-day pilgrims through their educational progress and childhood's end.

In a work the purpose of which is *to educate our aspirations, valuations, and sensibility* rather than to give us information and instruction, Nietzsche considers it fair game to make use of ideas that serve to reorient our thinking regardless of their mere "truth-value" (or lack thereof). The notion of the *Übermensch* is one, and the image of eternal recurrence is another. Indeed, the very figure of Zarathustra "himself" is a third. They are neither the literal truth nor illusions, nor are they even "noble lies," but rather something like the salient forms of imagery figuring centrally in myths. Their "truth" or justification is a matter of their value as means of enabling us to come to understand something important about life and the world that they do not *literally* describe or designate. Nietzsche does not tell us things about Zarathustra, and have Zarathustra proclaim and "teach" things about the *Übermensch* and eternal recurrence, in order to have us "learn" them. Rather, he does so in the course of (and as part of) his effort to prompt us to the sort of response that may foster and further the enhancement of our lives.

VII

The *Übermensch*, eternal recurrence, and Zarathustra himself thus are tropes that all have their places *within* the educational process Nietzsche crafts for us, rather than at its end, as its results. They are among the materials of a ladder that is to be dispensed with once it has been climbed. If we become fixated upon them, we have made mere means of this education into its end; for their role is not to capture and hold our attention, but rather to aid us in reaching the developmental point at which we can go on without them—as Zarathustra himself suggests often enough.

Nietzsche earlier (in the time of *Birth*, and even in *Uses and Disadvantages of History*[15] two years later) had been much concerned with the role of myth in making life possible and worth living and humans capable of flourishing. He had initially been convinced that, for better or worse, its efficacy in this respect depended upon *illusion*. As was earlier observed, however, he subsequently had second thoughts on this matter. While he continued to make much of the ubiquity and indispensability of fictions, lies, and errors in human life, I believe that he came to understand that he had been guilty of a number of oversimplifications here, and that in particular it is a mistake to suppose that everything in the entire domain of human thought must be either flat-out "true" or simply "false." But this is a false dichotomy. And what is important about the contents of myth and art alike is something else altogether— namely, their power to shape our dispositions and ways of thinking, feeling, and esteeming.

Nietzsche subsequently moved away from the celebration of myth, and during his "free spirit" years flirted with the idea that we may have to learn either to get along without it or to resign ourselves to the inescapability and necessity of all-too-human forms of "untruth." He retained the conviction that no healthy and vital culture and humanity can be attained and sustained without *something* of the sort. But he would seem to have come to the realization that the "something of the sort" need not be either myths of the kind by which we long have lived or the newer myths of scientism, nationalism, and Wagnerianism. Something like the device of *Zarathustra* might do the job, in a way that does not exact too high a price, does not entail the sacrifice of honesty and intellectual integrity—and does not self-destruct at its own hands when the truthfulness it promotes is brought to bear upon itself.

To do the kind of job that myth has done, compelling images and representations of alternative interpretations are still required. Something on the order of the fare Nietzsche serves up in *Zarathustra* is needed, if our thinking is not to remain confined to the dead end of mere critique. It is a myth-substitute for the modern world, intended for a humanity (or at least for its vanguard) in transition, ready to be weaned away from its dependency upon myths, and yet still not fully mature—either too cavalier or too desperate at the prospect of having to make do without them.

Zarathustra engenders a new naturalistically based enthusiasm, and then provides its own antidote (in the form of the fourth part) to ensure that the new enthusiasm does not congeal into a new dogmatism. For Nietzsche understood that we must be able eventually to distance ourselves from *the means of our education*, even if we must initially be seduced and induced to engage with it and take it seriously enough to be affected by it. As in the case of myth, literal truth is not what it is all about; and a fundamentalist turn of mind with respect to the "teachings" of Zarathustra would have been no more welcome to Nietzsche among would-be disciples than among detractors.

The fourth part makes it clear, if the first three parts do not (as Nietzsche may have feared after writing them), that these teachings are not intended to be embraced as gospel truth. Its irony, parodies, grotesqueries, and humor are more than sufficient for this purpose. But the whole of the work shares in this double effect, as a kind of self-parodying quasi-myth that we are expected *both* to take seriously *and* to see for what it is. It is offered to us as no mere self-parody, however, as Nietzsche's hyperbolic hype with respect to it in *Ecce Homo* renders obvious. He realized that it would take something approaching a miracle to enable humanity to get from where it is to where it needs to go without meeting one or another of the sorry fates he envisions—and *Zarathustra*, he believed, *is that miracle*.

But it can do its work only if it is taken seriously. Getting anything of the kind taken seriously, however, especially by the very readers Nietzsche wanted most to reach (with their modern and perhaps nascently postmodern sophistication), might seem to be a virtual impossibility. But this is a part of the genius of the work he came up with: its self-parodic character is neither what it is all about nor a hopeless stumbling block to sophisticated readers. Rather, it is the very device that *enables* such readers *to take it seriously*. We bear witness to that fact ourselves.

In short: By the time of *Zarathustra*, Nietzsche both felt the need for something more than the ever-increasing sophistication of the "free spirit" series, and knew better than to think that anything on the order of Wagner's new mythology—or any of the older ones around, including that to which Wagner had returned—could be embraced by anyone like himself. He therefore sought to come up with something that would incorporate the means of coming to discern and attain an appropriately transformed and promising sensibility, in a form that protects it as well as possible against dismissal for reasons of intellectual integrity.

Zarathustra is the result. We can take it seriously precisely because it is made clear that we are not expected *to believe it,* in any literalistic way. What is to be taken seriously in and about it is not the cognitive content of the images and ideas by means of which our attention is attracted and our thinking is engaged (let alone the story line). Rather, it is the human possibilities that are reconfigured and opened up to us as the work unfolds, and as we respond.

VIII

NIETZSCHE AS EDUCATOR:

A BRIEF PEDAGOGICAL READING OF *ZARATHUSTRA*

Prologue

Education is thematized from the outset; and the kind of education that is at issue is clearly distinguished from both indoctrination and mere instruction. Zarathustra sets out to impart his "wisdom" to others, having already been transformed himself; for in place of the ashes he carried into the mountains, it is now "fire" that he would bring to humanity in the valleys below. Or rather: "I bring men a gift" (Z P:2)[16]—a gift for all or none, depending on their receptiveness. His gift is a new sensibility and way of thinking that endows life with greater value than it has under prevailing modes of interpretation and evaluation. His formula for it, expressing his conviction of the importance of "remaining faithful to the earth" and making the most of life as an earthly affair, is that "the *Übermensch* is the meaning of the earth [*der Sinn der Erde*]" (Z P:3).

Zarathustra knows (because the Nietzsche of *JI* 335 already knew) that love needs to be learned, and so attempts to educate his hearers in the matter of learning how to love that in ourselves which relates to the enhancement of life (Z P:4). Dismissing what ordinarily passes for "education," and also disparaging the sorry excuse for humanity (the "last man") that aspires to nothing more than an insipid happiness, he advocates a different kind of education, the thrust of which is to inculcate and cultivate *aspiration* (Z P:5). As things stand, he observes, "Human existence is uncanny and still without meaning" [*Unheimlich ist das menschliche Dasein und immer noch ohne Sinn*] (Z P:7). Yet its transformation into something meaningful is humanly possible, he proclaims, if only we will heed him.

But Zarathustra's preaching these things to the multitude is to no avail. It is not in this way, and with such an audience, that any meaningful education can occur. Perhaps, however, it can occur between Zarathustra and the reader, who both may come away somewhat the wiser from the all-too-believable failure of this attempt (and any such attempt) to transform the way people are disposed to think simply by *telling* them things they are neither prepared nor interested to hear. Zarathustra now understands that real education requires a different approach, and that he needs *companions* rather than just an audience if he is to have any success as an educator. So he proposes "to lure many away from the herd," with the thought that "I shall show them the rainbow and all the steps to the *Übermensch*" (*Z* P:9). But his optimism is tempered: "That I might be wiser!" (*Z* P:10).

And with this the prologue concludes. The first steps in the education of the educator (and reader) have now been taken, and the stage is set for those to follow—beginning with a series of sermonettes ("Speeches" [*Reden*]), this time presumably addressed not to the multitude but to those who might be responsive to the kind of rhetoric in which the first part consists. It is only a beginning; but unless a beginning is made, nothing further can happen.

First Part

In the twenty-two speeches of which the first part of the work consists (written and published in 1883), we see what Zarathustra's initial wisdom amounts to—and also what sorts of things Nietzsche associates with the ideas of "remaining faithful to the earth" and of the *Übermensch* as "the meaning of the earth." It is with these ideas that Zarathustra starts out in the prologue; and it is with their reaffirmation that the first part ends, in a concluding reflection on "the gift-giving virtue" [*der schenkenden Tugend*]—which is "power" [*Macht*] and its affirmation and expression (*Z* I:22).

Much good naturalistic sense and worldly wisdom is to be found in these speeches, beginning on a high note with the famous discussion "On the Three Metamorphoses" (of the mature human spirit)—metaphorically speaking, starting out in the manner of a burdened camel, then rebelling in that of a courageous lion, and finally attaining a second innocence akin to that of a playful child (*Z* I:1). This is revealing of the kind of thing Nietzsche has in mind in speaking of the enhancement of life, and of what is involved in the transformative transition from animality toward higher humanity and *Übermenschlichkeit*; and it also provides a sketch of a model of the multistage educational process that is his point of departure.

It is significant, however, that this is *only* Zarathustra's point of departure rather than his summary statement on this topic, and that the first part of the work ends with Zarathustra's withdrawal from those to whom he has been preaching, bidding them to "lose me and find yourselves" (*Z* I:22:3). Their education has only begun, he realizes, even if they have comprehended and taken to heart the entire content of the intervening score of speeches. This content ranges from disparagement of the anti-worldly, the otherworldly, and the ascetically minded and puritanical to celebration of the body, sublimation (as opposed to repression) of the passions, love, friendship, fighting the good fight, and creativity, with a mixture of barbed commentary (on various all-too-human and insidious tendencies and developments) and Nietzsche's own all-too-human musings (on such topics as women, marriage, and children).

What are we to make of all of this? A part of the answer to this question surely is suggested by the fact that Nietzsche neither stopped with the first part nor merely continued to churn out more of the same preaching. Zarathustra's concluding rejection of discipleship with respect to all that has gone before (*Z* I:22:3) is also relevant and revealing. It is not mere instruction in the precepts of living humanly well that is imparted in these speeches, but rather also a general outlook reflecting the fundamental reinterpretation and revaluation Nietzsche had been seeking (prior to *Zarathustra*) to carry out with respect to human life, and continued to promote and pursue subsequently. The soundness or unsoundness of any particular piece of advice or observation matters less than their collective drift, which is all well and good as far as it goes—but which, for Nietzsche (as the next parts show), does not go nearly far or deep enough.

Some of these speeches give vivid expression to ideas that are central to Nietzsche's thought. They serve to enhance both the comprehension and the appreciation of these ideas in any reader who is at all receptive to them. Among the best are "On the Despisers of the Body" (*Z* I:4), "On Enjoying and Suffering the Passions" (*Z* I:5), "On the Thousand and One Goals" (*Z* I:15), "On the Way of the Creator" (*Z* I:17), and "On the Gift-Giving Virtue" (*Z* I:22). But Nietzsche seeks to do more than get these ideas across; and mere agreement with them is not sufficient either. One needs to *earn one's right* to them; and by themselves they do not add up to a firmly rooted way of thinking that can dispense with all external support and withstand any doubt.

Second Part

Zarathustra's task in the second part of the work (also published in 1883) is to begin to try to come to terms with various threats to this way of thinking and its affirmative character that are quite capable of subverting it. He is represented as having changed; for we are told that "his wisdom grew," and had become a "wild wisdom," at once "pregnant" and "foolish," with Dionysian overtones and undercurrents (*Z* II:1).

Zarathustra's first major speech in this second part ("Upon the Blessed Isles") is one of the high points of the entire work, reaffirming the basic thrust of the first part, and also extending it by both celebrating creating [*Schaffen*] and emphasizing the inseparability of creation and destruction (*Z* II:2). Much of what follows, however, is troubled, both by skirmishes and distractions and by deeper worries about the problematic relations between life, spirit, and wisdom. There are many things that pass for education that do more harm than good, and they need to be dealt with and dispatched. Even if one manages to avoid becoming caught in their snares, however, it is still deeply worrisome whether there is any educational antidote to the doubts, anxiety, and incipient despair that cast a deepening shadow over this second part, culminating in the crisis with which it ends.

A hint of a solution is offered in the central section "On Self-Overcoming" (*Z* II:12); but it is with profound dissatisfaction, distress, and foreboding that Zarathustra once again withdraws at the second part's conclusion. Nothing he has understood or conveyed up to this point is adequate to the challenges that dawn upon him in "On Redemption" (*Z* II:20) and "On Human Prudence" (*Z* II:21).

This, however, is itself an important educational advance. Coming to know what one does not know or understand, to comprehend the nature and magnitude of the problem one faces, and to grasp the inadequacy of ways of thinking already at one's disposal in relation to it, may be no solution; but one will never find a solution if one does not understand the situation, and is not impelled to seek some way of doing something about it.

Third Part

In the course of the sixteen sections of the shorter third part (written and published in 1884), a provisional solution is achieved, in the form of a profound transformation of the way in which life and the world and one's own existence are regarded, both interpretively and evaluatively. It begins with a renewed call (in "The Wanderer") to self-overcoming, the enhancement of life, and the aspiration to human greatness (*Z* III:1). It ends with the Dionysian "Other Dancing Song" (*Z* III:15) and "Seven Seals" hymn, to which Nietzsche gave the alternate title "The Yea and Amen Song" (*Z* III:16).

This remarkable concluding double climax gives quasi-musical expression to an ecstatic affirmation of life and the world, viewed as they are in their fundamental eternal nature (Nietzsche's version of them *sub specie aeternitatis*, in the perspective of eternity). The idea of "eternal recurrence"—of life recurring eternally in the same (specific or general) way, unredeemed by anything beyond or after it or by any significant alteration of its basic character—ceases to be experienced as a devastating, unbearable, and "most abysmal thought" that cannot be faced. Indeed, this idea comes to be not only celebrated but drawn upon to provide the outlook elaborated previously (in the first part and earlier in the second) with legs to stand on.

This outlook and the polemics accompanying its initial elaboration are recapitulated and reaffirmed in the early speeches of the third part, following Zarathustra's first intimation—in "On the Vision and the Riddle" (*Z* III:2)—that it may be possible after all to come to terms affirmatively with the notion of eternal recurrence. These speeches culminate in two of the most notable perorations in the entire work: "On the Three Evils" (*Z* III:10) and "On Old and New Tablets," with its paean to creativity as the key to the enhancement of life and its meaningfulness: "he who creates [. . .] creates man's goal and gives the earth its meaning and its future" (*Z* III:12:2).

Accompanying this reaffirmation of these ideas is the elevation to prominence of what had been a relatively minor theme in the first part. As it is developed here, with applications at all levels (up to that of the eternal recurrence itself), it becomes clear that it is crucial to the transformation that occurs in the third part. It is also of profound educational importance, and is one of the keys to the conception of the kind of education with which Nietzsche is concerned. This is the idea that the basic condition of the possibility of all affirmation is *learning to love*. (That had been the subject of one of the concluding sections of the 1882 version of *Joyful Inquiry, JI* 334.)

In "On Passing By" (*Z* III:7), the point is made that "passing by" is the best thing to do where one cannot love; and then, as the third part unfolds, the idea of the importance of loving and learning to love is explored in a variety of contexts, from "learning to love oneself" (*Z* III:11:2) to learning to appreciate the "many good inventions [*Erfindungen*] on earth" and grasp that "on their account the earth is to be loved" [*derentwegen ist die Erde zu lieben*] (*Z* III:12:17), to loving "life" (*Z* III:15) and even "eternity" (*Z* III:16). The "three evils" rehabilitated and celebrated—sex, lust to rule, and self-centeredness [*Wollust, Herrschsucht, Selbstsucht*]—are three elemental forms of loving that we must both learn to affirm and learn to cultivate beyond their simplest forms of expression.

Zarathustra's wisdom is powerless to sustain him by itself. What he can love, however, he can affirm, and find meaningful; for love bestows value and meaning. Here life expresses itself as the fundamentally Dionysian phenom-

enon Nietzsche takes it to be. And at the conclusion of the third part, he attempts to construct a means not only of *conveying* this point but also of *enabling* us to ascend his version of the ladder of love to its ultimate height,
from which even a world viewed under the aspect of eternal recurrence can
be affirmed.

Fourth Part

One cannot live, however, at such a height. How can the spirit of such a Dionysian love be preserved in some way when one descends to the plane of life
as we must live it? That is the basic question Nietzsche is attempting to answer in this fourth and last part of the work (written, but only privately published, in 1885). He may not have intended at first to extend *Zarathustra* past
its first three parts after having completed them; but had he not done so, the
educational project of the work would have been seriously incomplete. Like
a great symphony or grand opera, the third part ends with a rapturous and
glorious climax. But even if it succeeds in momentarily transporting us along
with Zarathustra as we reach that point, what then?

Nietzsche knew very well that even exceptions to the human rule will continue to have much of the all-too-human about them; and if depression is not
to set in once again with this recognition, one's education will have to continue further, to provide one with ways of coming to terms with this circumstance without illusions. If one is well advised to turn away and pass by where
one cannot love, where does this leave one who is acutely aware of the "all-
too-human" general character of humanity with dawning of the cold, clear
light of day, when the raptures evoked in the concluding songs of part 3 have
subsided?

Thus, the motley collection of so-called higher *Menschen* Zarathustra as-
sembles in the fourth part serves the purpose of providing another kind of
test, somewhat analogous to the recurrence test (posed by Nietzsche in the
penultimate section of the fourth Book of *Inquiry* [*JI* 341], immediately prior
to its final section, with which *Zarathustra* literally begins). If "higher humanity" were to amount to nothing more than the sort of thing this strange and
ludicrous crew represents, could one still affirm it with open eyes, and adhere
to the way of thinking that ties the "meaning of the earth" to the enhancement
of life? In the end Zarathustra passes this test; and if the fourth part accom-
plishes its educational task for us, we should be able to pass it as well.

In that event, one would not have to be in the throes of rapture of the "Seven
Seals" hymn to be able to embrace the conception of "higher humanity" as

the upshot of the idea of the *Übermensch* and the basis of a fundamental and comprehensive affirmative stance. One may have to learn to overcome the susceptibility to be overwhelmed by feelings of "pity" for "higher humanity," such as it is; and indeed this "temptation" may actually be heightened in the aftermath of the third part. Yet here we see that this is humanly possible, even if the only "higher" types around leave a great deal to be desired *and* are viewed utterly without illusions.

This requires yet a further "ripening" of Zarathustra's nature, and another chapter in the educational process with which Nietzsche is concerned. The section "On Higher *Menschen*" ("*Vom höheren Menschen*") (*Z* IV:13), with its twenty subsections, makes it clear that Nietzsche still means the idea of "higher humanity" to be taken very seriously, despite the comical procession of "higher" types to which we have been introduced. But a part of what *enables* it to continue to be taken seriously is that Nietzsche is effectively countering any tendency one might have to take it seriously *in the wrong way*, using comedy and absurdity to overcome "the spirit of gravity" (*Z* IV:17).

This is one expression of a central points of the fourth part: that one must learn not only to love but also to *laugh*, and to dance. It is with this theme that the last half dozen subsections of the discourse "On Higher *Menschen*" are concerned (*Z* IV:13:15–20). To be sure, they are followed immediately by the "old magician's" (Wagner's?) anguished "Song of Melancholy" (*Z* IV:14); but this only serves to underscore the point. The magician has not yet managed to incorporate the very lesson Zarathustra has just taught. His real education is still incomplete.

But not all laughter is of the same kind, as Zarathustra observes: "And if they have learned to laugh from me, it is still not *my* laughter that they have learned" (*Z* IV:17:1). And the same applies with respect to *his* kind of life affirmation, which can easily be parodied.[17] Indeed, it even applies with respect to the affirmation of the idea of eternal recurrence (*Z* IV:19:1). Zarathustra himself is still struggling with all of this right to the very end of the fourth part, falling back on the theme of the third part's end to fortify himself in "The Drunken Song"—albeit with greater self-consciousness this time, and with more explicit awareness of its implications for human life.

It is only at the conclusion of the final section that Zarathustra seems finally to arrive at the human maturity toward which his educational course has been tending. The conclusion clearly affirms that course, and shows that the fourth part is by no means a reductio ad absurdum of the entire work. But it also resists any reduction of the educational project of Zarathustra/ *Zarathustra* to a formula; for like creativity, maturity admits neither of any complete description nor of any specific prescription.

IX

Where does this leave Zarathustra? And how are we to imagine him after he again leaves his cave, "glowing and strong as a morning sun that comes out of dark mountains," having finally "ripened" and arrived at his realization of what finally does and does not matter (Z IV:20)? His education has been extraordinary: "The ladder on which he ascends and descends is tremendous," Nietzsche tells us three years later (*EH* "Books," Z:6). Nietzsche's retrospective apotheosis of him in *Ecce Homo* actually only serves to underscore his profound commitment to what Zarathustra and *Zarathustra* are all about.

Zarathustra may fall short of deserving Nietzsche's more extravagant claims for it, and may have fallen short of his hope for it as well; and as a literary vehicle for his philosophical ideas it may leave a good deal to be desired, as anyone who has tried to use it to "teach Nietzsche" in a philosophy course can attest. Yet regarded as an educational device of the kind I have been describing, and assessed by any more modest standard of success than Nietzsche's own, it would seem to me to be a truly remarkable accomplishment.

Most of humanity has been and is likely to remain untouched by it (for better or worse); and it has lent itself to uses and abuses both silly and sinister, as well as to others less awkward to acknowledge. Yet it does have the power to do—at least for some—the sort of thing Nietzsche attributed to his encounter with Schopenhauer. It can have a great and profound educational effect upon the sensibilities of kindred spirits. *Zarathustra* deals in consciousness-raising and attitude adjustment. And it may be in a class by itself among efforts of this kind in the philosophical literature after Plato.

This may be a far cry from saving humanity from the Scylla and Charybdis of fanaticism and nihilism, on whose rocks we may yet founder. But I do believe that the kind of education one *can* get from *Zarathustra* can help—at least as much as anything else we have—those who worry about such things to navigate through and beyond those straits.

Yet it is "a book for all—and none." For even the greatest of educational opportunities will be to no avail to those who are unresponsive to it.

5

The Nietzsche of *Beyond Good and Evil*:
Prelude to a Philosophy of the Future

JENSEITS VON GUT UND BÖSE:
VORSPIEL EINER PHILOSOPHIE DER ZUKUNFT

> Where, then, must *we* reach with our hopes? Toward *new philosophers*; there is no
> choice; toward spirits strong and original enough to provide the stimuli for opposing
> [*entgegengesetzten*] valuations and to revalue and invert "eternal values"; toward fore-
> runners [*Vorausgesandten*], toward *Menschen* of the future, who in the present tie the
> knot and constraint that forces the will of millennia upon *new* tracks.
> *Beyond Good and Evil*, 203

> This book is in all essentials a *critique of modernity*, not excluding the modern sciences,
> modern arts, and even modern politics, along with pointers to a contrary type that is as
> little modern as possible—a distinguished [*vornehmen*], a Yes-saying type. In the latter
> sense, the book is a school for the *gentilhomme* [gentleman, higher type], taking this
> concept in a more spiritual and radical sense than has ever been done before.
> *Ecce Homo*, "Books," BGE

Nietzsche's self-proclaimed "prelude" to philosophy's future, *Beyond Good and Evil*, has long been one of his most celebrated works. Yet prior to its publication in 1886, all of his previous books notwithstanding, he was virtually unknown to his contemporaries—and its appearance did nothing to change that. The sales of his books initially were so poor that, from *Beyond* onward, he was obliged to become his own publisher.[1] At the time of his collapse in January 1889, neither this book nor any of the others he had published after *The Birth of Tragedy* had attracted even the minor flurry of attention that *Birth* had received.

In the years just before and immediately following his resignation from his professorship at Basel in 1879, Nietzsche had published a number of aphoristic works that he came to think of as his "free spirit" series, discussed above, beginning with *Human, All Too Human* and concluding with *Joyful Inquiry*, both discussed above. By the time of the first version of *Inquiry* (1882), however, Nietzsche already had begun to outgrow that identity, as well as his infatuation with Schopenhauer and with Wagner's related special brand of late romanticism, discerning the need for new and more penetrating forms of analysis and critique. But he had not yet found an adequate way of articulating the possibility and character of an intellectually conscionable *affirmative* alternative to Schopenhauerian pessimism and its strange Wagnerian operatic cousin that he had earlier celebrated in *Birth* and (rather artificially) in *Richard Wagner in Bayreuth* (1876).[2]

For a time, therefore, Nietzsche ceased further writing—for publication, at any rate—of the sort he had been doing. In its place, he devoted himself to something completely different, in an attempt to express and convey that alternative: the subject of the previous chapter, *Thus Spoke Zarathustra*. It was with *Beyond*, in 1886, that he then returned to philosophical prose publication. A year later Nietzsche published an expanded version of *Inquiry* with a new Fifth "Book," in which he finally returned to the projects of the initial four-Book version. (See the addendum at the end of this chapter.) His only subsequent publication, however, apart from prefaces to his earlier works and prior to the polemics and diatribes of the final year of his productive life (1888), was *On the Genealogy of Morality*, which also appeared in 1887, as a kind of supplement to *Beyond* and partial preparation for a portion of the project of a "revaluation of values." (It is the subject of the next chapter.) The Nietzsche of *Beyond* thus was nearing what turned out to be the high point of his philosophical trajectory during the time of its composition.

Like most of Nietzsche's other books, from the "free spirit" series onward (other than *Zarathustra* and *Genealogy*), *Beyond* is a book of an aphoristic nature. It consists of groupings of relatively brief reflections that began in the workshop of the notebooks, in which he would first jot down and then work out, rework, and refine his ideas, as his inspirations, health problems, travels, and other personal circumstances permitted. While nothing like systematic treatises, however, these aphoristic books were invariably carefully composed, often very strategically. Virtually everything Nietzsche ventured to say in them was tentative, experimental, perspectival, and disjointed, displaying differing and changing as well as developing ways of thinking and lines of thought with relative or sometimes extreme brevity. Yet it is quite possible to discern in them emerging directions and positions in his treatments of many of the matters with which he deals.

I

Nietzsche gave *Beyond* the subtitle *Prelude to a Philosophy of the Future* [*Vorspiel einer Philosophie der Zukunft*];[3] and it is above all as a harbinger of a provocative, intriguing, and radically revisionist conception of the future of philosophy that both he and this work are deserving of a place of major importance not only in the recent history of philosophy but also in its actual future. But just what that conception is, and what is to be made of it, remain matters of intense controversy, among his diverse admirers and his many detractors alike.

Beyond is commonly and understandably regarded as the single most important of Nietzsche's prose philosophical works. It stands out among them as the book in which he most clearly conveys his hard-won new understanding of the character and tasks of the sort of "philosophy of the future" that will be most urgently needed in the human future that is now dawning, and that will itself be most deserving of a future. Yet it is also in some respects perhaps the most unnerving of his prose works; and it does no more than suggest and briefly sketch the sorts of reinterpretations and revaluations toward which he is inclined, as he looks beyond those he considers and finds wanting.

Its author is both emphatic and persuasive, however, in his insistence that interpretation (and reinterpretation) and evaluation (and revaluation) must henceforth be recognized to be the main tasks of philosophy; that there is virtually nothing in our intellectual and cultural inheritance and present self-understanding that is not in need of such reconsideration; and that the very forms and strategies of such endeavors themselves require to be reconsidered, as best we can.

Beyond is neither a monograph nor even (as *Genealogy* is) a set of essays. It is another of his "aphoristic" works, and consists of nearly three hundred consecutively numbered aphorisms or sections, ranging in length from a few lines to several pages, divided into nine *Hauptstücke* (major parts), and framed by a short preface and a poetic postlude. The first part, "On the Prejudices of Philosophers," sets the stage for Nietzsche's kind of philosophical thinking, the previous character of which is the subject of the second part, on "The Free Spirit." Its evolving character is then discussed and elaborated in the sixth and seventh parts, "We Scholars" and "Our Virtues."

The fourth part is a collection of (actual) aphorisms, "Epigrams and Interludes," providing a sort of intermission[4] between the heavy-going third and fifth parts, which deal both analytically and subversively with "religiousness" and with the "natural history" of morals. In the final two parts, Nietzsche turns his attention first to matters relating to the "peoples and countries" of his Europe and then beyond them, in a concluding part on the question "*Was ist vornehm?*"—that is, on the character of various *vornehm* ("exceptional," "distinguished," or "noble") human types, how they may have come to be humanly possible, and what the conditions of their possibility may continue to be. (I shall comment in more detail upon each of these parts of the book in due course.)

Nietzsche began working on *Beyond* in earnest in mid-1885 (immediately after finishing the privately circulated fourth part of *Zarathustra*); and he published it a year later, a scant thirty months before his collapse. As I observed above, the last thing he had written for publication before *Zarathustra* and *Beyond* was the four-part first version of *Inquiry*; and the first thing he published after them was an expanded second version of it. This suggests that *Beyond* belongs within a trajectory that is framed by the two versions of *Inquiry* and also within another that is framed by *Zarathustra* and the final series of his writings relating to the project of a "revaluation of values," beginning with *Genealogy*.

But Nietzsche's publication history during these years tells only a part of the story. The full history of *Beyond* began almost immediately after the appearance of *Inquiry* in 1882; for in his notebooks of summer and fall 1882 we find a collection of 445 aphorisms under the very title he used four years later: "*Jenseits von Gut und Böse*." Nietzsche may not have *published* another prose work until the appearance of *Beyond* itself in 1886; but his notebooks from the years between the publication of the first edition of *Inquiry* in 1882 and of *Beyond* in 1886 run to some 1,450 pages in the critical edition of his writings (*KGW*), greatly exceeding the number of pages of these two works combined. And he did not stop with that first collection of 445 aphorisms; for his notebooks of the winter of 1882–83 contain an untitled collection of another 273 aphorisms relating to the conception of "will to power" as a biological as well as a psychological conception. (Thus its first aphorism reads: "Will to life? In its place I found only will to power" [*KGW* VII 5:1].)

Nietzsche's *Zarathustra* years (1883–85), although devoid of prose publication, were full of further plans for new major works, culminating in the announcement (in 1886), on the back cover of *Beyond*, of a forthcoming book—first envisioned in a notebook entry of 1885—to be entitled "The Will to Power: Attempt at a New Interpretation of All Happening" [*Versuch einer neuen Auslegung Alles Geschehens*] (*KGW* VII 39:1). His notebooks from these years contain a great many entries indicating ideas for books, many of which feature titles or subtitles anticipating the actual title and subtitle of *Beyond*, and in which one can see its conception taking shape. They also include a great deal of material relating to these ideas. These ideas and this material—from the period leading up to the composition of *Beyond* and extending through the time of its publication—are only notebook entries; but they do provide convincing evidence for a number of points relating to his thinking at this time.

They include material on the importance and possibility of transcending the bounds of dogmatic moralistic "good-and-evil" dichotomizing and absolutizing, both with respect to putatively "moral" matters and also more generally; the importance and necessity of transcending both rationalist and empiricist dogmatisms, and also scientistic imperialism purporting to be capable "in principle" of "explaining" everything, and of replacing them with an "interpretive" approach to the understanding and comprehension of ourselves and of what is going on in the world of which we are a part.

Further examples of what Nietzsche concerns himself with in his notebooks from this period: The viability and preferability (by the best of humanly possible intellectually conscientious standards) of a broadly applied interpretation of all that transpires in this world in terms of something Nietzsche here and elsewhere calls "will to power"; and the possibility of a new orientation to matters of value, making possible a way of depriving nihilism of the last word with respect to values, and setting the stage for a critique, revaluation, and supersession of prevailing modes of valuation. All of these themes figure significantly in what became the book *Beyond Good and Evil* itself, and are developed in ways going well beyond anything Nietzsche had done with them previously.

Nietzsche's hopes for the book were high, even though he now felt compelled to act as his own publisher. He had the first copies printed at the press of C. G. Naumann in Leipzig in August of 1886, with a print run of six hundred—which was as much as Nietzsche the newly struggling self-publisher could afford. Distribution of a self-published book, however, quite understandably proved to be a problem. In any event, and for whatever reasons, the plain fact of the matter is that the book attracted no attention whatsoever, until Nietzsche was past caring. After ten months, only 114 copies had been sold, with another sixty-six being either given away to friends or sent to potential reviewers and others he wanted to see it. A second printing was not needed (and therefore was not made) until 1891, two years after Nietzsche's collapse, when a run of a thousand copies was made, with another thousand following two years later. The status of a classic that the book now enjoys thus was slow in coming.[5] "Some," Nietzsche observes in *Ecce Homo*, "are born posthumously" (*EH* "Books," 1). That observation certainly applies in his case, and with respect to this pivotal work.

II

As Nietzsche's ideas for titles from the notebooks of 1883–86 make clear, the theme of a "philosophy of the future" (no doubt echoing Wagner's characterization of his own work as the beginning of a *Zukunftsmusik* or "*music* of the future") was an important one in the shaping of the project of *Beyond*. Ludwig Feuerbach[6] had earlier seized upon the idea, calling his 1843 manifesto for a new sort of post-Hegelian philosophy *Principles of the Philosophy of the Future* [*Grundsätze der Philosophie der Zukunft*].

Nietzsche chose to describe the relation of *Beyond* to this "philosophy of the future" as a "prelude" [*Vorspiel*] to or of it. As was previously noted, the conventional translation of the first words of Nietzsche's German phrase *Vorspiel einer Philosophie der Zukunft* as "prelude *to*" is problematic. "Prelude *of*" would be more apt as well as more accurate. In any event, the translation choice should not be allowed to settle the question of whether Nietzsche meant *Beyond* itself to *mark the beginning* of that new development, or merely to envision and set the stage for it.

Nietzsche's choice of this bit of musical language would seem to argue in favor of the former possibility. Musical preludes are *parts of* the works to which they are preludes, anticipating what is to come even as they herald and prepare the way for it, and often giving a kind of preview of it, as Nietzsche the musician and lover of opera knew full well. His *Zarathustra* quite obviously had been his artistic counterpart and counter-creation to Wagner's *Ring* quartet of operas; and it seems equally obvious that, like Wagner's music more generally, *Beyond* was to be his philosophical counterpart and countermove not only to Wagner's advocacy of a *Zukunftsmusik*, but also to his inauguration of it in his own music. And Nietzsche enjoyed the advantage of being able to combine what he was preaching with first steps in its practice in the same work.

Nietzsche's "philosophy of the future," however, like Wagner's writings on a music of the future, was to be no mere theoretical exercise or scholarly affair. In both cases (as Nietzsche had understood from the beginning of his relationship with Wagner), that ultimate practice had to do with nothing less than the possible renewal and transformation of contemporary culture and humanity. Its upshot was intended to be cultural and experiential renewal and enhancement—and thereby an enhancement of human life itself, as it might at least be lived by exceptions to the human rule, if not by all. This intent is reflected in Nietzsche's emphasis upon the twin themes and tasks of reinterpretation and revaluation, both in *Beyond* and subsequently, with reinterpretation setting the stage for revaluation, and the needs of revaluation guiding the focus of the reinterpretation. Nietzsche's kind of philosophy involves efforts along both lines—not only for purposes of their illustration, but also by way of their implementation.

In *Inquiry*, four years earlier, as I have noted, Nietzsche had followed his observation that "God is dead" with the comment that "we—we still have to vanquish his shadow too" (*JI* 108). He had gone on impatiently to ask when we finally will "have completely de-deified nature" [*die Natur ganz entgöttlicht haben*], and have begun to proceed to "*naturalize*" [*vernatürlichen*] our understanding of ourselves as human beings [*Menschen*], in terms of a "pure, newly discovered, newly redeemed nature" (*JI* 109). By the time of *Beyond* he had come to recognize that "de-deification" is not enough, and that we must (as it were) *de-moralize*—that is, "*un*-moralize"—our thinking as well. We must reinterpret

and revalue not only nature and our own human reality but also virtually everything associated with them in a post-moralistic as well as post-religious and
post-metaphysical manner. More specifically, we must do so in a manner "beyond" or purged of the moralism that centers upon the opposite categories
of "good and evil," as well as beyond the other-worldly absolutisms related to
it. Hence Nietzsche's choice of "Beyond Good and Evil" as the main title of
the book.

But he had also come to recognize the importance of guarding against
the nihilistic rebound that was all too likely to attend their abandonment. He
took this "nothing matters" nihilism to be the most dangerous withdrawal symptom of these most deadly addictions. He therefore now sought to supply the
"Yes-saying," life-affirming reorientation to which he had given literary expression in *Zarathustra* with a suitable new-philosophical repositioning and articulation. The "*Mensch* of the future" he envisioned a year later, at the conclusion of *Genealogy*'s second essay, who "must come one day," would be at once
"*Antichrist und Antinihilist*," anti-Christian and anti-nihilist, *and* a "creative
spirit" [*schöpferische Geist*] of "compelling strength" sufficient to "restore its
goal to the earth and his hope to man" (*GM* II:24). This post-religious, post-
moralist, and also post-nihilist type of human being requires a "philosophy
of the future" as midwife and educator, even if not necessarily as principal
occupation. And that—or at any rate, a first glimpse of it—is what Nietzsche
undertakes to provide in *Beyond*.

This is one of the respects in which Nietzsche's kind of philosopher and
philosophy in *Beyond* go beyond those to be associated with what he described
four years earlier as his "new image and ideal of the free spirit."[7] The kinds of
"free-spirited" inquiry exemplified and advocated in the series of books from
Human to *Inquiry* are by no means abandoned, and indeed are continued; but
for Nietzsche they are no longer enough. The "philosophy of the future" must
involve such inquiry *and more*. In addition to taking enlightenment to new
heights and depths, acquainting oneself as best one can with the sciences—
whose "scope and tower-building" [*Umfang und Turmbau*] have "grown enormously" [*in's Ungeheure gewachsen*]—is to be one part of it (*BGE* 205). And
venturing further along the paths of reinterpretation and revaluation: the kind
of philosopher Nietzsche now has in mind must have the self-confidence [*Ehr-
furcht*] that is necessary to "lead" in the pursuit of knowledge [*als Erkennender*].
And further still: such a philosopher must also "demand of himself a judgment,
a Yes or No, not about the *Wissenschaften* but about life and the value of life
[*über das Leben und den Wert des Lebens*]" (*BGE* 205).

The key to understanding the kind of "philosophy of the future" Nietzsche
envisions in *Beyond* is to understand *what this means*. And he presumably

already was convinced that (as he was to observe in *Twilight of the Idols* two years later) "judgments of value concerning life [*Werturteile über das Leben*], for it or against it, can in the end never be true," and have significance "only as symptoms" (*TI* "Socrates," 2). For the author of *Beyond*, genuinely philosophical thinking ultimately requires a kind of fundamental "affirmation" that is neither itself a cognition nor a conclusion that can be validated cognitively. This Nietzschean "affirmation" likewise is no mere assent to a proposition, but rather is conceived as an expression having to do with how one is or has come to be (perhaps as thinker as well as human being). And making it, for Nietzsche, signifies not being compromised in one's intellectual integrity, but rather on the contrary having sought and found "one's way" to a "right" and "even a duty" to such an expression (*BGE* 205).

III

The agenda of Nietzsche's "philosophy of the future," as he presents it in *Beyond*, is a rich one. It begins—but *only* begins—with a reassessment of philosophy past and present from which it will be departing, and a disentanglement from both religious and moralizing ways of thinking that might otherwise subvert it by means of a mode of analysis serving to subvert them. It then calls for a reconsideration of what matters and makes a difference in human life, how to think about it, and what might be done about it.

It further requires consideration of how one is to go on to think about truth and knowledge, science and philosophy itself, our human reality and the world of which we are a part, and a host of social, cultural, and intellectual phenomena that bear in various ways upon the character and quality of human life. And one is to do so not merely out of a kind of intellectual curiosity, but rather quite self-consciously, recognizing the magnitude and seriousness of the task. It involves attempting to set the stage for a serious reckoning with the question of the future of humanity, in the aftermath of the "death of God" and demise of all absolutes, the de-deification of nature and the naturalizing of our understanding of ourselves, and our dawning comprehension of how we have come to be as we are, what we have to work with, what our constraints and vulnerabilities are, what could become of us, and what we might yet make of ourselves.

Among the things that emerged along the way, for Nietzsche, is the centrality and importance of what might be called the project of a post-metaphysical, scientifically and historically sophisticated, and "naturalized" *philosophical anthropology*. Its first order of business would be to "translate man back into nature" [*zurückübersetzen in die Natur*] and "see to it that man henceforth stands before man as even today, hardened in the discipline of *Wissenschaft*, he stands before the *rest* of nature [*der* anderen *Nature*]" (*BGE* 230). But it also would undertake to do justice to the respects in which human reality and possibility are no longer merely "natural" and admit of enhancement.

Nietzsche makes it clear elsewhere *in Beyond* that he considers a number of kinds of inquiry and their differing perspectives to be indispensable to his kind of philosophical anthropology: historical, physiological, sociological, linguistic, cultural, and perhaps most importantly, psychological. He even goes so far as to call psychology (or at any rate, his version of it) "the path to the fundamental problems," and so "the queen of the *Wissenschaften*, for whose service and preparation the others exist" (*BGE* 23).

A part of this project is to take a new look at a variety of phenomena that have long been put on pedestals and revered as having divine pedigrees in the perspective of such a philosophical anthropology—but also to draw upon the analysis of these phenomena to enrich and develop that anthropology itself. Those examined by Nietzsche in *Beyond*, and drawn upon in this way, are of a moral, religious, social, political, and cultural as well as of an intellectual, scientific, and otherwise cognitive nature; and they extend even further afield, to human differences in abilities and of a psychological and physiological nature. And so it is that he even ventures—problematically, to say the least—into the treacherous domains of human trait determination, mutability, and transmission and of race, sexuality, and gender, where most philosophers have either feared or disdained to tread.

Thus Nietzsche would have his "new philosophers" take serious account of the natural as well as social and historical disciplines (*Wissenschaften*), as he himself was attempting to do—such as what appeared to him to be new developments and insights in the life sciences. The hazards of doing so are well illustrated by his Lamarckism (according to which traits acquired behaviorally in one generation could be transmitted biologically), which at the time seemed to be a scientific winner, but subsequently turned out to be an at least largely wrong turn.[8]

Nietzsche may have taken more than a few wrong turns in his wanderings in these minefields. What is more important than any of his missteps is his insistence that these are matters to be reckoned with philosophically in our efforts to understand ourselves—and further, that philosophers (and in particular philosophers of the future) must be prepared to back off from prior convictions and conjectures, and to stand corrected when further inquiry in these various disciplines discredits ideas that had previously seemed sound.

Further: "translating man back into nature" is only the first part of such a project. A subsequent and ultimately even more important part of it is to translate our humanity back *out of* (mere) nature again; to grasp the respects in which it is *no longer* a merely biological phenomenon; to understand how this could have come about in the course of merely naturalistically occurring human events; and to comprehend the consequences. All of this, too, is a part of what is going on in *Beyond*. And it is reflected in the strong interest Nietzsche evinces in social and cultural phenomena, and for that matter in moral and religious phenomena as well. For he is convinced that they have had a great deal to do with what might be called *the genealogy of our humanity*—and further, that they continue to have a profound influence upon the different ways human beings turn out, individually as well as collectively. But there is to be more to his "philosophy of the future" than this, formidable as it already is.

IV

An important topic to which both parts of this project (as described so far) are pertinent—and which is of obvious importance for philosophy itself as well as all other forms of cognitive endeavor—is that of *human thought*, and its relation to our constitution, resources, and circumstances. This is a topic directly relevant to the problem of knowledge, and more specifically of the possibility and nature of human knowledge. It therefore has clear and significant bearing not only on the question of what to make of the sciences, but also on the prospects and character of Nietzsche's philosophy of the future. In *Beyond* he shows himself to be clearly on the way to a form of *naturalistic epistemology* along with a more comprehensive naturalistic philosophical psychology and anthropology, linked in one direction to physiology and in another to social and cultural anthropology.

Nietzsche is quite prepared to reckon with the possibility that a considerable revision in our understanding of humanly possible knowledge will be necessitated, not only by the reconsideration of truth and of the sorts of things there are to be known he calls for, but also by the adoption of a naturalistic-anthropological perspective upon all human capacities. But he leaves no doubt that he remains committed to the meaningfulness and importance of the idea of knowledge, and to the conception of his "philosophy of the future" as a fundamentally cognitive affair, in aspiration and reasonable expectation of attainment.[9]

It is often supposed that Nietzsche's insistence upon the interpretive character of all thought, and on the affective origins and motivation of all interpretation, entails his abandonment of the very ideas of "truth" and "knowledge." The fact that he readily avails himself of both concepts throughout *Beyond*, however, runs counter to this understanding of him. And while he does insist that no interpretation is immaculately conceived, it also is one of his most important (but underappreciated) points that, their origins notwithstanding, some interpretations *can turn out* to be better than others cognitively speaking, with respect to the specific matters with which they deal, in the justice they do to them. Which is to say: in terms of such things as the depth, subtlety, astuteness, explanatory power, and comprehensive sense-making of the accounts of these matters they enable one to provide.

If such interpretations are developed in conjunction with a sufficiently strong "will to knowledge" and "intellectual conscience" (whatever *their* human origins and motivations may be); if they further can be refined by a sufficiently rigorous, precise, and sophisticated intelligence; if a substantial evidential, circumstantial, and methodological case can be made for them; and if they prove capable of withstanding critical scrutiny, that is all that should be desired to satisfy the demands of intellectual conscience. For that is as much as is humanly possible, and is precisely what cognitive significance amounts to—or at any rate, for Nietzsche, should be understood to amount to, in many domains of human reality and the world of human life and experience. Thus, in the preface to *Genealogy*, written just a year after *Beyond*, we find him expressing delight at his growing "assurance," with respect to his views relating to morals and their origins, that they have arisen in him "from a *fundamental will of knowledge*" [Grundwillen *der Erkenntnis*] (*GM* P:2).

The converse side of Nietzsche's philosophical-anthropological project is to give at least some consideration to the "nature" back into which all things human are to be "translated." For it would make little sense to interpret human reality in a manner that does not accord at least fundamentally with the larger reality of which it is a part. That "nature" is first and foremost organic nature, or the phenomenon of "life" as it has come to be in our corner of the universe; but this phenomenon, too, has emerged within and out of and a larger and more fundamental reality, with the general character of which its own nature presumably must also accord.

These are among the basic postulates of any "de-deified" naturalism. But Nietzsche clearly has a more specific version of such a naturalism in mind. He has relatively little to say about it in *Beyond*; but he does say enough at least to indicate the basic outlines of the interpretation of that larger reality of which human life is an instance, even if a rather extraordinary one. He frames it in terms of an interpretation of psychological, biological, and even physical phenomena featuring the general dispositional notion of "will to power," which looms larger in this book than it does in any of his other writings.

The status and intended scope of this concept and interpretation, as well as the meaning of its central concept, are matters of great controversy. It is clear, however, that at least at the time of *Beyond*, Nietzsche was seriously committed to this interpretation, convinced of its basic soundness and superiority to its rivals, and persuaded that it applies well beyond as well as within the domain of human psychology, and indeed (as has been observed), to "*Alles Geschehen*" [everything that happens]. And in the course of *Beyond* itself, for better or worse, Nietzsche quite explicitly employs the concept of "will to power" every bit as broadly as this expression suggests.

So, for example, he writes: "Life itself is *essentially* [*wesentlich*] appropriation, injury, overpowering of what is alien and weaker, suppression, hardness, imposition of one's own forms, incorporation and [. . .] exploitation," because "life simply *is* will to power" [*Leben eben Wille zur Macht* ist]. And he strikingly adds for good measure: "If this should be an innovation as a theory—as a reality it is the *primordial fact* of all history [*als Realität ist es das* Ur-Faktum *aller Geschichte*]" (*BGE* 259). Indeed, Nietzsche indicates that he is prepared to go even further, to the world more generally: "In a world whose very nature is will to power [*in einer Welt, deren Essenz Wille zur Macht ist*]," he writes, the principle "Hurt no one, help all you can" is "insipidly false and sentimental" (*BGE* 186).

These passages make it evident that his hypothetically stated case for the idea that "the world viewed from within [*die Welt von innen gesehen*] [. . .] would be 'will to power' and nothing else" in *BGE* 36 is a case he considers compelling. This section, read in conjunction with these other passages, suggests that the Nietzsche of *Beyond* is convinced of the soundness of his interpretation of all events—in terms of the "development and ramification" of a single basic disposition of all force to express itself in an assertive manner establishing power relationships. He refers to it as "*mein Satz*" ("my proposition"). And it is his *Satz* because he believes it to be the simplest experience anchored (as the God-hypothesis is not) account sufficing to make sense of the profusion of phenomena of which we have experience: not only psychological and social but also cultural and intellectual phenomena, on the one hand, and biological and even physical phenomena on the other.

The gist of this interpretation is that "all that happens" in the world is fundamentally best understood not only dynamically but also in dispositional terms, with "will to power" characterizing the most basic disposition of all. Nietzsche's interpretive intuition is that *power relationships* are the bottom line at any level of description and in any context one may pick. And his theoretical wager is that, if one construes the stuff of this undeniably dynamic world of which we are a part in such a way that its dynamism is inherently disposed to the formation of power relationships, nothing more is needed to make sense of the kinds of change, development, organization, and dissolution that are to be observed at all levels of transaction we encounter within, among, and beyond ourselves.

The cognitive-interpretive claim that "the world viewed from within" is "'will to power' and nothing else" is an interpretation to which Nietzsche says one will have "gained the right" if one is able to succeed in the "experiment" of considering whether it is "*sufficient*, for understanding on the basis of this kind of thing," for "understanding" [*verstehen*] every sort of phenomena of which we do or may come to have any awareness (*BGE* 36). And the conviction with which he invokes this idea elsewhere in *Beyond* indicates that, at this juncture at any rate, he would seem to think that he has gained that right. Some think that his willingness to admit that this is "only interpretation" (*BGE* 24) indicates otherwise; but as has been observed, his insistence that all thought is "interpretive" does *not* entail the view that none is or can be *cognitively superior* to any other. In any event, it would not appear to have any such consequence for Nietzsche himself in *Beyond* (or any other major subsequent work, such as *Genealogy*).[10]

Finally, an important complement to this reinterpretive project also is accorded an important place in the book. That complementary project is implicit in its main title, and explicit from its opening sections to the topic of its final part: a new *theory of value*—also de-deified and naturalizing, but with a far greater positive reach and scope than one might have thought possible after "the death of God." This new value theory is sufficiently substantive to make possible a "revaluation of values" going well beyond a merely negative *devaluation* of (all) prevailing values—of which the intended dethronement of the morality of "good and evil" is indeed an instance. It further extends to that morality's proposed replacement—along with all other value absolutisms—by a quite different approach to morals and values. Its point of departure is the fundamental sort of life affirmation to the possibility of which Nietzsche had given powerful expression in *Zarathustra*; and its guiding ideas are those of "value for life" and "life enhancement." And since the notion of "life" thus figures centrally in it, its linkage to the task of reinterpreting life in general and human life in particular will be readily apparent.

V

But the first order of business for a post-religious, post-metaphysical, and postmoral philosophy of the future is to reconsider both the nature and the worth of the very thing that is presumed to be the goal of any sort of cognitive endeavor: *truth*. Neither its nature nor its value can be taken for granted; and for

Nietzsche nothing is more in need of reinterpretive and revaluative attention than the very idea and ideal of truth to which all cognitive inquiry presumably aspires. He therefore raises the first question in his remarkable preface to *Beyond*, and the second in the opening section of the first part of the book, and makes clear his revisionist intent in both respects.

Nietzsche begins the preface (and casts the first question) in a striking fashion: "Supposing that truth is a woman—what then?" [*Vorausgesetzt, dass die Wahrheit ein Weib ist—, wie?*] This trope has attracted so much attention for its problematic invocation and use of the word (or idea of) *Weib* (woman) that it has tended to obscure the very point it was intended to make vivid. The preface is a polemic against "dogmatism" in philosophical thinking. In German philosophy from Kant onward, and for Nietzsche here, "dogmatic" thinking is the sort of absolutist and essentially metaphysical thinking that models itself on mathematics, and proceeds by positing or taking for granted some principle or principles and making inferences from them that are as abstractly rigorous as possible, using concepts that are made as clear and distinct as possible. Old-style metaphysics offers cases in point, but for Nietzsche philosophical materialism—and in particular the mechanistic materialism that so many scientifically minded philosophers seemed to him to be taking for granted—is another. And his target extends to the tendency to conceive of truth and its pursuit in a manner attuned to such thinking, as a black-and-white affair and all-or-nothing endeavor in which rigorous proofs and certainty are required, or at least desired.

This way of thinking, Nietzsche suggests, is wedded to the fundamental "error" associated with "Plato's invention of the pure spirit and the good as such" [*Platos Erfindung vom reinen Geiste und vom Guten an sich*]. It involves a fictionalized account of the reality that is the proper object of thought and knowledge and of our status and relation to it, as well as a disastrous valorization of these fictions, to the detriment of life as we must live it. But this, he contends, "meant standing truth on her head and denying the *perspectival*, the basic condition of all life [*das* Perspektivische, *die Grundbedingung alles Lebens*]," where both "spirit" and value are concerned (*BGE* Pref.).

This way of thinking also leads to a "clumsy obtrusiveness" in the way in which philosophers "have usually approached truth [*die Wahrheit*] so far." Small wonder, therefore, that truth "has not allowed herself to be won." Why "herself"? Because in the gendered German language *die Wahrheit* is feminine (*weiblich*), which requires "truth" to be referred to as *sie sich* [herself]—a fact, however, that Nietzsche does choose to exploit. For it provides him with an occasion for wordplay, and to go on to suggest that, if *die Wahrheit* is *weiblich*, it could well be (figuratively speaking) *ein Weib* (oddly, in German, a neuter rather than feminine noun)—or at any rate something like one in certain respects, and to proceed to utilize some of its commonplace associations. For example: it provides him with a way of availing himself of ideas sure to be familiar to his readers about what is and is not likely to succeed in "winning a woman's heart," on his way to making—and trying to make plausible—what for him is an important point about "truth" as he would have it understood.

Nietzsche's point here is not that the very idea of truth must be abandoned, simply because it is not the kind of thing it has been taken—by "dogmatists" in particular—to be. Rather, on the contrary, it is that there is indeed something important to this idea—which, however, must be reconceived in a manner more appropriate to the contexts in which it has its most significant applications, with implications for the manner of its pursuit as well. And in these contexts we are dealing with the kind of reality of which our complex, diverse, contingent, emergent, changing human reality is a part and an instance. Appearances, surfaces, and relations are importantly if not entirely constitutive of this kind of reality, upon which there is no single definitive perspective, and of which there is no single complete, correct, and final description. We might wish that he had made his point in a different way; but it is the point that matters most.

The kind of truth that may be "won" or attained, moreover, in many domains of inquiry, is not something that can be captured once and for all, in formulations abstracting from all of this, by methods that are insensitive to much of it. It must be conceived undogmatically and even anti-dogmatically, as a matter of degree and perspective, of approximation and aptness, and of tentativeness and provisionality, without closure. And where such truth is concerned, interpretation must be the name of the game—with comprehension the aim, but with no illusions with respect to the possibility or even the meaningfulness of absolute knowledge, significant certainty, or ultimate explanation.

In opposition to the dogmatic rigor and kind of result to which philosophers have long aspired even if not often attained, Nietzsche looks ahead: "we good Europeans and free, *very* free spirits" who are to bring his philosophy of the future to life "are the heirs of all that strength which has been fostered by the fight against this error." It "has created in Europe a magnificent tension of the spirit the like of which had never yet existed on earth: with so tense a bow we can now shoot for the most distant goals." That tension is created by the passion for comprehension *conjoined with* the resolute rejection of dogmatism, and more: of the very aspiration to a kind of knowledge that would be absolute and certain; and of the very idea of a kind of value that would be something unto itself, above and beyond this life in this world.

VI

Having set the stage in this way, Nietzsche's very first next question, at the out-set of the first part of the book ("On the Prejudices [*Vorurteilen*; literally, "pre-judgments"] of Philosophers"), is the companion question to that of the *nature* of truth. Supposing that there is indeed a significant sort of truth that might be sought and won, "What in us really wants 'truth'?" he asks. And further: "Suppose we want truth: *why not rather* untruth? and uncertainty? even ig-norance?" This, for Nietzsche, is "the problem of the *value* of truth" (*BGE* 1), rather than of the *nature* of truth.

He offers no thoughts on the matter here, other than to remark on the great "risk" involved in recognizing the value of truth to *be* a problem or live issue. But he could not make it clearer that he wants to *emphasize* (rather than col-lapse) *the distinction* between the *nature* of truth and its *value*, of one sort or another. And in the following numbered aphorisms or sections he underscores the distinction between these two issues, even as he begins to address them. So, for example: "For all the value that the true, the truthful, the selfless may deserve," he observes that their opposites might deserve to be ascribed "a higher and more fundamental value for life"—and further, that they might ac-tually be "insidiously related" to these "seemingly opposite things."

These are among the sorts of questions Nietzsche's "new species of philos-ophers" would want—and dare—to raise (*BGE* 2). And he goes on to indicate what he takes to be the appropriate (very general) standard of value to be used in attempting to answer questions of the former sort: namely, their "value for life"—or, more fully, their value in relation to the preservation, flourishing, and development of "a certain type of life [*Art von Leben*]" (that is, of some "type of life" or other) (*BGE* 3). "The falseness of a judgment is for us not necessar-ily an objection to [it]," he writes; nor is the truth of a judgment necessarily a mark in its favor. "The question is to what extent it is life-promoting, life-preserving, type-[*Art*]preserving, perhaps even type-cultivating." And he makes clear the meaning of the book's main title when he goes on to observe that a kind of philosophy prepared to "resist accustomed value feelings" to the extent of being prepared to "recognize untruth as a condition of life" for us, at least in various significant respects, "would by that token alone place itself beyond good and evil" (*BGE* 4).

In the next several aphorisms or sections, Nietzsche reflects upon a related matter: his suspicion that ulterior motivations are often at work in the moves philosophers and scientists make (*BGE* 5–6). And he then offers critiques of such moves in a wide range of familiar developments that he takes to be cases in point, from the Stoics, Kant, idealism, and Schopenhauer to examples drawn from the various natural sciences—showing a decidedly greater sympathy, it should be noted, for the latter than for the former (*BGE* 9–22).

VII

The second part of *Beyond* is a series of reflections on the idea of "the free spirit" [*der freie Geist*] as Nietzsche now understands it, and begins in a strikingly tentative manner after the strong conclusion of the first part just remarked upon. Yet it, too, ends strongly, even if on a different note, with a half dozen aphorisms that do much to flesh out aspects of the picture of his kind of philosopher, in a preliminary way. (There is more to come, in the course of the book.) His "new philosophers" are to be "free spirits" of the sort he himself had been and envisioned previously—*and more.* "They, too, will be free, *very free* spirits, these philosophers of the future," he writes, speaking here as one of those "who are their heralds and precursors, we free spirits." But he then adds: "though just as certainly they will not be merely free spirits but something more, higher, greater, and thoroughly different" (*BGE* 44).

A Nietzschean "free spirit" is already well beyond the shallow enlightenment of those who like to think of themselves as deserving of that accolade, who may be emancipated from unenlightened ways of thinking but basically are mere well-meaning "slaves of the democratic taste and its 'modern ideas.'" But now, for the Nietzsche of *Beyond*, that sort of more significant "free-spiritedness" is not enough; and he is conscious of having done little more than make a start in the right direction, at least by the end of this second part of the book.[11]

But it is a strong start. Nietzsche begins with a number of cautionary remarks concerning the conditions of inquiry and potential pitfalls of which his kind of enlightened and free-spirited thinker must be mindful (*BGE* 24–31). He then proceeds to provide a number of examples of the kinds of issues, inquiry, and conjectures with which such an inquirer might make a beginning. One concerns the understanding and assessment of human actions, and the "overcoming of morality"—or at any rate, of "morality in the traditional sense, the morality of intentions" [*Moral, im bisherigen Sinne, also Absichten-Moral*]—that this may now be seen to require (*BGE* 32–33). Another, for which the first in a sense prepares the way, has to do with the whole problem of "appearance" and "reality," and of how to think about "truth" and "knowledge" in relation to them (*BGE* 34–35). The next has already been considered; it concerns the interpretation of life and the world (for him, in terms of "will to power"), together with our own basic affective nature (*BGE* 36–37). And a further one concerns the question of interpretation and truth, particularly as it pertains to the interpretive activity of Nietzsche's kind of philosopher (*BGE* 38–43).

The chief point of the distinction Nietzsche marks between the "philosophers of the future" and their free-spirited philosophical "precursors" has to do less with the interpretive and reinterpretive part of the Nietzschean philosophical task than it does with the matter of value. Before he indicates what he has in mind, however, he does some further stage setting, beginning (in the third part, "*Das religiöse Wesen*" ["Religiousness"; literally, "The Religious Thing"]) with how to think about religion and religiousness. His objective here would seem to be both to dispose of it as a rival mode of interpretive and evaluative thinking, and to consider what can be learned from it and derived from it as a phenomenon.

Here Nietzsche's strategy of what might be called "genealogical subversion" is on display, as he subjects religiousness to a kind of psychological analysis that has the effect of undermining its credibility as anything more than a human psychological phenomenon (*BGE* 45–52, 55–60). Along the way, he remarks upon the associated impending demise of the twin pillars of traditional religious thinking, "theism" (*BGE* 53) and "the old soul concept" (*BGE* 54), even while observing that "the religious instinct" remains alive and well, and "is indeed in the process of growing rapidly" (*BGE* 53).

That "instinct," as Nietzsche understands it, is fundamentally a matter of a profound need for a reality differing from the basic character of this life in this world, on the part of those "who can find the enjoyment of life only in the intention of *falsifying* its image." He thus associates the "religious interpretation of existence" with "the profound, suspicious fear of an incurable pessimism" with respect to the consequences of "getting hold of the truth" about life and the world—or at any rate, for Nietzsche, of getting hold of it "*too soon, before man has become strong enough, hard enough, artist enough*" (*BGE* 59).

This recalls his earlier observation that "something might be true while being harmful and dangerous in the highest degree," and indeed that "it might be a basic characteristic of existence [*Grundbeschaffenheit des Daseins*], that those who would know it completely [*an seiner völligen Erkenntnis*] would perish." And it also amplifies his previous contrasting characterization of the "free spirit" precisely in this connection, in his suggestion that "the strength of a spirit should be measured according to how much of the 'truth' one could still barely endure." The issue in both cases is "to what degree one would *require* it to be thinned down, shrouded, sweetened, blunted, falsified" (*BGE* 39).

In saying that "the religious instinct" remains powerful, as he does, Nietzsche is observing that, even if "belief in God" is on the decline, this all-too-human need is as strong as ever. And if that is so, it is only to be expected that it will seek—and, one way or another, will find—other means of its sat-isfaction. That being the case, he draws an unexpected conclusion, going on to suggest that "the philosopher as *we* understand him, we free spirits," who both understands this piece of human reality and also has "the most compre-hensive responsibility" and corresponding "conscience for the over-all devel-opment of man," will *avail* himself of "the religious instinct" rather than ignore it, and in one way or another "will make use of religions for his projects of cultivation and education [*Züchtungs- und Erziehungswerke*]" (*BGE* 61).

Nietzsche takes this to be at least desirable, whether or not it can actually be done, because "one always pays dearly and terribly when religions [. . .] insist on having their own *sovereign* way." For when they do this, they tend to wind up adversely affecting the enhancement of human life, which is difficult enough at best, thus making a bad situation worse. In this connection he gives expression to a concern that motivates much of the rest of the book: "The higher the type of man that a man represents, the greater the improbability that he will *turn out well* [*dass er* geräth]. The accidental, the law of absurdity in the whole economy of mankind, manifests itself most horribly in its destruc-tive effect on the higher *Menschen* whose complicated conditions of life can only be calculated with great subtlety and difficulty" (*BGE* 62).

In speaking here of his kind of philosophers availing themselves of "the religious instinct" and "making use of religions for his projects of cultivation and education," Nietzsche could have in mind the existing religions familiar to us. That idea would seem to be even more implausible than his suggestion that this sort of philosopher will "make use of whatever political and eco-nomic conditions are at hand," and highly dubious even as a desideratum. But he may well have been—and, I would say, probably was—thinking of some-thing else. For he himself might be thought of as having very recently tried his hand at this very sort of "project"—in and by means of his *Zarathustra* project, which he had just completed.[12] That could be precisely what he had in mind. And if it was with that thought in mind—of there being a widespread "religious instinct" that he had thought it to be strategically wiser to try to tap into rather than to attempt to eradicate altogether—this would make a new and different (if also perhaps problematic) sort of sense of some of the most philosophically curious features of the work, that would seem to be intended to do just that.

In the previous chapter I suggested that *Zarathustra* may be thought of as an educational device, in the service of the project of fostering the emergence and development of a healthier sort of humanity. I am now suggesting that this would account for the strikingly religious character of that work, in its most intense moments, as well as the passage in question in *BGE* 61. But it is a very emphatically *this-worldly* sort of religiousness. Nietzsche's word for it is "pagan," and his occasional name for it is "Dionysian."

That is the one sort of human religiousness—shorn of any sort of otherworldliness—that actually appealed to him; and he at least toyed with the idea that its revival (rebirth?) might not only be humanly possible but actually realizable. His *Zarathustra* may have been intended to be at least a step in that direction. Its version of that "after-the-death-of-God" non-theistic religiousness features the figure of the *Übermensch* and the idea of *Übermenschlichkeit* (which Zarathustra proclaims to be the new "meaning of the earth") as the symbols or representations of a new conception of what is (or is to be regarded as) *divine*, centering upon "life," its enhancement, and their emotional as well as intellectual affirmation.

In short: what Nietzsche has in mind in *BGE* 61 might be the idea that, if a "religious instinct" is ineradicable and must be satisfied in some way or other, then better in this way than in traditional ways—and to the strategic advantage of "philosophers of the future" in their crucially important "projects of cultivation and education." In any event, this is as close as he comes to illustrating the part of the task of his future philosophers toward which he gestures here and elsewhere in the book, that has to do with "value" and goes beyond reinterpretation and revaluation, under the rubric of "value creation." That is something to which I will return.[13]

VIII

Having reached this point in the book, which might be thought of as the conclusion of the first act of the opera (as it were), the curtain falls and a kind of intermission ensues. But the "Epigrams and Interludes" of this fourth part are no mere pause in the action of the book; for they, too, contribute to its general projection and inauguration of Nietzsche's "philosophy of the future," even if in a different sort of way. These aphorisms are "arrows" (a term he considered as a title), shot at a variety of targets. These (usually) one- or two-liners are a common feature of his philosophical writing in his "aphoristic" works, from beginning (*Human*) to end (*Twilight*)—sometimes grouped, as they are here, and sometimes scattered. And they are more aptly referred to as "aphorisms" than the great majority of the numbered sections in these works.

One might well judge Nietzsche to miss the mark (or at any rate the bull's-eye) as often as he hits it.[14] These aphorisms do illustrate, however, that one can hit targets squarely without the aid of arguments, and that there is something to be said for taking such risks and hazarding such shots when one thinks one has had insights into the sorts of matters addressed here. For these are

matters relating to a wide range of real-life human situations and traits; and
these are among the kinds of things of which one must be mindful if one's
interpretive and evaluative efforts are to be properly connected with human
reality. Here astute observation and insight matter more than rigorous argument; for while argument may well be needed in the end, both to assess one's
observations and to make comprehensive sense of it all, there is no substitute
for insight, as grist for the mill of such efforts, even if not as their compass.

The fifth part of the book is something like an overture to *Beyond*'s second
act (again operatically speaking), which runs through the next two parts ("We
Sophisticates [*Gelehrten*]" and "Our Virtues"). In this part, "On the Natural
History of Morality," Nietzsche indicates how he proposes to come to terms
with and set aside traditionally and conventionally moral ways of thinking, just
as he had earlier indicated how he proposed to deal with and set aside their
religious counterparts. By the end of this fifth part, he has finished position-
ing himself "beyond good and evil"—that is, beyond the type of thinking not
only in morality but also in other matters influenced by it that bears the stamp
of the moralism of so many "moralists" [*Moralisten*] (*BGE* 186) that revolves
around the opposition of the evaluative categories "good" and "evil"—and is
ready to begin more directly repositioning himself for a post-moralistic "philosophy of the future."

The distinction between "master morality and slave morality" does not appear until considerably later, in the final part of the book. Here in the fifth part
Nietzsche is concerned to articulate a strategy for breaking the grip of familiar forms of morality upon us, by convincing us that "there is something
problematic here," that we should regard morality "*as* a problem" [*Moral als
Problem*], that "the real problems of morality [*die eigentliche Probleme der
Moral*] [. . .] emerge only when we compare *many* moralities [*Moralen*]"—
and that we should approach "the problem of morality" as the problem of what
to make of a peculiar sort of phenomenon that *has* a "natural history" (as opposed to a divine or otherwise supernatural origin and basis) in which social
and psychological factors have played major roles (*BGE* 186).

Thus Nietzsche suggests that moralities are "merely a *sign language of the
affects*" [*nur eine Zeichensprache der Affekte*] (*BGE* 187). But that is not all. For
he further contends that "what is essential and inestimable in every morality
is that it constitutes a long compulsion" and involves "the *narrowing of perspective* [*die Verengerung der Perspektive*] [. . .] as a condition of life and growth"
(*BGE* 188). After giving a variety of examples of how various moral phenomena may be illuminated by social and psychological analyses (*BGE* 189–98),
he gives a further general characterization of conventional moralities. They

are said to be "herd" (*Herde*) phenomena, reflecting group needs and dynamics (*BGE* 199–201).

Nietzsche then goes on to observe that "herd animal morality" [*Herdentier-Moral*] is "merely *one* type of human morality [*Eine Art von menschlicher Moral*], beside which, before which, and after which many other types, above all *higher* moralities [*vor Allem* höhere *Moralen*], are, or ought to be, possible" (*BGE* 202). And for him they include (but by no means consist entirely of) those that he subsequently (in *BGE* 260 and again the first essay of *Genealogy*) calls "master [*Herren-*] moralities" in their originally paradigmatic forms. (In German, this nicely contrasts the morals typical of *Herden* and *Herren*!)

What inspires Nietzsche's interest in this matter is, on the one hand, his concern "for the over-all danger that 'man' himself *degenerates*" into "the perfect herd animal" and, on the other hand, his sense of "what, given a favorable accumulation and increase of forces and tasks, might yet *be made of man* [*aus dem Menschen zu züchten wäre*]." The stage is thus set for him to ask, "Where, then, must *we* reach with our hopes?" and to answer: "Toward *new philosophers*; there is no choice; toward spirits strong and original enough to provide the stimuli for opposite valuations and to revalue and invert 'eternal values' [*um die Anstösse zu entgegengesetzten Wertschätzungen zu geben und 'ewige Werte' umzuwerten, umzukehren*]," and to set "the will of millennia upon new tracks" (*BGE* 203). It is to the consideration of what this may require—"the probable ways and tests that would enable a soul to grow to such a height and force that it would feel the *compulsion* for such tasks [*um dem* Zwang *zu diesen Aufgaben zu empfinden*]"—that Nietzsche devotes the concluding parts of the book.

Nietzsche's philosophical project thus encompasses matters of value, and extends even to considerations relating to value determination and the politics of value realization. So he accords an important place in *Beyond* (and subsequent writings) to the necessary complement of his reinterpretation of our humanity: a new *theory of value*, also de-deified and "naturalized" in conception and articulation, but with a far greater reach and scope than one might have thought possible after "the death of God." And it is to make possible a "revaluation [*Umwertung*] of values" going well beyond a mere nihilistic devaluation (that would be an Ent*wertung*) of all prevailing values. This revaluation is exemplified by Nietzsche's intended dethronement of the morality of "good and evil," and by its proposed replacement with a quite different set of evaluative concepts and approach to morals and values. Its basis (to the extent that it has one) is a fundamental sort of *life affirmation*, to the possibility of which he had given powerful expression in *Zarathustra*. Its guiding ideas are those of "*value for* life" and "life *enhancement*" [*Erhöhung*].

The "Yes or No [. . .] about life and the value of life [*den Wert des Lebens*]" (*BGE* 205), on which all ultimately depends for the Nietzsche of *Beyond*, presupposes and yet also surpasses the disillusioned *comprehension* of the basic character of life and the world that is humanly possible. Nietzsche conceives of this "Yes or No" in terms of the possibility of a form of fundamental *affirmation*, beyond all illusion and disillusionment, that is no mere assent to a proposition, but also is neither a piece of knowledge nor a conclusion that can be validated or even warranted cognitively. It rather has the character of a kind of fundamental *expression* reflecting one's basic *sensibility*, or how one is or has come to be constituted and disposed (perhaps as thinker as well as human being).

Arriving at and living that affirmation, for Nietzsche, far from betraying a readiness to compromise in one's intellectual integrity, is instead associated with having sought and found "one's way" to a "right" and "even a duty" to such an expression (*BGE* 205). It signals no abandonment of commitment to truthfulness, but rather the ascent to a further, highest humanly possible form of truthfulness—about oneself in relation to "life," as it fundamentally is and that relation can come to be. His formula for it is *amor fati* ("love of fate," echoing but replacing the traditional religious ideal of *amor dei*, "love of God"). His name for it is "Dionysian" (*BGE* 295); and his metaphor for it, in the language of *Zarathustra*, is "remaining true [*treu*] to the earth."

IX

"We Sophisticates [*Gelehrten*]," the sixth part, is the heart of the book. I therefore shall give it special attention. In its ten aphorisms (sections), Nietzsche offers a series of reflections on the character of his "philosophy of the future" and its distinction from other kinds of inquiry and intellectual sophistication. It is as clear a statement of his conception of it as he ever provides. In the first of them he contends that there is more to "the masterly task and masterfulness of philosophy" than mere scholarship, and also more to it than mere analysis and critique. With an eye to the neo-Kantianism that was already beginning what became the "analytical turn" in philosophy, he refers to "philosophy reduced to 'theory of knowledge'" as a mere "doctrine of abstinence [. . .] that never gets beyond the threshold and takes pains to *deny* itself the right to enter," and dismisses it as "philosophy in its last throes, an end, an agony, something inspiring pity" (*BGE* 204).

In the next section Nietzsche sums up what he thinks the "development" of the genuine philosopher requires, and the "dangers" and difficulties it presents. Interestingly and importantly, the first thing he mentions is familiarity with the various *Wissenschaften*, whose increasingly formidable "scope and tower-building" make it all too likely that the nascent philosopher "grows weary while still learning or allows himself to be detained somewhere to become a 'specialist'"—and so fails to attain the next requisite, above and beyond such sophistication: "his proper level, the *height* [*Höhe*] for a comprehensive look, for looking around, for looking *down* [*Überblick, Umblick,* Niederblick]" (*BGE* 205).

This is a point of equal importance, suggesting that the kind of *interpreting* the genuine philosopher is to do is conceived by Nietzsche as at once taking account of what the various *Wissenschaften* (natural, social, psychological, historical, and cultural) come up with, and also going beyond them in a manner made possible by the adoption of a higher-level and more comprehensive perspective upon the matters under consideration. It is also a point that is highly relevant to the question of what his talk of "perspective" in *Beyond* amounts to.

And there is more to Nietzsche's kind of philosophy than interpretation. It extends to matters of value—valuation, revaluation, and even value determination and value creation; and that in turn requires something more than the kinds of sophistication, perspective, and comprehension already alluded to. But even that is not all. It is in this context that he makes a point noted above, writing: "Add to this, by way of once more doubling the difficulties for a philosopher, that he demands of himself a judgment, a Yes or No, not about the *Wissenschaften* but about life and the value of life." This, he observes, is something the philosopher is likely to be "reluctant to come to believe that he has a right, or even a duty, to do"—no doubt because it involves going beyond all comprehension, which even the "free-spirited" philosopher's intellectual conscience may well find troubling.

Moreover, Nietzsche suggests (no doubt out of his own experience), the path to such a decision is not an easy one: if the philosopher is to arrive at "this right and faith [*Glauben*]" at all, he can do so only by way of "the most comprehensive [*umfänglichsten*]—and perhaps most disturbing and destructive— experiences." The "Yes or No" on which all ultimately depends for such a philosopher is a matter not of cognition or interpretation but rather (as noted above) of *affirmation or negation* of that which one comprehends; and the making of such an affirmation is to be understood not merely verbally or intellectually but (as it were) existentially, from and with the depths of one's being. And it is only out of such a fundamental affirmation that "the genuine philosopher" can then proceed (perhaps "*unwisely*" [unklug] but courageously and venturesomely) to "play *the* nasty game" [*spielt* das *schlimme Spiel*]—that is, the game of real life—in an attempt to make a difference in what becomes of us (*BGE* 205).[15]

In the next several sections, Nietzsche contrasts the genuine philosopher with the mere scholar and sophisticate [*der Gelehrte*], researcher [*der wissenschaftliche Mensch*], and "objective" type of person and thinker [*der objektive Mensch* and *Geist*]. The former may be capable of carrying out useful forms of inquiry; but they do not make the kind of creative contribution to the enhancement of human culture and life that he expects of "the *philosopher*, the Caesarian cultivator and driver of culture" [*dem cäsarischen Züchter und Gewaltmenschen der Cultur*] (*BGE* 206–7). He likewise contrasts this sort of philosopher with the mere "skeptic," in whom he discerns a "paralysis of the will," as opposed to "the strength to will, and to will something for a long time," that he takes to be required to make a difference in this respect.

It is in this context that Nietzsche goes on to envision a role for philosophers of this sort in what he calls the coming "fight for the dominion of the earth—the compulsion to great politics [*grossen Politik*]," as the culture wars of the future unfold in the collision both of "a will to negate" with "a will to affirm" and of differing expressions of the latter (*BGE* 208). That role is neither the fantasy of somehow managing to seize the reins of government and to rule as philosopher-kings, nor the daydream of becoming the power behind the throne. Rather, it is to make a difference in the battles not just for minds and hearts but also between *sensibilities*, on which much more ultimately depends.

Nietzsche conceives of this role as extending to what he calls the "creation" and even "legislation" of "new values," by way of the fostering of new sensibilities, altering and enriching the landscape of different regions of human life. The idea that philosophers of any sort might actually "lead" or even "dominate" in such matters (as he sometimes suggests) may be difficult to take seriously. Not so, however, the idea of the genuine philosopher as one who can and does find ways of influencing the direction, character, and quality of cultural life and sensibility formation. Nietzsche himself was one such philosopher.

X

It is also with reference to considerations relating to life enhancement that Nietzsche goes on in *Beyond*'s concluding, ninth part, "*Was ist vornehm?*" ["What Is Superior?"],[16] to suggest a reassessment of certain sorts of phenomena that undeniably have had (and could again have) dismaying historical and real-world manifestations. They include things he is prepared to call by the harsh names commonly associated with their rudest forms, such as domination, exploitation, and even "slavery." One may well wonder whether it is even conceivable that Nietzsche could be on to something worth taking seriously in passages of this sort. It should be noted, however, that much of what he says along these lines is actually presented in the form of observations of a genealogical nature, and of conjectures based upon them, rather than in the language of advocacy.

The fundamental question with which Nietzsche is concerned here is that of the *conditions of the possibility* of the attainment of superior or "higher" forms of culture and humanity. At one level of his discourse, he is attempting to make comprehensible that and how forms of life of all sorts contrive, by whatever strategies are available and conceivable to them, to preserve and assert themselves in relation to whatever the competition may happen to be. At another level, however, he is very clearly taking sides, exhibiting a kind of partisanship on behalf of the flourishing and development of human life in ways enhancing its worth, and in opposition to others detrimental to them.

Much of what Nietzsche has to say on both levels in *Beyond* derives from his conclusion and conviction that, realistically speaking, when it comes to enhancements of life, there is no substitute in human life for *being compelled* in one way or another. So, for example, as has been noted, he writes: "What is essential and inestimable in every morality is that it constitutes a long compulsion [*ein langer Zwang ist*]." For "given that, something always develops, and has developed, for whose sake it is worth while to live on earth [*dessentwillen es sich lohnt, auf Erden zu leben*]; for example, virtue, art, music, dance, reason, spirituality—something transfiguring, subtle, mad, and divine" (*BGE* 188). And while the compulsion need not invariably be externally imposed and physically enforced, that is how he supposes it first came into human life, and is what it often continues to require.

Nietzsche's observations and conjectures along these lines may well be questioned. But he does have a concern that at least warrants serious consideration. *Can* highly complex and demanding forms of cultural life be sustained, flourish, and develop in the absence of a variety of forms of compulsion (internal if not external) sufficing for the continuing infusion of human resources and dedication of human effort they require over the long haul? That is indeed a real and serious question, on which the jury is still out. Nietzsche is acutely aware of how much rides on it. He is right to insist that we face it squarely, not permitting ourselves the dodge of wishful thinking. And he is also right to maintain that this requires a willingness to take into account what can be learned both from human psychology and from human history.

XI

Philosophy as Nietzsche envisions and pursues it in *Beyond Good and Evil* (and subsequently) is a searchingly critical examination and assessment of many aspects of human reality and experience, of the interpretations and evaluations we have lived by, and of the resources and abilities by means of which we may go *beyond* them. And it is also an extraordinary attempt to begin to do so. If there is one word that sums up his thinking as it is exemplified in this book, it is this word "beyond" [*Jenseits*]: *beyond* good and evil, *beyond* old faiths and values and ideas, but also *beyond* the "death of God" and nihilism; *beyond* the all-too-human, *beyond* the merely natural, *beyond* the merely social and conventional, *beyond* the mere preservation and perpetuation of life as it already is. That is why he speaks so often of "overcoming" and "enhancement." They are by no means inevitable, but they are humanly possible. Nietzsche seeks to be the herald and midwife and stimulus of such further development—of human life and philosophy alike.

Nietzsche's entire philosophical thought is what the subtitle of *Beyond* proclaims the book to be: a "prelude" both heralding and marking the beginning of what at least *could* be philosophy's future. Complete accordance with it is as difficult to imagine as is indifference to it, on the part of anyone who shares something like his sense of philosophy's problems and tasks and his commitment to intellectual integrity. Nietzsche does not hesitate to rush in—recall that encouragement of readiness to do so even if it may be to proceed "*unklug*" [unwisely] in *BGE* 205—where angels may fear to tread; but that is no mere folly on his part. Nietzsche's kind of philosopher need not be as much of a risk-taker in new ventures of reinterpretation and revaluation as he himself was; but one who is no such adventurer is no such philosopher—and perhaps no true philosopher either.

There remains more to be said about Nietzsche's "philosophy of the future" and "new philosophers," as conceived in *Beyond* than what I have said so far. The word "beyond" applies yet again to it—in this case to this account itself, even though what more there is to be said is only hinted at, in its two penultimate chapters. They will be revisited in the last half of chapter 10 below (section VII and following). That should be regarded as a continuation of this chapter, as well as a discussion that also needs to be where it is in this book.

Addendum: The Nietzsche of *Joyful Inquiry* V

I shall now turn briefly to the next thing Nietzsche published (after *Beyond*): a new fifth Book that he added to *Joyful Inquiry* in 1887. I discuss it here, rather than in the chapter on the Nietzsche of the original (1882) version, because in the context of "Nietzsche Becoming Nietzsche," this is where it chronologically belongs. But it also is of no little interest and importance to see what kinds of things he is saying and doing in it, in the immediate aftermath of *Beyond*, and how it relates to the matters I have just been discussing. Its relation in form and philosophical content to his views and thinking in the original version of *Inquiry* is of course of interest as well; but for my purposes here, the other question takes precedence.

I would say that, read with that question in mind, the Nietzsche we encounter in this first thing he did beyond *Beyond* is a more sophisticated version of the kind of free-spirited philosopher he had been and discusses in *Beyond*, rather than anything significantly different (along the lines of what is distinctive about the "new philosophers" of whom he speaks, for example). But that is important, because it shows that his kind of philosophy has chiefly been *enlarged*, to extend to and include something *more*—both in principle and in practice—rather than radically changed, to the exclusion or marginalization of the kinds of things he had been advocating and doing previously.

As has been noted, a fifth Book had been a part of Nietzsche's 1882 plan for *Inquiry*, but had had to be deferred. And in the fifth Book he belatedly did write, we encounter Nietzsche at what is arguably his philosophical best. In its seventy *KSA* pages, he basically resumed the enterprise of the first four Books, in something like the same spirit. Moreover, written just before *Genealogy*, and followed only by the largely polemical works of 1888, it is his last discussion in print of a number of the important topics he touches upon in it. After it and *Genealogy*, the only actual bits of recognizably philosophical thinking he published were the brief thirty *KSA* pages in *Twilight* ending with "The 'Improvers' of Mankind." That gives this fifth Book additional importance. I do not do justice to it in this addendum; but what I do say should leave no doubt that the kind of philosophy he had been doing prior to *Beyond* retained at least an important *part of* the "philosophy of the future" he has in mind, if his own example is any indication.

I

Nietzsche gave this fifth Book a title of its own: "*Wir Furchtlosen*" ["We Fearless Ones"]. To make it clear that he means to be more or less picking up where he had left off in the project of the first four-Book version of *Inquiry*, Nietzsche begins this fifth by both reiterating his (continuing) concern with the consequences of "the death of God," and then giving rapturous expression to his *fröhlich* disposition nonetheless. (The heading he gives to its first section, loosely but aptly rendered, is: "Regarding Our Cheerfulness [*Heiterkeit*].")

In this one short section, Nietzsche tells us the basic point of his "death of God" idea (namely, "that the belief in the Christian god has become unworthy of belief [*unglaubwürdig*]"); indicates what he takes the most serious consequence to be ("how much must collapse now"); and reports—five years after his first announcement of it (*JI* 108)—that, perhaps surprisingly, the "consequences for *ourselves*" seem to be "not at all sad and gloomy," but rather the very opposite of that. Using the very word (*Morgenröte*, that is, "daybreak" or "dawn") that he had chosen for the title of his work immediately prior to *Inquiry*, he writes: "Indeed, we philosophers and 'free spirits' feel [. . .] as if a new *Morgenröte* shone on us; our heart overflows with gratitude, amazement, premonitions, expectation." For "all the daring of would-be knowers [*Erkennenden*] is permitted again" (*JI* 343). This makes it clear that, whatever more than this his kind of "new philosopher" is to be, this language will continue to be applicable to it. ("*Morgenröte*" initially was to have been the title of the five Books of *Inquiry* as well as its own five Books.[17])

What makes this Book 5 so important for present purposes is not the specific points Nietzsche goes on to make concerning the various matters he touches upon, interesting and astute as many of them are. It rather is the array of those topics and issues themselves, and the ways in which he chooses to frame them. They collectively show what he—at this culminating point—takes to be at least a significant portion of the agenda of his kind of philosophy and "philosophy of the future."

The very first issue Nietzsche discusses has to do with truth—but *not* with the *nature* of truth, or the *possibility* of truth; these are taken for granted. What he finds highly problematic is *obsession with it*. He does not question or object to regarding truth as the aim and central value of *Wissenschaft* (presumably not only in the natural sciences but in *the Wissenschaften* more generally). His concern here is with those who are obsessed with it, and what that says about them—those driven by an "unconditional will to truth," for whom it is "truth at any price," and for whom "in relation to it everything else has only second-rate value." That, he suspects, is something far more worrisome than a mere "slightly mad enthusiasm": namely, a modern-day expression of the "ascetic ideal." And what he has in mind is: "a principle that is hostile to life and destructive. 'Will to truth'—that might be a concealed will to death" (*JI* 344).

In the next section Nietzsche takes on morality, under the heading "Morality as Problem." His interest in "the *genealogy* of morality," about which he was simultaneously thinking and writing, was only a useful preliminary to another, more serious concern, related to the one he had just mentioned: "the *value* of that most famous of all medicines which is called morality." His "task," he says, is "for once to *question* it." And in this connection he makes a point of great importance, which applies to a great many of the things he discusses: "Even if a morality has grown out of an error, the realization of this fact would not as much as touch the problem of its value" (*JI* 346).

The following section (*JI* 347) should be required reading for anyone who wants to understand what Nietzsche thinks, in a broad and general way, about life and the world—about "the world in which we live" and about ourselves in relation to it and in it; and about how he proposes to reconsider "the value of the actual world"—and about the nihilism question as well. This is close to being his last word in print on all of these matters; and it is set forth with admirable candor, clarity, precision, and calm. It is as though he is saying: "Do you want to know what I think about this world of ours? This is what I think—or at any rate, my point of departure." It is the mature Nietzsche at his best, in a nutshell.

I I

Following these four extraordinarily important sections, indicating at least a number of his central concerns and views at this point, Nietzsche shifts gears and reflects on a variety of all-too-human tendencies he takes to be all too common among believers, scholars, moralists, and religious figures (*JI* I347–53).

Then, in section 354, he shifts again; and this lengthy section is one of the most significant philosophically in the entire work (comparable in that respect to *GM* II:16). It is, in effect, an update of his early incomplete *Truth and Lie* essay. In the first part of *Human*, he had envisioned the project of "a *history of the genesis of thought*," which would be the "greatest triumph" imaginable of *Wissenschaft* and his new kind of "historical philosophizing" in collaboration (*HH* I:16). Here he provides what would seem to be an excellent example of the kind of thinking he had in mind. His topic is "conscious thinking" and "the development of consciousness"—in which he suggests that "the need for communication" among human beings and the development of "the signs used in communication" (which is to say: language) have played crucial roles. In brief: "My idea is [. . .] that consciousness does not really belong to humankind's individual existence, but rather to its social or herd nature." Further: "It was only as a social animal that *der Mensch* acquired self-consciousness." Moreover, Nietzsche takes it to follow that human consciousness "developed subtlety only insofar as this is required by social or herd utility" (*JI* 354).

And that is not all. He takes it further to follow that, "owing to the nature of *animal consciousness*, the world of which we can become conscious is only a surface- and sign-world, a homogenized and coarsened world [*eine ver-allgemeinerte, eine vergemeinerte Welt*]"; and that "We 'know' (or believe or imagine) just as much as may be *useful* in the interests of the human herd" (*JI* 354). Or at any rate, that is all that we had to work with in the first place; and that is what we have had to find ways of refining and transforming for anything like *Wissenschaft* and philosophical comprehension in their various forms to become humanly possible. That is a topic to which Nietzsche turned again and again, from *Human* onward. What he says here is not, for him, the last word with respect to the entire matter of knowledge and comprehension, but rather only something like his point of departure—and a circumscription of what it is likely to be within the realm of human possibility. (I take that to be the sort of limitation he had in mind at the beginning of *Human* when he wrote: "Consequently what is needed from now on is *historical philosophiz-ing*, and with it the virtue of modesty" [*HH* I:2]).

Nietzsche then touches on several related matters, beginning with "the origin of our concept of 'knowledge' " (*JI* 355), and the transformation of human reality that has come about through the emergence of the ability of human beings to think of themselves as "acting" in the sense of "playing a role," rather than simply being a part of something larger, with the solidity of "a stone in a great edifice" (*JI* 356). And that is followed by a deeply probing and extraor-dinarily interesting lengthy discussion of "real achievements of philosophical thinking" that are generally thought to be "owing to Germans," but actually are owing to the Germans he cites—Leibniz, Kant, Hegel, and Schopenhauer—as "good *Europeans*" (*JI* 357).[18]

In the course of this discussion, Nietzsche lays a number of his own cards on the table, at least to the extent of crediting the ideas he cites as "profound" and as "insights." In that way it contributes significantly to the understanding of his thinking at this point. First, he cites "*Leibniz's* incomparable insight" that "consciousness is merely an *accidens* [contingent feature] of experience and *not* its necessary and essential attribute." Second, he notes "*Kant's* tremen-dous question mark" about the scope of "the domain within which the con-cept of causality makes sense." Third, Nietzsche lists "the astonishing stroke of *Hegel*," who "dared to teach that species concepts develop *out of each other*," and so "first introduced the decisive concept of 'development' into science." And fourth, he names *Schopenhauer*, with his recognition that "the triumph of atheism" raised "the problem of the *value of existence*" in a whole new and critical way: "*Has existence any meaning at all?*" What Nietzsche is saying here is that these ideas inform his own thinking, beyond its above-indicated point of departure (*JI* 357).

The next fifteen sections are devoted to critical analysis of a wide variety of the kinds of shibboleths the demise of which he foretells in his next and last book of any philosophical substance—*Twilight* (1888)—with one exception: *JI* 360, in which he discusses an important distinction between "two kinds of causes" that he says is "one of my most essential steps and advances." (It is noteworthy that this shows him to be convinced that both "kinds of causes" are very real.) One "kind of cause is a quantum of dammed-up energy" needing to be "used up somehow"; while the other is whatever the impetus is that sets it off in some specific way or direction: "a match versus a ton of powder" in quantity and substance, one a blind "*driving force*," the other a guiding "*directing force*." (His examples of the latter are interesting: "purposes" and "vocations"—the former relating to actions by individuals, but the latter relating to sociocultural forms of life.)

This section nicely exemplifies one of the ways in which Nietzsche pursues his kind of philosophy: by reflecting on and briefly working out a distinction or point that he considers to be worth making, which occurs to him very unsystematically, but is relevant to some larger philosophical topic or issue in which he is interested.

III

The fifth Book ends with a flurry of important points of that sort (sections 370–82). The first of them, "What Is Romanticism?," is another example of Nietzsche's philosophizing by way of *creative distinguishing*—distinction drawing, redrawing, elaborating, and exploiting to make a point. His basic point here is that it is important to distinguish—not only in the arts but also in many other areas of human cultural and spiritual life—between two very different kinds of "suffering" or need, in the "driving force" category: those impelled by what he calls "the *over-fullness of life*," needing somehow to discharge itself, and "those who suffer from the *impoverishment of life*," whose need is for "a certain warm narrowness that keeps away fear," providing security, comfort, tranquility, and contentment (*JI* 370).

Section 372, "Why We Are No Idealists," revolves around yet another creative distinction, or set of distinctions, one of which is drawn between traditional philosophical "idealists" and his general kind of modern-day philosopher. It is of no little interest that he here seems to see at least some significant continuity between his kind of philosophers at present (including himself) and his "philosophers of the future" (with whom he also presumably identifies, at least aspirationally). For the "we" referred to in the heading is "we in philosophy at present and in the future [*Zukünftigen*]," all of whom are said to agree upon the philosophical importance of the senses. Hence the distinction he is making here between earlier "idealists" and all of "us in philosophy" from now on in being—in practice even if not in theory—what he calls "sensualists" [*Sensualisten*].

This is a dubious generalization; but the contrast Nietzsche wants to draw here is between philosophers who abstract from real (sensuous) human life— as he thinks traditional philosophers in general have done, not just rationalists and immaterialists—and those who philosophically affirm and emphasize the "sensuality" of our human reality and world. And that for him also means: those who appreciate the extent to which "life is music" (that is, akin to the kind of reality music and the making of it are), and are attuned to "the music of life" (*JI* 372).

The next section, *JI* 373, is another of the most important sections not only in this Book but in the entirety of the work. Titled "'*Wissenschaft*' as Prejudice" (and here Nietzsche actually is thinking of "materialistic natural scientists" [*materialistische Naturforscher*], but emphatically not his kind of *fröhliche Wissenschaft*!), this section makes it perfectly and emphatically clear that, if he is some sort of philosophical "naturalist," he is not one of that sort. His contempt here for that sort of "'scientific' interpretation of the world" is scathing. It is said to be "a crudity and naivety if not a mental illness, an idiotism," and might be "one of the *dumbest* [*dümmsten*] of all possible world-interpretations." And in it Nietzsche pursues his likening of life to music in a very interesting way: "How absurd would such a 'scientific' assessment of music be! What of it would one have grasped, understood, comprehended [*begriffen, verstanden, erkannt*]! Nothing, really nothing, of what is 'music' in it!" (*JI* 373).

This section is immediately followed by another that is also of particular importance: "Our New 'Infinite' ['*Unendliches*']" (*JI* 374). And this one is as difficult to understand as it is important—in part because of the seeming strangeness of Nietzsche's use of the words *Auslegungen* and *Interpretationen* (synonymously) in this context and in the way he does. (This was not the first time he had done so—even though this is the first and last time he does so in this Book and work.) It therefore is in need of careful consideration and elaboration.

Nietzsche had just used *Interpretation* (as the German word this has become) in a more ordinary way in the previous section, in a way that makes clear his commitment to the idea that there can be better and worse "interpretations." Here, however, he is entertaining the quite different idea that, for all we know, there *could* be "infinitely" or "endlessly" many "interpretations," of anything and everything—in the sense that we are in no position to be able to rule that out. Or, as he puts it, it could be the case that "all existence [*alles*

Dasein] is by its very nature [*essentiell*] an *interpreting* [auslegendes] existence."
The idea could be summed up in the slogan: To be is to interpret. And Nietzsche takes the question here to be: how far the perspective character [that is,
perspective-taking or perspective-establishing character] of existence extends.

It is important to observe that the only thing he is *asserting* here is that we
cannot rule out the possibility that this is the case: "The world has become 'infinite' for us all over again, in the sense that [*insofern*] we cannot rule out the
possibility that *it admits of infinite* [*unendlich*, endless] *interpretations*." It is also
important to recognize that Nietzsche is here using the words for "interpretation" in a very broadly extended way, to mean something like the literal meaning of one of them—*Auslegung*: to "lay out," to *arrange* or *organize* in some way
or other. And to think of "all existence" as being disposed to do this is obviously
not to think of it as necessarily involving any sort of consciousness, delibera-
tion, choosing, or the like—that is, *not* to think of it the way we normally think
of "interpreting." In this extended way of speaking of "interpreting," *that* sort of
"interpreting" would be a great exception to the general rule.

There is much that could be said about all of this. For my purposes at the
moment, however, the importance of this section (*JI* 374) is that it is indicative of one of the kinds of questions that the Nietzsche of this Book includes
in his kind of philosophy, and one of the ways in which he considers it to be
possible and appropriate to pursue them.

                                   I V

Nietzsche devotes the next few sections (*JI* 375–79) to reflections on his experience of what it means and takes to be his kind of philosopher. But he
was not yet done. He returns, in *JI* 380, to what would seem to be the basic
task of this fifth Book, identifying yet another topic on his new-philosophical
agenda. And it is an important one, not only for what he has to say on its specific topic—how to go about thinking about "our European morality"—but
also for what it shows about that part of his kind of philosophy, and what he
thinks it is reasonable to aspire to attain by means of it. It is his answer to the
question of how one can get oneself into a position to assess some particular
way of thinking and judging in the absence of any absolute standard.

What is needed in this instance, Nietzsche observes, is "a position *outside*
[that] morality, some point beyond good and evil to which one has to rise,
climb or fly," if one's assessments are to be anything more than mere "prejudices about prejudices." "The question," he observes, "is whether one really
can get up there"—and if so, how. And his answer, while metaphorical and
far from clear, shows both what he thinks the best we can do is, and that he

considers it to be much better than nothing—and can actually amount to something like knowledge. "In the main," he says, "the question is how light or heavy
we are." Because "one has to be *very light* to drive one's will to knowledge [*Willen zur Erkenntnis*] into such a distance"—from which one can gain a (proper
higher-order) perspective upon those (object-level) prejudices below. He explains: "One must have liberated oneself from many things that oppress, in-
hibit, hold down, and make heavy precisely us Europeans today." But doing so
is not enough. One must use that liberation to go on "to create for oneself eyes
to survey millennia and, moreover, clear skies in those eyes" (*JI* 380).

But what, for this Nietzsche, can one realistically and coherently attain that
could be deserving of the name of knowledge? That he does not tell us here.
My guess is that it is the kind of knowledge that is attainable in a realm such as
that of music, in which extensive experience and involvement can enable one
to know it well enough to discern standards that evolve along with the form of
life, experience, activity, and creativity it has become and involves. That may
or may not be what he has in mind. But again, the point for present purposes
is that Nietzsche is here showing that questions of this sort, pursued in this
sort of way, are yet another part of his kind of philosophy and philosophizing.

In section 381, now definitely nearing the conclusion of this Book's resumption of his philosophical *fröhliche Wissenschaft* (following the hiatus of *Zarathustra* and his largely programmatic "prelude to a philosophy of the future"
in *Beyond*), Nietzsche steps back, and provides us with a very valuable commentary on his way of going about it. It does not admit of summarization; so
I will simply say of it that those who are serious about wanting to understand
him as a philosopher would do well to read *Inquiry* 381 early on, and often
again thereafter.

Finally, in the next and penultimate section, Nietzsche delivers a remarkable concluding peroration very different from any other of his conclusions, in
soaring rhetoric. This is no longer simply a renewed free-spirited philosophical de-deifier, re-interpreter, and re-valuer of values speaking; nor, on the other
hand, would it seem to be the kind of value-creating cultural dynamo called
for in *Beyond*. It is a self-proclaimed "argonaut of the ideal" who speaks here,
providing what that would seem to be a kind of update of his earlier ideal of
Übermenschlichkeit, combined with a sense of responsibility that is heavy indeed (*JI* 382).

But then, rather than ending on that high note, he concludes the Book,
and also the work, in a manner more befitting its proclaimed *Fröhlichkeit*—
with a kind of jest (*JI* 383), followed by a short addendum [*Anhang*] of lighthearted short poems, entitled *Lieder der Prinzen Vogelfrei*—"Songs of Prince
Free-as-a-Bird."

V

It is interesting that, in this entire Book, there is no use or mention of any of the tropes that loom so large in the works Nietzsche published between the 1882 version of *Joyful Inquiry* and this addition to it five years later—"will to power," *Übermensch*, "eternal recurrence," or even "free spirit" (although he invokes the idea without actually mentioning it in *JI* 380). It is as if he found himself to be no longer in need of them to do what he wanted to do and say what he wanted to say at that point. And that remained the case when he turned his attention to his *Genealogy* project. In relation to his previous writings, he seems to me in these two works to have arrived at a new level of philosophical and intellectual maturity.

The post-*Beyond* Nietzsche of 1887 that we glimpse in this fifth Book, in my opinion, was just hitting his philosophical stride. The subtitle he gave it, *Wir Furchtlosen* (*We Fearless Ones*), makes a nice match with the "cheerfulness" [*Heiterkeit*] he immediately expresses and remarks upon, and the joyfulness [*Fröhlichkeit*] of his philosophical *Wissenschaft* proclaimed in the work's title—its "great seriousness" [*grosse Ernst*] (*JI* 382) notwithstanding. But the fates were unkind; neither that seriousness nor that cheerfulness and joyfulness, nor his newly attained and hard-won philosophical maturity, nor all of them together, sufficed to enable him to do any more than make the beginning he did.

One can only wonder what Nietzsche would have both wanted and been able to do had his next year been a different one, and not his last one. This fifth Book of *Joyful Inquiry* and *Genealogy* together showed great promise. As late as *Genealogy*'s third essay, and even in correspondence with his printer only months before his collapse, he was still talking about "a work in progress: *The Will to Power: Attempt at a Revaluation of All Values*" (*GM* III:27). He subsequently seems to have abandoned that project, but might well have revived it. If not, there are many other ways in which he might have pursued the kinds of philosophical interests they exemplify.

Or, if 1888 is any indication of where he was heading, he might have devoted his future efforts entirely to polemics of one sort or another—for which he certainly had both a penchant and a major talent—and made the culture wars his venue. All we can know for certain is that Nietzsche's kind of philosophy was what it showed itself to be, in what he did write.

6

The Nietzsche of *On the Genealogy of Morality: A Polemic*

*ZUR GENEALOGIE DER MORAL:
EINE STREITSCHRIFT*

My ideas on the *origin* of our moral prejudices—for this is the subject of this polemic—received their first, brief, and provisional expression in [. . .] *Human, All Too Human*. [. . .] *That* I still hold fast to them today [. . .] strengthens my joyful assurance that they might have arisen in me from the first not as isolated, capricious, or sporadic things but from a common root, from a *fundamental will* of knowledge [Grundwillen *der Erkenntnis*], pointing imperiously into the depths, speaking more and more precisely, demanding greater and greater precision. For this alone is fitting for a philosopher.

> *On the Genealogy of Morality*, P:2

Let us articulate this *new demand* [*Forderung*]: we need a *critique* of moral values, *the value of these values themselves must first be called into question*—and for that there is needed a knowledge [*Kenntnis*] of the conditions and circumstances in which they grew, under which they evolved and changed [. . .], a knowledge of a kind that has never yet existed or even been desired.

> *On the Genealogy of Morality*, P:6

Nietzsche's *On the Genealogy of Morality* [*Zur Genealogie der Moral*] was written in 1887, at an important juncture: during the final three-year period after *Zarathustra* and before his collapse (in January of 1889), and midway between *Beyond Good and Evil* and the last frantic year of his productive life.[1] It was written and published in the same year as the expanded second version of *Joyful Inquiry*, with its important added fifth Book. In these two works of 1887, therefore, the Nietzsche we encounter is Nietzsche at his philosophical high tide and high noon, all too shortly before night abruptly fell.

Many Anglophone readings of *Genealogy* have tended to focus—sometimes approvingly, sometimes not—on its treatment of what Nietzsche had referred to in *Beyond* as "morality in Europe today" (*BGE* 202) in startlingly unconventional ways, and on the question of the historical plausibility (or implausibility) of the accounts Nietzsche offers of its "genealogy." Some subsequent studies have given more attention to its three essays [*Abhandlungen*] as studies in moral psychology, or as philosophical-psychological analyses of moral feelings, attitudes, and dispositions. Others have gone further, taking note of Nietzsche's frequent excursions into human psychological issues more generally.

A very different sort of reading (sometimes referred to as "the French Nietzsche") has seized upon *Genealogy* as a key text in the emergence of a poststructuralist, postmodernist, historicist, and deconstructionist subversion not only of that (or even all morality), but also much else in and about philosophy as we know it, from the concept of "*der Mensch*" (as well as of "God") to the very ideas of truth and knowledge.[2]

In this chapter I will be doing something rather different from most of the former, and very different from the latter (in which I find it difficult even to recognize the Nietzsche I know). I will instead be discussing this work to see what it says and shows about Nietzsche's kind of philosophy and philosophical thinking, with regard to human reality in particular.

I

First, some preliminaries. In view of the fact that Nietzsche cared greatly about titles and headings, it seems to me that we should likewise care about their renderings in translation. The title of this book has been translated variously. *Genealogie* (his German) is always (for obvious reasons) translated as *genealogy*; but *Moral* has been translated both as *morals* and as *morality*. The *zur* can be translated both as *on the* and as *toward a*, and is sometimes simply ignored in favor of the simple article *the*. Since the book deals centrally with the "genealogy" of the morality that Nietzsche says is commonly considered to be "morality itself," *Moral* is perhaps best translated as *morality* rather than as *morals*.

However, Nietzsche is by no means prepared to grant the status of "morality itself" to it. So he wrote, just a year earlier (in *Beyond*, his emphases): "*Morality in Europe today is herd-animal morality* [Herdentier-Moral]—in other words, as we understand it, merely *one* type of human morality [eine *Art von menschlicher Moral*], beside which, before which, and after which many other types, above all *higher* moralities [höhere *Moralen*], are, or ought to be, possible" (*BGE* 202). It might be best, therefore, to think of the word *morality* in the title as having scare quotes around it, as a reminder that it is really only that particular "type of human morality" to which the term there refers.

This point is of no little importance. Nietzsche not only holds that "moralities" and "types of moralities" other than "morality in Europe today" are possible, but discusses two of them at length in *Genealogy*—"master morality" [*Herren-Moral*] and "slave morality" [*Sklaven-Moral*], neither of which is what he refers to as "morality in Europe today." And both of *them* have *their own* "genealogies," as well as figuring in the "genealogy" of "morality in Europe to-day." The kind of morality Nietzsche calls "slave morality" may loom large in the genealogical family tree of what he calls modern-day European "herd-animal morality" [*Herdentier-Moral*] (*BGE* 202). It would be a mistake, however—and one that is often made—to equate the "slave" and "herd" types, as shall be seen. "Slave morality" may be *a type* of "herd morality"; but for Nietzsche there can be "herd moralities" that do not share the particular pathologies he discerns in what he here calls "slave morality," and that have different genealogies. The basic point here is that "moralities" have "genealogies" (rather than being time-less truths), that different moralities have different ones, and that none of them is "morality itself," because there is no such thing.

With respect to the other problematic term in the title (*zur*): since Nietzsche used it—rather than simply the definite articled "*die*"—he must have had his reasons for doing so. One such reason may well have been that he regarded the book's three essays as *contributions to* the understanding of the "geneal-ogy" of modern-day morality, but to be nothing approaching a complete and comprehensive treatise on the subject. That would make good sense, and makes an important point that should not be lost sight of.

Next: if *Genealogie* here means the *study of* the genealogy of (modern-day Western) morality, then something like *Toward a Genealogy of Morality* would be the best rendering of the title; while if it refers to that development itself, then *On the Genealogy* of it would be preferable. Since the latter construal would seem to be the more likely, the latter version of the title gets my vote.

The rendering of the German word *Genealogie* by the English word *geneal-ogy* is unproblematic—but what does this word in either language mean here for Nietzsche? Interestingly, he hardly uses the term in connection with moral-ity at all in the book itself (only twice, early on and very casually, in *GM* I:2 and I:4)—or anywhere else (as far as I know), for that matter. It is rather ironic, therefore, that much is made of it, as though it is a term to which he attaches some very special meaning. In the preface to *Genealogy*, Nietzsche uses other quite ordinary terms in its place. In its second section, he uses—with emphasis— one of several words generally translated as *origin*: *Herkunft*. He writes (and conveys something significant about the relation of the book to his earlier work in doing so): "My ideas on the *Herkunft* of our moral prejudices [*morali-schen Vorurteile*]—received their first, brief, and provisional expression in the collection of aphorisms that bears the title *Human, All Too Human*" (*GM* P:2). And in its fourth section, he uses (without emphasis) another such equally common word generally translated as *origin*: *Ursprung*. There he writes about "the first impulse to publish something [further] of my hypotheses concerning the *Ursprung* of morality" (*GM* P:4).

It would seem, therefore, that in speaking of the "genealogy" of modern-day morality in the title of the book, Nietzsche means little (if anything) more than this, and is opting for the more unusual term *Genealogie* simply to give the book an intriguing name (as he sought to do in the cases of nearly all of his books). There is, however, one connotation of this term that he may have wanted to exploit here, though he did not attempt to get any further mileage out if it elsewhere. The term is normally used to invoke the idea of the "family tree" of ancestors from whom someone is descended. Nietzsche may have wanted to use the title to suggest to the reader that (modern-day Western) morality should be thought of similarly—as something (entirely) *human*, to the character of which a multiplicity of (human and even all-too-human) moral—and other—phenomena may have contributed.[3]

II

This was not the first time that Nietzsche had given a book—with a theme of this sort—a title in which a term with similar connotations appears. He gave his very first book the title *The* Birth [*Geburt*] of *Tragedy*, with "Out of the Spirit of Music" as a title extension of the original edition. And its central thesis was that Greek tragic drama (and culture) had two immediate parents, to each of which it owed something important: the two art forms and impulses he called "Apollinian" and "Dionysian." In *Genealogy* the theme is both similar and different: the two types of pre-modern morality that figure most prominently and immediately in his exploration of the origins of modern-day morality are those that appear in the first of the three essays of which the book consists: "master morality" and "slave morality." But it is worth noting that he also identifies other moral phenomena in the other two essays that also have places in the story he tells: most notably the "*Sittlichkeit der Sitte*" (the ethic of custom), the "sovereign individual's" kind of individuality, the phenomenon of "bad conscience" (all in the second essay), and the genesis of the "ascetic ideal" in its various forms (in the third).

Further evidence and instances of Nietzsche's long-standing interest in origins and developmental accounts, from a very different quarter, is provided by another of Nietzsche's early writings—in this case the unfinished manuscript (written at about the same time as *Birth*) called *Truth and Lies in a Nonmoral* [*aussermoralischen*] *Sense*. In that essay it is "origins" again that are being considered—only in this instance the issue is the very human origin, under primitive and prehistoric conditions, of the ideas of "truth" and "knowledge," and of what they originally (and therefore fundamentally?) amounted to.

Nietzsche was not yet a philosopher when he wrote *Birth* and *Truth*; but he was on the way to becoming one during his years as a professor of classical philology at Basel University. As the reader will know by now, he made his philosophical debut in print with the 1878 publication of the first version and volume of *Human, All Too Human*, while still on the faculty there in that capacity. In that book he does indeed (as he freely admits) anticipate at least some of the ideas he developed in *Genealogy*, a decade later—most notably his master morality and slave morality concepts and distinction (*HH* I:45), and his conjecture with respect to the origin of justice (*HH* I:92).

But that is only the tip of the iceberg. In *Human* Nietzsche also had already arrived at the basic conception of the importance of thinking (and philosophizing) "historically" in dealing with a great many matters of philosophical and human importance—up to and including our cognitive abilities and human reality itself. That project—of reinterpreting our human reality and everything human naturalistically and "historically"—is announced prominently and programmatically at its very beginning (*HH* I:2). It is closely linked with his interest in the origin of morality in human life in *Human* (the second part of which bears the heading "On the History of Moral Feelings" ["*Zur Geschichte der moralischen Empfindungen*"]—a heading to which the title *Zur Genealogie der Moral* is strikingly and significantly similar). Morality, too, falls within the scope of what Nietzsche was talking about when he wrote in *Human* that philosophers by and large "do not want to learn that man has *become* [. . .]. But everything has *become*"; and that "consequently what is needed from now on is *historical philosophizing*" (*HH* I:2).

By "historical philosophizing" here Nietzsche clearly had in mind a kind of philosophical thinking that is attuned to the (socially and culturally as well as physiologically and psychologically) *developmental* character of human reality and of all things human. So, for example, extending the idea remarked upon above with respect to knowledge in *Truth*, he suggests that "the steady and laborious process of *Wissenschaft* [inquiry] [. . .] will one day celebrate its greatest triumph in a *history of the genesis of thinking* [*Entstehungsgeschichte des Denkens*]" (*HH* I:16). As he had already intimated in *Truth*, he takes human reality to be a piece of nature through and through, however remarkably it may have developed and been transformed.

For the Nietzsche of *Human*, this is true of all things human, moralities included. And so, too, for him subsequently. The reader will recall that this same project, of a "naturalizing" reinterpretation of our humanity, had been articulated four years earlier, in the first (1882) version of *Joyful Inquiry* immediately following Nietzsche's proclamation of the "death of God" (*JI* 108), in his call for us now to "begin to *naturalize*" our understanding of ourselves (*JI* 109). And he makes it clear, there again, that the kind of reinterpretation of human reality and of things human that he has in mind (and pursues in this book) is to be "historically" (as well as natural-scientifically) minded.

That reinterpretation, for Nietzsche, needs further to be attuned to the very "human" and even "all-too-human" origins and development of human phenomena that are often not thought of as having "developed" at all, let alone in ways reflecting human circumstances, needs, and limitations. So the sections immediately following this one deal with such matters as the "origin [*Ursprung*] of knowledge" (*JI* 110); the "origin [*Herkunft*] of logic" (*JI* 111); the "many things" that had to "come together for scientific thinking to originate [*entstehen*]" (*JI* 113); *and* what accounts for the development of "very different moralities [*Moralen*]" in different communities (*JI* 116). *Inquiry* is not organized by topic, as *Human* is; but if it were, the part dealing with moralities and their origins would be one of the larger ones in the work.

When Nietzsche returned to prose publication in *Beyond* (after the three-year hiatus in which he published only *Zarathustra*), he resumed consideration of this topic. He did so in a part of the book bearing the title "On the Natural History of Morality" ["*Zur Naturgeschichte der Moral*"], coming even closer to the German title of *Genealogy*. And he did so in conjunction with a reiteration of his call for a naturalizing reinterpretation of human reality more generally. He explicitly (on the title page, no less) considered *Genealogy* to be a kind of "clarification and supplement" to *Beyond*.

This sets its immediate context—as a whole, but more specifically by his demand, in *Beyond*, that beneath "the old mendacious pomp, junk and gold dust of unconscious human vanity [. . .], the basic text of *homo natura* [natural man] must again be recognized." He continues: "To translate man back into nature; to become master over the many vain and overly enthusiastic interpretations and connotations that have so far been scrawled and painted over that eternal basic text of *homo natura* [natural man]; to see to it that man henceforth stands before man as even today, hardened in the discipline of *Wissenschaft*, he stands before the *rest* of nature [. . .]—that may be a strange and crazy task [*Aufgabe*], but it is a *task*—who would deny that?" (*BGE* 230).

It is Nietzsche's evident intention in *Beyond* that one should proceed in that same spirit when dealing with *moralities* (or morals) as human phenomena—and with the specific configuration of such phenomena that is the morality of "good and evil" in particular—that the very title of the book is used to convey he would have us get "beyond." So he begins the part of *Beyond* "On the Natural History of Morality" with the suggestion that the first order of business for moral philosophy ought to be to proceed as an anthropologist or zoologist would in dealing with a variety of cultures or creatures: "to prepare a *typology* of morality [*einer* Typenlehre *der Moral*]"—and to that end, in an analytical spirit, "to collect material, to conceptualize and arrange a vast realm of subtle feelings of value and differences of value that are alive, grow, beget, and perish" (*BGE* 186).

It is near the end of this fifth part of *Beyond* that Nietzsche famously proclaims "morality in Europe today" to be "herd-animal morality." Oddly enough, however, it is only later, in its ninth and final part—"*Was ist vornehm* [superior]?"[4] or, in other words, what makes "higher" humanity "higher"—that he gives a new version of the distinction between "master morality" and "slave morality" and their genesis (*BGE* 260). His claim here that "two basic types" of morality "revealed themselves" to him [*sich mir verrieten*] and "one basic difference emerged" sits oddly with his assertion that a "typology of morality" is what "is now needed"—*unless* this sequel is meant to be a major contribution to it. And that would evidently seem to be the case. (The "one basic difference" is that "master moralities" are said to originate in a Yes of self-affirmation, whereas "slave moralities" originate in a No of antipathy to the very qualities that are affirmed by the "masters.")

In view of the use Nietzsche went on to make of this distinction in *Genealogy* a year later, it is important to observe that he goes on to say: "I add immediately that in all the higher and more mixed cultures there also appear attempts at mediation between these two moralities [*Moralen*]"—since our culture (or cultures) in the modern Western world would presumably be among these "more mixed cultures." That would imply that modern-day morality, the "genealogy" of which he is concerned with in *Genealogy*, might well turn out to have a somewhat mixed pedigree. (In any event, for anyone interested in *Genealogy*, these two parts of *Beyond*—5 and 9—should be required preparatory reading!)

III

It was with this combination of interests—in the development of both human reality and human moralities as we know them, among other things—that Nietzsche followed the publication of *Beyond* with both *Genealogy* and *Inquiry*'s Book 5 in the subsequent year. It is tempting to think that *Genealogy* is a kind of sequel and supplement to parts five and nine of *Beyond*, while the fifth Book of *Inquiry* stands in the same relation to the rest of it. In fact, however, *Genealogy* is significantly related to much of the rest of *Beyond* as well— and indeed has considerably more to say that pertains to the kind of naturalizing reinterpretation of human reality called for in *BGE* 230 than does *Beyond* itself. Nietzsche had long been convinced that moralities played a key role in the "dis-animalization" of humanity (see *HH* II:II:350). Thus his project of a de-deified, naturalizing, and historically minded reinterpretation of our humanity quite understandably led him to think *both* about human reality in the perspective of the ways in which moralities have affected it, *and* about moralities in the perspective of their relation to human life and human variables. This is particularly true of the second essay; but the entire book can appropriately and fruitfully be read in this way.

As has been noted, *Genealogy* consists of three essays [*Abhandlungen*; literally, "handlings" or treatments of topics]—which in itself is rather remarkable, since it is Nietzsche that we are talking about. What is remarkable about this is not so much the distinctness of the three discussions—which he makes no real attempt to relate, and which indeed give accounts that are rather difficult to integrate into a unified whole. It is rather the very fact that they are actually *essays*—notwithstanding that they have numbered sections, in the manner of his aphoristic works. Nietzsche's only book-length monograph (setting *Zarathustra* aside) was *Birth*, his very first book.

The set of essays he published separately during the next few years (1874–76), which he gathered into a single volume ten years later (1886) under the loose title *Unzeitgemässe Betrachtungen* (*Unfashionable Reflections*), were not book-length; but they nonetheless were essays of a sort, in genuinely monograph form. After the last of them, however, Nietzsche abandoned that form altogether in his prose writings, in favor of the aphoristic style he came to prefer—with the single exception of the three essays relating to moral phenomena that he published as *Genealogy* a year later, in 1887. This brief return to essay form may well have been owing to the fact that the monograph form is better suited to *telling stories* [*Handlungen*]—and he had three stories to tell, relating in different ways to the origin and development of modern-day morality.

Each of *Genealogy*'s three essays deals with a strand that Nietzsche believes to have become woven into the fabric of modern-day morality. He gave all of them clear but curiously dry (for him) titles. The first essay, " 'Gut und Böse,' 'Gut und Schlecht' " [" 'Good and Evil,' 'Good and Bad' "], explores those different dualities, and features the phenomenon that he calls by the French word *ressentiment*. That phenomenon might be thought of as a particular and especially virulent and pathological form of resentment, amounting to a kind of hatred of others to whom one is in thrall. The second essay, " 'Schuld,' 'schlechtes Gewissen,' und Verwandtes" [" 'Guilt,' 'Bad Conscience,' and Related Matters"], highlights this quite different pair of related phenomena and their genealogies. And the third, "Was bedeuten asketische Ideale?" ["What Do Ascetic

Ideals Signify?"],[5] explores a third topic: the phenomenon of the idealization by living human beings of various forms and sorts of abstinence and self-denial, that collectively and variously reflect a kind of profound aversion to everything fundamental and conducive to vitally flourishing life in this world—and what it signifies or says about those who embrace it, and demonize its target traits.

Each of these phenomena itself has its own "genealogy," to the understanding of which Nietzsche attempts to contribute in these essays, as a way of pursuing the larger goal of an understanding of the genealogy of modern-day morality. He also believes and suggests that some of the things involved in their genealogies had a significant impact upon the transformation of our proto-human animality into our attained human reality, with important implications for the future of humanity, by way of both the possibilities and the vulnerabilities that this manifold transformation has had among its results.

Nietzsche gave *Genealogy* the unsubtle subtitle: *A Polemic*. The book is certainly polemical at various points—even if considerably less consistently and unrelentingly than the three short books that followed it during the next and final year of his productive life (against Christianity, against Wagner, and against the philosophical tradition and shibboleths or "idols" of the age) were to be. But it is something more and different as well: some serious and thoughtful interpretation and case-making, that is as sustained and substantive as Nietzsche ever gets. In his autobiographical *Ecce Homo*, written a year later (just prior to his collapse), Nietzsche says, with respect to *Genealogy*'s three essays: "Every time a beginning that is *calculated* to mislead: cool, *wissenschaftlich*, even ironic, deliberately foregrounding, deliberately holding off. Gradually more unrest: sporadic lightning; very disagreeable truths are heard rumbling in the distance—until eventually a *tempo feroce* [furious tempo] is attained in which everything rushes ahead in a tremendous tension. In the end, in the midst of perfectly fearsome explosions [i.e., thunderclaps], a *new* truth becomes visible every time among thick clouds" (*EH* "Books," *GM*).

Nietzsche evinces his recognition of and interest in "truths" of a different order of magnitude with respect to morality in the very first section of the first essay, when he lauds "English psychologists" who have "trained themselves to sacrifice all desirability to truth, *every* truth, even plain, harsh, ugly, repellent, unchristian, immoral truth.—For such truths do exist" (*GM* I:1). Why they (or anyone else, such as himself) might *want* to do such a thing, and place such a *value* on truth, is another matter. And it is a matter with which Nietzsche is very much concerned, which he implicitly raises at the book's very beginning, and to which he explicitly returns in its third essay (as well as in *JI* V). But, he emphasizes, "such truths do exist"—and he plainly is intent upon bringing some of them pertaining modern-day morality to light.

IV

Genealogy begins with a preface that is of great importance to the book's understanding, and indeed to the understanding of the mature Nietzsche's kind of philosophy and philosophical aspirations. The first section[6] (*GM* P:1) is a very striking beginning, the intended upshot of which is initially far from clear. This section does not question the very ideas of truth and knowledge; indeed, it presupposes their meaningfulness. It raises a very different sort of question of an equally intriguing nature, however—a question of a more psychological nature. As was the case in the first substantive section of what he had just written, Book 5 of *Inquiry* (JI 344), its issue is related to the question about the "will to truth" and the value of truth that Nietzsche had raised in the first section of *Beyond* (BGE 1).

Its very first sentence is arresting: "We are unknown to ourselves, we knowers [*Erkennenden*, those who aspire to knowledge]—and with good reason. We have never sought ourselves—how could it happen that we should ever *find* ourselves?" Nietzsche at least seems to go even further, concluding this opening section of the preface with the assertion that we (as "[would-be] knowers" or seekers of knowledge—of whom he readily admits to being one) not only "do not comprehend ourselves," but moreover "*must* [i.e., have to] misunderstand ourselves"—perhaps in order to be able to remain motivated to carry on.

Yet Nietzsche certainly would appear to take this book (and its third essay in particular) to contribute to our self-understanding *as* "*knowers*"—as well as to an understanding of the "psychology of the priest" (*EH* "Books," *GM*). And by "priest" here he has in mind those who exploit the susceptibility of much of humanity to *ressentiment* and "bad conscience" to create and promulgate religions as well as moralities revolving around "ascetic ideals." And even more importantly, it is also intended to shed light on ourselves as *Menschen*—as the kind of creatures human beings have come to be—to the comprehension of which all three essays are explicitly said to be intended to contribute.

Nietzsche concludes his reflection on *Genealogy* in *Ecce Homo* by characterizing it as consisting of "three decisive preliminary studies by a psychologist"— that is, by the kind of philosophical "psychologist" he takes himself (among other things) to be—preparatory to something further: "a revaluation of all values" (*EH* "Books," *GM*). This "revaluation" is a task that Nietzsche had come at this point to consider the most pressing and important one on both his own philosophical agenda and that of the "philosophy of the future" he heralds in *Beyond*.

In the second section of his preface to *Genealogy*, Nietzsche says something that is both interesting and significant on a number of levels. As has been

observed, he grants that the ideas he is about to take up again in the three essays that follow are essentially "the same ideas" as those he had expressed on
the matters in question in *Human* (and presumably in *Inquiry* and *Beyond* as
well). What he now says is that he actually takes this to count *in their favor* (as
well as in his own favor as a philosopher), notwithstanding the question (of
what makes "us knowers" tick) he had raised in the previous section: "*That* I
still hold fast [*festhalte*] to them today [. . .] strengthens my joyful assurance
that they might have arisen in me from the first not as isolated, capricious, or
sporadic things but from a common root, from a *fundamental will* of knowledge [Grundwillen *der Erkenntnis*], pointing imperiously into the depths, speaking more and more precisely, demanding greater and greater precision. For
this alone is fitting for a philosopher" (*GM* P:2). This passage also says something important about Nietzsche's conception of philosophy, and about what
he takes it to be to think and express oneself philosophically—despite his penchant for vehement and hyperbolic rhetoric.

Nietzsche states the general problem he is pursuing in *Genealogy* in the preface's autobiographical third section. His early interest in "where our good and
evil really *originated*" is said to have been "transformed," in the course of his
developing historical, philological, and psychological sophistication, into other
questions: "Under what conditions did man devise these value judgments 'good'
and 'evil'? *and what value do they themselves possess?*" He glosses this second
question by the further questions with which he continues: "Have they hitherto hindered or furthered human flourishing [*Gedeihen*]? Are they a sign of
distress, of impoverishment, of the degeneration of life? Or is there revealed in
them, on the contrary, the plenitude, force, and will of life [*Wille des Lebens*], its
courage, certainty, future?" (*GM* P:3).

This is as good a statement as Nietzsche ever offers of the considerations
in terms of which he proposes to carry out the "revaluation of values" he calls
for. It is indicative of his basic value standard, deriving from the fundamental
"affirmation of life" or "Yes' about life" (*BGE* 205) that is the ultimate basis of
his naturalized value theory. And it is because the moral-psychological phenomena upon which he focuses in *Genealogy*'s three essays fare badly by these
criteria, on his analysis of them, that he rails polemically against them—and
against the morality and religion he takes to have been built upon them to sustain and promote them.

In the fifth and sixth sections of his preface, Nietzsche makes it clear that
this "revaluation" of the values associated with and promoted by modern-day
morality—and with other phenomena that affect people's lives, such as various religions, types of art, social institutions and practices, and ways of thinking historically, scientifically, and philosophically—matters to him much more

than "genealogical" inquiry pertaining to it per se. Even at the time of *Human* (a decade earlier), he says, "My real concern was something much more important than hypothesizing [*Hypothesenwesen*]—whether my own or other people's—on the origin of morality. Or rather, more precisely: the latter [that is, the question of the origin of morality] concerned me solely for the sake of a goal to which it was only one means among many. What was at issue was the *value* of morality [*den* Wert *der Moral*]. [. . .] What was especially at issue was the value of the 'unegoistic,' the instincts of pity, self-abnegation, self-sacrifice [. . .]" (*GM* P:5).

This issue continued to be Nietzsche's more fundamental concern to the end of his productive life, even as he was engaged in a task "preliminary" to it in *Genealogy*. When he speaks of "the value of morality," what he has in mind is the significance for (human) life of the various specific "moral values" associated with that morality, of which he here gives examples. The (higher-order) "value for life" of such (lower-order) traits or behaviors that have come to be "valued" in existing moralities, and by those who embrace them, is what needs to be ascertained, with a view to their "revaluation" (perhaps positively, perhaps negatively) accordingly. What matters most of all to Nietzsche, however, is not their "revaluation" per se, but rather that which it, too, is intended to serve: namely, the actual flourishing and enhancement of human life.

That highest concern is evident as Nietzsche goes on to observe that he had earlier seen, in the kind of morality (such as Schopenhauer's) that celebrates the "values" he mentions, "the *great danger* to mankind, its sublimest enticement and seduction—but to what? to nothingness? [. . .] to—*nihilism*?" For, he writes, "it was precisely here that I saw the beginning of the end [. . .], the will turning *against* life" (*GM* P:5).[7] That continues to be his worry in *Genealogy*—but now with respect to modern-day morality, and not just to that of Schopenhauer the arch-pessimist, of whose moral philosophy Nietzsche was specifically speaking here. So, in the next section, he states his fundamental worry more generally: "What if a symptom of regression were inherent in the 'good,' likewise a danger, a seduction, a poison, a narcotic, through which the present was possibly living *at the expense of the future*? [. . .] So that precisely [our revered modern-day] morality would be to blame if the *highest power and splendor* actually possible to the type man [*des Typus Mensch*] was never in fact attained? *So that precisely* [*this*] *morality was the danger of dangers?*" (*GM* P:6).

This anxiety pervades the three essays that follow. But to repeat: *Genealogy* is not itself offered by Nietzsche *as* his "revaluation of [modern-day] morality"—even though it is as close as he ever got to writing one before his lamentably brief productive life ended. As he knew full well, knowledge of the origins of things settles nothing with respect to their assessment. So he observes in the fifth Book of *Inquiry* (written just prior to *Genealogy*) that "the history of the origins of these feelings and valuations" is "something quite different from a critique," and that "even if a morality has grown out of an error, the realization of this fact would not so much as touch the problem of its value" (*JI* 345). On the other hand, such knowledge may well provide insights into the character of things like various "moral values" that are quite appropriately taken into account in assessing them; and so an awareness and understanding of them is to be sought, as part of the "due diligence" (as it were) that should be done preparatory to their revaluation.

Putting these points together, Nietzsche writes: "Let us articulate this *new demand*: we need a *critique* of moral values; *the value of these values themselves must first be called into question*—and for that there is needed a knowledge [*Kenntnis*] of the conditions and circumstances in which they grew, under which they evolved and changed (morality [*Moral*] as consequence, as symptom, as mask, as hypocrisy [*Tartufferie*], as illness, as misunderstanding; but also morality as cause, as remedy, as stimulant, as restraint, as poison), a knowledge of a kind that has never yet existed or even been desired" (*GM* P:6). It is first and foremost to the attainment of that kind of knowledge that Nietzsche means to contribute in the three essays that follow. Yet he also takes the occasion to attempt to contribute to the reinterpretation and comprehension of "the type *Mensch*," in ways both suggested by and relevant to his inquiries. And he further avails himself of this occasion to provide at least a preview of his promised "revaluation" of the morality and associated moral phenomena he discusses.

<h2 style="text-align:center">V</h2>

"The truth of the *first* essay," Nietzsche tells us in *Ecce Homo*, is "the birth of Christianity out of the spirit of *ressentiment*" (*EH* "Books," *GM*). Here he is playing on the full original title of his first book, *The Birth of Tragedy out of the Spirit of Music*. As the title he gives to the first essay itself indicates, however, he has something more in mind as well. Its title—" 'Good and Evil' ['*Gut und Böse*'], 'Good and Bad' ['*Gut und Schlecht*']"—shows that his further purpose is to contrast the two fundamentally different types of morality he calls "slave morality" (the morality whose basic contrasting value concepts are "good" and "evil") and "master morality" (the basic contrasting value concepts of which are "good" and "bad").

It is the upshot of the first essay that the former of the two types is inspired and pervaded by "the spirit of *ressentiment*"—precisely in reaction to domination by those whose type of morality (the latter) has a radically different character. It is that of *self-affirmation*, on the part of those who are dominant, and tending to focus upon qualities associated with their dominance. Nietzsche considers the *ressentiment* that manifests itself in "slave morality" to be a (very understandable) reaction on the part of the dominated group to the dominant group. And he further suggests that its concepts of "good" and "evil" and their content are the negative images of the dominant group's self-affirming concept of "good" and its pejorative opposite "bad," supplemented by values associated with the dominated group's survival strategies.

It is noteworthy that Nietzsche makes no mention in this first essay (or in *Beyond* 260 or *Human* I:45 either, for that matter) of a very different type of normativity that he frequently discusses in his earlier writings, and mentions again in the second essay. It is neither a "master morality" nor a "slave morality"—notwithstanding his contention (in *BGE* 260) that these are *the* "two basic types" of morality he has found to exist or have existed in the world. Rather, it is what is often referred to in English-language translations and discussions as "the morality of mores":[8] *die Sittlichkeit der Sitte*, better rendered as "the ethicality (or ethic) of custom." In that kind of morality the norms people live by are the "mores" or customs of their communities, and their norms have a different sort of normativity. Their communities may be "herd-like"; but they are not envisioned to have the structure of a self-affirming ruling group dominating a resentful ruled group. The reason for this seeming oddity may be that Nietzsche, along with Hegel and a good many other German-language philosophers after Hegel (perhaps under his influence), simply did not think of the *Sittlichkeit* type of norms and normativity as a type of *morality* [*Moralität*] at all.

At times, however, Nietzsche does use the term *Moral* to cover both sorts of phenomena. Thus it would seem that his assertion in *Beyond* that "European morality" [*Moral*] today is "*Herdentier-Moral*" (*BGE* 202) is making a different point about it than he is making when he emphasizes its kinship with *Sklaven-Moral* [slave morality]—of which he clearly takes what he calls "*Christian* morality" to be an instance. Nietzsche nowhere claims that the three essays of *Genealogy* give a *complete* account of the "genealogy" of modern-day moral norms and normativity, however. It could well be that a more complete account of it as he understands it would need to include separate and significant mention of the *Sittlichkeit der Sitte*—and of its Hegelian higher type of *Sittlichkeit* in which *Sitte* (customs) are superseded by the laws, imperatives, prohibitions, and rules of mature modern societies—as well as of "master" and "slave" moralities.

Nietzsche argues in the first essay, on etymological, historical, and psychological grounds, that the aristocratically self-affirmative concept of "good" (and its companion derisive counterpart concept of "bad," construed simply as the lack of "good"-making qualities) were prior in point of origin to the opposing conceptions of "good-versus-evil" that have long been the rivals of the "good-versus-bad" opposition, with differing conceptions of "good" as well as of its opposites. The conceptions and morality of "good-versus-evil" are said to have triumphed over those of the "good-versus-bad" pairing (both conceptually and normatively) in a "slave revolt in morality" several millennia ago, and to predominate in the genealogy of modern-day morality. But the latter came first, Nietzsche contends (presumably as a development out of one type of *Sittlichkeit der Sitte*). The morality and opposition of "good and evil" then emerged as a *ressentiment*-charged reaction against the "masters" and everything associated with them—including their value judgments (*GM* I:10).

But there is more than this to the first essay. The *morality* of *ressentiment* is inseparable from the *psychology* of *ressentiment*, which Nietzsche believes to have been occasioned in a very understandable sort of way, but to have resulted in the emergence of a new type of *human sensibility* or mentality—and therefore of a new type of *human reality*. "The man of *ressentiment*" is said to be a very different sort of human being from "the noble man"; and the secretive, furtive nature of the former, whose "spirit loves hiding places, secret paths and back doors," contrasts vividly with "the stronger, fuller nature" of the latter, "in whom there is an excess of the power [*Kraft*] to form, to mold, to recuperate and to forget" (*GM* I:10–11).

Nietzsche thus is supposing, in a Lamarckian sort of way, that what presumably began as a form and manner of behavior that was forced upon the dominated group, was "internalized"—and not just in the ways that customs are learned and become habitual. Rather (the story goes), this disposition became deeply *ingrained* in them—to such an extent and in such a way that it not only become "second nature" to its first generation, but moreover became capable of transmission to subsequent generations, and developed further in them.

What is Lamarckian here is the idea of the intensification through biological inheritance of intragenerationally acquired or heightened characteristics. The thought is this: something one needs or chooses to do repeatedly and become good at, using some ability one already has, becomes an incrementally enhanced version of that ability and the beginnings of a disposition. That disposition can become sufficiently ingrained in one's constitution to be passed on along with others of one's constitutional traits to one's offspring. And that is a process which, if repeated often enough, can yield cumulatively significant results.

Lamarckism was scientifically respectable and commonplace in the nineteenth century, and makes intuitive sense even today (even though we now know it to be mistaken). Nietzsche seems to have taken this way of thinking for granted, and often avails himself of it.[9] So, for example, he writes: "A race of such men of *ressentiment* is bound to become eventually *cleverer* than any noble race; it will also honor cleverness to a far greater degree: namely, as a condition of existence of the first importance" (*GM* I:10). Some such subset of humanity, on this account, is forced to be clever. It then makes a virtue of the necessity; and this reinforcement results in further development of the trait, which is presumed to be biologically heritable in that more highly developed form. In this way, Nietzsche suggests, the seed of cleverness—and thus of intellect—was planted and grew in portions of humankind. And so too the disposition to react with *ressentiment* when confronted with superiority.

The initial upshot of this set of developments, Nietzsche surmises, is that, under the influence of the kinds of cultural developments through which these "instincts of reaction and *ressentiment*" were expressed, and through the heritability of acquired characteristics, the greater part of humanity was "domesticated" to the core. Thus he is prepared to suppose that it "really is true" that "the *meaning of all culture* [Cultur]," at least in the first place and with respect to its original function, "is the reduction of the beast of prey '*Mensch*' to a tame and civilized animal, a *domestic animal*." And by this Nietzsche means not just a wild animal that has been broken, but a changed type of animal, as different from a "beast of prey" as a dog is from a wolf. Human beings now come with psychological attributes that equip them from the outset for forms of life geared to the demands of the cultural reality that has displaced and "reduced" our erstwhile affective constitution (*GM* I:11). On the other hand, it is part of the upshot of Nietzsche's argument that humanity has come to consist of a considerable variety of differing types, differently endowed as well as differently disposed, both by nature and by nurture. And to complicate things even further, it is taken to be a very open question how this or that particular configuration of human qualities and capacities will express itself.

Nietzsche couples this reasoning with a famous piece of his philosophical psychology, the point of which is to undercut the possibility of any objection to the account he is developing that would appeal to the idea of some sort of homuncular *agent self* within any of the types of human beings under consideration that is above the fray, that is inherently capable of resisting any and all such dispositions. He does not attempt to make a case for his position on this matter here, contenting himself with simply putting his cards on the table: "There is no 'being' behind doing, effecting, becoming; 'the doer' is merely a fiction added to the deed," he writes; and thus there is no "neutral substratum behind the strong man, free to express strength or not to do so." Further: "To demand of strength that it should *not* express itself as strength [. . .] is just

as absurd as to demand of weakness that it should express itself as strength"
(*GM* I:13).

Problematic though certain of its underlying assumptions may be, the first
essay thus has a good deal to say about the origins and character of what Nietzsche variously calls our "psychology," our humanly attainable "spirituality," and
our humanly realizable "soul." These developments are conceived not only to
be fostered and reflected in the values and revaluations on which Nietzsche
is commenting, but also to be gradually ingrained in the constitutions of the
strands of humankind in which they have taken hold, with nature and nurture
both modifying and reinforcing each other, in a manner the highly contingent
but real cumulative outcome of which is a very different sort of human being
than walked the earth before it all began.

VI

Genealogy's second essay opens with the suggestion that humankind (*der
Mensch*)—or at any rate some part of it—*has become* something our proto-
human ancestors were not: "an animal *that may promise* [*versprechen darf*]."
This ability—not merely to say the words "I promise" but to have them *mean
something*—is no mere fiction or illusion for Nietzsche. So he not only refers
to this as "the paradoxical task that nature has set itself in the case of man" and
"the real problem regarding man" (that is, regarding the shaping of our attained human nature), but also reflects on how "remarkable" it is "that this
problem has been solved to a large extent." And he supposes this to have been
done through a process of "breeding" [*Züchten*],[10] in the course of which our
prior nature—or at any rate, that of some among us—was altered, in a manner that can be (and therefore presumptively should be) understood naturalistically (*GM* II:1). The question of what that process might have been is the
central question of this essay.

It is Nietzsche's contention that "the animal *Mensch*," which not only tends
but also actually "needs to be forgetful" to be able to function well, "has bred
in itself an opposing faculty, a memory, with the aid of which forgetfulness is
abrogated in certain cases." It is no fiction, but rather a psychological reality.
But this modification of our psychic constitution in turn required others: "The
task of breeding an animal that *may promise* [*das* versprechen darf; that is, has
become capable of making and keeping promises] evidently embraces and presupposes as a preparatory task that one first *makes* the *Mensch* to a certain
degree necessary, uniform, like among like, regular, and consequently calculable." And this, Nietzsche contends, did in fact happen—at least to some significant extent, even if neither completely and perfectly nor irreversibly—through

a process that he envisions (perhaps for lack of an alternative) in a Lamarckian manner. It is said to be "the tremendous labor [. . .] performed by man upon himself during the greater part of the existence of the human race, his entire *prehistoric* labor [. . .], with the aid of the ethic of custom [*Sittlichkeit der Sitte*] and the social straitjacket" (*GM* II:2).

Moreover: while this "long story" might seem to be the genealogy of nothing more admirable than the "herd mentality" of which Nietzsche is so contemptuous, he is quick to observe that it actually and ironically turns out also to have set the stage for a radical supersession of *that very type* of mentality and humanity. For its "ripest fruit" is said to be "the *sovereign individual* [*souveraine Individuum*], like only to himself, liberated again from the *Sittlichkeit der Sitte*, autonomous and supra-ethical [*übersittlich*]" (*GM* II:2). This type itself is far from being that about the possibility of which Nietzsche waxes so rapturously enthusiastic at the end of *GM* II:16, and again near the end of the second essay itself (*GM* II:24); but it is clearly a preliminary form of "higher humanity," well beyond that of the "pack of beasts of prey" we meet again in this essay (*GM* II:17).

But the "long story" of that process is purported to have been a bloody as well as winding one, as Nietzsche immediately goes on to surmise. For it took more than "the *Sittlichkeit der Sitte* and the social straitjacket" *as norms* to bring about these changes in our nature. It took what he calls "mnemotechnics," or the "techniques of memory," in addition to the gentler persuasions of childhood socialization and acculturation; and he observes that "*pain* is the most powerful aid to mnemonics." Human memory is suggested to have begun as the unforgettability of great pain, burning in the consequences of not following the rules of the practice of promise-making and promise-keeping, and so providing a powerful incentive to do whatever it takes to avoid it. Eventually it may become "second nature" for one to do so.

In the longer run, the cumulative effect is suggested to have been that the elements of such a "second nature" have taken root in us, as "the type *Mensch*" was transformed into a kind of constitutionally "domesticated animal," with the mental equipment and psychological dispositions needed to turn out "fit for society." So Nietzsche writes, of this longer process: "With the aid of such images and procedures one finally remembers five or six 'I will not's' [. . .]— and it was indeed with the aid of this kind of memory that one at last came 'to reason'! Ah, reason, seriousness, mastery over the affects, the whole somber thing called reflection, all these prerogatives and showpieces of man: how dearly they have been bought! how much blood and cruelty lie at the bottom of all 'good things'!" (*GM* II:3).

Yet Nietzsche takes the sort of "conscience" associated with the capacity to make and keep promises—at first under socially monitored circumstances and then on one's own, responsible only to oneself—to be very different from what he calls "that *other* [that is, *different*] 'sinister thing' [*düstere Sache*], the consciousness of guilt, the 'bad conscience' [*das 'schlechte Gewissen'*]"[11] (*GM* II:4). Strangely enough, it is *this* "other" (and thus *different*) type of conscience, pathological though it may be, that he suggests to be of the greatest importance not only in the context of the genealogy of our humanity to date, but also with respect to the further enhancement of human life. For he takes it to have opened the way for a significantly different sort of transformation of it than the developments associated with the first sort of conscience alone could have made possible. It is that further development, and the human possibilities it has opened up, to which the rest of the second essay is largely devoted.

The "bad conscience" is not self-punishment as the internalization of the institution and practice of punishment Nietzsche associates in the first part of this essay with the creation of memory and reliability. Rather, he argues, it is *self-torment*, in which one does unto oneself a sublimated version of the violence one is unable to do unto others. And it is precisely the possibilities this opens up that he finds so fascinating and promising: "The existence on earth of an animal soul turned against itself, taking sides against itself, was something so new, profound, unheard of, enigmatic, contradictory, *and future-expanding* [Zukunftsvolles] that the aspect of the earth was essentially altered [. . .]. From now on, man is included among the most unexpected and exciting lucky throws of the dice" (*GM* II:16).

The road to the real possibility of the *übermenschlich* higher humanity that Nietzsche has Zarathustra envision—and proclaim to be "the meaning of the earth"—is purported to have begun with this game-changing happenstance. That eventuality had the phenomenon of "bad conscience" as a condition of its possibility. And this is to be understood not only negatively, as an unfortunate price that had to be paid to travel it, but also positively, as a kind of wrenching but transformative ordeal of the spirit, upon which the emergence of the possibility of attaining such a humanity depended.

That higher humanity, for Nietzsche, would transcend the "sovereign individuality" he had discussed earlier in the second essay—in a crucial respect for which again the phenomenon of "bad conscience" has been genealogically indispensable. For it is the key to the very *capacity for creativity* of the "creative spirit" to which Nietzsche looks with such fervent anticipation at its end (*GM* II:24). The qualities of the "sovereign individual" are a part of the constitution and "great health" of this envisioned form of higher humanity; but they are not enough—for, admirable as they are, they are neither a substitute nor a recipe for creativity, any more than is the inventive cleverness that Nietzsche considers to be one of the traits we owe to the "slave" mentality.

VII

Human reality had already been significantly altered in the ways Nietzsche discusses in connection with the use of punishment to "create a memory" in the human animal; but that line of development would not have led by itself to the emergence of this second kind of conscience, nor would it have sufficed to set the stage for the sort of higher humanity that is the focus of Nietzsche's highest hopes. "The 'bad conscience,'" he writes, "this most uncanny and most interesting plant of all our earthly vegetation, did *not* grow on this soil" (*GM* II:14). He suggests how it may have originated—very differently from the "conscience" of the "sovereign individual," but once again, entirely mundanely—in the extraordinarily important section 16 of the second essay: "I regard the bad conscience as the serious illness that man was bound to contract under the stress of the most fundamental change he ever experienced—that change which occurred when he found himself finally enclosed within the walls of society and of peace" (*GM* II:16).

"In this new world," Nietzsche goes on to surmise, "these semi-animals, well adapted to the wilderness, to war, to prowling, to adventure," could no longer give free rein to "their former guides, their regulating, unconscious and reliable drives" that had served their kind so well prior to the advent of "society and peace." They were blocked by "fearful bulwarks" so daunting—"punishments belong among these bulwarks"—that even these aggressive "semi-animals" were deterred from doing so. With the stage thus set, Nietzsche introduces his theory of drive or instinct inhibition and "internalization": "All instincts that do not discharge themselves outwardly *turn inward*—this is what I call the *internalization* of the human [*Verinnerlichung des Menschen*]: thus it was *that den Menschen* first developed what was later called the 'soul'" (*GM* II:16). The consequence was that these aggressive drives, without losing their basic character, came to be turned upon the only available target: they "turned against the possessors of such instincts." And, Nietzsche continues, "*that* is the origin of the 'bad conscience.'"

But that is not all; for Nietzsche goes on to suggest that there is pleasure in cruelty (repugnant though this may seem to our modern sensibility)—and therefore also not only in the self-torment of "bad conscience," but also in something that it in turn makes possible, which is one of the greatest of gifts and boons to humanity: "This secret self-ravishment, this artists' cruelty, this delight in imposing a form upon oneself as a hard, recalcitrant, suffering material," he writes, is "the actual womb [*eigentliche Mutterschoss*] of all ideal and imaginative phenomena," and so "also brought to light an abundance of strange new beauty and affirmation, and perhaps beauty itself" (*GM* II:18).

Nietzsche's very image in this passage is highly suggestive of how he conceives of this development: the "bad conscience" was not merely the impetus to this development, or even merely its catalyst; it was its very "womb." And if this is so, it is something profoundly important with respect to the genealogy and future of humanity; for this would mean that it was the addition of the phenomenon of the "bad conscience" to the psychological makeup of humanity as it had previously been constituted that made possible the kind of sublimation process that has opened the way to all subsequent enhancements of human life, to date and to come.

It was only in just such a "womb," Nietzsche is contending, that the kind of transformation or sublimation of our merely animal vitality into spirituality and myriad forms of creativity became humanly possible, warranting the extravagant language of the conclusion of section 16. For the key to all such transformation is a compulsion to turn oneself in to *something other than one is*. And this, he suggests, is a compulsion that, in its beginnings, had to take the form of a "war against the old instincts" and our "whole ancient animal self"—but in a manner impelled *precisely by* those "old instincts," and so involving the just-mentioned "delight in imposing a form upon oneself as a hard, recalcitrant, suffering material" (*GM* II:18). Hence Nietzsche's startling suggestion that all of "higher culture," "higher spirituality," artistic creativity, and even intellectual integrity is rooted in *cruelty*, and in the disposition to take pleasure in it (*GM* II:6). And hence also his concern that, were this disposition to be *bred out of* us, the motivational key to their difficult cultivation and pursuit would be lost.

The topic of the third essay is the phenomenon of the idealization of life-denying asceticism that is the dangerous flower of the strange plant of "bad conscience." It is not surprising, therefore, in light of the foregoing, that Nietzsche concludes the second essay by giving hopeful advance notice of a humanly possible antidote to it that the "bad conscience" itself also has made a human possibility: the "creative spirit" who will "redeem us not only from the hitherto reigning ideal but also from that which was bound to grow out of it, the great nausea, the will to nothingness, nihilism." And that, for him, is the key to our being able—wittingly and without illusions—to affirm this life in this world in an unconditional way that "liberates the will again and restores its goal to the earth, and to humankind [*dem Menschen*], its hope" (*GM* II:24).

VIII

With this impassioned rhetorical gesture, Nietzsche looks beyond genealogical inquiry, and beyond revaluation as well, not only to a "philosophy of the future," but also to a possible *humanity* of the future. In the third essay, however, he goes no further than to reflect upon the threat to it posed by "ascetic ideals" and that which inspires them, and to offer a further and more specific glimpse of the kind of alternative to them he envisions. Its title, as was noted at the outset, is in the form of a question: "What do ascetic ideals signify?" [*Was bedeuten asketische Ideale*?]. His question is not to be understood simply in the sense of asking what ascetic ideals valorize or "idealize"; for that is nothing particularly mysterious. Rather: he is interested in what they *signify* or *reveal*, and what is to be made of them.

By "ascetic ideals" (plural) Nietzsche means such "ideals" as the three paradigm examples he cites in section 8 and goes on to discuss: the embrace and celebration as ideals of "poverty, humility, chastity"—the three things that Christian monks have long "taken vows of" in "renouncing the world." He further takes these "ideals" to be reflected in certain valuations associated with traditional Christian morality and its modern-day secular cousin: that there is something sinful or reprehensible about unabashed wealth, pride, and sexuality. By "*the* ascetic ideal" (singular) he means the general ideal of "renouncing the world," things of "the flesh," and everything worldly, while assigning negative value to everything natural. So, at the essay's conclusion, he glosses it as "this hatred of the human, and even more of the animal, and more still of the material, the horror of the senses, of reason itself [. . .], this longing to get away from all appearance, change, becoming, death, wishing, from longing itself" (*GM* III:28).

"The ascetic ideal," in short, is the ideal reflected in the "longing" of which Nietzsche here speaks—the ideal of somehow existing in a way that involves distancing oneself from all of these things, escaping them, rising above them, leaving them behind. This "longing" is a response to the "hatred" of which he speaks in the first part of the passage. And that "hatred," as he suggests earlier in this section, is owing to the "suffering" associated with those things in the experience of those who embrace some version of this "ideal"—not simply to that "suffering" per se, however, but rather to the sense that it might all be *meaningless*. "The meaninglessness of suffering, *not* suffering itself, was the curse that lay over humankind [*der Menschheit*] so far—*and the ascetic ideal offered it a meaning* [*bot ihr einen Sinn*]!" (*GM* III:28). That ideal "placed all suffering under the perspective of *guilt*," which is already to give it (and one's existence) *a kind* of meaning. In doing so, it further signifies that the reality (both within oneself and in which one finds oneself) associated with suffering was to be hated, negated, rejected, and transcended—and that such repentance, denial, and transcendence endows one's existence with further meaning and worth, as the only way of mitigating one's guilt.

Such a suffering-prompted, meaning-craving, and guilt-fueled "will to transcendence" is so widespread, in one form or another, that Nietzsche suggests an extraterrestrial observer might conclude that "the earth was the distinctively *ascetic planet*, a nook of disgruntled, arrogant, and offensive creatures filled with a profound disgust at themselves, at the earth, at all life" (*GM* III:11). It is commonly dressed up in positive interpretive clothing, but actually is a will to "nothingness," there being nothing beyond this life in this world to transcend *to*. Even that recognition, however, is not enough to break the spell—and for deep human psychological reasons. For Nietzsche's answer to the question of "what ascetic ideals signify" and their grip on humanity—stated at the essay's outset (*GM* III:1), and essentially restated at its conclusion (*GM* III:28)—is that they are "an expression of the basic fact of the human will, its *horror vacui* [abhorrence of a vacuum]: *it needs a goal*—and it will rather will *nothingness* than not will."

Nietzsche recognizes and dreads one possible human future: a wasting away of "the human will" to the point of its actual, fatal extinction. The only other solution, he suggests, is for humanity to find its way to a genuine alternative to "the ascetic ideal" that *would give* "the human will" a "goal" of the sort that *would satisfy* that "need" inherent to it, but that would be as conducive to human flourishing as "the ascetic ideal" is detrimental to it. He dismisses *Wissenschaft* as a candidate provider of such an alternative: "No! Don't come to me with *Wissenschaft* when I ask for the natural antagonist of the ascetic ideal, when I demand: 'where is the opposing will expressing the *opposing ideal*?'" For that requires "a value-creating power," which *Wissenschaft* lacks. Moreover—and worse still—he contends that "modern science" actually is "the *best* ally the ascetic ideal has at present." For its fundamental effect is to "dissuade humankind from its former respect for itself" without repairing the damage, resulting in a "*penetrating* sense of our nothingness," and because its unconditional "will to truth" is in fact the ultimate and noblest but potentially fatal expression of the "ascetic ideal" (*GM* III:24–25).

Interestingly, Nietzsche also has similar reservations about "the last idealists left among philosophers"—the very "free-spirited," kindred-spirited "naysayers and outsiders of today [. . .], these last idealists of knowledge in whom alone the intellectual conscience dwells and is incarnate today" (*GM* III:24). A lively intellectual conscience, by itself, will not be enough. (Nor will the proud conscience of the "sovereign individual," admirable as it may be.) Something further is needed, of which his description of the "*Mensch* of the future" he envisions as a "creative spirit" provides a hint. So it comes as no surprise when he writes parenthetically, toward the end of the essay: "*Art*—to say it in advance, for I shall some day return to this subject at greater length—art, in which precisely the *lie* is sanctified and the *will to deception* has a good conscience, is much more fundamentally opposed to the ascetic ideal than is *Wissenschaft*," and "modern science" in particular (*GM* III:25).

Nietzsche did not live to "return to this subject"; but the general idea is clear enough. He contends that the "ascetic ideal" has prevailed precisely because "it was the only meaning offered so far"; but he was being uncharacteristically restrained, by not continuing: "until my *Zarathustra*." For in that work his protagonist had already been made to proclaim "the *Übermensch*" to be the best available life-affirmative candidate for "the meaning of the earth" (*Z* I:P), standing for the new anti-ascetic and anti-otherworldly ideal of the "enhancement of life" through "value creation." In that new dawn, this-worldly *creativity* emerges as the master value, animated by an "artistic conscience" rather than a truth-obsessed "intellectual conscience" hostile to anything that does not pass its muster. For the latter as a master passion and if not accompanied and animated by the former, is actually *hostile* to life and its enhancement, and is thus the "ascetic ideal" once again—in yet another (and perhaps most insidious) guise.

It thus may seem that the third essay gives an answer to the question posed at the very outset of the book—with respect to what makes those tick who as "knowers" devote themselves to the pursuit of knowledge—that is rather grim. As such, Nietzsche writes, even those "hard, severe, abstinent, heroic spirits [. . .] are far from being *free* spirits: *for they still have faith in truth* [sie glauben noch in die Wahrheit]." However, upon closer examination, one sees that the kind of "faith" or "belief" he is talking about here is that which is akin to religious faith, and treats "truth" as a kind of God-substitute and new absolute value: "it is the faith in a *metaphysical* value, the absolute value of *truth*." Thus "this unconditional will to truth is *faith in the ascetic ideal itself*," even if it is no longer explicitly associated with the traditional idea of "God." The value of "truth" can be considered "absolute" if "truth" is associated and even fundamentally identified with that God. But "from the moment faith in the God of the ascetic ideal is denied, *a new problem arises*: that of the *value* of truth" (*GM* III:24).

It by no means follows, however, that Nietzsche thereby gives up on the very idea of "truth," or abandons the further idea that a "will to truth" is possible—and may be worth having and cultivating. And in fact *Genealogy* itself makes it quite clear that he is neither giving up on the former nor abandoning the latter. He most certainly believes that both of them must be significantly modified; but he also would appear to think that both, when so modified, will have important places in his (and our) "philosophy of the future." Neither truth and knowledge nor the value of truth and its pursuit (by would-be *Erkennenden* and "philosophers of the future") *stand and fall* with the idea of their unconditionality and absoluteness. And as Nietzsche makes clear in his preface, they are actually *required* for the very idea of a "revaluation of values" to be undertaken, or even to make any sense. They do, however, need to be cut down to human size and shape.

Midway through the third essay, in what is almost an aside, Nietzsche steps out of his genealogical account for a few moments to say some things about truth and knowledge as he conceives of them. I suggest that he does so precisely here in an attempt to make it clear that he does *not* mean the things he is saying about them in their ascetic-ideal bondage to apply *to their viability and value entirely*. One does well to bear these remarks in mind when considering what to make of this essay, the entire book, and his mature thought more generally:

> But let us, precisely as *Erkennenden*, not be ungrateful to such resolute reversals of accustomed perspectives and valuations with which the spirit has, with apparent mischievousness and futility, raged against itself for so long: to see differently in this way for once, to *want* to see differently, is no small discipline and preparation of the intellect for its future "objectivity"—the latter understood [. . .] as the ability to *control* one's pro and con and to dispose of them, so that one knows how to employ a *variety* of perspectives and affective interpretations *in the service of knowledge*. [. . .] There is *only* a perspective seeing, *only* a perspective "knowing"; and the *more* affects we allow to speak about one thing, the *more* eyes, different eyes, we can use to observe one thing, the more complete will be our "concept" of this thing, our "objectivity." (*GM* III:12)[12]

IX

One may well ask: What is the status of the kinds of claims that Nietzsche makes in *Genealogy*? He professes, in its preface, to aspire to contribute in it to "a knowledge of a kind that has never yet existed or even been desired"— namely, "a knowledge of the conditions and circumstances in which [moral values] grew, under which they evolved and changed" (*GM* P:6). His actual contribution, however, may be something that is both less and more than that. I take him to be venturing a number of "conjectures" and "hypotheses"—as he explicitly calls them in the preface (*GM* P:5)—with respect to aspects of "the origin of morality" as we know it, and various moral phenomena. His aim is not to establish the historical soundness of the particular "hypotheses" he proposes with respect to the unfolding of this genealogy. It is rather, I suggest, to convince his readers that it could have been and probably was nothing grander than developments *of the sort* he relates in his rather imaginative accounts that shaped their development. He also draws upon and imports into his story certain biological and psychological ideas that he believed to be sound scientifically, independently of the account he offers, which influence his telling of the story.

Nietzsche proceeds by appropriating some ideas and coming up with others that seem plausible and promising, and running with them interpretively—mindful of the possibility that many of his proposed accounts are only hypotheses and conjectures, and that there may turn out to be good reasons to reconsider and revise them. He proceeds in this way because he thinks that this is the way to conduct one's "historical-philosophical" experiments. If one wants to think outside the box, one has no alternative—or at any rate, no better way to conduct such experiments. The results often may not deserve the name of "knowledge," puristically speaking; and at times they may even go wide of the mark, not only historically but also psychologically and scientifically. But this for Nietzsche is the kind of thinking and interpreting that needs to be done if we are to advance our *comprehension* of moral phenomena or anything else about human reality, let alone position ourselves as best we can to undertake a naturalizing "revaluation of values."

Nietzsche thinks that these are some of the most interesting and important things a philosopher can and should be thinking about; and he tries to show us how he believes one might best go about doing so. He ventures his best guesses, and thereby challenges us and anyone else who might be interested to enter the fray and attempt not only to fault him but to improve upon his attempts and experiments. That, I suspect, is precisely what he would be doing if he were to return and join us today in reconsidering *Genealogy* and its topics, and others of his texts and their topics—just as he himself did in his 1886 preface to his reissue of *Birth of Tragedy* and on other subsequent occasions.

What *would* count for Nietzsche as "knowledge" here—the kind of *Erkenntnis* of which he speaks in *Genealogy*'s preface and to which he aspires to contribute in its three essays—may never be more than accounts of the kinds of moral-psychological and related human phenomena he is discussing that "ring true" as we consider them, and that continue to do so as we reconsider them. But where things human are concerned, that is often the best we can do. That's "knowledge" in the interpretation business—always an uncertain and even fallible work in progress, but still the name of the game.

Addendum: The Nietzsche of 1888

Nietzsche wrote five books in 1888, the last and increasingly fraught year of his productive life, all of them polemical: two of them against Wagner (*The Case of Wagner* and *Nietzsche contra Wagner*), one against Christianity (*The Antichristian* [*Der Antichrist*]), one against many targets beginning with Socrates (*Twilight of the Idols*), and one aggrandizing himself (*Ecce Homo*). (Several were completed but were not published until well after his terminal collapse in January 1889.) I have already taken account of the things he says in *Ecce Homo* that are relevant to the understanding of his kind of philosophy, in the chapters on the five works discussed in the first half of this book. The second polemic on Wagner is basically just a recycling of things he had written about Wagner in other books.

As I have already noted, there is a portion of *Twilight* in which Nietzsche addresses himself briefly but vividly to a number of recognizably philosophical issues. I consider the remainder of these polemics—insofar as they are coherent and less than half-mad—to be relevant to an understanding of his kind of philosophy chiefly in an illustrative sort of way. For they provide examples or instances of the kinds of cultural values, pathologies, diagnostics, and combat that he appears to expect of the "new philosophers" he is talking about in *Beyond*. What sets these "new philosophers" above and apart from their otherwise kindred Nietzschean-philosophical spirits, it seems, is that they are to strive to *make a difference*—a real human-life qualitative difference—not only through "value creation," but further through the related *value reformations and realizations*. And this is his way of going about it.

This, for my purposes in this book, is as much as need be said and understood about these last works—except for two things. The first is that, even in the midst of it all, and even in as his self-control was fraying, Nietzsche chose to engage in a series of reflections in *Twilight* that would not have been out of place in *Joyful Inquiry*'s fifth Book. They occupy only a quarter of *Twilight*'s modest length, and they show signs of the haste in which they were conceived and written. (He claimed to have written the entire book in ten days, and certainly did so within two months' time.[13])

The fact that Nietzsche can't have given much thought to the five parts of *Twilight* in question (from "'Reason' in Philosophy" through "The 'Improvers' of Mankind"), let alone to all of the specific things he says in them, should give one pause before supposing that these "last words" on these matters deserve to be regarded as his considered conclusions and final positions on them. (Many are provocative simplifications and radical generalizations of things he discussed with more care previously.) But they do show that, to the end, the kinds of issues and thinking with which he had been concerned both in the first version of *Inquiry* and in its later fifth Book remained an important part of his kind of philosophy.

The second thing is of great importance. It concerns Nietzsche's trope of "the *Übermensch*"—or rather, his idea of *Übermenschlichkeit*, which that image is used to invoke and betoken in his image-rich, literary-philosophical *Zarathustra*—and what became of it in his subsequent philosophical thinking. Nietzsche says something very important about it near the beginning of the part of *Ecce Homo* that he (so modestly) titles "Why I Write Such Good Books," after having made *no* use of it at all, or even any mention of it, in any of his post-*Zarathustra* writings.

He begins (in *EH* "Books," 1) by bringing up "the word *Übermensch*" and expressing some exasperation that "it has been understood almost everywhere" *not* in accord with the "values Zarathustra was meant to represent," but rather as their very "opposite": as "an 'idealistic' type of a higher kind of man [*höheren Art Mensch*], half 'saint,' half 'genius.'" And how *should* it have been understood? Nietzsche puts it quite simply: "to represent *eines Typus höchster Wohlgeratenheit*, in contrast to 'modern' men, to 'good' men, to Christians and other nihilists." The contrasts show that the *Übermensch* is not to be thought of as something that is no longer a human being, or even as a new and higher species of human being, but rather as *a type of human being* that, in contrast to those types, would represent humanity's "*höchster Wohlgeratenheit*." And what does that mean?

It does not mean "a type of supreme achievement" (Kaufmann's rendering of it in his long-favored translation). It does not mean anything like that. It means a type of human being who instead "has turned out supremely well." And *that*, Nietzsche tells us here, quite matter-of-factly, in his last word on the subject, is what he intended "the word *Übermensch*" in *Zarathustra* to stand for—its very "*Bezeichnung*" [description].

Nietzsche does not elaborate here on *what he means* by that phrase, other than to suggest that it is what the figure of Zarathustra, "the annihilator of morality" (in its present form), is seeking to make humanly possible. But it seems quite clear (to me, at any rate) that he has in mind the very thing he had described so eloquently at the conclusion of Book 5 of *Inquiry* that he had written the year before (1887), in its penultimate section bearing the title "The Great Health." (I drew attention to the section, without explicitly citing it, at the conclusion of the addendum to the previous chapter.)

It will be recalled that Nietzsche advertised his pre-*Zarathustra* "free spirit" series as "writings whose common goal it is to erect *a new image and ideal of the free spirit*"—and that he expressly stated that *Joyful Inquiry* was its "conclusion." What succeeded it and took its place was his next "series of writings"—namely, the four parts of *Zarathustra*. That remarkable work might be thought of as having the educational "goal" of erecting its successor (either in place of or subsuming and surpassing the previous "image and ideal"): namely, that betokened the *Übermensch*—understood in precisely the sense indicated by Nietzsche above.

I suggest that this remained his goal after *Zarathustra*, but that he ceased doing so under that name—and that here, two years later, he gave it a new one: "*The great health*" [*Die grosse Gesundheit*]. I shall conclude by citing from what he says about it here.

> Another ideal runs ahead of us [. . .]: the idea of a spirit who plays naively—that is, not deliberately but from overflowing power and abundance—with all that was hitherto called holy, good, untouchable, divine [. . .]; the ideal of a human-suprahuman [*menschlich-übermenschlichen*] [!] well-being and well-willing [*Wohlseins und Wohlwollens*] that will often appear *unhuman* [*unmenschlich*]—for example, when it confronts all earthly seriousness so far [. . .]—and yet it is perhaps only with that that *the great seriousness* [der grosse Ernst] really begins [. . .], that the destiny of the soul changes, the hand moves forward, the tragedy *begins*. (*JI* 382)

The ending is enigmatic; but it should be recalled that Nietzsche had the highest regard for tragedy as an art form (and life frame). His concept of "life affirmation" includes embracing its fundamentally and inescapably tragic character (properly understood), by way of the attainment of a sensibility that is tragic—and, nonetheless, joyful!

PART II

Nietzsche Becoming—What?

7

Nietzsche as Nihilist?

This *Mensch* of the future, this anti-Christian and anti-nihilist, this victor over God and
nothingness—*he must come one day* . . . [*Dieser Mensch der Zukunft, dieser Antichrist
und Antinihilist, dieser Besieger Gottes und des Nichts*—er muss einst kommen . . .]
On the Genealogy of Morality, II:24

It was as a kind of "existentialist"—of the French sort—that Nietzsche was reintroduced to the English-speaking world and philosophical community in the
aftermath of the Second World War, by interpreters and translators like Walter
Kaufmann, who were seeking to rescue him from his lamentable appropriation
by the Nazis. They were remarkably successful among the literati, who were generally well disposed to (French-style) existentialism in many quarters—but that
didn't help much among philosophers in the Anglo-American analytic mainstream, in which "that sort of thing" was deemed both odious and insidious.
That was, at least in part, because they considered what passed for philosophy
on the European Continent (hence: "Continental philosophy") to be a kind of
"cult of the irrational," and a menace to all that right-thinking people hold dear.
And they took the word of enthusiasts of that cult that Nietzsche, if not a proto-
Nazi, was something almost as reprehensible: a proto-existentialist!

Yet oddly enough, it was as the same kind of nihilistic menace existentialists
were thought to be that Nietzsche was reintroduced yet again (in the mid-
1960s), with a very positive spin, to the Anglophone philosophical community—by one of analytic philosophy's own most prominent proponents: Arthur Danto, in his now classic *Nietzsche as Philosopher*.[1] Danto, too, sought
to rehabilitate Nietzsche—not from the charge of nihilism, but rather from a
worse sin among philosophers: that of irrationalism! Nihilistic menace though
he might be, Danto argued in his favor that he at least was no disreputable ir-
rationalistic existentialist, but rather a cogent and rather formidable rational
(albeit unsound and worrisome) thinker. So he deserved to be (and had better be) taken seriously—"as philosopher"—even if only to be taken on, and
taken down.

Danto did gain Nietzsche some grudging respect among some analytic philosophers in this way, even if little esteem. There was, however, a price. It was all very well and good for him to be acquitted of the charge of being a bad philosopher (or none at all); but Danto reinforced the idea that, viewed from another angle, Nietzsche was actually something even worse than a raving existentialist. And that was (insidiously): a coherent—even analytically minded!—advocate of a radical sort of nihilism, for whom the very ideas of reality, truth, knowledge, morality, value, and meaning of and in life, must go over the side (along with God). Danto's Nietzsche was not simply announcing that "the advent of nihilism" was at hand, in the aftermath of the demise of the God-idea; he was radical nihilism's foremost proponent and proselytizer.

Danto himself took that in stride, almost lightheartedly; but for many others in the philosophical mainstream, it was generally thought to be reprehensible. And what made it all the more galling was that this radically nihilistic way of thinking seemed to be catching on in the Continental post-existentialist opposition to the mainstream, under the banner of "poststructuralism," which was styling itself as—Nietzschean! Hence the salience of the question: "Nietzsche as nihilist?" The question of whether Nietzsche's kind of philosophy can be appropriately characterized as a kind of "existentialism" will then be taken up in the next chapter.

I shall begin by briefly and succinctly stating my position on the matter, and then shall proceed to make my case for it. I shall frame my summary of my position in a way that I believe to be helpful: that is, by relating it to what I consider to be Nietzsche's kind of philosophical *naturalism*—the topic of chapter 11. For on the face of it, nihilism and naturalism would seem to preclude each other.

I

The term *nihilism* obviously derives from the Latin *nihil* ("nothing"), and so literally means "nothing-ism." And the *-ism* clearly conveys that it is a stance that involves (pardon the pun) "making much ado about nothing"—in the sense of insisting, with respect to some category or type of putative thing, that *there is* "nothing of the kind!" So, for example, Nietzsche's "God is dead!" slogan and idea is intended to convey very forcefully, with respect to the God-idea, that that is a concept whose time has come and gone, and that the truth of the matter is that "there is nothing of the kind"—no such thing or kind of thing as the sort of transcendent supreme being or reality that "God" was thought or imagined to be. So if holding that there is nothing of that sort makes one a kind of "nihilist" (where such things—and other such things that presuppose them, like "Divine Providence," "sin," and "heaven"—are concerned), Nietzsche certainly *was* at least *that* sort of "nihilist."

Broadly and abstractly speaking, there would seem to be two *sorts* of philosophical nihilism, and two *degrees* of each of them. One *sort* is what might be called *truth* nihilism: nihilism with respect to reality and knowledge. The other might be called *value* nihilism: nihilism with respect to value and meaning. (This accords with Danto's analysis.) As for the two *degrees*: one is limited to the denial or repudiation of *absolutes*—eternalities, immutabilities, unconditionalities, universalities, and the like—of the relevant sorts in their respective domains, and so might be called *metaphysical* nihilism, of one or both sorts. It might also be thought of as a *limited* nihilism—limited, that is, to the rejection of the idea that there is anything nonfictional to which absolutist versions of truth and value concepts refer. The other extends to the denial or repudiation of the very ideas of reality, knowledge, value, and meaning and anything to which those ideas might be coherently applicable—and so may be called *radical* nihilism, of one or both sorts. (Many interpreters, Danto among them, seem to think that Nietzsche collapses this distinction. I grant that he tended for a time to do so, but maintain that he came to know better, and never fully did so in any of his published writings—as I mean to show.)

Metaphysical nihilism is essentially the negative side of the view Nietzsche proclaims at the outset of *Human, All Too Human*. Elaborating this idea briefly, in a Nietzschean sort of way: this kind of nihilism is a dismissal of the idea of the existence or meaningfulness of anything "supernatural" ("otherworldly" or above and beyond the world of spatiotemporal "becoming")—with the Kantian as well as Christian ideas of "God, the soul, and immortality" at the top of the list. And the list extends to (ideas of) forms of reality (and existing), knowledge (and truth), value (and normativity), and meaning (and significance) transcending and independent of the contingencies and bounds of "this world" as we do or may encounter it in "life and experience." (This might be glossed as: above and beyond what has come about and is constituted physically, materially, historically, socially, creatively, linguistically, psychologically, or otherwise arising and happening within the world of which we are a part.)

Radical nihilism *extends* or broadens this denial to the *general* denial or repudiation of the meaningfulness or soundness of all categories of "this-worldly," de-deified and de-absolutized *versions* of such things, which might be deemed appropriately and usefully applicable for both cognitive and practical human purposes. It in effect accepts the absolutized versions of them, but contents itself with rejecting them as fictions or absurdities, and proclaiming that nothing less counts, strictly (and so, philosophically) speaking. One could, of course, be a radical nihilist with respect to some or all types of instance of either truth nihilism or value nihilism, but not both. The expression "*complete nihilist*" would therefore best be reserved for those who are radical nihilists of both sorts.

Now: it is already clear, from what was said above about Nietzsche and the "God-idea," that he could appropriately be said to have been at least one sort of nihilist: a truth nihilist and a value nihilist *with respect to* the existence or reality of anything supernatural of the "God-sort," and anything that is de- pendent upon it. But that by itself does not make him a *radical* nihilist of either sort, let alone a *complete* one. There are other types of nihilist that he might or might not be (or have been). So what are the wider parameters of *his* nihilism— and how should or can that be best determined?

I suggest that the best way of answering this question is to be guided by the maxim "Nihilist is as nihilist does"—with the corollary "*Doing* what real nihilists of some sort would *not* do means one is no nihilist of that sort." For example, consider the case of someone like Nietzsche, doing as he does in his various works from *Human* (1878) onward. What he *does* in these works—as I believe the previous chapters make quite clear—is to beat the drum for anti- otherworldly and anti-metaphysical thinking, *and* to proceed to chart and begin to pursue a different course for philosophy (and for his own thinking in the first instance), that is both reinterpretive and revaluative, and aspires centrally to a variety of sorts of comprehension, that he clearly believes to be humanly possible.

My answer to the question of what kind of nihilist Nietzsche shows him- self to be, therefore, arrived at by taking a comprehensive view of these works, is this (in terms of the typology sketched above): the Nietzsche we encounter, not just in some of these works but in all of them, *was* an emphatic *metaphysi- cal* nihilist but was *not*, generally speaking, a *complete radical* nihilist—and, for that matter, was neither a radical *truth* nihilist *nor* a radical *value* nihilist. He did, from time to time, flirt with both versions; but he did so primarily in an experimental way, in his notebooks, and before he got clearer than he was at times about the crucially important point that his *metaphysical* nihilism did not commit him to a *radical* nihilism, of either sort.

There is, for Nietzsche, no single ultimate absolute really real, really true Reality (or kind of Reality); and the same goes for Truth (or kind of Truth), Knowledge, Value, Meaning, Morality, Law, or anything else. But there are, in our world of life and experience, many variants and versions of all of these things that have "become" and "come to be," and that are deserving of our at- tention and admit of lesser or greater comprehension. (They undoubtedly are the actual mundane phenomena from which those concepts seem to have been idealizingly derived.) And they—rather than their *abstracted and absolutized derivatives*, and *their* nihilizing critique and deconstruction—are what Nietzsche proposes to have replace these abstracted absolutes in his "philosophy of the future."

In short: as I construe the general tendencies of his thought, Nietzsche is *both* a *kind* of nihilist *and* a *kind* of naturalist. (And by the latter I mean, roughly speaking: a "naturalizing" reinterpreter and reconceptualizer, for whom the origination and "becoming" of everything there is and everything that goes on is to be so understood.) Indeed, there is an interesting and important respect in which these two aspects of his thought actually go together. For *his kind* of nihilism, as I construe it, serves to clear the way and set the stage for *his kind* of naturalism—which is the kind of reinterpretation of human reality that he considers to remain a philosophically possible and important task in the aftermath of what he calls "the death of God." One might say that Nietzsche's naturalism is, in a sense, the Hegelian *Aufhebung* of nihilism—by which I mean: his nihilism is at once its negation, its transformation, and its preservation.

But as I understand him, there is *another kind* of nihilist, and also *another kind* of naturalist, that Nietzsche is *not*—even though he says things at times that make him sound (at times) like that other kind of nihilist and (at other times) that other kind of naturalist. My Nietzsche *is* the kind of nihilist for whom "God is dead," and for whom there is no "true world of being" God-substitute either—that is, no "true world" of absolute, timeless, and immutable entities, substances, structures, order, values, or "meaning." In *that* sense, for him, the world in which we find ourselves is a kind of "chaos" or orderlessness rather than a persistingly ordered cosmos. But he is *not* (or at any rate did not remain, even if he may for a time have been or thought himself to be)—the kind of radical nihilist who *further* thinks that the very ideas of reality, structure, order, truth, and knowledge, all stand and fall with the ideas of God and any such surrogate absolutes, and must be abandoned as well; and that the same is the case with respect to the very ideas of value and meaningfulness *of any kind*. And he further is *not* the kind of nihilist for whom the demise of all such absolutes settles the question of whether sense can be made of life affirmation—in the negative.[2]

II

The promotion of the former, more limited sort of nihilism—*metaphysical nihilism*—is by no means the whole story philosophically for Nietzsche, and does not, for him, mean the end of philosophy. What then remains of a positive nature, for him to go on to reconsider, reinterpret, and reassess? To answer this question, I suggest that one need only look at the things *he* continues to think about, reinterpret, and reassess, to the very end. They include (among other things) our human reality as it has come to be; the contents of the world of human life and history as they have come to be, as we live them, encounter them, and deal with them; the kinds of meanings and values with which they have been and can be endowed; and the ways in which this can happen and may have happened.

These things—these "matters" [*Sachen*], as Nietzsche sometimes calls them— are no "true world" absolutes. They are no Kantian *Dingen an sich* either. But such *Sachen* (that is, anything and everything that there is or goes on, in some way or context), for him, *are realities*, their contingency, mutability, and humanity-relatedness notwithstanding.[3] They are all of the many kinds of realities we are left with when we recover from our religious and metaphysical addiction to absolutes, and from the susceptibility to ascetic ideals to which that addiction contributes.

They include our human constitution and our human differences, and our environing world in which we live, act, and interact. They are realities that have "become" [*geworden*] (*HH* I:2)—which is to say: have *come to be, come to exist, become what they are and as they are.* And for Nietzsche, explicitly from *Human* onward, there is much about them and their "becoming"—and about the human possibilities their "becoming" has engendered—that is worth thinking about, and can be humanly comprehended. We need only develop the eyes—"the *more* eyes, different eyes"—needed to see them. They can be (and generally tend to be) misunderstood or only superficially and simplistically understood. But they also can come to be comprehended, more or less fully and well, from and by means of perspectives attuned to various of their features—even if never completely or with finality, or with any other (absolute) sort of "objectivity" (*GM* III:12).

Their attempted deepening comprehension is one of the central tasks of the kind of philosophy we find Nietzsche advocating and attempting to put into practice. That is the sort of task, for example, of which he speaks when he writes, in *Beyond Good and Evil*: "To translate man back into nature [. . .]; to see to it that man henceforth stands before man as even today, hardened in the discipline of *Wissenschaft*, he stands before that *other* nature [. . .], deaf to the siren songs of old metaphysical bird catchers who have been piping at him all too long, 'you are more, you are higher, you are of a different origin!'—that may be a strange and crazy task [*Aufgabe*], but it is a *task*—who would deny that?" (*BGE* 230). This "task" is one part of the project of *Nietzsche's kind* of naturalism. And on my reading of him, *his kind* of (limited anti-absolutist) nihilism not only does not preclude it, but actually sets the stage for it, by doing the critical work not only of vanquishing the God-idea but also of banishing "true world" ideas and ideals of reality, knowledge, and value that he calls that idea's "shadows" (*JI* 108). His naturalism picks up where his persisting metaphysical nihilism leaves off—thereby going beyond it, and also, in that sense, leaving it behind.

But what kind of nihilism-superseding naturalism, more fully characterized, *is* Nietzsche's kind of naturalism? That is my topic in the final chapter of this book. Here I will simply say: There is a well-known kind of *scientistic* naturalism that takes the natural sciences (and other disciplines that model their modes of description and explanation on those of the natural sciences) to be dispositive for all matters pertaining to human as well as natural reality. But that is not the only possible naturalism—and I would insist, that it is *not Nietzsche's.* For the moment, I will simply make a few remarks to convey the gist of it.

It is my contention that the game-changing phenomenon of the cultural saturation and transformation of human life is as central to Nietzsche's reinterpretation of human reality as is his call for its "translation back into nature." That is because he regards it as the key to the developmental story of how humanity—*der Mensch*, humankind—has come mundanely to make something no longer merely natural of itself. It has (unwitting but serendipitously) transformed itself, by these cultural means of its own devising, availing itself of its acquired capacity for sublimation, and assisted by social arrangements imposing constraints and reconfiguring options. Nietzsche's ways of dealing with it and with cases of it—analytically, interpretively, historically, imaginatively, and scientifically when possible and illuminating—are very much a part of his kind of philosophy.

That, in brief, is what I take Nietzsche's kind of "naturalizing" (and naturalism) to be. And it seems to me that there is much to be said for the idea of a naturalism that is not dogmatically wedded exclusively to the model of natural-scientific theory and explanation, and is prepared to become whatever it needs to become interpretively to make sense of the ways in which human reality has become what it is. But there also is much to be said for a naturalism that not only is scientifically informed and sophisticated, but also is attuned (both substantively and methodologically) to the reality of features of it that have transformed and emerged out of our basic human reality—those pertaining to or made possible by various kinds of cultural phenomena and content in particular.

III

My topic in this chapter, however, is my response to the question of Nietzsche's purported nihilism, and more specifically, my contention that his nihilism does not (comprehensively speaking) extend beyond his anti-metaphysical (and anti-supernaturalist) anti-absolutism. To make my case, I will look at what he is actually doing (and says he is doing) in his various philosophical writings throughout the course of his brief philosophical life.

My strategy here is to invite the reader to consider whether what Nietzsche is doing and saying in his works can be squared with the idea that he was a more radical nihilist than this, specifically in what he has to say and does with respect to various sorts of *realities and knowledge of them*. My survey of his works will show that he has a pervasive and continuing commitment to some sort of significant cognitivism. By that I mean simply: a commitment to the ideas that there are things (in the broad sense of *Sachen*) in and about ourselves and the world in which we find ourselves that we may or may not comprehend, more or less well, and that comprehension or understanding, in various ways, is humanly possible. I contend and will try to establish that the case for the latter response is clear: The Nietzsche we encounter in these works shows that commitment, and so cannot properly be characterized as a radical truth nihilist.

I hasten to add, first, that this is not to say that *this* (knowledge-and-reality) model is appropriate to all (or any) matters of value and meaning, at least as it stands. Some matters of value and meaning may be or relate to such things, while others may have a different status in our relation to them and in their relation to us. Nietzsche's thinking about this is something I intend to discuss on another occasion. For now I will simply suggest that it may well be something *other than a knowing* relation of any sort (that or how or by acquaintance), but a no less significant one in human life. And I will also say that I believe there to be a comparable but different sort of case from the case I will be making here, for the claim that Nietzsche is not a radical *value* nihilist either—even though he is properly regarded as an anti-absolutist (and so metaphysical nihilist) with respect to matters of these sorts.

My way of making that case would be the same: by showing that, throughout his philosophical life, Nietzsche was as importantly committed to the retention of revised (non-absolutist) versions of the ideas of value(s) and meaning(s) as he was to revised versions of the ideas of realities and their comprehension. A radical value nihilist would be one who gives up on and attempts to dispense with these ideas altogether. That is not Nietzsche—who actually championed (rather than repudiated) both, when suitably reconceived, and makes much use of various forms of both.

On my understanding of him, moreover, metaphysical nihilism for Nietzsche was not the end of the line. It became for him a kind of "transitional stage," as he himself said of nihilism generally in a note of 1887 (*KGW* VIII 9:35)—and not "transitional" to *radical* nihilism. He was not merely a kind of career nihilist militant. He may have been tempted along the way by the combination of the seductive "God-or-bust" dichotomy and his metaphysical nihilism to embrace a more radical comprehensive nihilism—but he *got over* that temptation, recovered from it, and became an explorer and champion of the "brave new world" in which we now find ourselves intellectually and philosophically. And this included experimenting with revised versions of ideas and concepts whose traditional versions he rejected, to see which of them might turn out to have significant uses and applications in our lives and thinking in this newly de-deified (*entgöttlicht*), de-absolutized, and de-"moralized" world.

In that sense, on my comprehensive reading and interpretation of him, the emancipated and enlightened *Mensch* and philosopher of the future will not just be, as Nietzsche put it in *Genealogy* (*GM* II:24), "*Antichrist* [Anti-Christian] *und Antinihilist*," but more importantly, *post-Christian and post-nihilist*, having left both behind—albeit in different ways. For this reason, it is actually misleading (even if not mistaken) to characterize him as "a nihilist"—of a drum-beating sort—to the end. For even when understood as a salutary philosophical housecleaning, metaphysical nihilism was for him no end point, but rather only a necessary (although also dangerous) "transitional stage"—to a healthier sort of humanity that did not revolve around a negation (either lamented or celebrated).

Even that kind of nihilism, for Nietzsche, is ultimately commendable only insofar as it is *on the way* to something fundamentally *affirmative*, that revolves around *what there is* rather than *what there isn't*, and what knowing can be rather than what it can't be. But it is important to him that his kind of philosophy and philosopher cease to be preoccupied with the void left by the abandonment of the ideas and ideals of the (religious, metaphysical, and moral) absolutes of old—or, as Nietzsche puts it, by the "death of God" and the demise of these *Götzen* [idols]. In the end, he might have said if he had written Book 3 of *Joyful Inquiry* five years later, nihilism, too—even (and perhaps especially) metaphysical nihilism—is one of the "shadows of God" needing to be "vanquished" (*JI* 108).

IV

I take Nietzsche's thinking with respect to knowledge to be an evolving attempt to replace a metaphysically oriented and modeled conception of knowledge with his version of a (broadly speaking) "naturalizing" epistemology that takes seriously the idea that "everything has *become*." This does mean, for him, that "there are *no eternal facts*: just as there are no absolute truths"; that "man has *become*"; and that so also our human "capacity for knowledge has *become*" (*HH* I:2). But he also attempts to do justice in a positive way to what human knowing *can be*.

To be sure, Nietzsche was scathingly critical of *certain ways of conceiving of* truth—and of *associated ways of conceiving of* knowledge—and was more than ready to abandon and excoriate them and their proponents. But he was no less eager to lay claim and proclaim allegiance to the ideas and realities (and even, under appropriate circumstances, the value) of truth and truthfulness, and of knowledge and knowing, *when properly construed and assessed*.

As I read him, Nietzsche was much more concerned to get things straightened out with respect to knowing and knowledge than he was with respect to truth per se, making certain conceptions of truth his targets because they have come to distort the way in which knowledge is understood, and stand in the way of its proper understanding and appreciation. I therefore consider it appropriate to characterize him as a kind of "cognitivist" (and a mistake to characterize him as a "cognitive nihilist") because, as shall be seen, he was firmly and importantly committed to the ideas of the possibility and reality of significant forms of *knowing* and *knowledge* throughout his philosophical life.

It has been common among philosophers through the ages to conceive of "knowledge" in terms of "truth," to define "knowledge strictly speaking" in terms of "truth strictly speaking," and then to construe the latter in a way that makes it difficult for very much if anything about the world and ourselves to pass muster. Nietzsche has little patience with such rarefied conceptions of "truth," and is deeply suspicious of preoccupation with them; and he accordingly is harshly critical and dismissive of ways of thinking associated with them. Indeed, I take him to be trying to get us to focus upon "knowing" rather than "truth" as the more central of the two. To put the point succinctly: if you want to understand *the reality of knowledge*, don't get hung up on the *ideality of truth*. Or, to paraphrase Kant (and even in a Kantian sort of way): Nietzsche finds it necessary to deny Truth (with a capital *T*) in order to make room for knowledge (with a lowercase *k*).

It is part of the philosophical training of many of us to suppose that we have to get clear (and rigorous) about "truth" in order to be in a position to go on to give a proper characterization of "knowledge." This way of thinking was already common enough by the time Nietzsche came along that he took it to be one of those many ways in which philosophers have long tended to go astray. If, for whatever reasons (or with whatever motivations), one conceives of "truth" in a manner that, "strictly speaking," turns out to have no nontrivial real-life satisfaction, and defines "genuine knowledge" in terms of it, one is asking for trouble. Dreaming this sort of impossible dream is dangerous, Nietzsche warns us; for that way nihilism lies, and the impossible dream turns into a seemingly impassable nightmare.

But this (as Wittgenstein would say) is self-bewitchment; and for Nietzsche there is a way out of the nihilistic nightmare that is simple enough, if only we can get ourselves to do it: to wake up. Human knowing is not a myth; it is a reality. Or rather, it might be better to say, there are a variety of sorts of human knowing and knowledge, which have come to be human possibilities and realities in the course of human development and human events. What they variously actually amount to, and what they might further amount to if refined and extended in various ways, are among the things it makes good Nietzschean sense to think about and try to understand.

I take Nietzsche to be trying to convince us that, to understand knowledge, one should think about the practice of *interpretation* rather than the paradigm of *proof*; forget about certainty and immaculateness; stop thinking in black-and-white, all-or-nothing terms; get comfortable with the idea of provisionality; come to terms with the humanness of all humanly possible knowing; start with commonplace paradigms of accounts in contexts in which sense can be made of their being more or less accurate, sound, and adequate; and work your way out from them as best (and as far as) you can. Think of "truth" as a floating designator for provisional outcomes of more or less successful but generally ongoing cognitive endeavors or varieties of knowing. And expect the knowledge they yield to have a diversity of character reflecting that of the differing matters with which they are concerned (or: to fit which they are tailored) and our differing relations to them.

In orienting ourselves to Nietzsche's thinking about these matters, we do well to attend closely to the language we find him using and sorts of things we find him saying along these lines, particularly in his published writings.[4] It should be noted that the German terms he uses in speaking of knowledge, from beginning to end, are for the most part either *Erkenntnis* (alternately spelled *Erkenntniss*) or occasionally *Kenntnis*, and their variants and derivatives, such as the verb *erkennen* [(come) to know] and *wir Erkennenden* ("we knowers," that is, we who go in for "knowing," of one sort and in one context or another). He sometimes uses other terms as well: for example, the various forms of *wissen* (and *Wissenschaft*), *begreifen* [comprehending] and *verstehen* [understanding]. It is striking how often Nietzsche uses this language of knowing and knowledge, and how comfortable he seems with it. There are indeed kinds or ideals of putative knowing and knowledge that he repudiates;

but there are others toward which he quite evidently is much more favorably disposed.

In what follows I will be both using and mentioning all of these terms a great deal. Much of the time I will be using and mentioning these German terms themselves, rather than their common English translations, because they are the terms Nietzsche uses; and it is important for English-speaking readers to get comfortable with them, and to know which ones he is using in particular instances and contexts. This is particularly important in the case of the term *Wissenschaft*, because it had a broader compass for Nietzsche than does our term *science* (its usual translation), as it has long had in German more generally.

Wissen means both "knowing" and "knowledge," and Nietzsche uses it more or less synonymously with the first set of words above, built around *erkennen*. The suffix *-schaft*, when used in this sort of way, simply means something like some sort of activity or endeavor. And *Wissenschaft* literally means "the knowledge business" or "the knowing endeavor"—the activities associated with the generation and attainment of knowledge. That includes the natural sciences; but it also includes many other developed ways of doing so, many of which differ significantly from the natural sciences, their methods, and their kinds of knowing and knowledge.

Wissenschaften are best thought of as *cognitive disciplines*—refined and developed forms of knowing, coming to know, and pursuing knowledge of various matters, in various contexts. They determine what counts as "knowing" and "knowledge" in those contexts (to the extent that anything does). Physics, of course, is one such discipline Nietzsche recognizes and talks about; and chemistry and physiology are others. But so are psychology, history, philology, and linguistics. (And let us not forget his own "*fröhliche Wissenschaft*"!) In frequently leaving *Wissenschaft* in German, my purpose is to remind the reader of this. Likewise *Erkenntnis* and the like, as shall be seen. And there is no company in which Nietzsche more frequently places himself than *wir Erkennenden* [we who go in for knowing]. I trust that readers will quickly accustom themselves to my use of these original terms to be in direct contact with his usage in speaking of these matters.

We also do well to consider and be mindful of some of the more notable ways in which we find Nietzsche using cognitive language and concerning himself with cognitive phenomena of various sorts. And as we shift our attention from his epistemological critiques themselves to what survives them, it is instructive to consider what unstated qualifications of the scope of these critiques are suggested by some of the kinds of things he clearly does not feel obliged by them to cease to say and do.

In what follows I shall take note of (and comment on) a number of cases in point, from Nietzsche's writings both early and later. I shall proceed in somewhat chronological fashion, to make my case for my contention: there is no point in his philosophical life when he does not make significant positive use of cognitive language, and does not show himself to be something quite other than a complete epistemic nihilist. And although that is the sort of nihilism I am focusing on here, I would reiterate that the same is true with respect to the idea that he was a complete value nihilist.

V

Nietzsche's early incomplete manuscript *On Truth and Lies in a Nonmoral Sense* (1873) has gained both celebrity and notoriety (in different quarters) for its critique (with seemingly radically subversive intent) of "truth." It is basically a polemic against the viability of the idea that there is or ever can be anything like the philosophically envisioned and prescribed literal *correspondence* of the way we perceive and describe and conceive of things with the way they are in themselves (or even of the contents of these different stages of the operation with each other)—and so against the idea of "truth" construed in terms of such a correspondence, along with any conception of knowledge based upon it.

Even if this critique is taken at face value, however, Nietzsche quite evidently is not deterred by the argument he presents—in this essay itself, as well as subsequently—from asserting quite a number of things about our constitution and the manner in which this all works, with evident confidence. More importantly, the author of this essay is undeniably *early* Nietzsche—still very much a rather Schopenhauerian Kantian, and just beginning to try his philosophical wings. The account he sketches is one that he subsequently rethought in fundamental and important ways. It was some time before it dawned upon him that the dream of knowledge against which he here inveighs is based on a picture that is deeply flawed; and that when this is recognized, both the dream and its critique are mooted. It is both true and important to recognize that Nietzsche began by thinking in this way, as well as in the way he does in *The Birth of Tragedy*. Yet it does seem to me that he shows himself in this essay already to be on the way to his eventual (rather Wittgensteinian) self-extrication from the corner into which he here seems to paint himself.

Shortly thereafter, in *On the Uses and Disadvantages of History for Life* (1874), the second of his subsequently titled *Unfashionable Reflections*, Nietzsche quite evidently takes it for granted that there is (and therefore can be) such a thing as knowledge—at least of *historical* phenomena. What interests him in this essay is the subsequent question of the various ways in which such knowledge and knowing may be conceived, pursued, and used, and their advantages and disadvantages for human life. We *need* such knowledge, he observes in the foreword—and not for the sorts of reasons it is sought by the mere "idler in the *Garten des Wissens* [garden of knowledge]," as an amusement or diversion (*UDH* foreword). It is "only for the purpose of life," or for its ability to be of such service, that "every man and every nation, in accordance with its goals, energies and needs, requires *eine gewisse Kenntnis* [a certain (sort of) knowledge] of the past" (*UDH* 4). But this allows for several rather robust forms of such knowledge, on different levels, in addition to the several different forms of historical knowledge Nietzsche goes on to distinguish and assess.

In *Human*, Nietzsche continues to insist upon the importance of raising "the question concerning the utility of *Erkenntnis* [knowledge]" (*HH* I:6). And he again concerns himself with the problem of whether "the aftereffect of *Erkenntnis*" is something to worry about (*HH* I:34)—which obviously can only *be* a problem if one thinks that *Erkenntnis* in some meaningful sense of the term is a human possibility that conceivably might *have* real "aftereffects" in the lives of those who go in for it. But his focus shifts in the direction of the contrast he discerns between the kind of knowledge that is attainable through *wissenschaftlich* inquiry, and another kind envisioned "in the Socratic schools" and their descendants down to the present, in which the question was posed, so fatefully for the history of philosophy: "What is the kind of *Erkenntnis* through which man can live most happily?" For, he laments, preoccupation with *this* question constricted and continues to constrict "the arteries of *wissenschaftlichen* inquiry" (*HH* I:7).[5]

It is one of the main themes of the several parts of *Human* that such *wissenschaftlich* research can and does contribute meaningfully and significantly to the advancement of human knowledge, where not only historical phenomena but also life and the world more generally are concerned. Indeed, Nietzsche contrasts it in precisely this respect both to ordinary language, which has long been erroneously supposed to afford "*Erkenntnis* of the world" and indeed "the highest *Wissen* [knowledge] of things," and to the formalisms of logic and mathematics, to which "nothing in the real world [*wirklichen Welt*] corresponds" (*HH* I:11). So he is also prepared here to say that, while people may think that humanity's "arts and religions" enable one to "get closer to the actual true nature of the world [*wirklichen Wesen der Welt*] and to *Erkenntnis* of it" than one can otherwise, they are mistaken: one "actually does so," he significantly adds, "through *Wissenschaft*" (*HH* I:29). And here it would seem that he has in mind the *Naturwissenschaften* [sciences of nature] in particular.

This is not, however, because Nietzsche thinks that such research can uniquely lead us into a comprehension of "things in themselves" or of the very "essence of things." Rather, it is because he already has become convinced "that the thing-in-itself is worthy of Homeric laughter: that it appeared to be so much, indeed everything, and is actually empty—that is to say, empty of significance [*eigentlich leer, nämlich bedeutungs-leer ist*]" (*HH* I:16). And he has already begun to understand that this has profound implications for the understanding of what there may meaningfully be said to be, and of our situation and cognitive prospects with respect to it.

Another hint of the direction Nietzsche's thinking was taking, both modifying his focus in thinking about what there is to be known and broadening his understanding of the character of the knowledge of it that is humanly possible, is to be found in one of his "Assorted Opinions and Maxims" from the next year (1879), which became the first part of *Human*'s second volume. There he observes that, "for us to know ourselves [*um sich kennen zu lernen*], we need history, for the past continues to flow within us in a hundred waves"; and that "self-knowledge thus becomes all-encompassing knowledge [*so wird Selbst-Erkenntnis zur All-Erkenntnis*] with respect to everything past" (*HH* II:I:223).

In his next book, *Daybreak* (1881), Nietzsche strikingly suggests that "no sacrifice is too great" in relation to "the one tremendous goal" of "the knowledge of truth" [*die Erkenntnis der Wahrheit*]. He recognizes that the "drive for knowledge" [*Erkenntnistrieb*] in most human beings is not strong enough to impel them to do much "to advance knowledge" [*die Erkenntnis zu fördern*], and that it would take some doing to raise "enthusiasm for knowledge" [*die Begeisterung der Erkenntnis*] to the point at which it could actually become the object of "the tremendous idea" of "self-sacrificing humanity" (*D* 45). But he seemingly proudly proclaims that, in him and his kindred spirits, matters stand otherwise: "*Erkenntnis* has in us been transformed into a passion which shrinks at no sacrifice and at bottom fears nothing but its own extinction" (*D* 429).

Nietzsche also shows himself here to be convinced not only of the real possibility and disillusioned desirability of knowledge, but also of its multifariousness: "There are no exclusive knowledge-generating methods [*keine alleinwissendmachende Methode*] in *Wissenschaft*! We have to deal with things [*den Dingen*] experimentally, sometimes severely and sometimes gently, and alternately with justice [*Gerechtigkeit*], passion and coldness" (*D* 432).

VI

The first version of *Joyful Inquiry* was published a year later (1882). In it these same themes are galvanized by the crystallization of a new insight, anticipations of which have already been noted. It finds its most succinct expression in the second section or aphorism of the second "Book" of this work. In that Book's opening section (*JI* 57), having already dismissed any and all forms of metaphysical "thing-in-itself" or "higher-reality" realism, Nietzsche derides the "realism" of the *naive* realist who supposes that things "really are" as we experience, oblivious to our "human contribution" to their constitution. He then goes on, in the next section, to state his new insight, remarking: "it has given me the greatest difficulty, and continues to give me the greatest difficulty [*die grösste Mühe*]" to grasp and fully comprehend the point: that is, "to realize that *what things are called* [wie die Dinge heissen] is incomparably more important than what they are [*was sie sind*]"—or rather, he might more cautiously have said: than what they might be supposed to be independently of their coming to figure as they do in our experience. He continues:

> The reputation, name, and countenance, the importance, the usual weight and measure of a thing [*der Ruf, Name und Anschein, die Geltung, das übliche Maass und Gewicht eines Dinges*] [. . .] gradually grows to be part of the thing and turns into its very body [*allmählich gleichsam an- und eingewachsen und zu seinem Leibe selber geworden*]. What at first was appearance [*Schein*] in the end almost invariably becomes *Wesen* [the thing's very nature], and *functions* [wirkt] as such. How foolish it would be to suppose that one only needs to point out this origin [*Ursprung*] [. . .] in order to *destroy* the world that counts as genuine [*die als wesenhaft geltende Welt*], so-called *reality* [*Wirklichkeit*]. We can destroy only as creators.—But let us not forget this either: it suffices [*es genügt*] to create new names and esteemings [*Schätzungen*] and probabilities in order in the long run to create new "things" ["*Dinge*"]. (*JI* 58)

Nietzsche here recasts both the idea of "reality"—as the world in which we find ourselves and with which we have to deal—and the picture of our relation to it in a manner that opens the way to a new lease on life for a revised but nonetheless significant and substantial conception of knowledge and its attainability. I have previously characterized this conception in terms of *doing justice* (to a greater or lesser extent) to something in one's account of it.[6] With this passage before us, I might more fully gloss it in terms of doing so paradigmatically with respect to something that has (as it were) "come true" in a constitutive manner rendering it accessible to our subsequent efforts to make sense of it.

So, in a Viconian vein,[7] Nietzsche wrote in a note several years later, in 1884, "We can *comprehend* only a world that we ourselves have *made*" [*Wir können nur eine Welt begreifen, die wir selber gemacht haben*] (*KGW* VII 25[470]; *WP*

495[8]). Even if he were not to have come (as he did) to think that this limitation can be stretched, this for him already gives the *fröhlich Wissenschaftler*[9] plenty to do; for it encompasses our entire human world, a great deal of ourselves included. And, as he wrote in another note in the same year of ourselves as aspiring *Erkennenden*: "This contradictory creature has in his nature a great method of knowledge [*Methode der Erkenntnis*]: he feels many pros and cons, he raises himself *to justice—*to comprehension *beyond assessment in terms of good and evil* [*er erhebt sich zur Gerechtigkeit—zum Begreifen jenseits des Gut- und* Böseschätzen]" (i.e., to post-moralistic assessment) (*KGW* VII 26[119]; *WP* 259, emphasis added).

In the third Book of *Inquiry*, Nietzsche engages in a number of extended reflections concerning the origin and character of such knowledge as an actual human possibility, beginning with one on the "Origin of Knowledge" [*"Ursprung der Erkenntnis"*]. The human intellect "long produced nothing but errors," he writes, some of which were "useful and species-preserving"; but this was not the end of the matter: "*Erkennen* [coming to know] and striving after the true [*das Streben nach dem Wahren*] eventually took their place [*ordnete sich*] as a need among other needs." This was a development of profound significance:

> *Die Erkenntnis* thus became a piece of life itself, and hence a continually growing power—until eventually *die Erkenntnisse* [plural] collided with those primeval basic errors: both as life, both as power [*beide als Macht*], in the same human being. The thinker [*Der Denker*]: that is now the being in whom the drive for truth [*der Trieb zur Wahrheit*] and those life-preserving errors clash for their first fight, after the drive for truth has *proven* itself also to be a life-preserving power [*sich als eine lebenerhaltende Macht* bewiesen *hat*]. Compared to the significance of this fight, everything else is of no consequence [*Im Verhältniss zu der Wichtigkeit dieses Kampfes ist alles Andere gleichgültig*]. (*JI* 110)

Several sections later Nietzsche contends that there is indeed something qualitatively real and significant that "distinguishes us from older stages of *Erkenntnis und Wissenschaft*"; but it is a matter of "description" rather than "explanation." "We describe [*beschreiben*] better; we explain [*erklären*] as little as everyone previously" (*JI* 112). He may have come to aspire to do more than that; but his commitment to differences along these lines is evident, and is indicative of what the *Erkenntnis* of which he is continually speaking amounts to.

In the next section (*JI* 113), Nietzsche offers an account of how the capacity for "scientific [*wissenschaftliches*, rigorously cognitive] thinking"—and so for such knowledge—could have arisen in the sort of creature we once were, whose original abilities cannot have included anything of the kind. He casts his account in terms of the separate development and eventual confluence of a variety of drives or impulses [*Triebe*], which themselves came to be parts of our affective repertoire for quite different reasons. He concludes this section with a reflection on the possibility that a "higher organic system"—presumably of yet greater cognitive power—might yet arise in us, through a further joining of "artistic powers and the practical wisdom [*Weisheit*] of life" to "*wissenschaftlichen* thinking." This portrait is an anticipation of the sort of new-philosophical thinking Nietzsche subsequently not only preached but himself attempted to practice. And in the following section he significantly adds two more ingredients to the mix, the importance of which to the efficacy of the outcome cognitively speaking is not gainsaid by their problematic moral pedigree: "our *Redlichkeit* [intellectual integrity] and *Gerechtigkeit* [justice]" (*JI* 114).[10]

Toward the end of the first version of *Inquiry*'s last (fourth) Book, Nietzsche returns to this topic in an aphorism entitled "What Knowing Means" ["*Was heisst erkennen*"]. At its conclusion he observes that "precisely philosophers are most apt to be led astray about the nature of *Erkennen*" by the fact that the kind of thinking with which *they* are most familiar—namely, their own—is so "calm" and "mild" that the roles played by the affects in all thinking and knowing are virtually invisible to them. In criticism of Spinoza, who had contrasted "knowing" [*intelligere*] with "laughing, lamenting, and cursing," Nietzsche contends rather that it actually is a kind of thinking involving something like all three at once:

> Before *ein Erkennen* [an instance of knowing] is possible, each of these instincts first must have presented its one-sided view of the thing or event; after this comes the fight of these one-sided views, and occasionally this results in a mean, a calming, a right-granting [*eine Mitte, eine Beruhigung, ein Rechtgeben*] to all three sides, a kind of justice and contract [*Gerechtigkeit und Vertrag*] [. . .]. We suppose [. . .] that *intelligere* [knowing] [. . .] stands opposed to the instincts, while it is actually nothing but a *certain behavior of the instincts toward one another* [*ein* gewisses Verhalten der Triebe zu einander]. (*JI* 333)

Nietzsche is here making not just one point about *Erkennen*, but two: the point he emphasizes in the last sentence cited, about what he supposes to be going on when knowing occurs, and a second one: namely, that this first point notwithstanding, *it does occur*. We may lack any God-given organs of immaculate conception and cognition; but this lack has been made good, at least to an extent, thanks to our very "maculate" psychology, which is capable of working in a way that serendipitously (if also dangerously) makes possible certain sorts and degrees of human knowing (conceived on the model of "doing justice").

In elaboration of this point, Nietzsche immediately goes on with two of the most striking (and, for present purposes, highly relevant) aphorisms or sections in the entire work: a first one (*JI* 334) on "learning to love" [*lieben lernen*], and the next in praise of natural science (entitled—in the manner of a celebratory salutation—"*Hoch die Physik!*" or "Here's to Physics!"). The gist of the first of these sections is that, if we are ever to come to love a piece of music (his example) or anything else, we must (and can) open ourselves up to it and attend to it with all the care and sensitivity we can muster. In so describing what "learning to love" involves, Nietzsche is describing a humanly possible form of *learning to know* as well, and characterizing both its manner and something of its nature.

In the second of these sections (*JI* 335), Nietzsche turns to something seemingly radically different: to the natural sciences, paradigmatically exemplified for him by "physics"—which he deems to be valuable not only as a kind of activity that is as indisputably cognitive in nature and upshot as anything can be, but also as a corrective to moralistic prejudices and ways of thinking about ourselves. So, after proclaiming that "we *want to become those who we are* [wollen Die werden, die wir sind]—the new, the unique, the incomparable, the self-legislators, the self-creators!," he continues: "To that end we must become the best learners and discoverers [*Lerner und Entdecker*] of everything that is lawful and necessary in the world [*alles Gesetzlichen und Notwendingen in der Welt*]: we must become *physicists* in order to be able to be *creators* in this sense—while hitherto all valuations and ideals have been based on *Unkenntnis* [ignorance] of physics or were constructed in *contradiction* to it. Therefore: here's to physics! And even more so to that which *compels* [zwingt] us to it—our *Redlichkeit* [honesty, intellectual integrity]!" (*JI* 335).

One can hardly imagine a more ringing endorsement of the idea that something deserving of the name of "knowledge" is humanly possible, involving our coming to think about things as diverse as music and the phenomena with which physics deals in ways doing more justice to them than is ordinarily done. Yet Nietzsche does offer another that goes even further, in this same concluding part of the first (1882) version of *Inquiry*; and in doing so he importantly suggests another way in which the pursuit of knowledge can be motivated—no less healthily, and perhaps even more powerfully—without subverting its cognitivity: "And *Erkenntnis* itself: let it be something else for others [. . .]; for me it is a world of dangers and victories in which heroic feelings, too, find places to dance and play. '*Life as a means to* Erkenntnis'—with this principle in one's heart one can live not only boldly but even joyfully [*fröhlich*], and laugh joyfully too!" (*JI* 324).

It may be that this "principle" is not Nietzsche's last word on the subject even in *Inquiry*, and that his bottom line is (or at any rate soon came to be) that knowledge actually *matters* only as a means to or occasion of something else (here "learning to love" and "becoming those who we are"; subsequently also "creating"). But making that point about knowledge is not denying its human possibility (which it actually presupposes), or the possibility of its coming to be powered by our affective nature in the way Nietzsche here expresses (with clear relevance to the understanding of the work's title).

VII

In *Thus Spoke Zarathustra*, the first two parts of which were published the next year (1883), knowers and knowing come in not only for recognition but for praise—even though one of the basic themes of this entire work is that the most important kind of spirituality is not knowing but *creating*. So Nietzsche has Zarathustra say: "*Geist* [spirit] is the life that itself cuts into life," and: "with its own agony it increases its own *Wissen*." *Geist* is said to "move mountains"; but for Nietzsche's Zarathustra, "*der Erkennende* [the knower] shall learn to *build* with mountains," putting the formidable mass of hard-won knowledge attained to creatively constructive use rather than merely continuing to add to it. Knowing per se may not be "the meaning of the earth"; that is here proclaimed to be *Übermenschlichkeit*—humanity surpassing itself. But it is seen as both a means to it (in a crucial supporting role) and, in its more refined and developed forms, as an instance of it.

So Nietzsche has Zarathustra report having been told by "life itself," in the famous speech "On Self-Overcoming," that "you, too, *Erkennender*, are only a path and footprint of my will; truly, my will to power walks also in the boots of your will to truth!" (*Z* II:12). This passage echoes a point made in a note from the same period (1884) that is of considerable importance for the understanding of Nietzsche's thinking with respect to both the human possibility of a "will to truth" and the possibility of its emancipation from its moralistic genealogy: "If the morality of 'thou shalt not lie' is rejected, the 'sense for truth' [*der 'Sinn für Wahrheit'*] will have to legitimize itself before another tribunal: as a means of the preservation of humankind, as *power-will* [*Macht-wille*]" (*KGW* VII 25[470]; *WP* 495). (What earns it its place among the jewels in the crown of enhanced forms of higher spirituality—the admirability of its various forms—is one thing [or type of thing], however; the specific cognitive import of its outcomes is another. They are, for Nietzsche, independent variables.)

A further extension of this line of thought is to be found in the speech "On Immaculate *Erkenntnis*."[11] The point Nietzsche has Zarathustra make here is that there is nothing unsullied or "immaculate" [*unbefleckten*] about the interest that animates the pursuit of knowledge, and that it is hypocritical of those who would be "immaculate" or "pure knowers" [*Rein-Erkennenden*] in their contemplation of all things to profess that they "want nothing from them, except to be allowed to be present before them like a mirror with a hundred eyes." Where there is interest, he contends, there is desire; and such desire in its most truly pure and innocent form is unashamedly creative and procreative. Knowing actually devoid of all desire, were it to be humanly possible, would be utterly sterile. But its interestedness, far from inevitably and hopelessly distorting and so invalidating it, is actually what opens its eyes, and then makes something of what comes to be seen. And so Nietzsche has Zarathustra conclude by saying: "And this is what *Erkenntnis* means to *me*: all that is deep [*alles Tiefe*] shall be raised—to my height!" (*Z* II:15).

Finally, one of the last topics on which Nietzsche has Zarathustra express himself, near the end of the fourth (and last) part of the work, is none other than *Wissenschaft*. This section shares the strangeness of most of the rest of the Fourth Part; but it makes several broad and important points very vividly. It begins with an attempt on the part of a character called "the Conscientious of Spirit" [*der Gewissenhafte des Geistes*] to lay claim to *Wissenschaft* on behalf of the timid, small-minded fearfulness Nietzsche has in mind, as heir and product of the tradition of the same sort of mentality in morality. But Nietzsche has Zarathustra refuse to accept the claim. Zarathustra instead appropriates the mantle of *Wissenschaft* in the name of a radically different sort of spirituality, characterized by a transfigured form of the "courage" of our most daring and adventuresome progenitors.

There may indeed be a kind of *Wissenschaft* and an approach to it that is of the small-minded sort; but *Wissenschaft* at its best, for Zarathustra and Nietzsche, is a very different sort of thing. Zarathustra is in the process of describing it—"*This* courage, finally refined, spiritualized, spiritual, this human courage with eagles' wings and serpents' wisdom"—and is obviously about to call it by the name "*Wissenschaft*" when his unruly companions interrupt to name *him* instead, to his evident annoyance (*Z* IV:15, "On *Wissenschaft*"). But there is something to their confusion, because for Nietzsche that sort of spirituality is common to both. He thus winds up according this sort of endeavor a high rank among activities of which human beings are capable, even if it is

deemed *to matter* chiefly as a means toward or an instance of the enhancement of life, rather than as an end in its own right or owing to the intrinsic
worth of its various outcomes.

VIII

Nietzsche's critique of the ideas of "truth" and "knowledge" in his next book,
Beyond Good and Evil (1886), may be seen actually to be directed primarily against absolutizing artificial *versions* of them that he contends have long
found favor among the metaphysically minded and their latter-day philosophical and scientistic kindred spirits. And their critique in turn is preparatory to their replacement by alternative versions, according better with what
is actually possible along these lines. This *Prelude to a Philosophy of the Future* (as it is subtitled) involves a critical reckoning with general tendencies of
philosophy to date, to set the stage; and the ways in which philosophers have
tended to conceive of "truth" and "knowledge" are prominent among them.

So Nietzsche attempts to problematize what he takes to be philosophers'
usual way of conceiving of "truth" in the preface, and extends this treatment
to what has become of the idea of "knowledge" in their hands in the first part
of the book. In its first section, he raises the question of the "value" of truth
(and so also of knowledge) of any sort (*BGE* 1). In the second, he suggests that
philosophers commonly have been led by a "faith in opposite values," and by
a longing for a reality more perfect and congenial to them than "this transi-
tory, seductive, deceptive, paltry world," to "bestir themselves about '*Wissen*'
['knowing'], about something that is finally baptized solemnly as '*die Wahrheit*'" (*BGE* 2). Nietzsche does not always use scare quotes to make it so clear
that he is referring to what he thinks of as the *metaphysical construal* of these
notions, as he does here; but once one realizes that this is one of his main targets, his uses of them in scare-quoted fashion become fairly readily discernible.

Thus he here throws down the gauntlet to philosophers who have bought
into absolutizing conceptions of truth and knowledge, in effect saying: "If
that is what you mean by 'truth' and 'knowledge,' then there is nothing that
answers to them." And he continues this running battle both in subsequent
books and in his notebooks, in which a good deal of material along these lines
is to be found. But that is only a part of what he here and subsequently has to
say and tries to do in this general connection. The other and more important
side of the coin is to rescue and rehabilitate these notions, construing them
in a manner *according with their paradigmatic instances*, and enabling significant distinctions to be made within the parameters of human possibility.

One of the passages that has vexed the understanding of Nietzsche's thinking with respect to truth and knowledge is the penultimate section of the first part of this book. In this section he discusses the "physicists'" conception of the world in terms of "laws of nature" and nature's "conformity" to them, and an alternative conception of the world dispensing with such notions in favor of power relationships and the disposition to enter into them (his "will to power" idea and hypothesis). He refers to the former as "no matter of fact" but rather the physicists' *Ausdeutung* [construal]—and then indicates that he is quite prepared to grant that the alternative cast in terms of "will to power" is "only interpretation [*nur Interpretation*] as well" (*BGE* 22).

As I read this section, it has no dire or radical consequences at all for the idea that Nietzsche is committed to a significant form of cognitivity, and indeed contributes usefully to its elaboration. First, it should be noted that Nietzsche begins by characterizing himself as "an old philologist," who can't help pointing out "bad ways of interpreting" [*schlechte Interpretations-Künste*]— thereby implying that "interpreting" is something that can be done *more or less well*, and that different interpretations of something not only may differ from each other but also stand in qualitatively different relations of *justice* to that which is being interpreted. (Recall Nietzsche's 1884 note [*KGW* VII 26[119]; *WP* 259] in which he writes of our having in our nature "a great method of *knowledge*" [*eine große Methode der* Erkenntnis]—namely, that we "feel many pros and cons," and are able to avail ourselves of that capacity "to raise ourselves *to justice* [zur Gerechtigkeit]"—that is, to richly informed and well-considered comprehension that "does justice" to the matter under consideration [*Begreifen*].)

Second: the alternative interpretations under consideration are very broad-scale and general, and so are far from typical examples of candidates for positive cognitive verdicts. Even if one were to conclude that neither of them nor any other such sweeping interpretive claim is or could be deserving of such a verdict, therefore, this would settle nothing with respect to the viability of the candidacy of more modest claims.

But third, and perhaps most important: one of the lessons to be learned here is that doing some measure of justice to whatever is under consideration is what coming to know (and therefore knowledge and comprehension) basically amounts to. And this is something differing interpretations can do, more or less well and fully, and in differing respects or at differing levels of consideration. One doesn't have to get something exactly and exhaustively right to *get it at all*. Moreover, the idea of "getting it exactly right" does not even have to make sense in many instances (e.g., a war, work of literature, or episode in cosmological or evolutionary history) for the ideas of "knowing something about it" and "understanding something of it" to make perfectly good sense.

And, in any event, if there can be "schlechte [bad] *Interpretations-Künste* [ways of interpreting]," it must be possible for there to be *better* ones as well, that are not to be equally faulted, even if they, too, remain "interpretations" none of which may be the last word on their subjects, rather than plain and perfect articulations of unadorned fact.

In the very next section (*BGE* 23), Nietzsche turns to another domain in which it does not have to make sense to imagine getting things exactly right for it to make good sense to speak of comprehension and knowledge, and he specifically cites it as just such a domain par excellence: namely, "psychology." "This immense and almost new domain of dangerous *Erkenntnisse* [plural; instances of knowledge]," he contends, is now to be recognized as "the queen of the *Wissenschaften*" as well as "the path to the fundamental problems." And it is of no little interest that, in this section, he moves comfortably between speaking in terms of both *Hypothese* [hypothesis] and *Lehre* [theory] in connection with his own overtly professed understanding of psychology "as study of the forms and *theory of the development of the will to power*" [*als Morphologie und* Entwicklungslehre des Willens zur Macht].

It is clear that Nietzsche here is deeming it appropriate to lay claim to *Erkenntnis* when there is warrant to suppose that an account (hypothesis, theory, interpretation) does at least some measure of justice to whatever is under consideration—notwithstanding its being provisional, less than certain, less than complete, perhaps somewhat metaphorical, and capable of being refined and developed or improved upon. If one is so fastidious in one's use of the terms *truth* and *knowledge* that one is loath to apply them ("strictly speaking") in any case in which far more rigorous standards are not met, one is free to abstain; and if one will settle for nothing less, so be it. But Nietzsche is not of that company, even if he sometimes speaks its language to show the consequences of their doing so; and as far as he is concerned, those consequences are *their* problem, not his. And he is by no means prepared to relinquish the very idea of knowledge to them, or to forswear his own claims to comprehension, let alone to deny them to the *Wissenschaften* and to other forms of inquiry into things historical, cultural, and human—even though he readily allows and often insists upon the often limited, perspectival character of the comprehension in question.

It is in this spirit that I suggest *Beyond*'s famous section 36 should be understood—culminating, after the indication of a variety of suppositions that conceivably could turn out to be satisfied, in the proclamation: "Then one would have gained the right to determine *all* efficient force univocally as: *will to power*" [*So hätte man damit sich das Recht verschafft* alle *wirkende Kraft eindeutig zu bestimmen als*: Wille zur Macht] (*BGE* 36). In this instance, however, Nietzsche is more tentative than he is in section 23, and does not venture (at least here, on this occasion) to explicitly affirm this extension of the "will to power" hypothesis from candidacy for cognitive standing to the status of purported *Erkenntnis*.

It is clearly Nietzsche's surmise in this passage, however, that something like *his* "proposition" to this effect is the case ("*wie es* mein *Satz ist*"); and he makes it equally clear that he considers this interpretation to be at least a genuine candidate for that status. Indeed, he even contends that making the "experiment" [*Versuch*] of considering whether it "suffices" to enable one to "understand" [*verstehen*] all physical and biological as well as psychological processes is "commanded by the conscience of *method*" [*vom Gewissen der* Methode *geboten*]. And while he does not claim to have done so, this is indicative of one of the things he considers to be relevant to the establishment of cognitive warrant.

This echoes Nietzsche's previous reference to "method, which must be essentially principle-thriftiness [*wesentlich Principien-Sparsamkeit sein muss*]" (*BGE* 13). (Interestingly, he makes this remark in connection with another reference to the same "will to power" interpretation he suggests here—on that occasion, however, not tentatively and hypothetically, but rather quite straightforwardly: "Life itself is will to power" [*Leben selbst ist Wille zur Macht*], he flatly asserts, and continues: "Self-preservation is only one of the indirect and most frequent results thereof.")

But *BGE* 36 supplements that point with the addition of another: that this condition ("principle-thriftiness") only comes into play in conjunction with the requirement that one start with something one is sufficiently well acquainted to place one's invocation of it beyond dispute. The opening lines of the section clearly indicate that Nietzsche supposes this requirement to be satisfied in this instance. Even if that supposition is questioned or even disputed, however, the point itself remains a significant one *for his conception of knowledge and its attainability*. Knowledge, for him, is in the first instance knowledge by acquaintance; and the stronger one's claim may be to authenticity of acquaintance, the strong one's "right" to lay claim to knowledge will be.

In the opening section of the part of *Beyond* entitled "*Wir Gelehrten*" ["We Sophisticates"], Nietzsche observes that "*Die Wissenschaft* is flourishing today," while philosophy has abstemiously and pathetically been "reduced to [mere] 'theory of knowledge' ['*Erkenntnistheorie*']"; and he laments this "unseemly and harmful shift in the respective ranks of *Wissenschaft* and philosophy." He does so both because this has led the sciences "with an excess of high spirits and a lack of understanding" to presume to "play the 'master,'" overestimating themselves, and because it represents an abdication of philosophy from its own responsibilities "beyond the threshold" at which it stops (*BGE* 204).

Devoting itself to "theory of knowledge," the neo-Kantian academic philosophy he has in mind abstains from substantive cognitive endeavor, leaving that to the *Wissenschaften*; while these disciplines, with their ever-increasing flood of results, are nonetheless limited, by the restricted scope and forms of such endeavor in which they specialize. But for Nietzsche there are things to be comprehended that matter and yet are invisible to or inadequately discernible in their cognitive lenses. The kinds of knowledge they can and do afford may neglect more than they capture, and so, if not supplemented and put into perspective, may lead us astray.

The problem with which Nietzsche is concerned here is not the impossibility, unreality, or artificiality of all knowledge, but rather the *profusion* of certain forms of it and the *neglect of others* that are humanly possible but differently attainable. As he goes on to observe in the next section, "The scope and the tower-building of the *Wissenschaften* has grown to be enormous," while the differing course and requirements for a philosopher to "attain his own height"—namely, one sufficing to make possible achieving an overview (*Überblick*), developing a comprehensive picture (*Umblick*), attaining a higher-level perspective (*Niederblick*)—are becoming ever more difficult (*BGE* 205).

Difficult—but not impossible; and Nietzsche goes on to proclaim the possibility of exceptions surpassing even the first-rate "*philosophische Arbeiter*" [philosophical worker] norm (*BGE* 211). Those he heralds as "philosophers of the future" are to be not only astute "skeptics" and "critics" but also *Versucher* (experimenters and [at]tempters), impelled by a "passion for *Erkenntnis*" even to the point of "audacious and painful experiments." They must (and so can) come to "be *able* to see with many different eyes and consciences, from a height and into every distance, from the depths into every height, from a nook into every expanse" (*BGE* 210). And so they must be capable of many forms of acquaintance, comprehension, and understanding.

Nietzsche observes that there is a kind of madness in the departure from established ways of thinking ventured in the reinterpretive undertaking within which his kind of psychology finds its place. Yet it also involves and paradigmatically exemplifies the sort of cognitive project he does not want to leave entirely to the *Wissenschaften*, and places high on the philosophical agenda he both adopts and bequeaths to his "future philosophers": "To translate man back into nature [. . .]; to see to it that man henceforth stands before man as even today, hardened in the discipline of *Wissenschaft*, he stands before the *rest* of nature [. . .] that may be a strange and crazy task, but it is a *task*—who would deny that?" (*BGE* 230). Nietzsche goes on to remark that to ask "Why did we choose this crazy task?" is in effect to ask "Why [strive for] knowledge at all?" ["*warum überhaupt Erkenntnis?*"]. He professes to "have found and find no answer" to this question—perhaps meaning: none that is not problematic with respect to its "value for life." He speculates on a genealogical answer to it in an early section of the fifth Book added to *Inquiry* in the expanded version published the next year (1887).

But that answer—in terms of a suspiciously motivated "metaphysical faith" and predilection for "another world than the world of life, nature, and history" (*JI* 344)—is only a part of the whole story for him, as has already been seen. There may indeed be a tale to tell about the origin of the "*will to* truth" in this type of all-too-human condition, and about its kinship with what he calls the "ascetic ideal" in the third essay of *Genealogy*. But Nietzsche also understood that this complex and artificial and yet nonetheless real human interest can be grafted onto a deeper and stronger part of our affective constitution. And it is at least his hope, if not his confident expectation, that it can be further sublimated and transfigured, and given new employment in the service of human life and its enhancement.

IX

In the opening section of this 1887 fifth Book of *Inquiry*, Nietzsche reflects upon the situation in which "we philosophers and 'free spirits'" find ourselves in the aftermath of "the news that 'the old god is dead,'" and declares himself to be in a celebrative mood—notwithstanding the daunting magnitude and possible long-range consequences of the event. Why? Because "all the daring of the *Erkennenden* is permitted again; the sea, *our* sea, lies open again" (*JI* 343). And however motivationally problematic the "unconditioned will to truth [*Wille zur Wahrheit*]" may be, for the reasons Nietzsche suggests in the following section (*JI* 344), he does not appear to have any doubts about the prospects of "we *Erkennenden* of today" who are impelled to venture out upon these newly open seas, and into what he here refers to as "the *Reich* [realm] of *Erkenntnis*." It may remain to be seen how extensive this *Reich* will turn out to be; but Nietzsche clearly is not thinking small here. So also he asserts, a few sections later: "We know it well [*Wir wissen es*], the world in which we live is ungodly, immoral, 'inhuman'; we have interpreted it far too long in a false and mendacious way" (*JI* 346).

There are several subsequent sections, akin to some notes in his notebooks from this period, in which Nietzsche expresses himself in a seemingly very different and indeed contrary manner, with respect to what passes for knowledge both in ordinary contexts and among the more sophisticated. So, for example, in the very important section entitled "On the 'Genius of the Species'" (*JI* 354), he offers an account of what might be called "the genealogy of human consciousness" in terms of the imposition upon our originally merely "animal consciousness" of language as a "net of communication" that was needed for social purposes. And he concludes by asserting that we therefore "simply lack any organ [*Organ*] for 'knowing' ['Erkennen'], for 'truth' [*die 'Wahrheit'*]"—that is, *as purists imagine them*. Continuing to use scare quotes, he writes: "We '*wissen*' ['know'] (or we believe or imagine) just as much as may be *useful* in the interests of the human herd, the species."

But this dismissive account of the scare-quoted versions of these notions leaves the door quite open to the emergence of a serendipitous psycho-historically engendered *substitute* for such a cognitively dedicated special "organ" (such as our sight-dedicated eyes), rendering conceivable and attainable a measure of genuine comprehension of at least some of what goes on in, among, and around us. Indeed, if Nietzsche is at all on target in this section, it itself represents a case in point. We also "simply lack any organ" for flying; but in the course of human events we have nonetheless contrived ways of doing so.

Similarly, in the next section, on "The Origin of Our Concept of '*Erkenntnis*,'" Nietzsche observes that what ordinary people and philosophers alike typically "understand by *Erkenntnis*," and "want when they want *Erkenntnis*," is basically nothing more than being able to "relate something strange to something familiar [*etwas Bekanntes*]." But this is by no means the end of the matter for him, as is clear from his comment on this circumstance that "the familiar [*Bekannte*] is the accustomed [*Gewöhnte*], and the accustomed is the most difficult of all to know [*erkennen*]" (*JI* 355). It is evidently both humanly possible and cognitively desirable for Nietzsche (by *wissenschaftlich* and also Nietzschean-philosophical standards), to aspire to forms and measures of comprehension that go well beyond what commonly passes for *Erkenntnis*, even if *Erkenntnis* did start out as nothing more than that.

It is a part of Nietzsche's purpose here to reiterate that there is—or at least can and should be—more to human comprehension than "*naturwissenschaftlicher Erkenntnisse*," the scope and "ultimate validity" of which he suggests to be questionable two sections later (*JI* 357). His point is *not* that such *Erkenntnis* is not really *Erkenntnis* at all. Rather, it is that at least in many instances it leaves a good deal to be desired in the justice it does to its objects; and it is limited to the bounds of its specific domain of inquiry.[12]

Nietzsche presses this point in one of most notable sections in the fifth Book, entitled "'*Wissenschaft*' as Prejudice" (*JI* 373). Here he derides "the faith [*Glaube*] with which so many materialistic natural scientists [*Naturforscher*] rest content nowadays," namely, that they are dealing with a world "that can be mastered completely and forever with the aid of our square little human reason." He contends rather that, where "existence" [*das Dasein*] is concerned, "one should not wish to strip it of its *multiply interpretable* [vieldeutigen] character." Why? Because this is "demanded by good taste"—that is, Nietzsche says, addressing the *Naturwissenschaftler* [natural scientist], "the taste of reverence for all that lies beyond your horizon." For that way of thinking, while it might do considerable justice to some features of things, may be oblivious to others.

Thus Nietzsche does not deny the "correctness" of interpreting the world as natural scientists do, *as far as it goes*; but he chastises them for their "crude and naive" idea "that only a world-interpretation [*Welt-Interpretation*] is right through which *you* are vindicated [*zu Rechte besteht*], and that can be scientifically pursued and researched in *your* sense"—that is, one that "allows counting, calculating, weighing, seeing and touching, and nothing more." His problem is *not* with the "counting" and "calculating" as such; it is with the "nothing more." A "'scientific' world-interpretation" attentive to *nothing more* than this sort of thing, Nietzsche surmises, will grasp only what "quite probably" [*recht wahrscheinlich*] is "precisely what is most superficial and external about existence [*das Oberflächlichste und Äusserlichste vom Dasein*]."

This is *not* to deny that such research yields *knowledge*; rather, it is to suggest that the knowledge it yields may only scratch the surface. So Nietzsche goes on to observe that, the genuineness of that knowledge as knowledge notwithstanding, *if* the interpretation based upon it is taken to be *the whole story*, it "might still be one of the *stupidest* [*dümmsten*]—that is, most meaning-impoverished [*sinnärmsten*]—of all possible world-interpretations." He drives home his point by means of a particularly well-chosen example: "Supposing that one assessed the *worth* [*Wert*] of a piece of music in terms of how much of it could be counted, calculated, and expressed in formulas: how absurd such a '*wissenschaftliche*' assessment of the music would be! What would one have comprehended, understood, known [*begriffen, verstanden, erkannt*] of it? Nothing, nothing whatsoever, of what is actually 'music' in it! [*was eigentlich an ihr 'Musik' ist!*]" (*JI* 373). Nietzsche's choice of music as his example is striking: it is something undeniably real, but it also is something the reality of which is very evidently a part of *human* reality, even if also involving a considerable variety of physical and physiological phenomena and processes.

X

In *Genealogy*, Nietzsche's next book (also 1887), Nietzsche focuses his attention upon the attainability of a new and important sort of *Erkenntnis* with respect to another type of phenomenon that likewise is both undeniably real and evidently human: namely, human moralities (*die Moral*). But his concern in this book is not only with them; for he makes it quite clear from the outset that he intends thereby also to contribute to the deeper and better comprehension of ourselves as *Erkennenden*—and further, of ourselves more generally, as the kind of creature we human beings have become. So he begins his preface to the book with the reflection that "we *Erkennenden*" are "unacquainted with ourselves" [*uns unbekannt*], and "do not understand ourselves" [*verstehen uns nicht*]. Indeed, he remarks, "we are not 'knowers' with respect to ourselves" [*für uns sind wir keine 'Erkennenden'*] (*GM* P:1). But that is not because the very idea of such comprehension is meaningless or incoherent, or because there is nothing to be known. This is a criticism for which "we" are to be faulted.

That is a situation Nietzsche had been trying to remedy in his philosophical writings from the very outset, in *Human*—which he also begins with the lament that it is a common failing of philosophers that they do not know themselves, and "do not want to learn that *der Mensch* has *become* [*geworden ist*], that the ability to know [*Erkenntnisvermögen*] has *become*" (*HH* I:2). (A propos of a point just made above: but this is also to say that that ability *has* "become," our lack of any "organ" for it notwithstanding.) And there is no better example of the kind of "historical philosophizing" he calls for in that very context and aphorism than *Genealogy*.

Nietzsche frames each of the three essays in terms of a fundamental question about a significant aspect of our attained humanity; and in the course of each he touches upon others, sometimes at length. Our comprehension of ourselves in these various respects (as well as the kind of morality that has come to prevail) is something to which he is clearly intent upon contributing, through the inquiries in which the book consists. And he characterizes it as, at least in one respect, a further development of what he calls "my ideas on the *origination* [*Herkunft*] of our moral prejudices" (*GM* P:2).

Nietzsche's preface to *Genealogy* is of particular interest for present purposes. He may think that "we *Erkennenden*" are lacking in self-understanding; but he leaves no doubt that he considers himself to be one of them, to be proceeding as one of them in writing this book, and to be getting somewhere in doing so. Recall, for example, the previously cited passage in which he says that he finds himself still convinced of the soundness of these genealogical ideas, which had first occurred to him much earlier; and that this strengthens his "joyous [*frohe*] assurance" that they arose in him "from a *fundamental will* of *Erkenntnis* [literally, "knowledge-will"], pointing imperiously into the depths, speaking more and more precisely, demanding greater and greater precision. For this alone befits a philosopher" (*GM* P:2).

Coming immediately upon the heels of the publication of the expanded version of *Inquiry*, this might well stand as the credo of Nietzsche as just such a philosophical "*fröhlich Wissenschaftler*" [joyful inquirer]. For he is precisely intent upon coming up with interpretations of things that will do more illuminating justice to them than can be expected of the kinds of interpretations favored by the type of *Wissenschaftler* [scientific inquirer] he disparages in *JI* 373. It is clear from this passage that he is convinced of the possibility of *Erkenntnis* in cases of this sort, however incomplete, and of the reality and possible strength of motivation to attain it, however checkered the origins of that motivation might be.

Interestingly, in view of the way Nietzsche frames the music example in *JI* 373, he asserts here that his real interest is and long has been in "something much more important" than "hypothesizing about the origin of morality [*über den Ursprung der Moral*]": namely, "It had to do for me with the *value* of morality" [*Es handelt sich für mich um den* Wert *der Moral*] (*GM* P:5). That is something he does not purport even to address, let alone to settle, in this book. But he is very explicit about the conceivability and presumptive attainability of something he is prepared to call "knowledge" of the matters *preliminary* to it with which this book is immediately concerned. "We need a *critique* of moral values," he writes; "and for that there is needed a *Kenntnis* [knowledge] of the conditions and circumstances in which they grew, under which they evolved and changed."

It is this sort of *Kenntnis* to which the book's three essays in the first instance are intended to contribute: "a knowledge of a kind [*eine solche Kenntnis*] that has never yet existed or even been desired" (*GM* P:6). It is said to be the outcome of the "new questions, inquiries, conjectures, probabilities" he referred to a few sections earlier, that were prompted by his interest in the "origination of our moral prejudices," of which he had remarked: "how fortunate we are, we *Erkennenden*," if only we have the patience to let such inquiries ripen (*GM* P:3).

I shall not examine *Genealogy*'s three essays in detail here, having discussed them at some length in the previous chapter; but I would make several general observations with respect to them. First: Nietzsche is quite emphatic on the point that, unlike armchair, blue-sky moral theorizing, "*ein Moral-Genealogie*" has something *real* with which to deal: "the documentable, the actually confirmable, that which actually existed, in short the entire long hieroglyphic record, so hard to decipher, of the human moral past!" (*GM* P:7).

Second: his three-essay format—in each of which he takes a quite different tack—itself makes an important point: Nietzsche not only deems a multiply perspectival approach compatible with his avowedly cognitive aspirations here, but evidently considers it to be conducive to their advancement.

Third: the character of Nietzsche's presentations in the three essays shows that he thinks interpretive accounts of those sorts—that are at least as much exercises in imaginative sense-making as they are documentable digests of the historical record—can have cognitive significance of the kind he is after. And fourth (in keeping with these last two considerations): the sort of *Kenntnis* that is at issue here is not an all-or-nothing affair. Rather, it is a matter of a broadening and deepening comprehension of the basic character of the phenomena under consideration, to which other sorts of investigations and reflections might contribute further.

XI

One of Nietzsche's most important pronouncements, with respect to knowers and knowing. occurs in *Genealogy*'s third essay, on "The Meaning of Ascetic Ideals." There he begins by posing the question of the form one might expect "the ascetic ideal" to take if it is (so to speak) "induced to *philosophize*." He suggests that it might well take the form of "looking for *error* precisely where the instinct of life most unconditionally posits truth." And he concludes by expressing gratitude rather than antipathy for this further addition to the stew of ingredients that has rendered us both motivationally and intellectually capable of comprehending things in ways not only indifferent to but actually at variance with our vital interests, contrary to what one might (naturalistically) expect:

> But let us not be ungrateful, precisely as *Erkennende* [would-be knowers], with respect to such resolute reversals of accustomed perspectives and valuations [*gewöhnten Perspektiven und Wertungen*] [. . .]: to see differently in such a way for once, to *want* to see differently [*dergestalt einmal anders sehn, anders-sehn-wollen*], is no small discipline and preparation of the intellect for its future "objectivity"—the latter understood not as "contemplation without interest" (which is nonsensical and absurd), but rather as the ability *to control* one's Pro and Con [*das Vermögen, sein Für und Wider* in der Gewalt zu haben] and to engage and disengage them [*aus- und einzuhängen*]: so that one knows precisely how to make the *diversity* of perspectives and of affect-interpretations [*die* Verschiedenheit *der Perspektiven und der Affekt-Interpretationen*] useful for *Erkenntnis*.[13] (*GM* III:12)

The section proceeds to an exhortation to philosophers henceforth to guard against "the dangerous old concept-fable [*Begriffs-Fabelei*] that posited a 'pure will-less, painless, timeless subject of *Erkenntnis*'" and against such related and "contradictory concepts as 'pure reason,' 'absolute spirituality' and '*Erkenntnis an sich*' ['knowledge in itself']." For "these always require that we think of something that simply cannot be thought"—namely, "an eye turned in no particular direction, in which the active and interpreting forces, through which alone seeing becomes seeing *something*, are supposed to be lacking." Nietzsche then goes on to say: "There is *only* a perspective seeing, *only* a perspective '*Erkennen*'; and *the more* affects we allow to speak about the same matter [*dieselbe Sache*], *the more* eyes, diverse eyes, we know to bring into play upon *dieselbe Sache*, the more complete our 'concept' ['*Begriff*'] of it—and our 'objectivity'—will be" (*GM* III:12).[14]

In this passage Nietzsche restates a point he had made in the note of 1884 cited above, about the "great method of *Erkenntnis*" we have at our disposal thanks to our complex nature, owing to which we "feel many pros and cons," by means of which one at least has the possibility of "raising oneself to justice" (*KGW* VII 26[119]; *WP* 259). This is not to say, of course, that every perspectival "seeing" and "knowing" is on a par with every other, where some *Sache* [matter] or other is concerned; and it is not to say anything at all about whether it might make sense to suppose that some are more fully knowable in this way than others, and why. But it certainly is to imply that it makes good and important sense to attempt to proceed in this way (as Nietzsche himself happens to be doing) if coming *to know something better* is what one is after, and to suppose that it is possible to do so in at least some significant cases. And for Nietzsche, the genealogies of the kinds of "moral" phenomena he discusses are cases in point.

Another case in point for him, of a very different nature, has to do with our human constitution, and more specifically with the status of that into which he as "psychologist" and philosophical anthropologist inquires. So, for example, in *The Antichristian*, he writes: "We no longer *derive den Menschen* from '*Geist*' ['spirit'] or '*Gottheit*' ['divinity']; we have placed him back among the animals. [. . .] The 'pure spirit' is a pure stupidity: if we subtract [*abrechnen*] the nervous system and the senses—the 'mortal shroud'—*then we are making a mistake* [so verrechnen wir uns]—that's all [weiter nichts]!" (*A* 14). Here Nietzsche echoes a note of the same year (1888): "To know [*wissen*], e.g., that one has a nervous system (—but no 'soul'—) is still the privilege of the best informed [*Unterrichtetsten*]" (*KGW* VIII 14[179]; *WP* 229). His late writings contain many examples of cognitive claims of this sort—and also of indications of the cognitive significance of properly disciplined empirical observation, as when he writes, in *Twilight of the Idols*: "Today we have *Wissenschaft* precisely as far as we have resolved to *accept* the testimony of the senses—as we have learned to sharpen them, arm them, and think them through [*schärfen, bewaffnen, zu Ende denken lernten*]" (*TI* "Reason," 5).

Among Nietzsche's late works, *Genealogy* is particularly instructive, when one considers just how many things Nietzsche brings up in it, concerning which *enhanced comprehension* is suggested to be possible if properly pursued, and of what sorts they are. They include the sorts of psychological matters more generally into which tough-minded "investigators and microscopists of the soul" inquire, having "trained themselves to sacrifice all desirability to truth, *every* truth, even plain, harsh, ugly, repellent, unchristian, immoral truth," since "such truths do exist" [*Denn es gibt solche Wahrheiten*] (*GM* I:1).

These sorts of presumptively attainable comprehension also include the historical sources of various moral concepts (e.g., *GM* I:2; the important note at the end of the first essay; and II:6); the origins of various moral value judgments (*GM* I:3, 10, and the same note); the circumstances under which "man first became *an interesting animal*," and "the human soul in a higher sense acquired *depth* and became *evil*" (*GM* I:6); the manner in which *der Mensch* came to be "a tame and civilized animal, a *domestic animal*" (*GM* I:11); and the character of human action, such that "there is no 'being' behind doing, effecting, becoming; 'the doer' is merely a fiction added to the deed—the deed is everything" (*GM* I:13).

That is all just in the *first* essay! Matters Nietzsche goes on in the second essay to attempt to illuminate include "the paradoxical task that nature has set itself in the case of man," namely, "to breed an animal *that may promise* [*das versprechen darf*]" (*GM* II:1), and "how *responsibility* originated" (*GM* II:2); the human possibility not only of various all-too-human forms of humanity but also of "the *sovereign individual*" [*das* souveraine Individuum] (*GM* II:2); the phenomena of human "memory" and of various sorts of "conscience" (*GM* II:3–6 and 16 in particular); the various "prerogatives and showpieces of man" more generally, such as "reason, seriousness, mastery over the affects" (*GM* II:3); "the origin and purpose of punishment" (*GM* II:12); "the *Wesen* [very nature] of life, its *Wille zur Macht*" (*GM* II:12); and the phenomenon of "the *internalization* of man" [*die* Verinnerlichung *des Menschen*], through which "man first developed what was later called his 'soul'" (*GM* II:16).

And then, of course, in the third essay, what Nietzsche is after is comprehension of "the meaning of ascetic ideals," and their involvement in a considerable number of phenomena as diverse as *ressentiment*, hypermoralism,

Wagnerianism, religious enthusiasm, the passion for scientific research, and even the psychology of the "last idealists of *Erkenntnis*" with their "faith in truth" (*GM* III).

It is quite a list—and a very interesting and revealing one. For it consists almost entirely of *human phenomena*, and things *with a human history*: things that have occurred in the course of human events, things that are humanly possible, and things associated with human relations, human practices, human action, human language—in a word, things having to do with *human reality*. (The only partial exception is "the *Wesen* of life" [*GM* II:12]; but "life," too, even if generalized, is something of which human life is an instance and a part.) And human reality, while it has a history rife with contingencies, displays great diversity, and (for better or worse, or both) remains mutable, is nonetheless a reality sufficiently stable, rich, and reachable to keep would-be *Erkenner* busy for as long as it itself keeps going.

XII

In short: in his published writings from first to last, Nietzsche thus comes across as strongly committed to the attainability of a number of forms of *comprehension*, of matters of considerable diversity. Disparagements of what human knowledge generally amounts to do make an appearance here and there in these writings; but they are typically couched in a manner that leaves open the possibility of exceptions to the general rule, and that does not preclude the legitimacy of claims to cognitive significance in many further instances (for example, in the *Wissenschaften*), if and when these claims are appropriately qualified.

Where does this all leave us? What emerges from this comprehensive reading of Nietzsche on knowers and knowing? Several things, I believe, of no little significance both for the "nihilism" question and for our understanding of Nietzsche and his kind of philosophy more generally. First: Nietzsche's critical comments about certain philosophically refined conceptions of "truth" and "knowledge" notwithstanding, he clearly is convinced that all talk of knowledge is *not* much ado about nothing. It should be evident that for him, however problematic its "value for life" may be, its *attainment*—properly understood in the more "modest" sort of way he suggests to befit "historical philosophizing" (*HH* I:2)—is a real human possibility.

Second: "knowing" and "knowledge," and "true" and "truth" along with them, amount to something different in different contexts of discourse and reality, but *do* make sense to speak of *in* a number of these different contexts. It likewise makes sense to speak of ignorance, error, distortion, and superficiality in such contexts, but with somewhat different failures or shortcomings indicated in each case: for example, with respect to historical, cultural, social, psychological, biological, and physical phenomena.

Third: knowing (comprehension) for Nietzsche is not a black-and-white, all-or-nothing affair, but rather—at least in most of its forms and contexts (the *wissenschaftlich* included)—is typically a matter of degree and respect, as are the sorts of truth that are involved. The basic idea in all such cases would seem to be that of the extent to which or respects in which an account *does justice* to something, in its appropriately contextual sort of way, and a relevant sort of case can be made for it. But both the sort of justice that can reasonably be expected to be done and the sort of case that can reasonably be expected to be made vary considerably from one context to another.

Fourth: Nietzsche clearly regards the *Naturwissenschaften* (natural sciences) as forms of inquiry and practice that can and do yield such enhanced comprehension. They do so by way of refined forms of redescription of much that transpires in the world of which we are a part (our corporeality included). This also involves (and is warranted by) marshaling experience relating to what their practitioners come to know how to do, measure, and bring about (which is as much as most contemporary *Wissenschaftler* would claim for their disciplines anyhow). And the same applies, mutatis mutandis, to other *Wissenschaften* (both formal and historical), with respect to their domains.

Yet fifth: Nietzsche also considers the sorts of knowledge that are attainable along these lines to be far from the whole story in many kinds of cases, particularly where things human are concerned. In such cases knowledge might rather be said to be a matter of greater or lesser, broader or narrower, shallower or deeper, cloudier or clearer *understanding*, often by way of interpretive accounts drawing upon language bound up with the character of the phenomena in question, and informed by relevant sorts of acquaintance with them. The key idea in all of these sorts of cases is that of the possibility of attunement between forms of humanly engendered language and things coming to be what they are and to happen as they do, owing to their entwinement.

I take the upshot of all of this to be that knowing of various sorts, in Nietzsche's kind of philosophy from beginning to end, is certainly humanly possible, and can be meaningfully pursued. It is, very generally and loosely speaking, a matter of doing some measure of conceptual justice to something or another in the relational world of human reality, activity, and experience. That might be expanded to say: in our dealings with states of affairs either linked in their constitution with prefigurations of our thinking, or in which our involvements in other ways establish a basis for the development of a like attunement. That attunement may run thin as we extend our inquiries into phenomena that owe ever less to human contributions to their constitution; but most of the phenomena with respect to which Nietzsche either claims knowledge or proclaims its possibility—from the historical to the moral to the psychological and anthropological—are within this arena, either in whole or in significant part.

The key to Nietzschean-naturalized knowing, I suggest, and to understanding his kind of cognitivism, is a *shift of paradigms* of the cognitive situation. That shift is from the model of a *subject-object relation*, in which the paradigmatic "object of inquiry" is some sort of "things out there," to the model of an *involvement relation*, in which acquaintance with things we have made, deal with, take part in, or know how to do or bring about, becomes paradigmatic. Human reality is a reality that has come to be (and continues to be) constituted in the many ways it is through myriad developments both making possible and made possible by a host of such involvements, which themselves paradigmatically feature human language. We are on the inside, in the thick of it all—and so our problem is not to gain access, but rather to come to be able to *get our bearings hermeneutically* from within. And that is precisely where Nietzsche, "the old philologist" and *post*-nihilist, comes in, with his kind of philosophy.

XIII

I will sum up what I have said and tried to show in this chapter, with respect to the "Nietzsche as nihilist?" question (and to the question of its compatibility with and relation to his "naturalism"), in two versions—one preliminary and the other suitably qualified and restated—of my "thesis," with twenty elaborative propositions. I simply now state them here in summary fashion. My general case for them is the preceding comprehensive discussion of what he says about knowers and knowing in his published writings from beginning to end.

Thesis (preliminary version): Nietzsche's (kind of) naturalism is the *Aufhebung* of his (kind of) nihilism. (That is: its negation, preservation, transformation.) Propositions:

1. Nietzsche *is* a nihilist—if a nihilist is one who rejects the idea of a "true world of being," of "eternal facts" and essences, and "absolute Truths" (an "anti-absolutist"). (He does that.)

2. Nietzsche is *not* a nihilist—if a nihilist is one who not only rejects that idea, but *also* for whom the very ideas of reality, truth, and knowledge stand or fall (and so: fall) with it. (That's not him.)

3. Nietzsche *is* a nihilist—if a nihilist is one who rejects the idea of any sort of immutable absolute value/values (a "True Value denier"). (That's him.)

4. Nietzsche is *not* a nihilist—if a nihilist is not only one for whom there is no such thing, *but also* for whom any value/valuing that does not have that status is no real value at all. (Not him.)

5. Nietzsche *is* a nihilist—if a nihilist is one for whom "God (the God-idea) is dead," and the same applies to all other postulated absolutes (a metaphysical nihilist). (That's Nietzsche.)

6. Nietzsche is *not* a nihilist—if a "nihilist" is one for whom the "death of God" makes nonsense of the very ideas of reality, truth, knowledge, value, morals, and meaning. (That also is not him.)

7. The radical nihilism that gives up on these very ideas is one Nietzsche takes seriously, associates with "ascetic ideals," regards as pathological, deems a danger, and would overcome.

8. A "God's-shadows"-vanquishing metaphysical nihilism is both itself one of those "shadows" and a preparation for a "de-deified" post-absolutist and post-nihilistic recasting of these ideas.

9. Nietzsche's call for a "naturalizing" reinterpretation of human reality is indicative of what for him it is possible and important to do philosophically beyond that anti-absolutes nihilism.

10. What matters most to Nietzsche is what we might go on to do *humanly*—beyond that nihilism *and* reinterpretation—by way of "value creation" and "life enhancement."

11. Difference-making possibilities for doing so center upon transformations of human reality, through *Lebensformen* development and associated *sensibility* cultivation.

12. Human reality (*der Mensch*) is no fixed and immutable form; it is something that "has *become*"—contingently and transiently, but actually—and remains a work in progress.

13. Human reality not only is something that "has become"; it also has *become something*, the comprehension of which requires "*historische Philosophieren*."

14. What human reality has become is something about which there is much that *is the case* and can be discovered/ascertained; likewise the world in which we find ourselves.

15. Their interpretation is itself a human possibility, to which forms of perspectival experience and inquiry attuned to various of their forms and aspects may contribute.

16. These forms of humanly possible experience and inquiry include what have become the various *Wissenschaften* (social, cultural, and historical as well as natural-scientific).

17. Nietzsche's kind of "naturalizing" philosophy needs to be *scientifically informed*, but *is not scientistic* (not modeled and reliant entirely upon on natural-scientific thinking and findings).

18. This philosophical *fröhliche Wissenschaft* is to be an interpretive endeavor aspiring to comprehension, partnering with but not taking its cues entirely from the *Wissenschaften*.

19. Nietzsche's kind of nihilism (metaphysical nihilism) does not preclude or subvert this "naturalizing" reinterpretation, but rather enables it, yet by itself is not sufficient for it.

20. Thesis restated: *Nietzsche's naturalism (properly understood) may be conceived as a kind of philosophical* Aufhebung *of his nihilism (properly understood), in which that nihilism is incorporated into but also superseded by this reinterpretive project.*

Nietzsche as Existentialist?

The greatest recent event—that "God is dead," that the belief in the Christian god has
become unbelievable—is already beginning to cast its first shadows over Europe [. . .].
But in the main one may say: [. . . not] many people know as yet *what* this event really
means—and how much must collapse now because it was built upon this faith, propped
up by it, grown into it; for example, the whole of our European morality.

Joyful Inquiry, 343

Nietzsche has long been considered to have been one of the first "existentialists." For a time, in the aftermath of the Second World War, that identification seemed to make good strategic sense, both to his humanistically minded
friends and to his analytically minded foes. To his friends, placing him in the
philosophical company of the (French) existentialists, who had been on the
"right side," was a good way to counter the stain of his appropriation by
the Nazis and Fascists; while to his detractors, doing so was an equally effec-
tive way of dismissing him as undeserving of serious philosophical attention.
Nietzsche's subsequent appropriation by the poststructuralists provided
an alternative way of accomplishing the same two objectives, after the waning
of "existentialism" as a philosophical fad and fashion. (It came to be known
for a time in Anglo-American circles as "the French Nietzsche."[1]) To many
in the philosophical community who found both the poststructuralists and
their appropriation of Nietzsche to be uncongenial, however, the previous association of him with the serious and more philosophically respectable tradition of existential philosophy (or *Existenzphilosophie*) seemed to make better
sense. And that has remained the case among those who appreciate the growing interest in Nietzsche in the analytic philosophical community, but find
"the poststructuralist Nietzsche" to be barely recognizable as the "Nietzsche"
they thought they knew, and harder to take seriously.

I have long been troubled by and dissatisfied with all of these appropriations and associations of Nietzsche. To my way of thinking, none of them
comes anywhere close to doing justice to the Nietzsche (and his kind of philosophy) I know. Indeed all of these construals of his thought and philosophical concerns have seemed to me to be serious *mis*construals, in important
respects. In what follows, I will attempt to make this clear in the case of his

association with what I consider to be the most important of them philosophically: both "existentialism" and "*Existenz*-philosophy" as I have characterized them. For on my reading of him and understanding of them, his kind
of philosophy and philosophical thinking needs to be clearly distinguished
from both of them. I will begin with a preliminary discussion of what I take
to be distinctively characteristic of these very different alternatives to what
Nietzsche was up to, their points of linkage notwithstanding.

I. Existentialism, Existential Philosophy, and Existenz-Philosophy

There can be no doubt that Nietzsche figured importantly in the genealogy of
existentialism. Along with Kierkegaard, he is commonly considered to have
been one of its fathers—or perhaps grandfathers, if its paternity is to be attributed to Martin Heidegger and Karl Jaspers in the next generation. An
argument can certainly be made that Kierkegaard deserves the characterization "existentialist," his passionate Christianity notwithstanding. He virtually
defined the program of the movement with his famous criticism of "modern
philosophy" (by which he meant Hegelianism—but the shoe also fits high-
tide analytic philosophy to a T). Kierkegaard accused it of "having forgotten,
in a sort of world-historical absent-mindedness, what it means to be a human
being [. . .], each one for himself." He himself maintained that "If [one] is
a human being then he is also an existing individual," and contended that a
human being does best to "concentrate his entire energy upon the fact that
he *is* an existing individual."[2] But is the reinterpretation of human reality that
Nietzsche calls for and undertakes to be understood at all similarly?

There certainly is a great gulf between them. Nietzsche considers this reinterpretation to be mandated by what he terms the "death" of the sort of God
upon whom Kierkegaard considers everything to depend, while Kierkegaard
links his conception of the kind of "subjectivity" he considers to be the "truth"
of human "existing" to the idea of a "God-relationship" requiring a "leap of
faith"—which Nietzsche explicitly disparages.[3] Moreover, Kierkegaard construes human "existing" in terms of a strong conception of "subjectivity" and
makes much of an associated conception of selfhood, while Nietzsche scorn-
fully exclaims: "Is there anyone who has never been mortally sick of everything
subjective and of its wretched ipsissimosity [i.e., self-fetishism]?" (*BGE* 207).

If "existentialism" is defined as what Kierkegaard, Nietzsche, Heidegger,
and Sartre *have in common*, it becomes a word with little if any positive meaning. That is all the more the case if the list is expanded to other major figures associated with the existential philosophical movement in (Continental) Europe.[4] They would seem to have little more in common than a critical

relationship to classical modern philosophy from Descartes to Hegel, and overlapping sets of philosophical admirers, adversaries, and detractors. If, on the other hand, "existentialism" is defined as the *totality* of what and how they think, the upshot would be utterly incoherent. So Sartre himself complained (already in 1947!) that the word "is now so loosely applied to so many things that it no longer means anything at all."[5] In attempting to deal with this situation, I consider it useful to distinguish between "existentialism" and "*Existenz*-philosophy" and "existential philosophy"—all of which are further to be distinguished from a competing development that also emerged in Europe at about the same time that goes by the name of "philosophical anthropology" (from which Heidegger explicitly distinguishes his enterprise in *Being and Time* in that very book,[6] but with which the post-existentialist Sartre of *Search for a Method* actually allies himself).[7]

"Existentialism," as an "-ism," is a term that has come to be strongly associated with a certain view of human existence and the human situation, to which it therefore might as well simply be considered to refer, as a terminological fait accompli. It is basically the picture one gets from Sartre, Camus, and their literary and philosophical kindred spirits. On this view, we are "home alone" in a godless and alien universe. There are no absolutes in the realms of value and morality. There is no heavenly "happily ever after" beyond death, and no real possibility of one. Human life is ultimately meaningless, and the human condition is fundamentally hopeless. In the immortal words of Monty Python's "Bright Side" song: "Life is quite absurd, and death's the final word."[8] So far, at least, Nietzsche would not be out of place in their company. So if subscribing to this basic description of the human condition is both necessary and sufficient to be considered an existentialist, he could be said to be one (although Kierkegaard would be disqualified, Jaspers would be doubtful, and probably Heidegger as well).

But there is more. Quite centrally, for Sartre and company, we are *free* in a most radical sense, the limitations and contingencies of our abilities and lives and circumstances notwithstanding—free in the decisions and choices we make from among the possibilities open to us. We are completely responsible for our decisions and choices, and all that really matters is the integrity or authenticity with which we are capable of making them as we exercise our freedom. The fundamental absurdity and futility of it all make our lot a difficult one to bear, and many avoid facing up to them by fleeing into various forms of self-deception and inauthenticity. But there is a kind of dignity, value, and even happiness attainable by rising above the temptation to do so and realizing our absurd freedom, thereby giving our existence the only kind of human meaning that is not an illusion.

This is without question a possible construal and assessment of human existence—and, as fleshed out in the associated literature (novels, short stories, plays, movies), a vivid and gripping one. It enjoyed considerable vogue in the decades following the Second World War, and still does in some quarters. It undeniably addresses the question of "what it means to be a human being" and, more specifically, to be "an existing individual."

It certainly was not Kierkegaard's view of the matter, however—even though he was well aware of it as a human possibility (as one of the most extreme forms of "despair," serving as the springboard for his "leap of faith" that alone can remedy it). It was not shared by such major figures as Heidegger and Jaspers either, for whose thinking provision certainly must be made in this general connection. That is one reason why they so emphatically rejected the label of "existentialist" and sought to disassociate themselves from "existentialism."

That poses a problem, since an apt rubric for what they all are doing would be useful. Fortunately, a solution is readily available, in the form of the notion of "*Existenz*-philosophy," or the "philosophy of *Existenz*," that is commonly used for this purpose in German-speaking Europe. The term *Existenz* here is used to refer specifically to "existing" in the manner that a human being "exists"—but not merely in the sense of simply having been born and still being alive. Rather, it refers to something like living one's life highly self-consciously, with an acute awareness of oneself as (as Kierkegaard puts it) "an existing individual," "each one for himself," responsible for one's choices, and reflectively *leading* one's life, all the while recognizing and taking seriously the inescapability of one's finitude and mortality. Both Heidegger and Jaspers make major use of the German term *Existenz* in this connection, and make its analysis or elucidation the central task of their major contributions to the literature under consideration.

More generally characterized: *Existenz*-philosophy is the analysis or elucidation of human self-conscious "existing" viewed from a first-person standpoint, beyond simply being a living instance of our species—of human reality as "lived" as both subject of experience and agent in the human world, and of the various possible ways of doing so (and of assessing them). I shall appropriate the term and use it (without italics) accordingly.[9] It has to do with what Kierkegaard called the irreducible "subjectivity" of human "existing," with the experiential character and general circumstances of such "first-person singular" existing, and (at least in some instances) with its purported basic ("ontological") structures.

Existenz-philosophy, so construed, is thus to be conceived in terms of what this part or sort of philosophy deals with (like "philosophy of mind"

244   CHAPTER EIGHT

and "philosophy of action"), rather than in terms of any conclusions about its topic, or any particular construal of human existing (such as the one just sketched). Its only general assumptions are that its topic is a *real* one (something that is humanly real or possible), a *fundamental* one (something that is part of the very fabric of human reality), and a *key* one (something that is of special significance in the makeup of human reality). So understood, Heidegger, Jaspers, Kierkegaard, and Sartre can all be considered Existenz-philosophers (or philosophers of Existenz). Some (such as Heidegger and Sartre) think that human Existenz can be analyzed in appropriate special concepts, often introduced as technical terms specifically for this purpose; while others (like Kierkegaard and Jaspers) think that it can only be indirectly elucidated, in fairly ordinary language.

"*Existential* philosophy" is an expression used by many commentators as a synonym or alternative version of "Existenz-philosophy." It may also (and, I believe, more helpfully) be used to refer to the sort of approach, perspective, or way of proceeding that tends to be favored by Existenz-philosophers, but that can be used to analyze or elucidate realities in addition to human Existenz itself. One version of it is the adaptation of Husserl's phenomenological method[10] that is often referred to as "existential phenomenology," which analyzes phenomena from the perspective of the way in which they are experienced by the "existing" human being. The other main version of it involves the use of more literary and informal forms of language evocative of kinds of such experience to elucidate the matters under consideration. Existential literature (novels, plays, short stories, cinema) offers many cases in point; but so do the Existenz-philosophical writings of Kierkegaard and Jaspers, and of Sartre at times as well.[11]

It is characteristic of Existenz-philosophy to take such existential-philosophical (that is, existential-phenomenological or existential-literary) perspectives not only to be most appropriate to the consideration of human Existenz, but also to be privileged (given priority of some sort) over all others in the interpretation of human reality—even though the possibility of other (e.g., biological, social, cultural, historical, psychological) perspectives upon human reality that are relevant to its comprehensive interpretation may be acknowledged.

This is in marked contrast with a rival development in European philosophy in the middle two quarters of the twentieth century that came to be known as "philosophical anthropology." Philosophical anthropology—for which human reality is most properly conceived and approached as a form of (fundamentally even if no longer entirely biological) life—takes other such perspectives upon human reality equally seriously, and indeed tends to regard first-

person singular perspectives and phenomena to be very much in need of supplementation and interpretation by way of what can be learned about human
reality from biological and social perspectives.[12] This difference has made
philosophical anthropology's developing rivalry with Existenz-philosophy in
the reinterpretation of human reality a deep one.

Finally (for present purposes), it is common for Existenz-philosophers
to distinguish between different fundamental ways in which it is possible for
human beings to "exist," one of which is taken to be distinctly superior to the
other or others. So Kierkegaard distinguishes between different types of "subjectivity"; Heidegger between "authentic" and "inauthentic" existing; Jaspers
between genuine "Existenz" and the failure to attain it; and Sartre between
existing in "bad faith" or "self-deception" and existing with what might be
called "integrity" with respect to one's radical freedom and responsibility.

Nietzsche's introduction to philosophy was by way of Schopenhauer, for
whom all "representation" [*Vorstellung*] (basically meaning "perception") in
consciousness was in stark contrast with the fundamental reality of "the
world as will," and all individuation was a kind of illusion. The twin origins
of Existenz-philosophy, in Kierkegaard's passionately Christian championing
of the radically subjective "self" and in Husserl's intensely anti-naturalistic
neo-Cartesian program of a "pure phenomenology," are radically different—
and would have been equally (but for very different reasons) repugnant to
Nietzsche. Yet Nietzsche did come to loom large in the thinking of many philosophers in the twentieth-century existential tradition. Indeed, it is probably
fair to say that he was at least something like the catalyst that was necessary
for Existenz-philosophy to be born of the unlikely coupling of Kierkegaard
and Husserl, with genes from each of them that one might think could not
possibly have been viably combined.[13]

In what follows, I will briefly discuss a number of aspects of Nietzsche's
thought—some of which were relevant to the emergence and development of
Existenz-philosophy, while others render his association with it problematic.[14]

II. "The Death of God"

Nietzsche's thought might very broadly be regarded as an attempt to work
out what he took to be the profound consequences of what he famously
called "the death of God." It is that, more than anything else, that made him
one of the forerunners and initiators of existentialism and existential philosophy, together (ironically) with the God-idea's greatest champion in the
history of modern philosophy, Kierkegaard—his exact opposite in this very
respect! (That helps to make sense of the fact that there is a—sometimes

vehemently—Christian existentialism and Existenz-philosophy, as well as—often vehemently—atheistic versions.)

Nietzsche, of course, is most warmly embraced by atheistic existentialists. For him the demise of the "God-idea"—as an idea deserving of being taken seriously, together with loss of viability of everything that depended upon it—changed everything. It was his chosen preliminary task to try to make this clear. And it was his larger chosen task to take on the whole question of where we go from here, and whether it is possible to affirm life without it—in a way that would grant the basic truth of Schopenhauer's grim basic assessment of the human condition but would find a way to be as profoundly affirmative of life as Schopenhauer was negative about it. The existentialists took up both of these tasks. In these respects, Nietzsche and the existentialists (the French existentialists in particular) were kindred spirits (although it might be more appropriate to consider them and existentialism to have been among his philosophical progeny rather than full-blooded kin—along with a number of other, quite different subsequent philosophical developments).

Nietzsche first announced this demise quite matter-of-factly in the first (1882) version of *Joyful Inquiry*, at the beginning of the third of its four "Books"; but he made it clear (in figurative language) that he took it to have major implications for the agenda of philosophy: "*New Struggles* [Kämpfe].—After Buddha was dead, his shadow was still shown for centuries in a cave—a tremendous, gruesome shadow. God is dead; but given the way of men, there may still be caves for thousands of years in which his shadow will be shown.—And we—we still have to vanquish [*besiegen*] his shadow too!" (*JI* 108). By God's "shadow" Nietzsche means, at least in part, the many ways in which the God-idea has influenced our interpretations and evaluations—some of which he proceeds immediately to indicate and address, beginning with ways in which we tend to think about the world and ourselves. (It also includes the radical rebound from the demise of that idea that goes by the name of "nihilism," discussed in the previous chapter; see *JI* 109.) Nietzsche takes up the theme again a few pages later, in a way that is anything but matter-of-fact, in the famous "Madman" section (*JI* 125), the point of which is to make clear what a traumatic development the "death of God" could turn out to be. It appears again at the beginning of his next book, *Thus Spoke Zarathustra*, early in its prologue, with less anguish but in a way that indicates that it is the entire work's point of departure (*Z* I:P:2).

The year after Nietzsche returned to philosophical prose publication with the appearance of *Beyond* (in 1886), he published a second (1887) expanded version of *Inquiry*, with a new fifth "Book." And he began that added Book by sounding the same theme again, making clear in passing what he means by that phrase more specifically: "The greatest recent event—that 'God is dead,' that the belief in the Christian god has become unbelievable [*unglaubwürdig*; literally, "unworthy of belief"]—is already beginning to cast its first shadows over Europe." He goes on to indicate that what makes this "event" chilling is the thought of "how much must collapse now that this faith has been undermined [*untergraben*] because it was built upon this faith, propped up by it, grown into it; for example, the whole of our European morality [*Moral*]" (*JI* 343).

Nietzsche's basic point in speaking of God's "death" is that the idea of God is an idea whose time has come and gone—or at any rate, is on its way out. "Why atheism today?" he writes in *Beyond*, and answers: "'The father' in God has been thoroughly refuted [i.e., debunked]; ditto, 'the judge,' 'the rewarder'" (*BGE* 53). What remains of the God-idea is a mere abstraction that has nothing to be said for it; and there is a strong (if not direct) case that weighs against it, in the form of a combination of problematic origins and motivations that render it undeserving of even being taken seriously.

Nietzsche indicates how he proposes to dispose of it in a passage in *Daybreak* (1881): "In former times, one sought to prove that there is no God— today one indicates how the belief that there is a God could *arise* and how this idea acquired its weight and importance: a counter-proof that there is no God thereby becomes superfluous.—When in former times one had refuted [i.e., critically demolished] the 'proofs of the existence of God' put forward, there always remained the doubt whether better proofs than those just refuted might not be found: in those days atheists did not know how to make a clean sweep of it [*reinen Tisch zu machen*]" (*D* 95).

That is: atheists previously had not figured out how to get the whole issue *off the table* and lay it to rest: namely, by depriving it of all credibility, showing that its origins and motivations weigh against it rather than for it, and thus—in the absence of countervailing supportive evidence or arguments— *subverting* it. Nietzsche indicates some of the sorts of things he has in mind two sections earlier, when he writes: "What if God were *not* 'the truth' and it were precisely this that were shown [*bewiesen*]—if he were the vanity, the lust for power, the impatience, the terror, the enraptured and fearful delusion of men?" (*D* 93). This may not amount to a "disproof" or "refutation" in the logical sense of these terms; but for Nietzsche it disposes of the God-idea compellingly and decisively, and should be convincing for any "free spirit" of sufficient sophistication and intellectual integrity. The real task of "the philosophy of the future" that he heralds and seeks to inaugurate is not to dwell on the matter and belabor the point. It is rather to proceed to reckon with its interpretive and evaluative consequences.

III. The Advent and Overcoming of Nihilism

I have already discussed this general topic in my previous chapter. Here I will briefly recap my view of the matter in a way that brings it more directly to bear on the question of Nietzsche's relation to the kind of nihilism that is commonly regarded as one of the basic tenets of the "existentialism" with which he is thought to be associated. (It should be obvious that, as I have characterized "Existenz-philosophy," it simply does not engage with that issue.)

Nietzsche had a great deal to say about "nihilism"—some in his published writings, and much more in his notebooks from 1886 onward.[15] One of his great concerns was with what he called "the advent of nihilism"—the "rebound from 'God is truth' to the fanatical faith 'All is false'" (*KGW* VIII 2[127]; *WP* 1). He believed that a certain sort of nihilism—that is, the rejection of all metaphysical, religious, evaluative, and moral absolute principles transcending this life in this world in their status and reality—can be a healthy thing philosophically and humanly (for those capable of doing without them, at any rate). But he considered it also to be a great danger; for it is profoundly negative in its basic thrust, and susceptible of metastasizing, and so must be superseded if it is not to become a life-negating fatality for humanity. "Nihilism represents a pathological transitional stage," he observed in another note from the same period (1887); "what is pathological is the tremendous generalization, the inference that there is no meaning at all" (*KGW* VIII 9[35]; *WP* 13).

So Nietzsche concludes the second essay of *On the Genealogy of Morality* with an impassioned evocation of the possibility of a post-nihilistic humanity of "creative spirit" and "compelling strength" sufficient to overcome it: "This man of the future, who will redeem us not only from the hitherto reigning ideal but also from that which was bound to grow out of it, the great nausea, the will to nothingness, nihilism [. . .]; this anti-Christian and anti-nihilist; this victor over God and nothingness—*he must come one day*" (*GM* II:24). The "hitherto reigning ideal" is that of a transcendent God considered to be the absolute basis of all value, meaning, and truth; and "that which was bound to grow out of it" is nihilism—the conviction that, in the absence of any such basis, the ideas of value, meaning, and truth collapse—here diagnosed as a kind of withdrawal symptom resulting from previous addiction to that ideal. "A nihilist," Nietzsche quips, "is one who judges of the world as it is that it ought *not* to be, and of the world as it ought to be that it does not exist" (*KGW* VIII 9[60]; *WP* 585A).

The key to overcoming nihilism, Nietzsche came to understand, is ironically somewhat similar to his strategy for disposing of the God-idea: that is, by a kind of *cure*—in this case by coming to understand and freeing ourselves from the (false but seductive) "God-or-bust" ("nothing matters") dichotomy, and from the absolutism addiction that disposes one to give up on and disparage anything that does not satisfy the craving for it. Liberation from that addiction by itself, however, is not enough. Truth and value must be given a new footing. And that, for Nietzsche, is possible—by shifting their locus to this life in this world. Life itself holds the key to the meaning of life; for the meaning of life, beyond its self-renewing vitality, is nothing more or less than its own enhancement and enrichment.

Nihilism for Nietzsche thus is not to be overcome by way of the discovery of some new transcendent absolute reality, truth, or value standard beyond this life and world to replace God, by reference to which they and our own existence can be assessed and are endowed with meaning and worth. It is to be overcome instead by learning to think of reality, truth, and value differently, in a manner attuned to the basic character and developmental possibilities of life as they reveal themselves in human life and history and in the life around us—and to come to *affirm* them for what they are and have it in them to become, rather than to condemn them for not being otherwise.

So, Nietzsche writes, a genuine philosopher "demands of himself a judgment, a 'yes' or 'no' [*ein 'Ja' oder 'Nein'*], not about the *Wissenschaften* but about life and the value of life" (*BGE* 205). That judgment can go either way; for it is neither a cognitive judgment nor a value judgment in terms of some standard of value external to life. Rather, it is an expression of one's basic disposition with respect to life as one takes it to be. Schopenhauer had said No to it, and that is what Nietzsche takes the nihilist fundamentally to be doing. The overcoming of nihilism for him is a matter of finding a way to a "yes" to life that is genuine and deep. And that sort of affirmation is not merely intellectual; it is a matter of acquiring a *sensibility* that is attuned to it, and so coming or learning to *love* it, for what it fundamentally is, as it fundamentally is.

At a basic level, Nietzsche takes it to be the case that a healthy living creature, "being alive, loves life" (*BGE* 24). It is, in some more or less primordial dispositional way, "affirming" life and the kind of life it is (even if that may involve doing things that risk or result in its own individual "going under," as he has Zarathustra put it). But for creatures like ourselves, Nietzsche observes (near the end of the first version of *Inquiry*), there is nothing that is more important and needful where our dispositions are concerned than "learning to love" (*JI* 334). And several sections later, at that edition's conclusion, he uses one of his most famous images—that of "the eternal recurrence" of everything in and about life and the world, and even (in his thought experiment) in and about one's own life—to construct a kind of test to reinforce it in its application in the larger context of the affirmation of life: "How well disposed would you have to become to yourself and to life *to crave nothing more fervently* than this ultimate eternal confirmation and seal?" (*JI* 341).

A part of what "the death of God" entails is that life can have no meaning bestowed upon it from on high—because there is nothing "on high" that might bestow it. Some take that to render nihilism unavoidable. For Nietzsche, however, life can come to have another kind of meaning, beyond that of its own mere preservation and continuation. That meaning has to do with what Nietzsche calls its *enhancement* (*Erhöhung*; literally, "heightening" or making "higher"). This idea is what he memorably conveys by means of another of his most familiar images—that of "the *Übermensch*" (his emblem of a self-surpassing higher humanity)—when in *Zarathustra*, he has Zarathustra begin his preaching and teaching by saying: "*I teach you the Übermensch. The Übermensch is the meaning of the earth. Let your will say: the Übermensch shall be* the meaning of the earth [sei *der Sinn der Erde*]! I beseech you, my brothers, *remain faithful to the earth*, and do not believe those who speak to you of otherworldly hopes!" (*Z* I:P:3).

Nietzsche employs the figure or image of the *Übermensch* here as a kind of symbol of the enhancement or creative transformation of human life, elevated above and beyond the plane of merely animal existence, and yet again above and beyond that of life that is human but "all too human," to the level of forms of exceptional humanity that he considers to be "higher" than ordinary human life typically is in one qualitative way or another. In using it, Nietzsche refers to no particular specific type of human being but points in the same sort of general direction as he does in the passage from the end of the second essay of *Genealogy* cited above. There he envisions the possibility of a form of humankind that would be characterized not only by greater health and vitality but also by higher and richer spirituality and creativity than has been attained even by the most notable of exceptions to the human rule previously (including the "sovereign individual" discussed in *GM* II:2). This is the idea of a humanity continually "overcoming" and surpassing itself, and further transforming and enriching human life on this earth. That conception of human possibility is the heart of Nietzsche's response to the danger posed by nihilism, in the aftermath of the "death of God."

In short: Nietzsche's way of responding to and dealing with the challenge posed by "the death of God" does not align well with the basic response of the proponents of atheistic existentialism. Their solution to the advent of nihilism is not to seek a way to "overcome" it and leave it behind but to embrace it, and find a way to defy it from within it and within oneself that can be self- and life-affirming enough to live by and for. That is what came to be described as "the challenge of existentialism."[16] These existentialists agreed upon the problem, but differed radically with respect to the solution. And it is not clear that one can or should be considered an existentialist whose response to "the problem of existentialism" is not to somehow meet "the challenge of existentialism" but rather to find one's way to a standpoint from which the existentialist sort of response becomes unnecessary, and a very different sort of way to affirmation is found and deemed viable. In what follows I will provide a sketch of what I take Nietzsche's response to have been.

IV. A "Philosophy of the Future"

Nietzsche wrote *Zarathustra* to give expression to his discovery of this new post-religious, post-metaphysical, and also post-nihilist way of thinking, which he believed heralded a new dawn for humanity and for philosophy alike. He gave his next book, *Beyond Good and Evil*, the subtitle *Prelude to a Philosophy of the Future*. In it he attempted to set the stage for the new kind of philosophy, to indicate what some of the main tasks on its agenda would be and how it would pursue them, and to get on with it. Is it anything like any of the versions of existential philosophy discussed at the outset of this chapter?

As its title is meant to suggest, Nietzsche's "philosophy of the future" is to be *post-moral* (as well as post-religious, post-metaphysical, and post-nihilist), in the sense of being purged of the "moralism" of thinking in a moralizing way about everything, human reality very definitely included, and of doing so under the influence of "good-versus-evil" morality and of moral values that are assumed to trump all others. It is to be analytical and critical; but its twin basic tasks are constructive *interpretation* (and reinterpretation) and *evaluation* (and revaluation).

It is one of the themes of *Beyond* that Nietzsche's kind of interpretive and evaluative philosophy is to be carried on in an "experimental" rather than "dogmatic" manner, recognizing that no interpretation or evaluation of anything of significance will ever be beyond the possibility of challenge and improvement. It is another that such inquiry needs to be multiply "perspectival," in the case of anything as complex and diversely relational as art, music, morality, human reality, or life more generally, let alone such notions as "truth," "value," and "creativity."

A related point, sounded as early as *Human*, is that in dealing interpretively and evaluatively with most matters—and in particular with anything relating to human reality—one is dealing with things that have *become* what and as they are and thus must be approached not only analytically but also "genealogically" or "historically"—which is to say, developmentally. So, as has been noted above, he contends that "everything has become: there are no eternal facts, just as there are no absolute truths." The conclusion Nietzsche draws is that "consequently, what is needed from now on is *historical philosophizing*," in partnership with the natural sciences (*HH* I:1–2). In contrast, for existential philosophy what is needed is a newly intensified focus on what Kierkegaard characterized in terms of "subjectivity" and "inwardness," and to first-person experience that became the focus of an adaptation of Husserl's radically non-naturalistic and even anti-naturalistic science-circumventing "phenomenology."

The theme of the need for philosophy to take a kind of naturalizing turn as it emancipates itself from metaphysics is one that recurs in Nietzsche's subsequent writings. He insists that philosophers of the kind he calls for and attempts himself to be must be as sophisticated scientifically as possible, and that scientific inquiry is essential both to the reinterpretation of human reality and to the attempt to foster the enhancement of human life and the attainment of a "higher" humanity. So, in *Inquiry*, he celebrates "physics" (shorthand for natural science generally) precisely for this reason. Proclaiming that "*we want to become those we are*—the new, the unique, the incomparable, the self-legislators, the self-creators [*die Sich-selber-Gesetzgebenden, die Sich-selber-Schaffenden*]!," he then continues: "To that end we must become the best learners and discoverers of everything that is lawful and necessary in the world: we must become *physicists* in order to be able to be *creators* in this sense—while hitherto all valuations and ideas have been based on *ignorance* of physics [i.e., natural science] or were constructed so as to *contradict* it. Therefore: here's to physics [*hoch die Physik*]! And even more so [*höher noch*, higher still], to that which *compels* us to turn to physics—our intellectual integrity [*Redlichkeit*]!" (*JI* 335).

Here again, it is hard to imagine any existential philosopher saying anything of this sort. Nietzsche is by no means prepared, however, to grant the natural sciences the last word with respect to many matters, and in particular with respect to human reality and the human world. So, for example, he writes: "A 'scientific' interpretation of the world" in which it is supposed that "mechanics is the doctrine of the first and last laws on which all existence must be based as on a ground floor," would be "a crudity and naiveté, if not a lunacy, an idiocy," driving home his point by way of the example of "how absurd" a purely "'scientific' assessment of music would be" (*JI* 373). In this, at least, Nietzsche and existential philosophy are in strong agreement.

The same would apply, for Nietzsche, to a purely "scientific" understanding of his idea of "becoming those we are" [*Die werden, die wir sind*]—that is, have it in us to become—and his explication of it in the characterization of the "new" sort of human being he envisions that follows. It is "to that end" [*dazu*]—that of "becoming *creators* in that sense"—that we are said to need to learn and discover everything we can about ourselves and the world by way of the sciences. "Becoming *creators* in that sense," however, and the results of such creativity, are different matters. They both require to be comprehended (and appreciated) in different ways than those of scientific analysis and explanation, and involve forms of endeavor for which scientific knowledge is insufficient. This point is of great importance in connection with the question of how Nietzsche's kind of "naturalism" is to be understood. And, for better or worse (or perhaps simply differently), this is something quite alien to the spirit and general thrust of existential philosophy.

V. Nietzsche's "Naturalism"

Existential philosophy and Husserl's kind of "science of consciousness and experience" that he called "pure phenomenology" also agreed on one thing, at least: their opposition to any sort of philosophical "naturalism." Nietzsche insisted upon the need for a "naturalizing" turn (of the right sort). I have made frequently mention and characterization of what I take to be his kind of "naturalism" throughout this book, and will be discussing it at length in chapter 11. I will give a brief preliminary account of it here, because it is one of the key respects in which his thinking is radically different from the approaches to and treatments of human reality that are characteristic of Existenz-philosophy and its offshoots.

As Nietzsche says time and again, one of the most important tasks on his philosophical agenda is *the reinterpretation of human reality*—and that, for him means: of humankind or "the type *Mensch*," as the form of life it has come to be. So, earlier in *Inquiry*, after announcing "the death of God" (*JI* 108), he goes on immediately to call first for a "de deification [*Entgöttlichung*] of nature"—a purging of our conceptions of the world and nature of all of the "shadows of God" and related anthropomorphisms that have long characterized our thinking about them—and then for a thoroughly "naturalizing" reinterpretation of ourselves as human beings who are a part of this newly understood nature: "When may we begin to '*naturalize*' ourselves [*uns Menschen zu* 'vernatürlichen'] in terms of a pure, newly discovered, newly redeemed nature!" (*JI* 109). His implicit but clear answer is: here and now—for this is the general project of the book. The sections that follow—"Origin of Knowledge" (*JI* 110), "Origin of the Logical" (*JI* 111), on the origin of "scientific thinking" (*JI* 113), on the origin of our "humanity" (*JI* 115), on the origin of "morality" (*JI* 116)—provide immediate illustrations of what he has in mind.

Nietzsche considers it to be beyond dispute that human reality is originally and fundamentally a form of animal life; and, in the aftermath of the "death of God," the upshot seems to him to be unavoidable: Everything it has "become" has come about through developmental processes of an entirely mundane (worldly) nature. So he has Zarathustra proclaim: "Body am I entirely, and nothing else; and soul is only a word for something about the body" (Z I:4). Putting the point more prosaically in *The Antichristian* (1888), he writes: "We no longer *derive den Menschen* from '*Geist*' ['spirit'] or '*Gottheit*' ['divinity']; we have placed him back among the animals. [. . .] The 'pure spirit' is a pure stupidity: if we subtract [*abrechnen*] the nervous system and the senses—the 'mortal shroud'—*then we are making a mistake* [so verrechnen wir uns]—that's all [*weiter nichts*]!" (A 14).

Beyond, like *Inquiry*, revolves around the project of reinterpreting human reality naturalistically—such human phenomena as morality and religion included. These phenomena may well have been among the "many chains [that] have been laid upon humankind [*dem Menschen*]," as Nietzsche figuratively puts it, "so that it should no longer behave like an animal"—and that have indeed resulted in the actual "separation of humankind from the animals" (HH II:II:350). But they nonetheless have their own "natural histories" that are parts of our own—indeed, the part of *Beyond* dealing with morality bears the title "Natural History of Morality"—and so are to be treated accordingly, even though they have contributed significantly to what Nietzsche calls our "de-animalization" [*Enttierung*] (D 106). "To translate den Menschen back into nature; [. . .] to see to it *that der Mensch* henceforth stands *before dem Menschen* as even today, hardened in the discipline of science, it stands before the *rest* of nature [. . .], deaf to the siren songs of old metaphysical bird catchers who have been piping at it all too long, 'you are more, you are higher, you are of a different origin!'—that may be a strange and crazy task, but it is a *task*—who would deny that?" (BGE 230).

This is a "task" Nietzsche continued to pursue in *Genealogy*—the topic of which is not only the "genealogy" or (very human) origin and development of a number of significant moral phenomena associated with modern-day morality, but also those of a number of salient features of human reality more generally. These developments include "the reduction of the beast of prey '*Mensch*' to a tame and civilized animal, a *domestic animal*" (GM I:11); "the labor performed by man upon himself" by means of the "ethics of custom and the social straitjacket" through which "humankind was actually *made* calculable" (GM II:2); the further process through which "nature" was able "to breed an animal *that may promise*"—that is, capable of making and keeping promises—which Nietzsche calls "the paradoxical task that nature has set itself in the case of humankind" (GM II:1); and the "*internalization* [*Verinnerlichung*]" through which "humankind first developed what was later called its 'soul'" and "entire inner world," by way of the "inhibition" of the "outward discharge" of aggressive drives (*GM* II:16).

Nietzsche's naturalism is to be scientifically attentive (as *JI* 335 makes clear); but it is by no means "scientistically" reductionist, in the sense of supposing that the whole of human reality can in principle be comprehended and expressed in terms of the technical languages, conceptual schemes, and empirical-theoretical explanations of the natural sciences. His diatribe in *Inquiry*'s fifth Book that bears the title "'Science' as Prejudice" (that is, natural-scientific thinking as dogma; *JI* 373), cited above, with "music" invoked as star witness, makes that evident as well. Nietzsche's naturalism is one that not only is open to the idea of emergent development (in which processes converge in a way that results in the emergence of something qualitatively different), but features it prominently. Indeed, it stands ready to meet the challenge of those who would point to various sorts of cultural, intellectual, and "spiritual" phenomena as evidence of something "more than" or "different from" anything of entirely "natural" origins by undertaking to make them naturalistically intelligible. But it *is* a kind of naturalism, and so is a fundamentally different way of conceiving and thinking about human reality than that of existential philosophy, which prioritizes the first-person perspective on and in human "existing" over every other.

Nietzsche's naturalism extends to his thinking with respect to value and morality. So, in a note from 1887 to which he gave the heading "Toward a Plan," the first item he lists on his agenda is: "In place of *moral values*, purely *naturalistic* values. Naturalization of morality" (*KGW* VIII 9[8]; *WP* 462). So also, in *Twilight of the Idols* a year later, he writes: "Every naturalism in morality—that is, every healthy morality—is dominated by an instinct of life; some commandment of life is fulfilled by a determinate canon of 'shalt' and 'shalt not'" (*TI* "Morality," 4). He and existential philosophers are in accord in rejecting the idea of any absolute values somehow existing independently of this life and world. Very unlike them, however, he is intent upon a naturalizing reorientation—although not a reduction—of value theory, and of moral theory as well in derivative association with it. And this is a matter in which he and existential philosophy would seem to diverge even more greatly, as I shall next be showing.

VI. Nietzsche's "Aestheticism"

This characterization—"aestheticism"—is intended to underscore the crowning importance Nietzsche attaches to aesthetic and artistic concepts and values in his thinking with respect to life and the world in general, to human reality and possibility more specifically, and the overcoming of nihilism (and finessing "the challenge of existentialism") in particular. It is related to his emphasis on the ideas of the "enhancement" [*Erhöhung*] of life and its quality, and of the kind of humanity he calls "higher" [*höher*] and "superior" [*vornehm*] in relation to the all-too-human general rule in human life, of which his image of "the *Übermensch*" is the apotheosis and symbol. Can it be seen as at all akin to anything in existentialism? Or are they simply on different wave lengths here?

The term "aestheticism" here refers more specifically to the way in which Nietzsche conceives of the difference-making characteristics at issue—difference-making not only in terms of what he calls "ranking" or "order of rank," but also with respect to their human-experiential significance. What renders the term appropriate in this context is Nietzsche's emphasis on the idea of creation and creativity, his heavy reliance upon artistic imagery and upon art and the artist as paradigms of what he has in mind (and seeks to generalize), and his identification of culture as the dimension of human reality that is the locus of all such differentiation and development.

The expression "aestheticism" is thus both useful and apt as a further positive indication of the general direction of his post-moralism, and of the development of his kind of post-absolutist as well as post-nihilist value theory. It is not in conflict with his value naturalism, and actually can even be seen as an outgrowth and extension of it. His fundamental aesthetic values are not independent of what he refers to above as "naturalistic values" but rather are grounded in and developed out of the latter, which animate them even as they are transfigured in them. They thus remain naturalistic values, while yet also involving and displaying their creative transfiguration and supersession.

Nietzsche's aestheticism is on full display in *The Birth of Tragedy* (1872), in which he writes that "it is only as an *aesthetic phenomenon* that existence and the world are eternally *justified*" (*BT* 4, repeated in *BT* 24); and that "art is not merely imitation of the reality of nature but rather a metaphysical supplement of the reality of nature, placed beside it for its overcoming" (*BT* 24). By "metaphysical" here he means something transcending and contrasting with the merely natural—and yet he also considers the two basic impulses he identifies in art, "the Apollinian and its opposite, the Dionysian, as artistic energies which burst forth from nature herself," thus making the "overcoming" of nature in or by means of art its own self-overcoming through its self-"transfiguration" (*BT* 2). Moreover, he writes, in the Dionysian arts of music and dance one "is no longer an artist, he has *become* a work of art," and that "we have our highest dignity in our significance *as* works of art" (*BT* 1 and 24, emphasis added).

Nietzsche subsequently abandoned the characterization of art as a kind of "metaphysical" activity, but not the idea of art as the creative transformation of the natural, through which the natural—and we as its transformers and loci of its transformation—attain significance and worth it and we would otherwise lack. This idea is at the heart of what he means by "value creation." He likewise retained the idea of the redeeming transfiguration of nature through man's artistic self-transformation, writing in a note from 1885 that "man becomes the *transfigurer of existence* when he learns to transfigure himself," and calling this "the great conception of man" (*KGW* VII 7[37]; *WP* 820). And he further retained the idea of "becoming a work of art," writing (in an aphorism in *Inquiry* entitled "One Thing Is Needful"): "To 'give style' to one's character: a great and rare art! It is practiced by those who survey all the strengths and weaknesses of their nature and then fit them into an artistic plan" (*JI* 290).

On the other hand, Nietzsche subsequently came to think less of art in the sense of "the fine arts" in this connection than of the artistic character or quality that can be extended and cultivated more broadly in human life and experience—for which, however, he stresses our indebtedness to art in this narrower sense. So he writes: "*What One Should Learn from Artists.*—How can we make things beautiful, attractive, and desirable for us when they are not? [. . .] Here we could learn something [. . .] from artists who are really continually trying to bring off such inventions and feats[. . . . But] with them this subtle power usually comes to an end where art ends and life begins; *we* want to be the poets of our lives—first of all in the smallest, most everyday matters" (*JI* 299). A little later in the same work, Nietzsche expands upon the idea of a transformation of human reality in such a way that "all nature ceases and becomes art" in the passage (by now very familiar) in which he sounds one of his favorite themes, that is also relevant in this context: "We *want to become those we are*—the new, the unique, incomparable, the self-legislators, the self-creators" (*JI* 336). Here he joins characteristics commonly associated with true works of art to two other characteristics, which he associates with true artists: autonomy and creativity.

Creativity is one of the central themes of *Zarathustra*, as Nietzsche through Zarathustra elaborates upon his meaning in having Zarathustra proclaim the *Übermensch* to be "the meaning of the earth": "He who creates, creates humankind's goal and gives the earth its meaning and its future" (*Z* III:12:2). That same thought is reflected more prosaically in a later (1887) note in which Nietzsche considers "to what extent one can endure to live in a meaningless world *because one organizes a small part of it oneself*" (*KGW* VIII 9[60]; *WP* 585A). It remains central to the reconsideration of values for which *Beyond Good and Evil* prepares the way, and to his elaboration of the "new language" with respect to value—centering it upon "value for life" (*BGE* 4)—with which Nietzsche proposes to replace moralistic thinking, even of a hedonistic or utilitarian kind: "All those ways of thinking that measure the value of things in accordance with *pleasure* and *pain* [. . . are] naivetes on which everyone conscious of *creative* powers and an artistic conscience will look down, not without derision, nor without pity."

Nietzsche then goes on, in a memorable passage in this same section, to contrast "all-too-human" humanity and the higher humanity of which the *Übermensch* is emblematic: "In humankind *creature* and *creator* are united: in humanity there is material, fragment, excess, clay, dirt, nonsense, chaos; but in the human there is also creator, form-giver, hammer harness, spectator divinity, and seventh day: do you understand this contrast?" (*BGE* 225). This "contrast" illuminates Nietzsche's conceptions of what he calls the "all-too-human" and the "enhancement of life." The latter involves the overcoming of the former, and the developmental attainment of a higher humanity, the general character of which is summed up in his phrase "union of spiritual superiority with well-being and an excess of strength" (*KGW* VII 35[27]; *WP* 899). And spiritual superiority for him is by no means something purely or even primarily inward. Rather, it is fundamentally a *cultural* matter. The enhancement of life, for Nietzsche, essentially involves the enhancement of human cultural life; "higher humanity" and "higher culture" are concepts that for him go hand in hand.

That interest is already evident in *Birth*; and it becomes very explicit in *Schopenhauer as Educator* (1874). This third of Nietzsche's four *Unfashionable Reflections* is of particular interest in the present connection, because it is in effect Nietzsche's aestheticist manifesto, setting the stage for *Zarathustra* and the "philosophy of culture" that is a crucial feature of his developing reinterpretation and reassessment of human reality. He begins in a way that would seem to make his association with existentialism appropriate: "*The Mensch* who does not wish to belong to the mass needs only to cease taking themselves easily: let each follow their conscience, which calls to each: 'Be your self! All you are now doing, thinking, desiring, is not you yourself'" (*SE* 1). However, Nietzsche immediately takes this thought in an unexpected direction. The "self" that one is encouraged to "be" (or become), setting oneself apart from "the mass" of all-too-human humanity, is no distinct identity one is to discover and be true to, or even to establish as one's own by way of an authentic choice or decision: "Your true nature is not concealed deep within you but immeasurably high above you, or at least above that which you usually take yourself to be" (*SE* 1). Nietzsche does not immediately explain what he means by this, but his language here hints broadly that he has in mind the attainment of a significantly "higher" sort of humanity than "the mass" represents.

Nietzsche's underlying thought in this essay is that "man is necessary for the redemption of nature from the curse of the life of the animal," which (in the spirit of Schopenhauer) is said to be the fate of meaningless striving and suffering. Our challenge is to rise above an existence that is no better than this, to a humanity that transcends animality in a way that lifts this curse and thereby "redeems" nature. And it does so through the transformation of our animality—in ourselves and our lives—into something that is more than merely natural, by endowing our own striving and suffering existence with a kind of meaning that merely natural existence (and its striving and suffering) lacks. But, Nietzsche asks, "Where does the animal cease, where does *der Mensch* begin?" For, he contends, in our all-too-human ordinary existence, "usually we fail to emerge out of animality, we ourselves are the animals whose suffering seems senseless." Genuine humanity is *"higher"* humanity: "We are pressing toward humanity as toward something that stands high above us" (*SE* 5). This perspective on human reality, and this conception of higher humanity, would seem to be incommensurable in relation to existential-philosophical issues of "existing," "authenticity," and the like.

Nietzsche then goes on to contend that those who point the way, provide a glimpse and anticipation of that higher and truer humanity and thereby "lift us up," are "those true *Menschen, those who are no longer animal, the philosophers, artists and saints*" (*SE* 5). These three types are singled out because they represent three ways of transcending the plane of fundamentally animal existence: by way of insight, creativity, and self-mastery. And it is the cultivation and combination of these traits that are said to make possible *"the completion and fulfillment* [Vollendung] *of nature."* This, Nietzsche says, enables us to *"discover* a new circle of duties"—duties involving our doing whatever we can to advance the cultivation of these traits, through the "production" and assistance of those exceptional human beings through whose efforts they are furthered. Moreover: "These new duties are not the duties of a solitary [individual]; on the contrary, they set one in the midst of a mighty community held together, not by external forms and regulations, but by a fundamental idea. It is the fundamental idea of *culture* [Kultur]" (*SE* 5).

It is in these terms that Nietzsche here answers the question: "How can your life, the individual life, receive the highest value, the deepest significance? How can it least be squandered?" His answer is: "by *consecration to culture."* He elaborates: "Anyone who believes in culture is thereby saying: 'I see above me something higher and more human than I am; let everyone help me to attain it, as I will help everyone who knows and suffers as I do.'" And unless one happens to be among the "rarest and most valuable exemplars" of humanity and culture in and through whom they are further enriched and enhanced, "consecration to culture" means "living for the good" of those who *are* such "exemplars" in whatever way one can (*SE* 6). The centrality of culture to Nietzsche's thinking about human reality and higher humanity is then further reflected in the fact that the centerpiece of his science-friendliest book *Human* is its fifth part, an extended discussion of "Higher and Lower Culture" (*HH* I:224–92, discussed at length in chapter 2 above). And that preoccupation continued subsequently, through *Beyond* (as shall be seen in chapter 10), to and including *Twilight* and the other polemics of 1888.

Nietzsche undoubtedly had Richard Wagner—his paradigmatic creative genius—in mind when he wrote this. He subsequently outgrew that bit of "great man" romanticism, and generalized the idea along the lines of Zarathustra's exhortation that one do whatever one has it in oneself to do to contribute to the advent of the *Übermensch* (*Z* I:P:4)—that is, to the enhancement of human life. The emerging focus of his concern, as he puts it in his preface to *Genealogy*, was with the attainment—or nonattainment—of "the *highest power and splendor* actually possible to the type man [*Mensch*]" (*GM* P:6). It remained the case, however, to the end of his productive life, that the kind of human greatness he has in mind is to be conceived in terms of both human-spiritual and human-cultural "power and splendor," as two sides of the same coin. They together are the twin loci of his conception of the "highest" humanity conceivable and attainable. "What matters most," he wrote in *Twilight*, just before the abrupt end of his productive life, "always remains culture" (*TI* "Germans," 4). It would seem that nothing could be farther from existential-philosophical thinking and appraising.

The key to getting beyond nihilism in the aftermath of "the death of God" (and finessing "the challenge of existentialism" by way of this aestheticism), for Nietzsche, is not making life in this world fundamentally different and better than it is. That is an impossible dream. Rather, it is a combination of availing oneself of these real human possibilities to the best of one's ability, and attaining and sustaining a sensibility (involving good use of the ability to "learn to love") in which this can be experienced as more than sufficient. But for this to have a chance of working, it has to be done in a very powerful way. Nietzsche's version of it is the subject of the next section.

VII. Nietzsche's Dionysianism

Finally, mention must be made of Nietzsche's distinctive this-worldly alternative to (or kind of) religiousness, which is perhaps best characterized (following his own characterization of it) as "Dionysian." It could not be more different from Kierkegaard's radical God-centered Christianity—or, on the other hand, from the flatly secularist, utterly de-divinized worldviews of Sartre and Camus. The philosophical theologian Paul Tillich liked to refer to him as an "*ecstatic* naturalist." That characterization is well warranted. In the spirit of Zarathustra's proclamation that "body am I entirely, and soul is only a word for something about the body," one might say that for Nietzsche "divine" is only a word for something about life and the world—but that "something" is an *important* "something" in each case.

So Nietzsche feels in need of such notions as "joy," "affirmation," "faithfulness to the earth," "*amor fati*," and "eternal recurrence" to characterize the kind of fundamental attitude and relation to life and the world that he considers not only to be humanly possible but to be *humanly optimal*. They are expressive and indicative of what he calls a "Dionysian" kind of sensibility— one that rises emotionally to the level of a this-worldly religiousness—that is as far beyond nihilism as it is beyond all religious and metaphysical "other-worldliness" and life-inhibiting (or even -negating) "ascetic ideals." If human life is to flourish beyond the possibility of all disillusionment, we must not only become capable of *enduring a recognition* of the fundamental character of life and the world, and of the human condition in this life and world. We must come to be able truly and deeply to affirm, embrace, and love them, even in the face of loss and death.

Nietzsche's Dionysianism is, for him, that kind of sensibility, and that kind of love and celebration. So, in a late (1888) note, he speaks of "a Dionysian value standard for existence," and writes:

> Such an experimental philosophy as I live anticipates experimentally even the possibilities of the most fundamental nihilism; but this does not mean that it must halt at a negation, a No, a will to negation. It wants rather to cross over to the opposite of this—to a Dionysian affirmation of the world as it is, without subtraction, exception, or selection—it wants the eternal circulation [i.e., recurrence]: the same things, the same logic and illogic of entanglements. The highest state a philosopher can attain: to stand in a Dionysian relationship to existence—my formula for this is *amor fati*. (*KGW* VIII 16[323]; *WP* 1041)

Amor fati (love of fate) is Nietzsche's counterstroke to the Judeo-Christian idea of *amor dei* [love of God] as the formula for the essence of religiousness. Thus "For I love thee, O eternity!" [*Denn ich liebe dich, oh Ewigkeit!*] is the repeated refrain of the "Yes and Amen Song" with which Nietzsche has the third part of *Zarathustra* ecstatically conclude. *Love* is quite probably the most often-used word in the entire work. And the most important sort of love at issue, for Nietzsche, is not just *amor fati*. It might perhaps better be called *amor mundi*—an expression more fully evocative of Nietzsche's idea of profound "faithfulness to the earth" and love of life and the world that are what *amor fati* means to him. It is his envisioned alternative to making the unconditional love of a God imagined to exist beyond this life and world the cornerstone of the living of one's own life in this world—and also to a nihilistic negation of this life and world in the absence of such a God, and to their mere emotionless cognizing as objects of scientific knowledge.

Nietzsche envisions the alternative of an unconditional affirmation and loving embrace of what we are in any event stuck with: the world as it fundamentally is and will ever continue to be—notwithstanding the fact that our own individual and collective human existence cannot change the way it is and is itself but a fleeting ephemeral instance of the kind of affair it is. "Saying 'Yes' to life even in its strangest and hardest problems," he writes at the conclusion of *Twilight*—"*that* is what I called Dionysian [in *BT*]," even referring to himself as "the last disciple of the philosopher Dionysus" (*TI* "Ancients," 5). Nietzsche's Dionysianism differs from what he calls by that name in *Birth*, however, in that it incorporates elements of what he had there called "Apollinian" as well, as does the "tragic" sensibility that he had conceived as the issue of their union; and in fact his Dionysianism might be seen as his version of that very sensibility.

As Nietzsche came to realize, one's *attained sensibility* makes all the difference. In *Birth*, looking at life and the world through the lenses of the Schopenhauerian interpretation and sensibility that he had adopted, he had written: "Suppose a human being has thus put his ear, as it were, to the heart chamber of the world will and felt the roaring desire for existence pouring from there into all the veins of the world [. . .]—how could he fail at once to *break*?" (*BT* 21). By the time of *Human* (six years later), however, he had attained the new sensibility that was to animate his thinking from then onward—which he credits to *art*:

> Above all, [art] has taught us for thousands of years to look upon life in any of its forms with interest and pleasure, and to *develop our sensibility so far* [unsere Empfindung so weit zu bringen] that we at last cry: "life, however it may be, is good!" This teaching imparted by art to take pleasure in life and to regard the human life as a piece of nature [. . .] has been absorbed into us, and now reemerges as an almighty requirement of knowledge. One could give up art, but would not thereby relinquish the capacity one has learned from it. (*HH* I:222)

As Nietzsche very importantly observes in *Inquiry*, "One must learn to love" (*JI* 334)—or at any rate, one must learn to do so if one's love is to be strong enough to survive the recognition of the things about life and the world that Schopenhauer took to warrant their condemnation and rejection. It is of the utmost importance for Nietzsche that they *can* come to be loved—at least in their totality, from which we are not at liberty to pick and choose—beyond all revulsion and disillusionment, and without the mediation of the various forms of illusion that he had deemed indispensable to the achievement of this result in *Birth*. And that, he is saying here, is something that it has become possible for us to do precisely through the further cultivation of the kind of sensibility for which we have the arts to thank.

In a note from the mid-1880s, Nietzsche suggests thinking of "the world as a work of art that gives birth to itself" (*KGW* VIII 2[14]; *WP* 796)—and, he might have added, that also destroys itself and then gives birth to itself yet again, in a never-ending alternation of creation and destruction. And again: "An anti-metaphysical view of the world—yes, but an artistic one" (*KGW* VIII 2[186]; *WP* 1048). Nietzsche's Dionysianism is thus conjoined with his aestheticism, as its generalization and celebration. It involves learning to think of oneself as— and to become—something along the lines of "a work of art giving birth to itself," in a culture and a form of life and world that each may likewise be so construed. And, it must be added: with an attained sensibility that enables one further to learn to love it all, for the aesthetic phenomenon it can come to be seen to be—its ephemerality notwithstanding, and somehow "redeemed" (to the extent that it can be) by the consolation of the idea of its endless recurrence.

VIII. Conclusion

So—is Nietzsche an existentialist? His thought is philosophically unconventional, post-religious, post- (and indeed anti-) metaphysical, sometimes polemical, and often passionate; but that does not answer the question in the affirmative, for the same things may be said of the thought of Bertrand Russell. His embrace by subsequent paradigmatic existential philosophers likewise does not answer the question; for he has also been embraced by others hostile to existential philosophy, of a variety of orientations.

In terms of the distinctions suggested at the outset, Nietzsche's Dionysian aestheticism is either his *alternative to* or his *version of* existentialism. His naturalizing, "historical" philosophical anthropology is either his alternative to or his version of Existenz-philosophy. And his science-friendly but historically, socially, and culturally informed interpretive genealogical-psychological *fröhliche Wissenschaft* is either his alternative to or his version of phenomenological existential philosophy.

Nietzsche's kind of philosophy, so understood, is certainly quite different from Sartre's or Heidegger's, not to mention Kierkegaard's. If it, too, *is* to be considered a possible *kind* of existentialism, Existenz-philosophy, and/or existential philosophy, however, so much the better—for them.

9

Nietzsche as Individualist?

We *want to become those we are*—the new, the unique, the incomparable, the self-legislators, the self-creators! [*Wir aber* wollen Die werden, die wir sind—*die Neuen, die Einmaligen, die Unvergleichbaren, die Sich-selber-Gesetzgebenden, die Sich-selber-Schaffenden!*]

Joyful Inquiry, 335

Truly, the individual himself [*der Einselne selber*] is still the most recent creation [*die jüngste Schöpfung*].

Thus Spoke Zarathustra, I:15

My philosophy aims at an ordering of rank: not at an individualistic morality [*individualistische Moral*].

KGW VIII 7(6); *WP* 287; 1886–87

If we place ourselves at the end of this tremendous process [. . .], where society and the ethics of custom [*die Sittlichkeit der Sitte*] at last reveal *what* they have simply been the means to: then we discover that the ripest fruit is the *sovereign individual* [*souveraine Individuum*], like only to himself, liberated again from the ethicality of custom, autonomous and supra-ethical [*das nur sich selbst gleiche, das von der Sittlichkeit der Sitte wieder losgekommene, das autonome übersittliche Individuum*] [. . .], in short, the *Mensch* who has his own independent, protracted will, who *may promise* [*der* versprechen darf].

On the Genealogy of Morality, II:2

Every particular individual [*Jeder einzelne*] may be regarded as representing the ascending or descending line of life. When one has decided which, one has thereby established a canon for what his selfishness is worth [*einen Kanon dafür, was seine Selbstsucht wert ist*]. If he represents the ascent of the line [*das Aufsteigen der Linie*], his worth is in fact extraordinary [*so ist in der Tat sein Wert ausserordentlich*] [. . .]. If he represents the descending development [*die absteigende Entwicklung*] [. . .], then he is to be accorded little worth [*so kommt ihm wenig Wert zu*].

Twilight of the Idols, "Skirmishes," 33

Nietzsche is sometimes thought to have been "the philosopher of individualism"—a champion and celebrant of "the individual" and "individuality." But is his "highest" type of human being the "sovereign individual" that he lauds in *On the Genealogy of Morality*? How does he conceive of human individuality? How much importance does he attach to it? And why? Does he take it to be something valuable and desirable for its own sake? Or does he esteem and commend it (to the extent that he does) only owing to what he supposes to be its association with something else that he takes to matter, either as a means to it, or as something inseparable from it, or as a consequence of it?

These are important questions. The answers to them have important implications for the understanding of Nietzsche's thinking with respect to human reality, and what he calls "higher humanity." Many make the mistake of supposing him to subscribe to a version of the radical individualism of Kierkegaard and the existentialists—or the much worse mistake of imputing to him the different sort of radical individualism espoused by Ayn Rand.[1] But it would be another kind of mistake to fail to understand the sorts of individuality that he not only recognizes as having come to be humanly possible but also considers to be humanly desirable (at least selectively)—and further, to fail to understand the kinds of significance that he attaches to them (and why).[2] I shall try to give these questions content and focus, and shall suggest the sorts of answers I believe to be truest to the direction of his thinking. I shall base my case primarily on a consideration of what he has to say on the matter in his published writings, although I believe that further support for it can be found in his notebooks and other *Nachlass*. The passages cited above are indicative of his strong interest in this question, and of the range of his thoughts on the matter.

I

It is worth recalling at the outset that Nietzsche cut his philosophical teeth on Schopenhauer; that Schopenhauer considered the *principium individuationis* (principle of individuation) to be fundamentally illusory;[3] and that Nietzsche associates the celebration of individuation with the "beautiful illusions" of Apollinian art in *The Birth of Tragedy*. And it also is worth noting that in that early work he further takes a considerable part of the power of both Dionysian and tragic art to derive from their ability to provide alternative and relatively more successful ways of coping with both the utter ephemerality and the "terror and horrors" of individual human existence in the kind of world in which we find ourselves. The issue of individuality was thus on his mind from the outset. And as he distanced himself both from Schopenhauer and from the standpoint of *Birth*, that problem loomed large among those that he undertook to revisit and reconsider.

Nietzsche next addressed this issue in a significant way in *Schopenhauer as Educator*, the third of his *Unfashionable Reflections*. At first glance this essay would seem to be a kind of individualist manifesto, in which he attempts to out-Emerson Emerson (another of his "educators").[4] Nietzsche proclaims at the outset of that essay that it is "artists alone" who "reveal everyone's secret bad conscience, the law that every man is a unique miracle," and that one need only "follow his conscience, which calls to him: 'Be yourself [*sei du selbst*]! All you are now doing, thinking, desiring, is not you [*das bist du alles nicht*]!' " (*SE* 1).[5]

As the last sentence just cited indicates, however, "being yourself" is no simple matter for Nietzsche even here, and means something quite different than merely keeping on being the self or sort of person one already is, or doing what comes naturally. "Being yourself" may require or involve "*becoming yourself*," and/or what he subsequently calls (and calls for) "becoming *who you are*" (which may or may not mean the same thing). So he asserts, shortly thereafter, that "your true nature [*dein wahres Wesen*] lies, not concealed deep within you, but immeasurably high above you, or at least above that which you usually take yourself to be [*dem, was du gewöhnlich als dein Ich nimmst*]," adding that "the true basic material of your being [*was der wahre Ursinn und Grundstoff deines Wesens ist*]" is "something completely unteachable and ineducable, and in any case difficult of access, bound and paralyzed: your educators can be only your liberators [*Befreier*]" (*SE* 1).

Nietzsche offers a hint of the sort of thing he has in mind when he refers to his (highly idealized) sense of Schopenhauer as "a whole, unified, self-affixing and self-moving, unconstrained and uninhibited natural being" [*ein ganzes, einstimmiges, in eignen Angeln hängendes und bewegtes, unbefangenes und ungehemmtes Naturwesen*] (*SE* 2). This rather fanciful Emersonian characterization may not describe Schopenhauer at all accurately, or even remotely; but it does offer a sketch of the kind of individuality that Nietzsche continues to admire to the end of his productive life, as is evidenced by his similar characterization of Goethe[6] and Goethe's ideal in *Twilight of the Idols*.

There Nietzsche describes Goethe as representing "a return to nature, through a going-*up* to the naturalness of the Renaissance," who "aspired to *totality*," and "strove against the separation of reason, sensuality, feeling, will." And as for Goethe's ideal (which is clearly his own at that point): Nietzsche writes, in a passage cited at the outset (but well worth repeating), of Goethe's conception of "a spirit that has *become free*." Such a person is not only "a strong, highly cultured human being" but also one who "has himself under control," and who therefore "may dare to allow himself [*sich zu gönnen wagen darf*] the whole compass and wealth of naturalness [*Natürlichkeit*], who is strong enough for this freedom" (*TI* "Skirmishes," 49). Nietzsche's naturalizing reinterpretation of human reality is one that not only allows for this qualitatively distinctive higher-human possibility, but moreover is intended to have the virtue of making its emergence and development comprehensible.

This characterization likewise is a variation on the same theme sounded in the passage from *Genealogy* on the "sovereign individual" (also cited at the outset, and frequently elsewhere). It undeniably conveys something of Nietzsche's conception of what he calls "higher humanity"; and a human being of that sort certainly would possess a very meaningful and significant kind of individuality. Whether individuality is the *central and defining feature* of that type of humanity, however, and whether it is what that type of humanity is all about, are different matters.

II

In *Schopenhauer*, at least at times, Nietzsche goes even farther in the claims he makes with respect to the kind of individuality of which human beings are capable. So he asserts: "Each of us bears a productive uniqueness within him as the core of his being [*eine productive Einzigkeit in sich, als den Kern seines Wesens*]," and that "a chain of toil and burdens derives from this uniqueness," pertaining to its realization (*SE* 3). But in the course of the essay, he gives this idea a number of interesting twists, which strongly qualify it in important ways.

At the beginning of the sixth section of *Schopenhauer*, Nietzsche puts forth the following "proposition" [*Satz*]: "'Humankind ought constantly to work to produce individual great human beings [*einzelne grosse Menschen zu erzeugen*]—that and nothing else is its task'" (*SE* 6). That certainly sounds like a kind of radical individualism. It should be observed, however, that he makes it vividly clear here that it is not *individuality as such* that he is championing, but rather *human greatness*—which, he is supposing, can only come to exist and remain vital in existence *in an individual manner and form*.

The associated "new circle of duties" Nietzsche envisions and advocates revolves around "the idea of *culture*" [*der Grundgedanke der* Kultur]—but in a rather specific respect: "insofar as it sets for each one of us but one task: to promote the production of the philosopher, the artist and the saint within us and beyond us [*in uns und ausser uns*] and thereby *to work at the perfecting of nature* [der Vollendung der Natur zu arbeiten]" (his emphasis). And "these new duties are not the duties of a solitary; on the contrary, they set one in the midst of a mighty community [*eine mächtige Gemeinsamkeit*]"—namely, that of those who are dedicated to culture's advancement (*SE* 6).

The figure of "the philosopher" here stands for the attainment of knowledge and wisdom of a fundamental and comprehensive kind, culminating in "the great *enlightenment* as to the character of existence." The type of "the artist" signifies the cultivation of creative powers through which nature's own creativity can be raised to a higher level. And "the saint," in this instance, interestingly represents the attainment of that self-mastery and self-overcoming in which, Nietzsche writes, "the ego is completely melted away," and individuality gives way to a "oneness and identity with all living things"—in which, he adds, a "final and supreme becoming-human" [*jene endliche und höchste Menschwerdung*] is achieved (*SE* 5).

Nietzsche seems to be suggesting here that (thanks to developments in the course of human events) we all may have something of each of these figures or capacities "within us," at least potentially. He goes on to contend, however, that at least for most of us, the best thing we can do with our lives is to do whatever we can to promote the emergence of the highest attainable human embodiment of all three human capacities through the advancement of culture. And that advancement can only occur, he apparently supposes, through the flourishing and activity of those "individual great men" who are at its cutting edge.

So Nietzsche poses what he takes to be the fundamental and crucial question for each and all of us who are up to it. "The question is this," he writes: "how can your life, the individual life, receive the highest value, the deepest significance [*wie erhält dein, des Einzelnen Leben den höchsten Wert, die tiefste Bedeutung*]? How can it be least squandered?" And he answers: "Certainly only by your living for the good of the rarest and most valuable exemplars [*Gewiss nur dadurch, dass du zum Vorteile der seltensten und wertvollsten Exemplare lebst*]." One who resolves to do this "places himself within the circle of *culture*." He importantly continues:

> Anyone who believes in culture is thereby saying: "I see above me something higher and more fully human than I am [*ich sehe etwas Höheres und Menschlicheres über mir*]; let everyone help me to attain it, as I will help everyone who knows and suffers as I do: so that at last the human being may appear who feels himself perfect and boundless in knowledge and love, perception and ability [*der Mensch entstehe, welcher sich voll und unendlich fühlt im Erkennen und Lieben, im Schauen und Können*], and who in his completeness is at one with nature, the judge and evaluator of all things." (*SE* 6)

We may and undoubtedly should understand "the *Mensch*" Nietzsche speaks of here as "the kind of human being" (rather than some particular person)—and more fully stated, as "the kind of human being embodying the highest conceivable sort of humanity," rather than as one particular individual.

It should be quite evident that what Nietzsche has in mind is the appearance of that highest type of humanity, conceived along the lines he indicates, rather than the ultimate in individuality per se; nor is radical individuality at all what his description of that type of humanity suggests it to be all about. And he makes it clear in the earlier part of this passage (cited just above) that individuality sundered from the attainment or pursuit or support of these culturally expressed and culturally realized human qualities is of no interest to him. Indeed, individuality and the pursuit thereof may even be detrimental to this highest of human goods, if its valorization or indulgence hinders that highest good's realization, or squanders human assets that might have contributed to its realization.

Moreover, the "individual great men" to whom Nietzsche here accords such importance in this connection have that importance *only to the extent* that they further the enhancement and realization of this highest human good—as they inevitably do only in some respects, and only for a time. So Nietzsche quips, in an aphorism in *Beyond Good and Evil*, perhaps with this very discussion in mind: "A people [*Ein Volk*] is a detour of nature to get to six or seven great *Menschen.*—Yes, and then to get around them" (*BGE* 126).

This general position with respect to individuality is one that Nietzsche continued to maintain throughout his productive life. Indeed, he goes even further in *Twilight*, in the section cited at the outset, in the course of making it clear that he by no means supposes egoism always to be a good and desirable thing. "The value of egoism," he there writes, "depends on the physiological value of the one who possesses it: it can be very valuable, it can be worthless and contemptible." He then goes on to observe that this is the case precisely because the same is true of human beings themselves, and of their individuality: "Every particular individual [*Jeder einzelne*] may be regarded as representing the ascending or descending line of life." In the former case, "his worth is in fact extraordinary"; while in the latter, "he is to be accorded little value" (*TI* "Skirmishes," 33).

What matters most, Nietzsche is contending yet again in this late passage, is *the kind of humanity* we have attained, that lives in us and is sustained and advanced through our lives, rather than our particular existences and identities, however individuated they may be. So he goes so far as to say that "the single person, the 'individual' [*Der einzelne, das 'Individuum'*], as people and philosophers have hitherto understood him, is an error [*Irrtum*]"; for the more fundamental reality is not the particular human being at all, great or small, but rather "the entire *single* line '*Mensch*' up to and including himself"—and extending beyond himself in prospect—which each of us briefly "constitutes" (*TI* "Skirmishes," 33).

It should be noted in passing that translators generally render both of the above expressions Nietzsche uses in this connection—*der einzelne* or *der*

Einzelne and *das Individuum* (plural *Individuen*)—as *the individual*, thereby obscuring a possible intended difference in meaning. While these expressions can be used more or less synonymously, as they are here, Nietzsche sometimes would seem to have something more specific, distinctive, and exceptional in mind when he uses the latter expression than he generally does when he uses the former, which can be applied to each and every one of us as *particular* human beings, whether or not we have become full-fledged "individuals."

At times, however, Nietzsche also uses the former expression (particularly in its capitalized form) to refer to something along the lines of that more uncommon sort of selfhood. It is with his conception of "individuality" as such a more distinctive human attainment—rather than with the sort of "incidental differences" individuality that may be attributed to every particular human being as such (and means nothing more than that)—that I am concerned here. It should not be supposed, however, that he wishes to distinguish only one type of individuality in this stronger sense from the garden-variety type all normally functioning human beings have. On the contrary: he would seem to discern a number of them, and to regard them rather differently. This is a point to which it is important to remain attentive.

In the above-cited passage (*TI* "Skirmishes," 33), as so often in his later writings, Nietzsche gives this point a physiological edge (rather than casting it in the language of culture and its life-transforming significance that he favors in his earlier writings), having become convinced that the human differences with which he is concerned have a physiological as well as cultural reality and basis. But it continues to be the case that it is the *qualitative differences* in the character of human life—into which both physiological and cultural differences translate—that matter to him, and lead him to attach the importance he does to these distinctions and tendencies.

III

We must learn to think "historically" about everything human, Nietzsche had maintained at the outset of *Human, All Too Human*, ten years earlier [1878]; for everything human—along with everything else—"has *become*" [*ist geworden*] (*HH* I:2). And that includes whatever sorts of human individuality are humanly possible. For there is nothing metaphysically essential either *about* a human being or *within* a human being that constitutes or defines or establishes that human being's individuality. And there is no sort of individuality with which all human beings are endowed, or some prescription from on high or from deep within of what kind of individuality all human beings as such ought to attain. Individuality is one of those conceptions that must be reconsidered, in the course and context of the naturalizing reinterpretation of human reality for which Nietzsche calls at the outset of the third Book of *Joyful Inquiry*.

Individuality is one of the topics upon which Nietzsche focuses his attention in *Inquiry*, which offers a wealth of reflections upon different aspects of human reality, human differences, and human possibility, from a wide variety of perspectives. And one of the points that emerges from his reflections upon it is that, insofar as human individuality is a matter of something more than the *particularity* of each human being's physical, behavioral, and biographical existence, it can mean a variety of different things, all of which are results of various sorts of contingencies, and some of which are not only different from others but also are more difficult to attain and more unusual than others.

Individuality, Nietzsche suggests, is a relatively recent human phenomenon. He even has Zarathustra say so, in the first part of *Thus Spoke Zarathustra*: "To esteem is to create [. . .]. First, peoples [*Völker*] were creators; and only in later times, individuals [*Einzelne*]. Verily, the individual himself [*der Einzelne selber*] is still the most recent invention" (*Z* I:15). This was one of the main theses of Nietzsche's Basel senior colleague and mentor Jacob Burckhardt, in his 1860 work *The Civilization of the Renaissance in Italy*—a great and fascinating book, which Nietzsche knew well.[7] Its second part is entitled "The Development of the Individual." And it is a thesis Nietzsche made his own, even following Burckhardt in tracing this phenomenon to the Italian Renaissance, with a nod to the Athenian Greeks.

(In this respect, it seems to me that both Burckhardt and Nietzsche are actually only being good Hegelians; for this theme is a very Hegelian one. Individuality, for Hegel, is a humanly possible type of more or less differentiated identity and spirituality, which—like all types of humanly possible identity and spirituality—is realizable only under certain social and cultural conditions, and which, like most, is of real but limited interest and significance in the larger scheme of things.[8] I take Nietzsche to be in basic agreement with this general Hegelian assessment—even though he and Hegel do differ considerably, with respect not only to the *conditions* of this possibility, but also to that about human reality that matters most.)

As the passage from *Zarathustra* just quoted shows, Nietzsche supposes that relatively anonymous and conformist "herd" humanity was long the general rule in human reality, whether the populations in question were bucolic or predatory. He may maintain that human life is fundamentally *particular*, and that it is the conditions of social life and the nature of language as a social medium that render human consciousness and conduct herd-like (*JI* 354); but those circumstances cannot be said to stifle and homogenize an *innately individuated* human identity. Nor are the appetites and self-protective and self-assertive tendencies we as living creatures have tantamount to a kind of proto-individuality, real though they may be—and true though it may be that drastic measures had to be employed to turn our pre-social proto-human ancestors into the socialized and "domesticated" herd-animal humanity that eventually became the human rule (as Nietzsche contends in the second essay of *Genealogy*).

The fundamental question with respect to individuality, Nietzsche suggests, thus is *not* how it comes about that essentially and significantly individual human beings are so often *dis*-individuated. He does not ask, in the manner of Rousseau: "How is it that human beings are born individuals, but are everywhere in herds?" The real question, for him, is a very different one: How could it have come about that any significant kind of individuality has become humanly possible *at all*, given that it originally was (or at any rate must be presumed to have been) utterly lacking? Or rather: this is *one* real question with respect to individuality. Another, of even greater importance for Nietzsche but subsequent to this one, is that of its worth, in the various forms it can take.

IV

The first of these questions—one might call it the "genealogical" question, to distinguish it from the "axiological," evaluative and revaluative question—is, like the second, one to which Nietzsche turned frequently. He does so perhaps most vividly in his evocation of the figure of "the sovereign individual," and characterization of it as the "ripest fruit" of the long development he discusses at the outset of the second essay of *Genealogy*. He had used the same figure of speech in the same general context in *Joyful Inquiry*, five years earlier, in a section interestingly entitled "The Signs of Corruption." At a certain point in the decline of a society, he there surmises, as "morals decay" and "corruption" spreads, "*those Menschen* emerge whom one calls tyrants"—and, he observes: "They are the precursors and as it were the precious harbingers of *individuals [Individuen]*." To this he adds: "Only a little while later this fruit of fruits hangs yellow and mellow from the tree of a people—and the tree existed only for the sake of these fruits" (*JI* 23).

On the other hand, one should recall Nietzsche's qualifying quip five years later, shortly before *Genealogy*, in *Beyond*, cited above: "A people is a detour of nature to get to six or seven great *Menschen*.—Yes, and then to get around them" (*BGE* 126). Peoples and individuals alike—even the exceptional sorts of individuals he has in mind here and elsewhere (for example in *Schopenhauer* and *Genealogy*, in the passages cited above)—derive their significance *not* from their mere existence as such, for Nietzsche, or as human beings per se, but rather from what they mean for the enhancement of human life, and for the realization of the highest attainable sort of humanity in it.

Nietzsche is interested in the kinds of exceptional circumstances and human types he discusses in this section of *Inquiry* because he is convinced that some such extraordinary dynamic was required to break the grip of the kind of "herd" mentality that made any sort of individuality seem reprehensible and abhorrent. So he writes, in a later section entitled "Herd Remorse": "During the longest period of the human past nothing was more terrible than to feel that one stood by oneself," and "it was egoism that was formerly experienced as something painful and as real misery." This may remain the case among "the herd"; but among those "free spirits" to and for whom he is writing and who as such share his minority sensibility, he observes that "there is no point on which we have learned to think and feel more differently," and that "today [. . .] one finds one's pride in oneself" (*JI* 117).

Thus Nietzsche suggests here there has been a profound revaluation of the sort of "individuality" that involves having a sense of oneself as meaningfully separate and different from others. But that is by no means the end of the matter, for him; for as has already been seen, he considers the commonplace modern "sense of self and pleasure in the individual" he discusses here to be problematic in more ways than one. It is a far cry from the difficult and rare autonomy of the "sovereign individual," for example; and in Nietzsche's eyes the self-importance that tends to be associated with the commonplace modern "sense of self and pleasure in the individual" is utterly ludicrous.

One of the kinds of human individuality that Nietzsche does consider deserving of being noticed and emphasized is the subject of a section that appears shortly thereafter, entitled "Health of the Soul." Its point is that human beings are sufficiently complex that, beyond certain fundamental parameters, "there is no health as such," either of body or of soul; that "there are innumerable healths of the body." And for him the same applies to our psychological and spiritual healths—and also to our capacities for intellectual development, which may not only vary from one person to another, but also have requirements that are at odds with those of our healths (*JI* 120).

These dimensions of individuality—which may distinguish some human beings from all others, but which more often distinguish some *types* of human beings from others—are of no little significance for Nietzsche. Their larger (rather than merely personal or social) significance, however, is suggested ultimately to be a function not merely of their importance in relation to the happiness, flourishing, usefulness to others, or other such consequences for the particular person *or* for that person's community, but rather in relation to the character and quality of human life.

In a later section of *Inquiry* bearing the heading "The Greatest Advantage of Polytheism," Nietzsche probes further into the genealogy of individuality and suggests that it may have been in the sphere of religion—and more specifically in polytheistic religions—that the way may have been opened to the possibility of a significant form of individuality in human life. "For the individual [*der Einzelne*] to posit his own ideal and to derive from it his own law, joys, and rights," he writes, "may well long have been considered the most outrageous human aberration," since a high premium was placed on the general acceptance of "*one* ultimate norm" for all members of a society. "But above and outside," he continues, *beyond* the human world, "one was permitted to behold a *plurality of norms* [*eine* Mehrzahl von Normen]," associated with different gods.

"It was here [in polytheistic religions] that individuals [*Individuen*] were first permitted," Nietzsche surmises; and, he suggests, "the invention of gods"— and also (notably) of "heroes, and *Übermenschen* [NB!] of all kinds," along with various other types of fantastic beings—"was the inestimable preliminary exercise for the egoism and sovereignty of the individual [*Vorübung zur Rechtfertigung der Selbstsucht und Selbstherrlichkeit des Einzelnen*]." In this way "the strength to create for ourselves our own new eyes—and ever again new eyes that are even more our own [*sich neue und eigene Augen zu schaffen und immer wieder neue und noch eigenere*]" began to be developed and cultivated. And this, for Nietzsche, was and remains an essential precondition of "human free-spiritedness and many-spiritedness [*die Freigeisterei und Vielgeisterei des Menschen*]" (*JI* 143)—and thus of any significant kind and degree of human individuality.

<h2 style="text-align:center">V</h2>

It is precisely this kind of individuality that Nietzsche goes on to celebrate in some of the most notable sections of *Inquiry*. Among the aphorisms with which he concludes its third Book, we find an initial statement of one of his mottos: "What does your conscience say?—'You shall become who you are' [*'Du sollst der werden, der du bist'*]" (*JI* 270). And he develops this idea in one of the concluding sections of its fourth Book, which I have had occasion to cite a number of times previously: "We *want to become those we are* [*Wir aber wollen Die werden, die wir sind*]—the new, the unique, the incomparable, the self-legislating, the self-creating [*die Neuen, die Einmaligen, die Unvergleichbaren, die Sich-selber-Gesetzgebenden, die Sich-selber-Schaffenden*]!" (*JI* 335).

This is individuality conceived both as autonomy (giving oneself one's own laws) and as what might be called "autogeny" (that is, fashioning an identity for oneself out of the materials and circumstances of one's life). It is this latter theme that Nietzsche sounds in another of *Inquiry*'s notable sections, bearing the heading "One Thing Is Needful." That "one thing," he writes, is "to 'give style' to one's character [*Seinem Charakter 'Stil geben'*]—a great and rare art!" He spells out what he means by this as follows:

> It is practiced by those who survey all the strengths and weaknesses of their nature and then fit them into an artistic plan [*einem künstlerischen Plane*] until every one of them appears as art and reason [. . .]. Here a large mass of second nature [*zweiter Natur*] has been added; there a piece of original nature [*erster Natur*] has been removed—both times through long practice and daily work at it [. . .]. In the end, when the work is finished, it becomes evident how the constraint of a single taste governed and formed everything large and small. (*JV* 290)

This passage is well worth bearing in mind, not only for the indication it provides of an important aspect of the kind of individuality to which Nietzsche attaches significance, but also because it shows quite clearly that he considers this sort of self-transformation *to be humanly possible*—even if only for some, only within limits, and only with effort and persistence. Pieces of one's "original nature" *can* be altered, he thinks, or even removed; and pieces of "second nature" *can* be added to what one is to start with. Such self-shaping may not be "creation ex nihilo"; but neither is any other kind of artistic creation. And Nietzsche's readiness to use the language of "creating" to characterize it is indicative of the appropriateness of invoking the artistic model here.

Indeed, Nietzsche explicitly invokes this model himself shortly thereafter, in a section bearing the heading "What One Should Learn from Artists." "How can we make things beautiful, attractive, and desirable for us when they are not?" he asks—which in some cases may simply mean: when they are not so to us in the first place, as we find them. We can and should learn from artists not only how to alter the aspect of things—the ways in which we experience them—but also how to alter the materials with which they work, in such ways that they admit of being experienced differently than they would have been had the materials not been artistically reworked. And he concludes by saying that we need to learn to carry this ability beyond the point at which "art ends and life begins," and that "we want to be the poets of our life—first of all in the smallest, most everyday matters" (*JI* 299).

If Nietzsche may here be seen to be advocating a form of individualism, it would seem to be a kind of *aestheticist* individualism. A measure of autonomous and distinctive individuality may be both a precondition of giving "style" and aesthetic quality to one's "character" and identity and the outcome of doing so, developing through this very self-transformative process. But it has or acquires significance and worth, for him, only to the extent that one actually is (in another of his favorite phrases) "turning out well" in this respect.

What matters, for him, is not merely changing, or even merely becoming more distinctive, but rather doing so in a manner analogous to that of the artistic endowment of what begins as mere material with aesthetic quality and worth. In the language of *Birth*, this is to transform human life into a kind of "aesthetic phenomenon." And it is the endowment of life with aesthetic quality—in ways involving and resulting in certain sorts of individuality— that matters and gives it the only sort of "justification" of which it is capable, rather than its individualization per se, in some instances of which aesthetic quality may happen to be found.

In *Thus Spoke Zarathustra* many of these ideas reappear. In "On the Way of the Creator," Zarathustra asks: "Can you give yourself your own evil and your own good and hang your own will over yourself as a law?" (*Z* I:17). But such autonomy is not an end in itself, for Nietzsche's Zarathustra; for the whole point is to make clear what sort of independence is required if one is to be capable of taking "the way of the creator." And it is "creation" that is taken to be the key to "the meaning of the earth" and the possibility of "the affirmation of life." So Nietzsche has Zarathustra proclaim: "Creation [*Schaffen*]— that is the great redemption from suffering, and life's growing light" (*Z* II:2).

Such creation is to involve or bring about not merely the production of works of art, but the artistic transformation of human reality: "I taught them all *my* creating and striving," Zarathustra states—"to create and carry together into One what in man is fragment and riddle and dreadful accident [. . .]. I taught them to work on the future and to redeem with their creation all that *has been*" (*Z* III:12:3). And it is only "you creators" who are deserving of being called "higher *Menschen*," and who have "the right" as well as "the strength" for "egoism." For the only justification of "egoism" is in terms of the creativity for which it is required, as "the caution and providence of the pregnant" (*Z* IV:13).

VI

Did Nietzsche subsequently change his mind about the possibility of the sort of creativity and self-transformation of which he speaks here? It is sometimes suggested that he did, and that he came to subscribe to a kind of materialistic and fatalistic determinism that would rule out anything of the kind. Certain passages in *Twilight* in particular are thought to provide evidence of this. So, for example, he there writes: "The individual [*Der Einzelne*] is, in his future and in his past, a piece of fate, one law more, one necessity more for everything that is and everything that will be" (*TI* "Morality," 6).

It seems to me, however, that passages such as these neither preclude nor retract the idea that these sorts of things are or at least may occasionally become humanly possible. For when Nietzsche goes on to indicate what he is talking about, it turns out that he typically has in mind various rather general circumstances and features of our existence and the manner in which we are constituted *in the first place*, rather than everything about ourselves, and everything that becomes of us or might become of us. So, for example, in the latter passage, Nietzsche goes on to elaborate the point he is making as follows: "*No one* is responsible for it being the case [Niemand *ist dafür verantwortlich*] that one exists at all; or that one is constituted in a certain way, or that one is in some particular circumstances and surroundings. The fatality of his nature cannot be disentangled from the fatality of all of that which has been and will be" (*TI* "Morality," 8).

If *this* is the sort of thing Nietzsche is talking about, it would seem to leave quite open the possibility of the kinds of self-transformation and creative activity of which we find him speaking in his earlier writings. For while considerations of these sorts do indeed constrain us, they do not preclude the possibility of such things as artistic creativity, responsibility, "giving style to one's character," "becoming poets of our lives," or "becoming those we are" in ways that will be more meaningful in some cases than in others. And the fact that he remains committed to the meaningfulness of such ideas as these— even after having made (and coherently with) the above assertions—is evident in his continuing use of versions of these conceptions later on in the very same work.

So, for example, we find Nietzsche speaking again of the "grand style" in architecture—and therefore in the spirituality of those whose architecture it is—in which "the highest feeling of power and security finds expression" (*TI* "Skirmishes," 11). In the sections on "My Conception of Freedom" and "Freedom I Do *Not* Mean," he offers reflections upon autonomy and individuality that show he believes it to continue to be meaningful to speak of "the will to self-responsibility" [den *Willen zur Selbstverantwortlichkeit*] as something one may or may not have; of the sort of "person who has *become free*" [der frei gewordene *Mensch*] (*TI* "Skirmishes," 38) and "making the individual possible" [*das Individuum möglich machen*] in the world today (*TI* "Skirmishes," 41). And his reflections upon Goethe near the book's end, mentioned above,

provide an ample corrective to any tendency to read too much into his remarks about fate and necessity. Indeed, there is no better paradigm for the
late Nietzsche of what human individuality at its best can amount to than the
Goethe he describes in these late sections (*TI* "Skirmishes," 49–51).[9]

VII

In *Beyond* there is relatively little discussion of individuality. It is of some interest, however, that Nietzsche is at pains to reject the metaphysical underpin-
nings and construal of the idea of the self commonly associated with the sort
of easy egalitarian individualism to which he is so strongly opposed. So he
dismisses "soul-atomism" [*Seelen-Atomistik*] (*BGE* 12), the idea of a subject or
"'I' that thinks" (*BGE* 17), and the very concept of some sort of "I" that each of
us is (*BGE* 19). He suggests that one of the main positive features of the entire
history of modern philosophy is its collective effort to dispose of "the old soul
concept, under the guise of a critique of the subject-and-predicate concept"
(*BGE* 54). He is concerned to replace preoccupation with the idea of such a
self, subject, or soul with attention to the character and quality of human life
and its possible enhancement (or decline). And they are conceived in the
perspectives of biology and culture, in both of which the individual matters
much less than the larger form of life of which the individual is a part. This is
a way of thinking that becomes even more prominent in Nietzsche's writings
during the last year of his productive life.

The "individual" actually only makes an appearance as such once in *Beyond*, in a version of the portrait that we have already encountered in Nietzsche's earlier writings—but a version that brings out what he takes to be both
its highly contingent and very problematic character. The section in question
(*BGE* 262) occurs in the ninth and final part of the book, in which Nietzsche
is concerned with the nature and genealogy of the "*vornehm*" (superior, foremost, higher, "noble" in that sense) type of human being. In this section he
distinguishes between the type of human being produced in social conditions
of stress "through the long fight with essentially constant *unfavorable* conditions," and the type for which the stage is set when this sort of stress has first
occurred and then has given way to a relaxation of social controls and imperatives. Under such more relaxed conditions, he suggests, the strength built
up within the stalwarts of a society in the face of such stress then finds other
outlets and modes of expression: "whether as deviation (to something higher,
subtler, rarer) or as degeneration and monstrosity [. . .]; the individual [*der
Einzelne*] dares to be individual and different."

Nietzsche elaborates upon this point as follows: "The dangerous and uncanny point has been reached where the greater, more manifold, more comprehensive life transcends and *lives beyond* the old morality; the 'individual'
[*das 'Individuum'*] appears, obliged to give himself laws and to develop his
own arts and wiles for self-preservation, self-enhancement, self-redemption"
(*BGE* 262). At such a juncture, he suggests, there are "all sorts of new what-
fors and wherewithals," with "no shared formulas any longer." Sociologists
would describe this social situation as one of "anomie," or "normlessness,"
and would characterize those Nietzsche characterizes (in scare quotes) as "individuals" as "anomic," or "normless"—for better or for worse. They may be
either "beyond" the generally prescribed norms that define what is "good"
and what is "evil," or they may sink *beneath* these norms in one way or another, ranging from degenerate self-indulgence to pathological monstrosity.

It is only "individuals" of the former sort whose attained individuality is of
any larger significance. They are those who not merely indulge socially deviant
inclinations of the latter sorts, but rather make something of themselves transcending their proto-human animality, their minimally human sociality, and
their all-too-human idiosyncrasy. It has a higher significance than mere "self-
preservation." It is that of what Nietzsche calls "self-enhancement" and even
"self-redemption." And, as he contends at the outset of this part of the book,
that has only happened and can only happen under certain sorts of social and
cultural conditions, in which the stage has been properly set. For, as he states
in the opening sentence of its first section: "Every enhancement of the type
'*Mensch*' has so far been the work of an aristocratic society." His reasoning is as
follows: "Without that *pathos of distance* which grows out of the ingrained difference between [social] strata [. . .], that other, more mysterious pathos could
not have grown up either—the craving for an ever widening of distances within
the soul itself, the development of every higher, rarer, more remote, further-
stretching, more comprehensive states—in brief, simply the enhancement of
the type *Mensch*, the continual 'self-overcoming of man'" (*BGE* 257).

The implications for individuality of this line of thought are clear, even
if Nietzsche's reasoning here may be less so, and even if the soundness of his
psychological-anthropological speculation here may be even more problematic. The only kinds and realizations of individuality that he considers to be
of positive rather than negative or merely indifferent significance are those
which are positively associated with the kind of "enhancement" of human
life and human reality that he here has in mind. For it is only in the realm
of culture and its various forms of reality, activity, and experience that such
transformations "within the soul itself" can be realized. And the significance

attaching to such sorts of individuality are entirely derivative and instrumental, in relation to the enhancement of human cultural reality, the dynamics of which dictate the kinds of individuality that are to be required, desired, expected, and tolerated.

VIII

Individuality makes another major appearance in *Genealogy*, Nietzsche's next book. Again, however, it does so only briefly—even if also very significantly. And its absence from most of the rest of the book is no less significant. The passage in question has already been cited at the outset and mentioned in the foregoing discussion. It occurs in its second essay, near its beginning, when (with no little fanfare) Nietzsche introduces the figure of "the sovereign individual" [*souveraine Individuum*] as "the ripest fruit" of "the tremendous process" of which he there is speaking. That "process" is "the long story of how *responsibility* originated"—which, he observes, "*presupposes* as a *preparatory* task that one first *makes* human beings to a certain degree [. . .] regular and calculable," by way of "the ethic of custom [*Sittlichkeit der Sitte*] and the social straitjacket" (*GM* II:2; emphasis added).

The "sovereign individual," as Nietzsche here characterizes this figure, has *internalized*—and has thereby attained—the kind of "regularity" and "calculability" that first had to be required and imposed *externally*, and then has somehow managed to turn external restriction and control into self-mastery and self-control, substituting *his own* internally centered and exercised "sovereignty" for that of the community. He has become "liberated again from the ethic of custom" and so has become "autonomous," his attained "autonomy" replacing the heteronomy of socioethical normativity, as that sort of governance had replaced the reign of the impulses, instincts, and drives by which our pre-socialized and pre-"domesticated" ancestors once were governed—but *without merely reverting* to their proto-human animality.

This type of human being who has "become free" [*dieser Freigewordene*], Nietzsche writes, "who *may promise*" [*der* versprechen darf], has become "master of a *free* will" [*Herr des* freien *Willens*], in thrall neither to natural compulsion nor to the dictates of merely social regulation and regimentation. (The word *darf* here is crucial to his point. To be one who *versprechen darf* is to be one who has *become capable* of doing what promising requires—namely, not merely of verbally *giving* one's word but of *keeping* it—and so has become *promise-eligible*.)

As "possessor of a protracted unbreakable will" [*Inhaber eines langen unzerbrechlichen Willens*], the sovereign individual has a new kind of freedom and power: "this distinctive freedom, this power over oneself and over fate" [*dieser seltenen Freiheit, dieser Macht über sich und das Geschick*] (in the form of both impulses and circumstances that continue to arise), at least to an extent that is both humanly possible and humanly significant. And one who has attained this kind of power is therewith said to be entitled to a "proud awareness of the extraordinary privilege of *responsibility*"—responsibility not merely in the context of social expectations and interpersonal relations, but rather in the very different context of one's expectations of oneself, framed independently from those of others, and involving the exercise of the capacity for independent commitment and disciplined persistence that Nietzsche here characterizes in terms of "will."

Nietzsche has relatively little to say here about the *use* of this exceptional sort of autonomy, other than to make reference to the fact that it really means something when human beings of this sort "give their word"—whether to others or to themselves. But he does go on to add significantly, in the following section, that such a person not only "may give his word" [*für sich gut sagen dürfen*] but "also *may affirm himself*" [*auch zu sich* Ja sagen dürfen] (*GM* II:3).

It seems clear, however, that what Nietzsche has in mind is the capacity to which he repeatedly refers with great emphasis elsewhere, of setting goals for oneself, and of being able to pursue the most ambitious and distant goals with a determination and discipline that can be supplied neither by mere nature nor by mere socialization. So he speaks of "giving laws to oneself" appropriate to the goals in question, and adhering to them in the face of both adversity and temptation. In a word: what he has in mind is the capacity to make and keep meaningful *commitments* to future courses of action—not only to others but (even more importantly here) commitments *to and of oneself*. And it is this capacity, rather than mere distinctiveness per se, that would seem to be the core feature of Nietzschean individuality.

To say this, however, is *not* to say that this is the core feature of Nietzschean higher humanity. On the contrary: I would contend that it is *only* the core feature of *one type* of humanity that Nietzsche would deem "higher" and "*vornehm*" [superior]—a type that is by no means the highest and most admirable of those he envisions—and only one of a cluster of features that he combines in the sketches he provides of that sort of more complete higher humanity.[10]

One of the most striking of these features is made vividly apparent at the end of *Genealogy*'s second essay. It concludes with an image that contrasts significantly with that of the "sovereign individual" with which that essay began, showing one of its major limitations. This surely was no accident or mere coincidence. Indeed, the second essay can be read as Nietzsche's account of the sort of *further* transformation of humanity that made the difference, and made that difference humanly possible. What the "sovereign individual" as described in *GM* II:2 lacks most crucially is summed up in Nietzsche's characterization of *"the Mensch* of the future" he is envisioning as a *"schöpferische Geist"* [creative spirit] (*GM* II:24). That is something the sovereign individual of *Genealogy* II:2—at least as such—is not.

IX

This is an important point that warrants brief elaboration. "Sovereign individuality" is not the feature that looms largest in the genealogical account to which the remainder of *Genealogy*'s second essay is devoted. That account is an account not only of certain "moral" phenomena, but also of what turn out to be *further* psychological conditions of the possibility of a further-enriched higher humanity. It is *not* autonomous, self-responsible, sovereign individuality about which Nietzsche waxes so enthusiastic toward the end of section 16, for example—"something so new, profound, unheard of, enigmatic, contradictory, *and future-opening* [Zukunftsvolles] that the aspect of the earth was essentially altered." It is rather something he takes the creation of the "bad conscience" to involve: "the existence on earth of an animal soul turned against itself" (*GM* II:16). And it is *that* phenomenon, I suggest, that moves Nietzsche to the soaring rhetoric with which the second essay itself concludes. It has no direct connection with "sovereign individuality"; but *when combined with it* in a certain sort of way, it held and holds extraordinary human [*menschlich*] and supra-human [*übermenschlich*] promise.

The *"Mensch* of the future" Nietzsche there (in section 24) envisions, who is to "redeem us not only from the hitherto reigning ideal but also from that which was bound to grow out of it, the great nausea, the will to nothingness, nihilism," is no mere "sovereign individual." Or rather: it is *that and more*: namely, a *"creative* spirit" [*der* schöpferische Geist], with a "compelling strength" [*drängende Kraft*] that must be actively expressed, and so "will not let him rest in any aloofness or any 'beyond'" (*GM* II:24; emphasis added). And so, once again, we find that for Nietzsche it is the element of *creativity*— for which we are indebted to the pathology of "bad conscience"—that is crucial. Sovereign individuality alone, like intellectual integrity alone, impressive and important as it is, is not enough—not enough to serve as an antidote to the "ascetic ideal" to the analysis of which he turns in the third essay, and "redeem us" from "the will to nothingness" in which he there contends it is bound to culminate (*GM* III:28).

NIETZSCHE AS INDIVIDUALIST?

Indeed, the will to individuality is as problematic as is "the will to truth," for Nietzsche, if it is not joined to something better suited to this role than either of them is. So, he tells us in the third essay, for guidance in this matter we must look to *art* rather than to either *Wissenschaft* (*GM* III:25) or the ethic of radical autonomy. And we are to look to art for reasons relating to both the creativity and the associated sensibility (including a clear conscience for the preference of what is *created* to what can be *discovered* about the way things are in the first place) that are its hallmarks and its great gifts to humanity.

The key to higher humanity and to the enhancement and affirmation of life, for the Nietzsche we encounter here, is neither intellectuality nor individuality, nor is it even autonomy and the ability to commit by themselves. Rather, it is the kinds of creativity and associated sensibility that are humanly possible that are the key. And they are what these other qualities must serve— and which must transcend them—if they are to be conducive rather than detrimental to life, and if they are to be capable of sustaining us.

X

The upshot of this reflection on what Nietzsche has to say about individuality is that he does not consider it to have intrinsic worth, and to be an end in itself. Rather, he regards it as a means, symptom, and attendant feature of the attainment of higher humanity—which is to say: of "the 'humaneness' of the future" (*JI* 337), "the 'great health'" (*JI* 382), and a "'Dionysian' faith" (*TI* "Skirmishes," 49) and "disposition toward life and the world" sufficiently affirmative to enable one to pass the ultimate test of the thought of "eternal recurrence" (*JI* 341) that he associates with it.

Individuality figures in Nietzsche's conception of higher humanity; but it is neither its defining characteristic nor the central value around which Nietzschean higher humanity revolves—*nor* a sufficient condition of its attainment. I believe that, if we pursue this line of reflection, we will achieve an understanding not only of his conception and assessment of the various forms of individuality that are humanly possible, but also of such different but related and important Nietzschean notions as the enhancement of life, higher humanity, and supra-humanity [*Übermenschlichkeit*].

Nietzsche as "Free Spirit"?

The truly free in spirit will also think freely regarding the spirit itself and will not shy away from anything dreadful pertaining to its source and tendency. [*Der wahrhaft Freie im Geiste wird auch über den Geist selber frei denken und sich einiges Furchtbare in Hinsicht auf Quelle und Richtung desselben nicht verhehlen.*]
Human, All Too Human, II:I:11

Goethe conceived of a strong, highly cultured human being [*einen starken, hochgebildeten Mensch*], skilled in all physical accomplishments, having himself under control and having reverence for himself, who may dare to allow himself the whole compass and wealth of naturalness [*Natürlichkeit*], who is strong enough for this freedom [. . .]. Such a spirit that has *become free* [*Ein solcher freigewordner Geist*] stands in the midst of the universe with a joyful and trusting fatalism, in the *faith* that only the particular is contemptible [*nur das Einzelne verwerflich ist*], that overall [*im Ganzen*] everything is redeemed and affirmed [. . .]. But such a faith is the highest of all possible faiths: I have baptized it with the name *Dionysus*.
Twilight of the Idols, "Skirmishes," 49

Nietzsche's first self-consciously philosophical book, *Human, All Too Human* (1878), was also the first of what he later described as "a series of writings by Friedrich Nietzsche, whose common goal is to set forth *a new image and ideal of the free spirit*."[1] He also gave the book the subtitle *A Book for Free Spirits* [*freie Geister*]. The idea of the "free spirit" and of the "free in spirit" were thus very much on his mind as apt characterizations of his kind of philosopher and philosophy from the outset of his brief but extraordinary philosophical career. They also figured explicitly and prominently in the most programmatic of his philosophical writings, *Beyond Good and Evil*.

But what does Nietzsche mean by *Freigeist* [free spirit] and related expressions? It should go without saying (but is worth reminding ourselves) that, in taking up this question, one must set aside whatever might come to mind when English-speaking readers see such expressions in translations of his writings (or even when German-literate readers see expressions like "*der freie Geist*" in Nietzsche's German texts), drawing upon common usage or our linguistic intuitions in either language. The question is: What does *he* have in mind when he uses such expressions? And for that our primary guides must be how *he* uses them, and what he says about what he means. So he insists (in *Beyond*) that "we 'free spirits' [. . .] are something different from '*libres-penseurs*,' '*liberi pensatori*,' '*Freidenker*,'" and the like (*BGE* 44). And he says in *Ecce Homo* that even before *Human*, in his *Unfashionable Reflections* (1874–76), "an altogether new type of free spirit thus gained its first expression" (*EH* "Books," *UR*:2).

"The Free Spirit" is the title Nietzsche gave to the important second part of *Beyond Good and Evil*, immediately following its opening critique of what he calls philosophical "prejudices." In it he discusses the kind of philosopher he considered himself at least in large part to be (throughout the book he speaks repeatedly of "we free spirits"), presumably in contrast to previous philosophers of whom he is so critical in the preface and the book's first part. One good way to approach the question of what Nietzsche was trying to do and be as a philosopher, therefore is to consider what he has to say about becoming and being a "free spirit" and "free-spirited" thinker in these works.[2]

Another important way to do so is to go on to consider what Nietzsche came to regard as the limitations of that sort of thinker and philosopher. For "free-spirited thinking" is not all there is to the kind of philosophy and philosophical thinking he came to champion, at least after the years of his "free spirit" series. Indeed, while he repeatedly characterizes himself as a "free spirit" in *Beyond*, he also makes it clear that, for him, to the extent that he and we are not *more than* free-spirited thinkers, we are only "heralds and precursors" of the full-fledged "new species of philosophers" he there envisions.

So Nietzsche writes that they "will be free, *very* free spirits, these philosophers of the future—though just as certainly they will not be merely free spirits [*nicht bloss freie Geister*] but something more, higher, greater, and fundamentally different [*etwas Mehreres, Höheres, Grösseres und Gründlich-Anderes*]" (*BGE* 44). This makes it all the more important that we consider both what his kind of "free spirit" is and what it lacks, in relation to what his conception of what this kind of philosopher is to be in *Beyond* (1886). That is the question to which I will turn at the end of this chapter.

I

I shall begin by recalling a bit of what was said in chapter 2 about the first version and volume of *Human, All Too Human*, Nietzsche's subtitled *Book for Free Spirits*, with which his "free spirit" series began. It was published in the centenary year of the death of the Enlightenment thinker and writer par excellence generally known simply as Voltaire, and was dedicated to his memory. This already says something about how Nietzsche thought of the "free spirit" at the time. It was now Voltaire, rather than his earlier idols Schopenhauer and Wagner, in whom he found a new kindred spirit and inspiration.

As was further noted in that chapter, Nietzsche also subsequently saw that book as something more: "the monument of a crisis." In writing it, he tells us in his autobiographical *Ecce Homo* (1888), he was struggling to *free himself* from many things that stood in the way of his (as he later liked to put it) "becoming who he was"—perhaps as a person, but more particularly as a thinker. "Here I liberated myself from what in my nature did not belong to me." It was initially the "freedom" of *his own* "spirit" that was most immediately at issue, and for the sake of which *writing* and publishing the book was needed. It was his public declaration of independence from Wagner, his former idol, intimate personal acquaintance, and spiritual mentor, whom he knew would not like it one bit.

Nietzsche also emphasizes in *Ecce Homo* that by "free spirit" he had meant the "spirit" of a person and thinker who has been "*freed*"—which is to say, liberated or emancipated from some sort of bondage or domination. And by this he means "a spirit that has *become free*, that has taken possession of itself again" (*EH* "Books," *HH*:1). At that point the "freedom" he had in mind and was concerned with had to be *attained*, through rebellion against and escape from influences that had previously held sway over him.

In the first instance, he further tells us, the influences from which he had to free himself were of a cultural nature, and related to "ideals" associated with his earlier preoccupations and attractions. Thus he refers to *Human* as a "monument of rigorous self-discipline with which I put a sudden end to all my infections with 'lofty swindles,' 'idealism,' 'beautiful feelings' [and the like]"—presumably meaning romanticism in general and Wagner in particular (*EH* "Books," *HH*:5). But the freedom Nietzsche was seeking—and, in the perspective of 1888, believed himself largely to have attained during the years of his "free spirit" series—was a liberation from other "ideals" as well, ideals associated with a broad range of attachments: professional (academic and philological) and philosophical (Schopenhauer) as well as cultural (art and music). And he tells us he did so with the aid of perspectives upon them developed by way of his avid pursuit of "physiology, medicine, and natural sciences" (*EH* "Books," *HH*:3). He describes his "liberating" strategy as one designed to deprive seductive ideals of their appeal: "This is war, but war without powder and smoke [. . .]. One error after another is coolly placed on ice; the ideal is not refuted—it *freezes* to death" (*EH* "Books," *HH*:1).

II

Nietzsche followed *Human* with another substantial volume of aphorisms in the developing series that he called *Morgenröte* [literally, "morning reddish glow," usually translated as *Daybreak* or *Dawn*; 1881]. He gave it that name to suggest that it marked the dawning of a new (free-spirited) day. In that book, he tells us in *Ecce Homo*, he expanded his "war" to "the prejudices [*Vorurteile*] of morality" (in the words of its subtitle), launching what he calls "my campaign against morality"—and, in particular, "against the morality of self-effacement [*die Entselbstungs-Moral*]." The aim of this "fight" is said to have been "a liberation from all moral values," opening the way to "saying 'yes' to, and having confidence in, all that hitherto had been forbidden, despised and damned" (*EH* "Books," *D*:1, 2).

By the end of *Joyful Inquiry* (Nietzsche's next work and *Daybreak*'s sequel), that liberation, too, is said to have become part of the new freedom of the "free spirit," enabling him to "dance right over morality," leaving it behind and beneath him (*EH* "Books," *JI*). He had in mind, more specifically, the moralism of judgmental "good-versus-evil" thinking, to which the title of *Beyond* also refers. It was only in retrospect, however, that he felt he understood what it was that he was striving to attain—and at that point he was still far from having attained it. His description in the 1886 preface he added to *Human* vividly depicts his progress toward freedom:

> From the desert of these years of temptation and experimentation, it was still a long road [. . .] to that *mature* freedom of spirit [reifen *Freiheit des Geistes*] which is equally self-mastery and discipline of the heart, and permits access to many and contradictory modes of thought [. . .], to that overabundance of formative, curative, molding and restorative forces which is precisely the sign of *great* health—an overabundance that grants to the free spirit the dangerous privilege of living *experimentally* and of being allowed to offer itself to adventure: the master's privilege of the free spirit! (*HH* I:P:4)

Nietzsche's "long road" to this "mature freedom of spirit" thus began but did not end with the form he describes, of which he here considers the first installment of *Human* to have been both the expression and the means of its own attainment, as it bootstrapped its way into existence (*HH* I:P:3). So he goes on in that preface to identify three *intermediary* stages in the progress of the developing "free spirit"—or at any rate in the emergence and development of his own "free spirituality." They follow (in the imagery of Zarathustra's parable of "The Three Metamorphoses") its initial, explosively rebellious "lion" stage, and precede the much later "mature" stage of ripened spirituality that by contrast (and somewhat ironically) has something innocently childlike and "playful" about it. All are "free-spirited"; but for the Nietzsche of this preface, all of the initial forms of this "free-spirited" spirituality still leave a good deal to be desired.

At the threshold of "mature freedom of spirit" but not yet well across it, Nietzsche's "free, ever freer spirit begins to unveil the riddle of that great liberation" itself, and grasps what it is all about: namely, *self-mastery*, and its employment in the enhancement of life. So he writes: "If he has for long hardly dared to ask himself: 'why so apart? So alone? Renouncing everything I once reverenced? Renouncing reverence itself?'" And he answers this question with the following envisioned reply: "You shall become master over yourself, master also over your virtues. Formerly *they* were your masters; but they must be only your instruments beside other instruments. You shall get control over your For and Against and learn how to display first one and then the other in accordance with your higher goal" (*HH* I:P:6).

In an important counterpart passage to this one in *Genealogy of Morality* a year later, the phrase "in accordance with your higher goal" is replaced by "useful for knowledge" [*für die Erkenntnis nutzbar*] (*GM* III:12). A concern with knowledge was already also central to Nietzsche's early conception of the "free spirit." Liberation from the many burdens and inhibitions he associates with the "Christian-moral" tradition—and also with the tyranny of "the *Sittlichkeit der Sitte*" [the ethic of custom] (*GM* II:2)—is another part of it. But subsequently, when Nietzsche speaks of the "free spirit," what he more specifically has in mind is the emergence and character of what he takes to be a distinctive new and important type of thinker and thinking.

That is certainly his focus in the second part of *Beyond* that bears "The Free Spirit" as its title. What is so important about all of the liberations that make the "free spirit" a progressively more completely "freed" spirit, for him now, is that they make possible a more *uninhibited* and irreverent kind of thinking than one finds in philosophers previously. So, in *Ecce Homo*, he refers to the kind of "free spirit" we find in *Human* as a "merciless spirit" that goes after all philosophical and moral prejudices, and "the ideal" in all of its guises, with gloves off and no holds barred. And it does so in alliance with any disciplines that are capable of shedding light upon and into the all-too-human "*underworld* of the ideal" (*EH* "Books," *HH*:1).

Moreover, if it is "truly free," for Nietzsche, a "free spirit" of his sort "will also think freely," in a completely unencumbered and candid fashion, even—and indeed especially—about the basic (and possibly disturbing) "origin and tendency" of *its own* spirituality. And this means eschewing all "dissembling" (such as that of taking refuge in euphemism and steering clear of hard psychological truths) (*HH* II:I:11). Nietzsche's "free spirit" is no "blithe spirit"—even if, at least by the time of *Inquiry*, it has acquired a sense of humor and a dancing style, has learned to enjoy and employ puns and wit, and loves to laugh. And the *Fröhlichkeit* [joyfulness] of his free-spirited philosophical *Wissenschaftler* is no stranger to bloody-mindedness. If this was already the case in his "free spirit" series, it is even more so in *Beyond*, in which the banner of the "free spirit" is again unfurled. So Nietzsche observes in *Ecce Homo* that, in it, "psychology is practiced with admitted hardness and cruelty" (*EH* "Books," *BGE*).

In short: pre-*Zarathustra* Nietzsche conceived of the "free spirit" first and foremost as one who engages in radically "dis-illusioned" inquiry aspiring to an unsparing comprehension of all things human, drawing upon all available disciplinary perspectives and resources, and animated by an unflinching "intellectual conscience" of a severity that he complains is all too rare (*JI* 2). And this for him is done more specifically—and most importantly—in league with the project of a "de-deified" and "naturalizing" reinterpretation of human reality that he announces at the outset of Book 3 of *Inquiry* (*JI* 109), and the associated project of what he came to call a "revaluation of all values" (*EH* "Books," *D*:1).

III

I now turn to Nietzsche's discussion and treatment and use of the "free spirit" idea in the second part of *Beyond*. *Beyond* was contemporaneous with his just-discussed prefaces added in 1886 to his earlier "free spirit" series works. This second part ("The Free Spirit") follows an opening (first part) critique of "Prejudices of Philosophers," to which Nietzsche evidently intended it to stand in contrast. It therefore is a kind of introduction to the rest of the book, and so to this "prelude" to his newly envisioned "philosophy of the future." He appeared to have retired that rubric with the announced conclusion of his "free spirit" series upon the publication of *Inquiry* in 1882.

When Nietzsche reintroduced the "free spirit" idea here, therefore, seemingly as the rubric under which he was choosing to position himself in this new and obviously programmatic book, he at least gave the appearance of having changed his mind. And the fact that he went on, the year after *Beyond* (1886), to add a new fifth Book to a reissue of *Inquiry*, is indicative of at least some continuity in his thinking between the project of the first four-Book version of this work (and of the "free spirit" series more generally), *Beyond*, and his proclaimed post-*Zarathustra* "philosophy of the future." So what is the relation—both the continuity and the difference—between them? That is the basic question I will be discussing in this chapter.

It seems clear that, in availing himself once again of the "free spirit" idea, Nietzsche had in mind something like the "mature freedom of spirit" he regarded as the culmination of the development of that idea, discussed in the previous section, rather than any or all of its preliminary forms. So we find him, in this second part of *Beyond*, taking this occasion to further elaborate that "image of the free-spirited philosopher," in what he regarded as its fully "mature" and developed form.

He does so by indicating various "traits" he associates with it (*BGE* 39). One of them, of course, is indicated by the very title of the book itself: such a philosopher is to be "beyond good and evil"—that is, beyond thinking moralistically, in ways influenced by the norms and values of the kind of morality he uses that duality to characterize. Another such trait is obviously freedom from the various other "prejudices of philosophers" he discusses in the previous (first) part of the book—as well as from the dogmatic tendencies and Platonistic errors with respect to human spirituality and value that he excoriates in the preface to it. But what else?

The first further or more specific trait in the portrait Nietzsche mentions is the ability to recognize, admit, and take in stride the idea that human life in general—including the human endeavor of scientific thinking and the free-spirited philosopher's own pursuit of knowledge—inescapably involves (and even requires) forms of strategic "simplification" and "falsification," and thus at least a measure of "will to ignorance" and "love of error" (*BGE* 24). He next (in *BGE* 25) makes the point that his "free-spirited philosophers" will of course be "friends of knowledge [*Erkenntnis*]"; but they are not to be fanatics or martyrs for whom nothing else matters or is more important, and no sacrifice is too great. (This marks a change; because he had spoken of *Erkenntnis* and commitment to its pursuit in just that way in *Inquiry*.)

Further (*BGE* 26): as would-be "knowers" nonetheless, seeking to comprehend human reality, they must concern themselves not just with exceptional and admirable human beings and possibilities, but also with the human rule and the all-too-human; and they must be ready to learn from the observations of "cynics" with respect to them, but without allowing themselves to become cynics themselves. They therefore need to be prepared to be misunderstood (*BGE* 27 and 30).

They further should be sensitive to how much depends on the contingencies and differences of languages (*BGE* 28). They of course will need to be independently minded and daring in their interpretive experiments, which requires strength of spirit (*BGE* 29). They need spiritual maturity as they proceed with their tasks, knowing better than to "venerate and despise" too quickly and superficially, and becoming adept at "the art of nuances" (*BGE* 31).

IV

At this point Nietzsche shifts gears for a half dozen sections, mentioning a number of topics and tasks in which he himself is very much interested and engaged, and interpretations he seems prepared to advance with respect to them. Their inclusion here may seem odd; for thinking about what he discusses in them obviously cannot be part and parcel of the very nature of "free-spirited" philosophical thinking. Sense can be made of it, however, by supposing that what he means to be doing is to provide *examples* of "free-spirited" philosophical thinking in action (while also taking advantage of the opportunity to put some of his own cards on the table).

The first (*BGE* 32) concerns the understanding and assessment of human action, and the need for "a fundamental shift in values" and associated "overcoming of morality," the stage for which is being set by the new "self-examination of man" that is required by the "de-deifying" of our thinking, "deepening" our comprehension of ourselves. Nietzsche refers to this "overcoming of morality" as a task that "has been saved up for the finest and most honest [*redlich*] consciences of today." Here he names what he subsequently (in part 7, "Our Virtues") identifies as the cardinal virtue of the "free spirit": *Redlichkeit*—commonly translated as "honesty," but better understood as *intellectual integrity* (*BGE* 227). And as he indicates in the next section (*BGE* 33), the "morality" that is to be "overcome" is "the whole morality of self-abnegation [*Selbstentäusserungs-Moral*]," along with "the aesthetics of 'disinterested contemplation,'" in which disinterestedness is idealized as a general standpoint.

The next example concerns what appears to be an epistemological point, for it pertains to what Nietzsche calls "the *erroneousness* of the world in which we think we live." In fact, however, it has to do with the importance of learning to think about such things free of the "moral prejudice that truth is worth more than appearance"—which is a prime example of what he means by associating the "free spirit" with liberation from the morality of "good and evil." That liberation frees philosophical thinking for an understanding and appreciation of the basic (perspective-dependent and interdependent) character of "life" and of value: "Let at least this much be admitted: there would be no life at all if not on the basis of perspectival valuations and appearances" (*BGE* 34).

Nietzsche pauses, in *BGE* 35, to suggest that the free-spirited philosopher will not be "too human"—that is, too earnest, demanding, dogmatic, simpleminded—about and in the "search for truth." He then proceeds (in *BGE* 36) to provide a striking and important example of an issue such a philosopher might legitimately try to tackle, and of the sort of interpretation such a philosopher might appropriately venture with respect to it. The issue is the basic character of all that transpires in life and the world; and the interpretation is his hypothesis—which he terms "my *Satz* [proposition]"—that this basic character may aptly be construed in terms of the fundamental disposition he calls "will to power."[3] The hypothetical but nonetheless substantive framing of this section may be intended to illustrate Nietzsche's idea of free-spirited philosophical thinking—and to make clear that his free-spirited philosopher is to be understood as no mere critic, but also as a robustly adventuresome interpreter.

V

After pausing again in the next section (*BGE* 37) to observe that the free-spirited philosopher will not be deterred by the vulnerability to caricature of such ideas by those who might wish to avoid taking these ideas seriously, Nietzsche returns (in *BGE* 38) to the further characterization of such a philosopher. The trait he mentions next is of particular importance for one who (like Nietzsche himself) recognizes that "everything has become," and that this calls for "historical philosophizing" (*HH* I:2). That trait is alertness to a temptation that is one of the most common sources of "misunderstanding": the tendency to interpret things that have developed historically "according to their own indignations and enthusiasms," with the consequence that "the text disappears beneath the interpretation." The free-spirited philosopher is not one for whom "anything goes"; for such a philosopher, alert to this tendency, the moment it is detected, "it is all over" for the self-gratifying interpretation in question. This sort of philosopher is allergic to all such wishful thinking.

The next trait Nietzsche mentions (in *BGE* 39) is "strength"—as in mental toughness and intellectual fortitude. Observing that "something might be true while being harmful and dangerous in the highest degree," and that "existence" might be such that "those who would know it completely would perish," he then suggests that "the strength of a spirit should be measured according to how much of the 'truth' one could still barely endure." The free-spirited philosopher needs as much strength of this sort as is humanly possible. And to this Nietzsche adds (also in *BGE* 39) "a final trait for the image of the free-spirited philosopher," citing Stendhal's[4] observation that "To be a good philosopher, one must be dry, clear, without illusion"—not least with respect to "seeing clearly into what ['making discoveries in philosophy'] is."

Nietzsche does not elaborate upon the point here, for he in effect has already been doing so all along; but the point warrants comment. "Discoveries in philosophy," he has been insisting (e.g., *BGE* 22, 23, 36), have the character of *interpretations*; but this certainly does not mean that they make no contribution to comprehension. There are interpretations and interpretations. Some are silly, or self-serving, or ill-informed, or deeply misguided. But others can be and are better informed, reasoned, more probingly thoughtful and carefully considered.

Nietzsche goes on in the next section (*BGE* 40) to suggest that interpretations of the latter sort are most likely to be developed by those of a philosophical disposition whose free-spiritedness has been translated and developed into the more penetrating thinking of a "deep spirit" [*tiefe Geist*]. So, in his preface to *Genealogy* (his next book), he wrote of his conviction that his "ideas on the origin of our moral prejudices" sprang from a "*fundamental will* of knowledge, commanding onward into the depths, speaking ever more precisely, demanding ever greater precision. For this alone is fitting for a philosopher" (*GM* P:2).

In the next section (*BGE* 40), Nietzsche reiterates the point that free-spirited philosophers must expect to be misunderstood. He then goes on to suggest that they will even welcome the disguise or "mask" to which such misunderstanding gives rise—presumably because it is just as well that most people do not have a clear sense of the thought of a truly "deep spirit," which he thought was sure to be unsettling to many (as he took his own to be likely to be, especially with respect to God and morality). And then, in the following section (*BGE* 41), he returns to the theme of the "independence" that is the heart of the "freedom" of the "free spirit."

Here Nietzsche emphasizes the *attained* character of that independence, and elaborates in a rhetorically powerful way upon the point that its attainment comes at a cost. It is said to require detaching oneself from various things to which one very probably and humanly will have been attached previously. The phrase "not to remain attached to" (or, more literally, "hanging onto," in the sense of "clinging to") is repeated again and again; and the repetition of the idea of *being able to let go of* is part of the power of the passage. Here I will compress it: "Not to remain attached [*hängen bleiben*] to a person [. . .], to a fatherland [. . .], to some pity [. . .], to a *Wissenschaft* [cognitive discipline]— even if it should lure us with the most precious discoveries [. . .], to one's own detachment [. . .], to our own [personal] virtues" (*BGE* 41).

It is quite a list; these are only examples from it. I would observe, however, that Nietzsche is not saying that the independence of the "free spirit" involves and requires the *rejection* of everything of the sort to which one has ever been attached, *turning away* from all such previously near and dear things altogether. Rather, his point is that a "free spirit" is one who is no longer *under their sway*—but to whom they nonetheless *remain available*, even philosophically, as resources and grist for one's mill.

VI

Nietzsche then turns, in the remaining three sections of this part (*BGE* 42–44), to the idea that "a new species of philosophers is coming up," of whom he says that "we free spirits" are the "heralds and precursors." These "new philosophers" themselves "also will be free, *very* free spirits," he says; but they "will not be merely free spirits" [*nicht bloss frei Geister sein werden*]. For, as was previously noted, he states they will be "something more, higher, greater, and fundamentally different" as well (*BGE* 44). Yet there also is considerable overlap. So, for example, Nietzsche begins by suggesting that the "new philosophers" will have similar "intentions and instincts" to the kind of "free spirit" he has been discussing; and he further observes that there is much else that may be said and needs to be understood about "us collectively" [*uns gemeinsam*]—that is, about "free-spirited" and "new" philosophers alike. For example, he writes:

> At home, or at least having been guests, in many countries of the spirit; having escaped again and again from the musty agreeable nooks into which preference and prejudice, youth, origin, the accidents of people and books [. . .] have banished us; full of malice against the lures of dependence [. . .]; curious to a vice, investigators to the point of cruelty [. . .], ready for every venture, thanks to an excess of "free will" [. . .]; inventive in [interpretive] schemes [. . .]; friends of *solitude*: that is the type of human being that we are, we free spirits! And perhaps you have something of this, too, you that are coming, you *new* philosophers? (*BGE* 44)

Further: like the free-spirited philosophers he has been discussing, Nietzsche considers it is "probable enough" that "these coming philosophers" will be "new friends of 'truth'"—but that they too "certainly will not be dogmatists," and will not even want "their truth" to be "supposed to be a truth for anyone and everyone [*Jedermann*]." (It is worth observing that by "truths" here Nietzsche means "judgments" [*Urteile*], in the sense of conclusions, interpretations, and assessments, such as the "proposition" in section 36 that he refers to as "mein *Satz*." His point is that, as he puts it, they are likely to be the sort of thinker who would say: "'My judgment is *my* judgment [*ist* mein *Urteil*]'; no one else is easily entitled to it" [*BGE* 43].)[5]

VII

What then is the difference between "we free spirits" and "you *new* philosophers"? Nietzsche hints at the difference he has in mind when he first announces that "a new species of philosophers is coming up," and goes on to say that "these philosophers of the future may have a right [. . .] to be called *Versucher*"—by which he may mean experimenters, attempters, tempters, or all three at once (*BGE* 42). But it has been seen that he conceives of free-spirited philosophers as being more than mere "scholars" and "philosophical laborers," and to have something of the "*Versucher*" about them as well—for example, in the inventiveness and experimental adventuresomeness with which they approach and pursue the tasks of reinterpretation and revaluation. And the final section of this second part of the book (*BGE* 44) ends on a chord of concord, with only a suggestion that there is to be a difference nonetheless.

Nietzsche hints at the difference again, a little more clearly, in the next (third) part of the book, on "Religiousness." There he envisions philosophers not only free-spirited enough to be liberated from religious modes of interpretation and scruples, but also "high and hard enough to be able to shape *Menschen* as artists do [*um* am Menschen *als Künstler gestalten zu dürfen*]" (*BGE* 62). This is said without elaboration, near the end of the part's concluding section, seemingly as little more than a rhetorical flourish. But it is actually a promissory note.

It is only later in the book—in its sixth part—that Nietzsche redeems this promissory note, revealing that he has something important in mind.[6] This part's title is "*Wir Gelehrten*"—literally, "we learned ones." Commonly translated as "We Scholars," this is better rendered here as "We Sophisticates" (in the sense of being well informed, astute, enlightened). But even that rendering is misleading, and makes sense as an indication of what follows only if it either is ironically intended, or is meant to refer to Nietzsche himself and the kind of reader he hoped to have, who would be equally sophisticated, enlightened, and capable of taking his point.

This part's topic is the central one of the entire book—and its mood is far from being that of Nietzsche's *fröhlich*, free-spirited *Wissenschaftler*. Its topic, about which he could not be more serious, is what—for him now, in *Beyond*—it means and takes to be a "genuine [*wirklich*] philosopher." And this, for him, has become something more than being a very good philosopher of the sort he has been discussing (and himself had become). His topic, more specifically, it is what it would mean to be the kind of creative thinker and influence he has come to envision, as a philosopher of the highest sort, above and beyond that already exceptional and admirable type. "Toward *new philosophers*," he writes in the final section of the previous part, preparing the way for what follows, addressing himself to "you free spirits" who might be capable of becoming—or at least of envisioning and fostering—something more: "new philosophers" who would not only be first-rate thinkers and interpreters but also would *make a difference*. Or, as he puts it: who would also be (in some significant sense) *"leaders"* (*BGE* 203).

There is no getting around the fact that the term Nietzsche uses here is *Führer*. Since subsequent history has made that a problem (and the Hitler type would have been an abomination to him), one might wish that he had chosen the other common German word for *leader*—namely, *Leiter* (were it not for the circumstance that subsequent events would have made that a problem as well!). However, such problems are ours rather than his; for at the time the former term was no more problematic than the latter—and most of Nietzsche's uses of it in this context are in the plural. Moreover, if there is anything problematic here, it should not be Nietzsche's word choice, but rather its meaning for him in this context. And so, once again, that must be ascertained not from what it has come to mean for us, or even from a diction-ary, but rather from what he does with it, and with the kind of leading that he shows he has in mind.

A start can and should be made with what Nietzsche immediately goes on to say in this very section: "It is the image of such leaders that *we* envision," he writes, who would not only "teach man the future of man as his *will*, as depen-dent on a human will," but also "prepare great ventures and overall attempts of breeding and cultivation [*Zucht und Züchtung*]," and who would be "hard" and "strong" enough to "endure the weight of such responsibility" (*BGE* 203).

In *"Wir Gelehrten"* Nietzsche goes on to elaborate upon the relation of this type of philosopher—now, for him, "the philosopher" in the fullest and new-est sense—to lesser types of thinker. They include not only the "philosophical laborer" who operates within previously established ways of thinking, and the mere philosophy "scholar" [*Wissenschaftler*], but also the philosophical *Freigeist* he had earlier discussed, and had previously himself exemplified as well as espoused. He writes:

> It may be necessary for the development [*Erziehung*] of a genuine philoso-pher [*des wirklichen Philosophen*] that he himself has also once stood on all these steps [. . .]. Perhaps he himself must have been critic and skeptic and dogmatist and historian and also poet and collector and traveler and solver of riddles and moralist and visionary and "free spirit" [. . .], and must be *able* to see with many different eyes and consciences, from and height and into every distance [. . .]. But all these are merely preconditions of his task: this task it-self wants [*will*] something different—it requires [*verlangt*] that he *create val-ues* [Werte schaffe]. (*BGE* 211)

One might think that we now have in hand Nietzsche's full answer—with respect to the difference—even if it may be puzzling what to make of it: the "task" [*Aufgabe*] of his "new philosophers," above and beyond being "free spirits" and first-rate "free-spirited" philosophers, would appear to be *value creation*. But that is not quite right. Their "task" is said to "want" and "require" that values be "created." But that implies that their actual fundamental "task"—which "wants" and "requires" value creation—is something other than simply value creation per se. It must be characterized differently: it must be something to which value creation is a means, or contributes. And that, for Nietzsche, can only be: the actual enrichment and enhancement of human life—the primary arena of which is human cultural life.

Moreover, since these are endeavors that both matter greatly, and in which competition rather than cognition is the order of the day, this makes them in an unusual but important sense *political*. So it is in this sense that Nietzsche contends, "The time for little politics [*kleine Politik*] is over," and we face a "*compulsion* [Zwang] to great politics [*grossen Politik*]" (*BGE* 208). And I believe that it is with this fateful impending contest for the future of the human spirit weighing heavily on his mind that he deems it to be the "task" of the new philosophers he envisions not merely to attempt to understand it all, but themselves to *enter the fray*.

So Nietzsche goes on to indicate—quite emphatically—the sense in which these new philosophers are to be "leaders" [*Führer*]: "*The genuine* [wirkliche] *philosophers are commanders and lawgivers* [*Befehlende und Gesetzgeber*]: they say 'thus it shall be [*so soll es sein*]!' [. . .] They reach with a creative [*schöpferischer*] hand toward the future." To this he further adds: "Their 'knowing' [*Erkennen*] is *creating* [Schaffen], their creating is a lawgiving, their will to truth [*Wille zur Wahrheit*] is—will to power [*Wille zur Macht*]." And he ends this (rhetorically soaring) section with the (rhetorically pointed) question: "*Must* there not be such philosophers?" (*BGE* 211).

VIII

There is certainly at least one respect in which the Nietzsche of *Beyond* is not the Nietzsche of the "free spirit" series: the Nietzsche of *Beyond* is much given to overheated rhetoric! And he became more so in the few years left to him. But sense can be made of that. And sense also can be made of what he is saying. I suggest that these unsettling lines are best read as simply an elaboration—as if with multiple exclamation points—of his point about these new philosophers being "value creators" (and promulgators) rather than simply excellent free-spirited inquirers and interpreters, and about "value creation" (and promulgation) being importantly different—in both character and significance—from comprehension.

Speaking for Nietzsche here, or on his behalf: "Value creation" may require and draw upon a great deal of knowledge and understanding of what is the case; but it involves going beyond what is the case, and its comprehension. It involves *making*—and *making different*. The kind of "knowing" that is most important for the creator is envisioning—and in that sense, "knowing"—what specific new and different outcome is envisioned; and that involves working out and laying out new ways of doing and experiencing things—and promoting them as persuasively and forcefully as one can. And it is a "lawgiving" in the sense that it is establishing a different game, to be played in a different way, with different rules and norms ("laws") for those who enter into it, following its creator's "lead."

The cultural creator, moreover, has to be something like a visionary mastermind—an astute strategist with imagination and a vision, a sense for new possibilities, a dominating intelligence, and great powers of persuasion. In short, an *überragender Geist* (in the language of *Schopenhauer*)—an extraordinarily "powerful spirit" expressing itself as a "cultural dynamo," of which Wagner had for Nietzsche been an instance. But now Nietzsche is envisioning that sort of human possibility conjoined with the sophistication of his *Gelehrten* (conceived as the "free spirit" at its philosophical best). And he is further envisioning that sort of supra-human agency taking the lead in the kinds of transformations of human life that not only would be most conducive to its perpetuation and refinement but also contribute most powerfully to its enrichment, well warranting the language and idea of its further "enhancement." It is in this context that I believe Nietzsche would have the vivid language he uses here be understood.

So, in the following section, we find him saying, with respect to the "task" of the new sort of philosopher he is talking about, that the genuine philosopher is "*of necessity* a man of tomorrow and the day after tomorrow," whose "secret" is "to know of a *new* greatness [*Grösse*] of man," and to be capable of envisioning some "new untrodden way to its greatening [*Vergrösserung*]." But this section ends with the question: "*ist heute—Grösse möglich?*" ("Is greatness today—*possible*?") (*BGE* 212).

The implication Nietzsche seems to have drawn is that it will be up to his new philosophers to make it so. The genuine philosopher's task and responsibility is not just to talk about and advocate the "enhancement of life" but to do something about it. That has to mean: to do something that will actually contribute to it, in more than a mere supporting or inspiring role. (As Marx put it in the eleventh of his "Theses on Feuerbach":[7] "The philosophers have *only interpreted* the world, in various ways; the point, however, is to *change* it."[8]) And that, Nietzsche is saying, will require something more than what he is calling "value creation," if anything is to come of it.

But why should this be up to any sort of philosopher at all? I suggest that this is not—or at any rate not only—because Nietzsche thinks that philosophers of any sort have it in them to be better at "value creation" than is anyone else. It is rather because he thinks that his kind of philosopher (and philosopher-psychologist) will have a better understanding of human nature and psychology than anyone else is likely to have.

That understanding (if attainable and attained)—of human nature generally and of various human types more specifically—would put them in a unique position. For, in conjunction with the ability to "*know of* a new greatness of man," this can and should enable them to envision and promote ways of countering human pathologies, and of enabling new life-enhancing "value creations" to come true. That is something Nietzsche thinks the right kind of philosopher is better able and equipped to do than anyone else. And that is what makes sense of his assignment of such importance and such a pivotal role to the "new philosophers" of which he so passionately speaks in *Beyond Good and Evil*.

In short: humanity's future, for the Nietzsche of *Beyond* is open, and is up for grabs. God is dead, so we're on our own, and both the preservation and the enhancement of life are up to us. And the alternative to making the most of what we've got to work with is too awful to contemplate—or rather, when contemplated, is too awful to take lying down, on our merely contemplative couches. This may be what accounts for his often rather overwrought rhetoric about the "new philosophers" he envisions there.

Nietzsche is seemingly content in *Beyond* to refer to himself as being among the free-spirited heralds and precursors of this "new" type of philosopher. Yet he does invite his readers to think about what anyone might do—or have tried to do, along these lines—when he asks: "Are there any such philosophers today?" (*BGE* 211). He rather remarkably makes no mention of the fact that he had spent the previous three years trying his hand at what might well be considered at least an instance and example of the very sort of thing he is talking about, in this discussion of what more the "new philosopher" would do than the free-spirited philosopher does.

But perhaps Nietzsche thought that his readers would hardly need to be reminded of it. I refer, of course, to *Also Sprach Zarathustra*. Recall that, in *Ecce Homo*, he describes it as a work that "stands altogether apart," not only from his other writings but also from just about everything else ever written: "My concept of the 'Dionysian' here becomes a *supreme deed*; measured against that, all the rest of human activity seems poor and relative." In his

Zarathustra and its protagonist, Nietzsche may well have thought, he not only has shown us an instance of what he means by value creation, but has done his best to initiate an instance of it, and provide the means of at least the beginning of its realization. His Zarathustra heralds the figure of the *Übermensch* as the new "meaning of the earth"; and so Nietzsche can refer to him as "one who first *creates* truth, a *world-governing* spirit, a destiny" (*EH* "Books," Z:6). And his *Zarathustra* was to be the means of the realization of this "value creation." A "book for all and none" indeed!

If Nietzsche does or would consider this to be a case in point of what he is talking about and advocating in *Beyond*—an instance of attempted value creation meant for realization in human life, with a would-be "new philosopher" taking the "lead"—it is a helpful one. Helpful, that is, at least to the understanding of what he is talking about. And helpful also to the consideration of what to make of the ninth and final part of *Beyond*, and of the question of his "great politics." For as Nietzsche sees it, the contest of old and new sensibilities and values always has been and always will be ultimately a kind of "political" one—in some broadened sense of the term.

IX

The answer to the question posed by the title of this chapter would seem to be clear. The rubric of *Freigeist*—understood to mean the kind of philosopher Nietzsche had in mind in his "free spirit" series and depicts and discusses in the second part of *Beyond*—does indeed characterize the kind of philosophy he had been pursuing to that point in his philosophical life, and largely continued to pursue during its next and last few years, to a very considerable extent. But it also is inadequate as a characterization of the kind of philosopher and philosophy he envisioned in the second half of *Beyond*, and to which he would seem to have aspired—and also as a characterization of the kind of "new-philosophical" endeavor he began to try to undertake in *Zarathustra*.

How so? In brief, because the chief concern of that kind of philosopher, and that Nietzsche, is not just the *comprehension* of human reality and human possibility—and, in particular, the recognition of "what might yet be *made of man*" [aus dem Menschen zu *züchten wäre*]. It is the actual *enhancement* of life, carried to the level of human reality transformation, as opposed to standing idly (or merely contemplatively) by as its opposite occurs, and its promise is squandered (*BGE* 203). Actually *doing* something about that is what I believe to be the "new *task*" that he envisions and announces at the very end of that section, just prior to "*Wir Gelehrten*." The guiding ideal of "*der Freigeist*," exercising itself in both thinking and living, was superseded by that of "*der schöpferische Geist*," expressing itself and fulfilling itself in the endowment of life as a living reality with value that it does not otherwise possess, even if only ephemerally—as everything human ultimately does and is.

But *doing* something requires something more than becoming the kind of "philosophical physician" he calls for[9]—"one who has to pursue the problem of the total health of a people, time, race or of humanity [*Menschheit*]"— which includes the pathologies of which they are susceptible (*JI* P:2). It involves actually engaging creatively in the "culture wars" that are "where the action is" (so to speak), both promoting one's favored outcomes and combating developments detrimental to them as powerfully as one can. And both require efforts of different sorts than those of the philosophical *Freigeist*. *Zarathustra* and Nietzsche's other literary efforts in subsequent publications (including his late *Dionysos Dithyrambs*) are examples of the former, as also are his frequent exhortations in those same works.

X

But post-*Freigeist* (and post-*Zarathustra*), philosophical-activist Nietzsche might be said to have done more than that—and more also than merely probing the pathologies of the spirit that he considered to be dangers to the flourishing and enhancement of human life. He further sought to actively combat and subvert a number of them, by way of a different sort of writing, for which he found that he also had a flair: polemic.

Few writers in the history of philosophy come even close to Nietzsche in this respect (although Schopenhauer does come to mind). *Beyond* does begin with a kind of polemic (against various "Prejudices of Philosophers"), and features a good bit of polemical writing in its second half; but a fair part of it is written in the measured mode of his *Freigeist* series—as is the fifth Book that he added to *Inquiry* in the next year. But he actually gave *Genealogy* the subtitle *A Polemic* [*Eine Streitschrift*]—which indeed it is, even though it does contain a good deal of similarly straightforward stretches of his kind of philosophical discussion and writing.

After that, it was essentially one polemic after another, in that final year of Nietzsche's productive life (1888)—*The Case of Wagner, Nietzsche contra Wagner*, and *The Antichristian* obviously so, but much of *Twilight of the Idols* as well. *Twilight* is more measured than the others (particularly in several of its parts), but only in the sense that it is less of a rant than they are. It begins with a polemic against Socrates, and proceeds to attempt to similarly demolish a whole array of other "idols" Nietzsche considers to be comparably insidious. Even *Ecce Homo* is basically a kind of polemic—on his own behalf!

These late works are often dismissed for this very reason (as well as because they seem increasingly to show signs of Nietzsche's approaching madness). But if I am right, he came to consider it to be a part of the business of his kind of "new philosopher" to engage in the "culture wars" on behalf of envisioned human possibilities deemed to be life-enhancing, employing the resources of language rhetorically as well as interpretively to do so. So by the same token it would seem to make sense for the "new philosopher" to do so in opposition to discerned human realities deemed to be detrimental to life as well. And that is precisely what Nietzsche was doing in these works.

Viewed in this light, Nietzsche's late polemics are in a kind of accord with both his ideas of "new philosophers" who are and do something above and beyond what even his own kind of (free-spirited interpretive and evaluative) philosophy had been, and the rather grandiose-sounding (and unsettling) rhetoric he uses in talking about it in *Beyond*. What he is envisioning and calling for there is philosophers who also would undertake to *make a difference* in the character and course of human life, not only as culture psychologists (especially with respect to pathologies), but also more actively, as culture dynamos, and further as culture warriors, actively engaging in both opposition (via polemics) and advancement (via promotional strategies). They are to be not only public (as well as philosophical) intellectuals, but also public (as well as intellectual) cultural *activists*. It's a tall order—but, for Nietzsche, a humanly possible one, and a crucial one, in view of the likely consequences for humanity of shirking it.

XI

In short: I do think that some sense can be made, in this way, of Nietzsche's late works and their relation to what he says in *Beyond* about what would set his "new philosopher" apart from his "free-spirited philosopher." I also think that sense can be made of his conception of human "greatness"—in terms of the cultural enrichment of human life conjoined with the idea of what he calls "wholeness in manifoldness" or "being capable of being as manifold as whole, as ample as full" (*BGE* 212).

I further think that sense can be made of his idea that its enhancement involves the emergence of new forms of human cultural and intellectual life (previously "untrodden ways"), which in turn both requires and results in "value creation"—and even of the thought that a certain sort of philosopher, with the needed sorts of creative abilities and powers, might be capable of it. I suggest that the key to doing so is understanding them and the importance he attached to the ideas of sensibilities and their formation and transformation, which I believe to be central to Nietzsche's thinking with respect to all of them.

Much of what most of us admire and value in Nietzsche's thought and work, however, seems to me to be encompassed in his conception of the kind of "free-spirited" philosophy we find not only in his "free spirit" series but also resumed in his post-*Zarathustra* writings (in the fifth Book of *Joyful Inquiry* and *Genealogy* in particular). The "philosophy of the future" to which *Beyond* is proclaimed to be a "prelude" is not something altogether different, but rather is that kind of philosophy continued and developed—and then some. There may well be a version of the "then some" that is much more modestly conceived than Nietzsche conceives of it there, and yet in the spirit of what he is talking about, that is humanly and even philosophically coherent enough and important enough to be worth aspiring to.

I am inclined to think that one reason why I (and perhaps many of us) think Nietzsche matters as much as he does, as a philosopher and philosophical conscience, is that he not only was as good a free-spirited philosopher as he was, but also himself aspired to that "something more"—and may actually have succeeded at least to some extent. For it is arguable that, not just in and by way of *Zarathustra* but also through his other writings, Nietzsche actually contributed—not polemically but significantly—to the emergence and development of a very important and much-needed *new sensibility* that is neither otherworldly nor anti-worldly, and an antidote to all versions of the "ascetic ideal."

This new sensibility is one that is *jenseits* (beyond) the moralism of "good and evil," and that Nietzsche seems to regard as having the best chance of countering other worrisome pathologies of the human spirit as well. (For example: those represented by "The Last Man" in *Zarathustra*, and exhibited by the providers and consumers of cultural narcotics with whom he is concerned in *The Case of Wagner*.) It is the sensibility that he calls "Dionysian" (discussed in chapter 8), and that I have characterized as "ecstatic naturalism," brought down to earth.

In the next and concluding chapter, I will be considering the appropriateness of characterizing Nietzsche's kind of philosopher and philosophy in a "naturalizing" sort of way, that that characterization presupposes. This is an issue that has loomed much larger in the Nietzsche world than that of the "something more" about what his "new philosophers" are to be or do than his kind of philosophy had been. It is the question of whether he can appropriately be considered to have been a philosophical "naturalist" of some sort—and if so, of *what* sort.

Nietzsche as Naturalist?

Wann werden wir die Natur ganz entgöttlicht haben! Wann werden wir anfangen dürfen,
uns Menschen mit der reinen, neu gefundenen, neu erlösten Natur zu vernatürlichen!
[When will we have completely de-deified Nature! When may we begin to *naturalize*
ourselves [in line] with a pure, newly discovered, newly redeemed nature!]
Joyful Inquiry, 109

It is by now abundantly clear that I consider Nietzsche to have been fundamentally a kind of philosophically *naturalistic* (or at any rate "naturalizing") thinker, whose kind of philosophy and philosophical agenda are best understood accordingly. This has been central to my understanding of him for as long as I have been thinking and writing about him. So, in my first Nietzsche book, I wrote that his basic project was: "to develop *a naturalistic conception of human reality* which takes as its point of departure our status as instances of a certain form of life among others, holds to this perspective in dealing with all aspects of our experience and activity, and shuns both the 'soul-hypothesis' *and* the 'thing-hypothesis' in doing so."[1]

This is a characterization with which many—in the analytically minded part of the philosophical community, at any rate—have come to agree. But there are many kinds of things called "naturalism" in the philosophical literature; and it would be a mistake to assume in advance that any of them in particular is what Nietzsche espoused or was moving toward—especially since there are some kinds of naturalism of which he himself is quite disdainful, and scathingly critical. For example, there is the scientistic "mechanistic" kind, that he calls one of "the *stupidest*" [der *dümmsten*] ways of assessing and construing such things as music (and other human phenomena) in *Joyful Inquiry*. And there is also the kind he attributes (in *Beyond Good and Evil*) to "*Naturalisten*" [naturalists] whose "clumsiness" [*Ungeschick*] is such that "they no sooner touch 'the soul' than they lose it" (*BGE* 12).

So we need to consider *what kind* of naturalism Nietzsche's is—particularly as it relates to science, as "science" has come to be understood, paradigmatically exemplified by the modern natural sciences. Philosophical naturalism and scientific thinking (so understood) are rightly conceived to be significantly linked. Just how tight that link is, however, and what sort of link it is, are matters concerning which philosophical naturalisms differ. I have needed to indicate and briefly elaborate my answer to this question in almost every chapter of this book, owing to its bearing on the matters under discussion in them. My aim in this concluding chapter is to spell out and elaborate my understanding of his kind of naturalism more systematically and (I hope) both plausibly and persuasively.[2] Readers of the previous chapters will already be familiar with passages cited again, and may recall points reiterated here; but that is unavoidable, and reminders of them may be useful—or in any case will do no harm.

I

As has been seen, Nietzsche makes positive use of the language of naturalism to characterize his own philosophical efforts and projects on a number of occasions. So, for example, at the outset of Book 3 of the first version of *Inquiry*, he writes (and this is the passage epigraphically cited at the outset): "When may we begin to *naturalize* ourselves [*uns Menschen zu* vernatürlichen] [in line] with a pure, newly discovered, newly redeemed nature!" By this he means: reinterpret ourselves as human beings, in a manner that accords with a reinterpretation of the reality of which we are a part that we call "nature," that has itself been reconceived in an "entirely de-deified" [*ganz entgöttlicht*] manner, purged of all traces of the God-idea (*JI* 109).

In *Beyond*, Nietzsche similarly proclaims (and quite evidently embraces) the "task" of "*translating Mensch* back into nature" [*den Menschen zurückübersetzen in die Natur*], and of seeing to it that "*Mensch* henceforth stands *before Mensch* as even today, hardened [*hart geworden*] in the discipline [*Zucht*; schooling, literally, "breeding"] of *Wissenschaft* [here: science] it stands before the *other* nature [*der* anderen *Natur*]." And by this he means, in particular, turning a deaf ear "to the siren songs of old metaphysical bird catchers who have been piping at us all too long, 'you are more, you are higher, you are of a different origin [*anderer Herkunft*]'!" (*BGE* 230). We *have* come to differ significantly from the rest of nature around us, for Nietzsche; but that, he is here insisting, is owing to something other than some sort of "different origin" altogether.

Nietzsche's many critical comments with respect to science (and *Wissenschaft* more generally) notwithstanding, I take his general disposition with respect to the *Wissenschaften* and their relation to his kind of philosophy to be a generally positive one—as long as they do not overstep their bounds and are not overestimated. From the first installment of *Human, All Too Human* onward, he attaches great importance to paying attention to the natural sciences (*Naturwissenschaften*), as well as to historical, cultural, linguistic, and psychological sophistication in philosophical thinking, and advocates taking into philosophical account what can be learned about ourselves and our world by way of any and all forms of *wissenschaftlich* inquiry, natural-scientific or other. (See, for example, *JI* 335.)

To mark and underscore that point, I suggest availing ourselves of the old but still useful English word *sciential*, and modifying it slightly for the purpose to *scientian*, to designate philosophical thinking of that sort.[3] All naturalisms presumably are "scientian" in that sense: they are intended to be natural-scientifically (as well as otherwise cognitively) informed, sophisticated, and attentive to what can be learned from such inquiry, and attach importance to this intention. Satisfying this description could reasonably be taken to characterize and define a sort of naturalism; and, if conjoined with various other criteria (including the rejection of any sort of supernaturalism, religious or metaphysical), it could be considered to constitute a potentially interesting one. If Nietzsche is to be considered a naturalist, his kind of naturalism would be one of that sort.

Naturalisms that go further in the specific direction of *privileging* natural-scientific thinking—supposing that everything about human reality is to be explained and understood in terms of the same sorts of deterministic causes encountered in natural-scientific theories and explanations more generally, and deeming such thinking unproblematic in the status of its kinds of knowledge, paradigmatic in its methods, all-encompassing in its scope, and decisive in its authority—may contrastingly be called "scientistic." As I understand him, and as I believe the "Nietzsche Becoming Nietzsche" chapters above make clear, the thinking of the Nietzsche we encounter in all of the works discussed is neither the simplistic "mechanistic," materialistic-reductionist naturalism that he explicitly derides on a number of occasions, nor any other more sophisticated *scientistic* naturalism.

Indeed, I would say that Nietzsche not only stops well short of such "scientism" but also sets himself in resolute opposition to it. He repudiates rather than embraces the idea that the natural sciences and thinking modeled on the natural sciences have a monopoly on the whole story with respect to everything, human reality and the whole panoply of the human world included. If he is a kind of naturalistic thinker, he is not one of *that* sort. He aspires to take account of scientific inquiry and what can be learned and understood by way of it. But his kind of philosophy does not limit itself to reliance upon them, or take all of its cues from them. He neither simply assumes nor posits nor concludes that there cannot be anything more to human reality and the world in which we find ourselves than the natural sciences can deal with and tell us about them.

In what follows, as in the previous four chapters, I will discuss the respects in which I do and do not consider the rubric in question to be an appropriate characterization of Nietzsche's philosophical thinking—even if one restricts attention to the reinterpretive and revaluative parts of it (setting aside the "new task" relating to "value creation" discussed in the previous chapter). And I further will elaborate upon the character of his quite distinctive and interesting kind of naturalism as I understand it.

II

Some interpreters of Nietzsche in recent years have taken him not merely to be a philosophical naturalist of a broadly "scientian" sort, but to be a "scientistic" naturalist. Brian Leiter is a case in point; and because he has figured so centrally in the popularization of that interpretation in the Anglophone philosophical mainstream, I will begin by commenting specifically on his influential version of it. I am in basic agreement with Leiter's contention, at the outset of his *Nietzsche on Morality*, that Nietzsche belongs "in the company of naturalists like Hume and Freud—that is, among, broadly speaking, *philosophers of human nature*."⁴ But then my problems with his account of Nietzsche's naturalism begin.

Leiter frames his discussion of Nietzsche by "distinguishing between two basic naturalistic doctrines: *methodological* (or M-Naturalism) and *substantive* (S-Naturalism)." He characterizes the "methodological doctrine" as the view that "philosophical inquiry should be continuous with empirical inquiry in the sciences"⁵—that is, "*continuous with* the sciences either in virtue of their *dependence upon the actual results* of scientific method in different domains or in virtue of their employment and emulation of *distinctively scientific ways of looking at and explaining things*."⁶

By the latter phrase Leiter means: looking at all that goes on in the world—human life included—as phenomena with "deterministic causes" of the sort that figure in natural-scientific theories and explanations. "The bulk of [Nietzsche's] philosophical activity," he asserts, was "devoted to variations on [the] naturalistic project" of "naturalistic explanation" of various human phenomena "that is continuous with both the results and [the] methods of the sciences."⁷ Leiter takes this to make Nietzsche a "methodological naturalist" in precisely that sense. He further considers Nietzsche to be what he calls a "*Speculative* M-Naturalist," like Hume, who (Leiter says) "constructs a 'speculative' theory of human nature [. . .] modeled on the most influential scientific paradigm of the day."[8] That, according to Leiter, is precisely what Nietzsche did as well—and that is how his naturalism is to be understood. Leiter's Nietzsche is committed to a "scientific picture" of everything that happens, including all of what goes on in human life.

This, I would say, is a paradigmatic case of construing Nietzsche's naturalism *scientistically*. I conceive his naturalism quite differently: as one that stands (and may even have been intended to stand) as an alternative—and indeed as an antidote—to that very (scientistic) kind of naturalism, of which he is scornful. As I understand him, Nietzsche subscribes to neither of Leiter's "two basic naturalistic doctrines"—the one with respect to "what exists," and the other with respect to "how things work" and are to be explained. But he does suppose that everything in the world (human reality included) started out as merely "natural."

Nietzsche does contend explicitly, from the very beginning of *Human* onward, that philosophical interpretation of everything human (along with everything else) needs to be "informed by the sciences" relevant to them. And he does suppose it to be the case that everything about human reality—and everything that goes on in human life and experience—has "become" as it is by way of developments of an entirely mundane character. But while these tenets are features of Nietzsche's kind of naturalism, they neither show nor entail that he is a *scientistic* naturalist. And the varieties and "doctrines" of naturalism that Leiter identifies are Procrustean beds that Nietzsche's naturalism does not fit. We do him and his kind of naturalism neither justice nor any favor, in my view, if we stretch or trim it to their contours. It is better added to the list of possible naturalisms, spared any such Procrustean modifications, as a significant and promising alternative to others.

III

I next will comment briefly on two other significant contributions to this discussion. Maudemarie Clark and David Dudrick share my discomfort with a scientistic construal of Nietzsche's naturalism. In "The Naturalisms of *Beyond Good and Evil*,"[9] they suggest that there is a "need for a distinction between two versions of naturalism, the one Nietzsche accepts and the one he rejects."[10] The one they say he rejects is one that couples acceptance of "true scientific explanations of human cognitive processes and behavior [...] with a denial that there is anything about human beings that cannot be seen from the empirical perspective," and dealt with scientifically. They, on the other hand, contend that (the mature) Nietzsche rejects the view that "everything can be explained scientifically,"[11] and more specifically that "although human beings are part of nature, Nietzsche's version of naturalism insists that science doesn't tell us all there is to know about their doings [...]; rather, it says that fully natural beings have developed in such a way as to admit of true descriptions that cannot be had from an empirical perspective."[12]

That seems to me to be quite right. However, I am less comfortable with the narrowness of what they have in mind, and with their ascription to Nietzsche of a completely scientistic naturalism with respect to everything else. They write: "The only things that stand outside the range of scientific explanation, on our account of Nietzsche's naturalism, are the thoughts and behavior of human beings"[13]—by which they appear to mean: "the thoughts and doings of particular human beings." And they construe that narrowly: "What remains veiled when one adopts the perspective of the natural sciences," on their view, is limited to "activities that take place in the space of reasons, the activities of rational interpreters and agents."[14] They attempt to link this exception to the otherwise purportedly ubiquitous scientistic rule to what they call Nietzsche's "will to value" by way of their contention that "truths about agents can be had only from a perspective constituted by values, by our understanding of how one ought to act or think," and that "to describe human beings using the language of agency (as acting, believing, knowing, etc.) is to see them in a network that is not merely causal but normative."[15]

This invocation and use of the (Sellarsian)[16] "space of reasons" strategy to make sense of the idea of our not being wholly within the dominion of the "merely causal" does strike me as a definite improvement upon Kant's earlier "two worlds" version of it (articulated so vividly and memorably in the conclusion of his second *Critique*).[17] There may even be something to it. Indeed, I am inclined to think that it is on the right track, even as a kind of reconstruction of Nietzsche's naturalism. It would, however, seem rather far removed from anything we find articulated or intimated in Nietzsche's writings—even if Clark and Dudrick are right about there being something similar to this idea in Afrikan Spir,[18] who is known to have influenced him in other respects.[19] As an account or interpretation of Nietzsche's naturalism, therefore, it would seem to be something of a stretch.

Moreover, and more seriously, this account seems to me to circumscribe the domain of the "not merely causal" almost as narrowly as Kant does, and far more narrowly than I take Nietzsche to do. If Clark and Dudrick had simply identified that domain as "the thoughts and behavior of human beings" and left it at that, they would have come closer; although even that characterization of it would still leave something to be desired. But their succession of glosses—presumably intended to indicate how they propose to justify that exception to the supposedly otherwise complete dominion of the "merely causal"—shows that they take it to include only those "thoughts and behavior" that can properly be described "using the language of agency." That turns out to mean, for them: in the language of the sort of "normativity" that characterizes "activities of rational interpreters and agents" framed in what can be construed as a "space of reasons." And they conceive such a "space" as a "perspective" reflecting—and indeed "constituted by"—a very special set or sort of "values," pertaining to "our understanding of how one ought to act or think."

This seems a rather slender reed on which to rest the entire structure of human deliverance from the complete dominion of the "network" of the "merely causal," and in terms of which to make sense of it and a case for its plausibility. One further might well wonder *whose* "understanding" is "our" understanding, and whether sharing it is a necessary condition of such emancipation. This is a particular concern because Clark and Dudrick seem to regard what they call the "value drive," from which the "values" in question and purported to spring, as a distinctive part of—and therefore presumably bound up with—the mentality of Nietzsche's kind of philosopher. Thus they speak of "the value drive, which aims to create or construct the world in accordance with *the philosopher's values.*"[20]

Clark and Dudrick could allow that this putative "drive" is and long has been far more widely distributed and active in this manner, sometimes to similar effect. Even so, however, one might still wonder how much of human reality—and more specifically, of what there is and goes on in human life and the human world—would fit their picture of the "not merely causal" part of Nietzsche's naturalism (in which life and world there are, for example, things like languages and their using, institutions and their functioning, contests and their contesting, sciences and their pursuing, and musics and their making). I would say: for Nietzsche as well as for me, not nearly enough. Something like what they have in mind may be a part of the story; but it seems to me that there is importantly more to it.

Christopher Janaway offers a sketch of Nietzsche's naturalism that I consider to be a further step in the right direction, in his book *Beyond Selflessness.*[21] He begins by characterizing it "in a broad sense" as follows: "[Nietzsche] opposes transcendent metaphysics, whether that of Plato or Christianity or Schopenhauer. He rejects notions of the immaterial soul, the absolutely free controlling will, or the self-transparent pure intellect, instead emphasizing the body, talking of the animal nature of human beings, and attempting to explain numerous phenomena by invoking drives, instincts, and affects which he locates in our physical, bodily existence. Human beings are to be 'translated back into nature,' since otherwise we falsify their history, their psychology, and the nature of their value."[22]

Janaway rightly observes and emphasizes that Nietzsche's methods are often "*dis*continuous with those of empirical scientific inquiry," rather than based or modeled on it;[23] and that "explanatory facts about me, even if somehow located in my psychophysiology, are essentially shaped by *culture*."[24] Further to the point, he writes: "If Nietzsche's causal explanations of our moral values are naturalistic, they are so in a sense which includes within the 'natural' not merely the psycho-physiological constitution of the individual whose values are up for explanation, but also many complex *cultural* phenomena."[25] Janaway here is looking in the right direction; but it seems to me that we need to move even further in that direction to bring out the full colors of Nietzsche's naturalism.

To do justice to Nietzsche's kind of naturalism, it seems to me that we need to distance ourselves even further from restriction to the causal-deterministic natural-scientific paradigm than Janaway does. He states his proposed liberalized (and pointedly *non*-scientistic) alternative to Leiter's position as follows: "Nietzsche can be read as a naturalist in that he seeks explanations that cite causes in ways that *do not conflict with* science."[26] It would be better, on my view, to drop all reference to "causes" in any such general statement; for while Nietzsche does use causal language at times, he has serious reservations about the concept of "cause and effect" when speaking strictly, and avoids it in many contexts.

I would amend and expand Janaway's statement to say (a little more fully): "Nietzsche can be read as a naturalist in that he seeks explanations and interpretations of all things human that do not conflict with science, are scientifically informed where appropriate, and make reference to nothing beyond entirely mundane developments and transformations of our original and fundamental human animality." (By "mundane" I mean simply to capture the drift of Nietzsche's themes of "this-worldliness" and the humble origins and stories of everything human.)

IV

My approach to Nietzsche's naturalism, as to his philosophical thinking generally, continues to be guided by a number of general considerations. Several of them are of particular relevance in the present instance. The interpretation of Nietzsche is a notoriously tricky business. He says things in various places that are hard to square with virtually every interpretation of his thought that attributes definite positions of one sort or another to him. In trying to decide what to make of them and how much weight to give to them, and in considering what lines of interpretation to favor and disfavor, I believe that considerable weight should be given to pervasive concerns and convictions of his that are evident in a broad range of his writings, even if he sometimes says things (in print or in his notebooks) that are at apparent or actual variance with them. One thus should proceed with care in considering what to make of any particular passages in his writings (both published and not), and is well advised to read him comprehensively before jumping to conclusions with respect to the import and upshot of any such passage.[27]

Next: as Nietzsche makes vividly clear in his preface to *Beyond*, and repeatedly elsewhere, dogmatism and doctrine-mongering are anathema to him. In deconstructionist days it was a common mistake to suppose that he never means what he might seem to be saying and doing when he puts forward some proposition, theory, or interpretation. Proposing as well as criticizing accounts and interpretations is standard fare in his writings, as is using striking phrases and images in doing so. It is also a misunderstanding, however, to construe him as dogmatically promulgating *doctrines*. In *Thus Spoke Zarathustra*, and on occasion elsewhere, we do find proclamations he characterizes with the word *Lehre*; and that is a word that can be and often is translated as "doctrine."[28] In *Zarathustra*, however, the *Lehren* (plural) Nietzsche puts in Zarathustra's mouth are clearly better regarded as something like "teachings" (another meaning of the word), exhortations, and powerful images. His pronouncements sometimes have this "my teaching" character elsewhere in his writings as well.

To be sure, there are other occasions on which Nietzsche makes assertions in a straightforward, unqualified, and emphatic manner that may tempt one to construe them as being put forward in a doctrinal way. In *Beyond*, for example, he refers to the idea that "our entire affective life [*Triebleben*]" is "to be explained" in terms of the basic disposition he calls "will to power" as "mein *Satz*" [*my* proposition] (*BGE* 36), and elsewhere in the same work states flatly that "life itself is *will to power*" (*BGE* 13). It seems to me, however, that even then they are to be understood not as settled "doctrines" to which he is unqualifiedly committed, but rather as theories, interpretations, accounts, or simply views that he holds or is advancing. But he does so always subject to the caveat of his general eschewal of dogmatism and embrace of the idea that all interpretive cognitive inquiry, even at its best, remains forever experimental and provisional.

What I now will be doing is giving an account of what I take Nietzsche's kind of naturalism to be, when spelled out and worked out in some detail. For the most part I will be summarizing themes and ideas from his writings that pertain to it, rather than citing specific passages (which would require a book-length presentation). My case for it is the comprehensive reading of him that I provided in my *Nietzsche*, that informs my *Making Sense of Nietzsche*, and that has been on display in the preceding chapters.[29]

V

Nietzsche takes as his point of departure what he calls "the death of God," announced in the first (1882) version of *Joyful Inquiry*. By this he means, in the first instance, the demise of the tenability of the Judeo-Christian God-idea; but he takes that to apply as well to ideas of any other sort of religiously, metaphysically, or morally envisioned different, "higher," and "truer" reality underlying or transcending the world in which we find ourselves and live our lives. He considers this "mass purge" (one might call it) to require that we undertake to "naturalize" our understanding of ourselves and all things human (*JI* 109). His naturalizing reinterpretation proceeds on the supposition that the kind of world "this world" is—"the world of life, nature and history" [*die Welt des Lebens, der Natur und der Geschichte*] (*JI* 344)—is the only *kind* of world and reality there is, with no particular configuration of it being essential or fundamental to it.

That project or "task" (*BGE* 230) further proceeds in accordance with the general "Guiding Idea" (as I shall call it) that everything that goes on and comes to be in this world is the outcome of developments occurring within it, that are owing entirely to its internal dynamics and the contingencies to which they give rise, and come about (as it were) from the bottom up, through the elaboration or relationally precipitated transformation of what was already going on and had already come to be.

This, I suggest, is Nietzsche's naturalism in a nutshell. It is no further particular "doctrine" or set of "doctrines" of *any* sort; and even its "Guiding Idea" is only that: a *guiding idea*. His embrace of it is definite but not dogmatic, grounded in his growing (through battle-testing) confidence that it will be able to withstand all challenges and deal plausibly with all proposed counterexamples (such as the cases of ascetic ideals, moral values, and religious ideas)—but it is open to them.

In a second preface ("Attempt at a Self-Criticism") Nietzsche added in 1886 to *The Birth of Tragedy*, he says of himself that, while his interpreting "eye" had in the interval become "much older [and] a hundred times more demanding" than it was when the book first appeared fourteen years earlier, it had not become "a stranger to the task which this audacious book ventured for the first time: to look at science in the optic [*Optik*] of the artist, but at art in that of life" (*BT* "Attempt," 2). And to this he added, two sections later, "its gravest question of all": namely, "What, seen in the optic of *life*, is the significance of morality?" (*BT* "Attempt," 4). These "questions" are not "doctrines"—nor is the conviction that they are worth pursuing. One could well take the asking and pursuing of such questions to be the basic project of Nietzsche's naturalism more generally.

Philosophy for Nietzsche involves attempting and proposing accounts of various sorts—some "genealogical" or otherwise developmental, others interpretive or otherwise sense-making. They are sometimes but by no means always—or even for the most part—modeled on natural-scientific modes of explanation, let alone based explicitly upon appeals to results of research of the sorts pursued in natural-scientific disciplines. These accounts are often developed imaginatively and proposed merely hypothetically, in order to help show the plausibility of what I am calling the "Guiding Idea" that all things human can be made sense of in this-worldly developmental terms, even though they may well be problematic as they stand.

In *Beyond*, speaking of the philosophical position he calls "sensualism" [*Sensualismus*],[30] Nietzsche advocates it "at least as a regulative hypothesis, if not to say as a heuristic principle" (*BGE* 15). This language (quite apart from the question of what he means by *Sensualismus* here) can be usefully employed in the present context. I suggest that, for Nietzsche, naturalism (construed as I have just sketched it) is *both* a "regulative hypothesis" (substantively speaking) *and* a "heuristic principle" (methodologically speaking). As a "regulative hypothesis," it is the hypothesis that this Guiding Idea will hold up well (in terms of continuing plausibility, viability, and sense-making) if one remains within its bounds as philosophical inquiry, reflection, and interpretation proceed. As a "heuristic principle," it is the thought that approaching things in this way will be helpful to interpretive and reinterpretive inquiry.

Nietzsche's naturalism, as we see it displayed in his various writings, is by no means wedded to the view that everything that happens in human life, and in the development and unfolding of human reality and experience, can be adequately explained and fully comprehended in terms of natural-scientific or natural-scientifically modeled concepts and processes—"causality" first and foremost among them. Indeed, he takes the refinement of and reliance upon causal thinking in the natural sciences to be at once their strength and their limitation in their partnership with philosophy in these matters.

Nietzsche would seem to share at least something of the deeper doubt of which he speaks in his remarks relating to Kant in his discussion of "The Old Problem: 'What Is German?'" in the 1887 fifth Book of *Inquiry*: "As Germans, we doubt with Kant the ultimate validity of natural-scientific knowledge and everything that *allows* itself to be known causally [*Allem, was sich causaliter erkennen* lässt]." For "what is know-*able*" [*das Erkenn*bare] in this manner, he continues, "seems to us to be of *lesser* worth" (*JI* 357). (That is: of lesser worth than that which does *not* "allow itself to be known causally," and thus natural-scientifically, because it is *more than merely natural*. This is an idea to which he himself evidently subscribes, but to which he gives a new and very different, "this-worldly" meaning, in terms of the meaning-endowing transformation of the natural.)

Nietzsche does not doubt for a moment that the developments through which human reality has come to be as it is, and the many different sorts of things that go on in human life, are shot through with necessities, influences, attractions, constraints, reactions, interactions, and power relations of many sorts. What he *does* doubt (and even ridicule) is the idea that natural-scientifically modeled *causal thinking* is capable of doing comprehensive justice to all of them, or even of being appropriate to a good many of them—notwithstanding his subsequent favorable contrast of "science" conceived as "the healthy concept of cause and effect" to the pathological mode of interpretation he associates with priestly Christianity in *The Antichristian* (*A* 49).[31] That sort of "causalism" (as I shall call it) is one of the cardinal tenets of the "scientism" to which I take him to be opposed.

"Translating man back into nature," for Nietzsche, and coming to terms with what he calls "the terrible [*schreckliche*] basic text of *homo natura* [natural man]" in a manner that has "become hard in the training of science" [*hart geworden in der Zucht der Wissenschaft*] (*BGE* 230), is something he strongly advocates.[32] But that, for him, does *not* mean treating human reality as if it were *no different now* than it was when our species first appeared, or dealing with it in a purely natural-scientifically modeled way. To be "hardened in the *Zucht* of *Wissenschaft*" for him is rather a matter of having been sufficiently disciplined and schooled by acquaintance with scientific thinking to become *redlich*—that is, not simply "honest" (as this favorite term of Nietzsche's is commonly translated) but intellectually conscientious, tough-minded, unsentimental, and on guard against wishful thinking—in our de-deified reinterpretation of human reality no less than of the world in which we find ourselves. And what interests him most is not simply what this "basic text" was in the first place and what remains of it, but also the *transformability* of which it has proven to be capable, and the further transformations of it that may yet be possible.

VI

The point just made is an important one, warranting elaboration. Nietzsche's naturalism countenances the possibility and reality in human life of qualitatively transformational episodes, occurring in the course of entirely *mundane* human events. By this I mean: episodes resulting in the emergence of various historically developing (and sometimes mutating), socially and linguistically structured and culturally configured *forms of life* (*Lebensformen*, human "life forms"). Nietzsche identifies and discusses many such phenomena, of differing types and subject to historical contingencies, that often differ significantly from their own and other historical as well as biological-evolutionary antecedents and contemporaries, and that further require to be understood in different terms from their physiological undergirdings.[33]

Nietzsche's naturalism is sensitive and attentive to the many sorts of *Lebensformen* (with their associated kinds of experience, activity, and objectification) that have come to be parts of human reality, and involves the attempt to comprehend them in a manner doing justice to their attained richness and diversity as well as their very human (and often all-too-human) origins. Those he mentions and discusses include various social, cultural, political, religious, artistic, scientific, and even philosophical phenomena. They all (along with "the type *Mensch*" in general) are to be both "translated back into nature" in their origins and basic constitution, *and also* comprehended in their emergently human character—as a kind of "transfigured nature" (in Nietzsche's manner of speaking), showing what some of the things are that our originally merely natural nature had it in it to engender and become. His resistance to causalistic scientism pertains both to the developmental emergence of such "forms of life" and to what goes on within them that is made humanly possible by them—which includes much (if not all) of human life.

In a sense Nietzsche's naturalism is a rather minimalist one, committed to little more than the Guiding Idea mentioned above. Yet it is also what I would call a robust naturalism, in the sense that it has eyes and appetite for the richly fleshed-out panoply of our human reality and world—quite unlike the kind of austerely barebones scientistic naturalism attributed to Nietzsche by Leiter, according to which everything in and about human reality is to be understood in terms of "a scientific picture of how things work."[34] Nietzsche's own version of naturalism, as it is on display throughout his writings, is much more expansive than this, both substantively (in terms of how he is prepared to talk about what exists and what goes on in the world of human reality) and methodologically (in his ways of approaching and dealing with it).

As was earlier observed, the world of Nietzsche's human reality—"the world that *concerns us*"—contains things like words, languages, books, pianos, operas, symphonies, plays, paintings, sculptures, cities, states, universities, armies, professions, games, laws, moralities, and *Wissenschaften*. These are all things the "existence" of which, for him, is or should be beyond dispute. While there is a sense in which they are "natural" (that is, have no supra-mundane origins and histories), there is another sense in which they are by no means merely so (that is, comprehensible in terms of the kinds of processes that suffice to explain what comes about and goes on in the rest of nature). The bits and pieces of "natural" reality that figure in them may in some sense be what they are "made of"; but *what they are* is a very different story—or rather, a wide variety of very different stories.

The ways in which such things need to be approached and talked about and interpreted in order to be comprehended must be appropriately attuned to these different stories—as Nietzsche tries to be when he deals with them. A barebones naturalist might object: "But strictly and philosophically speaking, things of these sorts do not *really* exist as such; what is *really* real is only the stuff of which they are made, what is *really* going on is only the causal processes in which they figure." To this objection the appropriate Nietzschean-naturalistic response would be first to laugh, and then to observe that that way of thinking is "true world" metaphysics once more, akin to the other dogmatic targets of the preface of *Beyond*.

While the kinds of things just mentioned are no "things in themselves," and are what they are only in the context of human life, they also are no "mere appearances" either, in contrast to fantasized "things in themselves" of some sort that might be imagined to have a kind of "true being" they lack. They exist—as the realities they have come to be in our lives and world, within which they have been engendered. Rather than either being or manifesting "things in themselves," they *are* the "things themselves." The kinds of reality they *are*—in our lives and experience and thought—are the kinds of reality they *have*. The engendering of such things, involving the humanly creative transformation of the natural resources of our bodies and environing world, is fundamental to the development and fleshing out of what is more than merely animal about human reality. Doing justice to it, and to the difference its results make in the attained character of that reality, is a central challenge and task of Nietzsche's naturalism.

VII

This has significant implications for the manner in which that task is to be pursued—as Nietzsche makes vividly clear in *JI* 373, using the example of music to powerful effect. His contention here is that a purely natural-scientifically modeled "world interpretation" (and especially a *Mensch* interpretation entirely of that sort, without supplementation) would be no better than the sort of strictly "scientific" analysis and conception not only of the "*Wert*" [worth or value] of "a piece of music" [*einer Musik*] but also of *what it is*—"what is actually 'music' in it!" [*was eigentlich an ihr "Musik" ist*]—that he here ridicules. That sort of naturalism for him would be "a crudity [*Plumpheit*] and naivete," and indeed (as he puts it) would be "one of the *stupidest* [*dümmsten*]" of interpretations.

What is "naive," "crude," and "stupid" about it, for Nietzsche, is that while a good deal of knowledge might well be attained thereby, *restricting oneself to* that sort of interpretation would be to take what he calls "precisely the most superficial and external aspect of existence" to be the whole of it. And that would be a great mistake in the case of every sort of thing that is *meaning-constituted*, even if also nature-based and incarnate in one way or another—things like dance, music, and works of the plastic as well as literary arts included, along with a wealth of other forms of gesture and expression.

In this passage Nietzsche has "mechanistic"-materialistic scientific thinking specifically in mind; but his basic point applies to natural-scientific (and natural-scientifically modeled) thinking more generally, where human reality and the human world are concerned: such thinking is inherently *meaning-blind*. It is attuned to observable aspects of things in which any meanings that may be constitutive of them are not to be found; and thus a world conceived accordingly would be, as he puts it, "essentially *devoid of meaning*" [*essentiell sinnlose*]. An interpretation of that sort would completely miss all of the layerings and texturings of meaning that make so much of what exists and goes on in our world and our lives the meaningful realities they are.

This may not matter all that much in the cases of the sorts of phenomena to which the various natural sciences are geared. It matters a good deal, however, if the same ways of thinking are brought to bear upon matters that cannot be at all adequately comprehended without taking account of the kinds of meanings that make sense of them and make them what they are. "Music"—presumably both as a richly differentiated phenomenon and at the level of particular instances of it—is Nietzsche's specific example here, but of which a great deal of human reality and experience is his larger case in point.

So he writes, using language that hammers home the epistemic (not just valuational) point he is making: "What would one have *comprehended, understood, discerned* of it [*von ihr* begriffen, verstanden, erkannt]? Nothing, really nothing of what is 'music' in it!" (*JI* 373; emphasis added). Nothing, that is, of what *makes it what it is*, as the kind of thing that has been *made out of* what it is made of. It is precisely that sort of reality, however, and that sort of difference, to which Nietzsche considers it most important for us as philosophers to be sensitive—and for us as developers of a sophisticated philosophical naturalism to be attentive.

To be sure, the case of music is a rather special one, in a number of re-spects; and it is undoubtedly true that there is much about human reality that can be more usefully and importantly illuminated by scientific inquiry—in ways that have significance for its Nietzschean-philosophical interpretation and comprehension—than "what is 'music' in music." There is much in and about something like music that can be discovered and learned only by ap-proaching it by way of the sort of intimate acquaintance and cultivated sen-sibility Nietzsche considers to be needed to understand this. But there also is much about even something like music that *can* be learned and discovered by availing ourselves of a variety of very different mentalities and perspectives that can be brought to bear upon the many aspects of music as a phenomenon and piece of human reality. And they are legion—some physical-scientific, physiological, neurological, and psychological; others anthropological, cul-tural, historical, biographical, sociological, and even technological.

This serves to illustrate and bring out an important point about Nietzsche's kind of naturalism. He himself makes it in a well-known passage in the third essay of *On the Genealogy of Morality*. There he writes, with respect to the requisite "*Zucht* [breeding, training] and preparation of the intellect for its future 'objectivity,'" that "the *more* eyes, different eyes, we can use to observe the same matter [*dieselbe Sache*], the more complete our 'concept' of this *Sache*, our 'objectivity,' will be." And he takes this to be desirable not merely for self-expressive or creative purposes, but rather "so that one knows how to make precisely the *diversity* [*Verschiedenheit*, differentness] of perspectives and affective interpretations useful *for knowledge* [*für die Erkenntnis*]" (*GM* III:12; second emphasis added). I take the differing sorts of ways of looking at things I have just mentioned to be paradigmatic examples of the "*more eyes, different eyes*" he is talking about here. And I take him to consider the kind of mentality he associates with natural-scientific thinking to be one of them (or rather, one cluster of them) that is very definitely needed—but by no means the only one, or the most important one.

This important passage is highly relevant to the question of the "method-ology" of Nietzsche's naturalism. Indeed, it may be his single best statement of it. It connects in an interesting way with a somewhat earlier reflection, in the first version of *Inquiry*, in which he is discussing both the genealogy of "*wissenschaftlich* thinking" and some of the ways in which it needs to be supplemented. He begins by suggesting that it is a phenomenon with a com-plex developmental story: "So many things must come together for *wissen-schaftlich* thinking to originate." He then remarks that "as long as [these many things] were still separate," it was often the case that "their effect was that of poisons"; but that "when integrated into *wissenschaftlich* thinking they hold each other in check," and so are able to work together to make humanly possible a very different (cognitive rather than merely lethal or chaotic) result.

Of particular interest, for present purposes, is Nietzsche's concluding remark in *JI* 113: "even now the time seems remote when artistic energies [*künstlerischen Kräfte*] and the practical wisdom of life will join with *wissenschaftlich* thinking to form a higher organic system [*höheres organisches System*]" or way of proceeding in which they complement and supplement each other. This sounds very much like an early recipe for the kind of thinking that would at least partially characterize Nietzsche's "philosophy of the future."

To mention just one further case in point: in the uncharacteristic and therefore striking "Remark" [*Anmerkung*] at the end of the first essay of *Genealogy*, Nietzsche provides what I take to be an excellent example of the kind of thing he is talking about in section 12 of *Genealogy*'s third essay (cited above). As in the book itself, the topic of this concluding remark is "moral concepts," which he proposes to approach—in keeping with his commitment to a (naturalistic) reinterpretation of all things human—in terms of their developmental "history" (*HH* I:2). He begins by suggesting that this is a matter that "deserves the attention of philologists and historians as well as that of professional philosophers." He then observes: "It is equally necessary to engage the interest of physiologists and medical experts [*Mediziner*]" when proceeding to the reconsideration of the "*value* of previous values" he advocates because, he writes, "the question: what is the *value* of this or that table of values and 'morals'? should be viewed from the most diverse perspectives [*unter die verschiedensten Perspektiven*]" (*GM* I:17n.).

The initial role of philosophers, Nietzsche says, and more specifically of "professional philosophers" (of whom he generally has little that is positive to say), "after transforming the originally so reserved and mistrustful relations between philosophy, physiology, and medicine into the most amicable and fruitful exchange," would be to act as "advocates and mediators" between these "diverse perspectives" and what can be discerned by way of these differing approaches and ways of thinking. Then those who have it in them, presumably availing themselves of insights gained in this manner, could go on to develop a more comprehensive reinterpretation and reassessment of the values and morals in question. And from there, some might even ultimately proceed to what he calls "the future task of philosophers" for which "all the *Wissenschaften* have from now on to prepare the way": namely, tackling "the *problem of value*" and of "the *rank order of values*" (*GM* I:17n.). One could hardly ask for a better indication of the character and larger agenda of Nietzsche's naturalism.

VIII

Nietzsche's kind of naturalism is predicated on his conviction that everything about human reality—along with everything else there is—has "become" (*HH* I:2). It therefore is centrally concerned not only with explanations and origins but also with *developmental* questions. And this includes attempting to identify and understand the qualitative respects in which human reality has become something significantly different from the sort of merely biological affair he presumes it to have been in the first place. His interest in the "*Ent-tierung*" or "dis-animalization" of "the type *Mensch*" is as strong and important as his emphasis upon our fundamental "*tierische*" [animal] nature and his interest in the respects in which it continues to constrain and shape human life.

Nietzsche's naturalism further is *historically* (as well as biologically) developmental; and his conception of our attained human reality is as much social and cultural as it is biological, physiological, and psychological. It is attuned as much to the emergent reality and indispensability of the former dimensions, and to developments with significant consequences at those levels, as it is to traits and dispositions of the latter sort, and to questions of their differences and mutability. Indeed, the main focus of his attention is upon the emergence and development of various sorts of human phenomena—forms of life and the many sorts of experience and activity they make possible—that have not only human-biological and physiological presuppositions and psychological dimensions, but also a historical character, in which social, cultural, and circumstantially contingent events may be presumed to have played major roles (upon which he delights in speculating). (The term "historical" [*historisch*] for Nietzsche, when used in this context, is to be understood to include what he calls "our human prehistory," prior to the advent of recorded history.)

So, for example, the title Nietzsche gives to the third part of *Beyond* is indicative and revealing on this score: "*Zur Naturgeschichte der Moral*" ["On the Natural History of Morality"]. It deals with the question of what the origins and developmental story of various moral phenomena may have been— supposing them to *be* historical phenomena that are to be understood in entirely "natural" (that is, mundane psychological and sociocultural) terms. Being able to make developmental sense of such phenomena is important to him, in part to strengthen the case for naturalism itself, by showing its sufficiency to account for even the loftiest forms of our spirituality. It also contributes importantly to our understanding of what we have both to work with and to deal with, as we concern ourselves with the further "enhancement of life," and address ourselves to the all-important Nietzschean question of "what might yet be made of man" (*BGE* 203).

In short: Nietzsche makes much of physiological as well as psychological considerations and conjectures, and seeks to counter the long-standing tendency of philosophers to be oblivious to the relevance of psychological and physiological considerations to the things about ourselves that they esteem most highly. But he also is quite evidently convinced that human cultural phenomena, while physiologically grounded, are historically developed forms of life differing qualitatively from the biological and physiological phenomena associated with their origination and ongoing occurrence. They reflect diversely articulated and elaborated expressions of unevenly realized aspects of human reality and varieties of human possibility, in differing social and historical circumstances.

Nietzsche's typical procedure (and the "methodology" of his naturalism, such as it is) therefore involves employing and drawing upon a multiplicity of differing perspectives, "optics," and mentalities, as was observed above, in the service of the interpretive attempt to broaden and deepen our comprehension of ourselves and of the human possibilities that have come to be realized and expressed in things as diverse as differing psychological types and traits, cultures and subcultures, societies and institutions, arts and literatures, morals and values, kinds of thinking and knowing, and various human sensibilities that have come and gone, in which all of these sorts of things are interwoven.

IX

These features of Nietzsche's naturalism are already anticipated, in clearly programmatic fashion, in *Human*. In the revealing final section of *The Wanderer and His Shadow*, its third and last installment, he writes: "Many chains have been laid *upon dem Menschen* so that it should no longer behave like an animal" (*HH* II:II:350). And at the very outset of its first (1878) installment he makes several crucial general points. He begins by proclaiming "natural science" [*Naturwissenschaft*] to be "the youngest of all philosophical methods," to which the kind of philosophy he is advocating (and contrasting with "metaphysical philosophy") needs to ally itself, and from which it "can no longer be separated" (*HH* I:1). But he then goes on to call this new kind of philosophy "*historical* philosophy," for an important reason he gives and elaborates in the next section (*HH* I:2): "Historical philosophizing," for Nietzsche, here and subsequently, is philosophizing in a way that is mindful that "everything has become," and is attentive to the *historical-developmental* character of whatever it deals with—human reality [*der Mensch*]—in particular.

Thus while he insists upon the relevance and importance of *Naturwissenschaft* and the various *Naturwissenschaften* in this undertaking, it is *historische* (rather than *naturwissenschaftliche*) philosophizing that he calls for. The "becoming" or development of things is held to be crucial to their comprehension and proper assessment; and by his use of the term *historische* Nietzsche is indicating that, while the kinds of development the natural sciences deal with must be taken into account by philosophers from now on, they are not the only kinds of development that may need to be reckoned with. Where all things human in particular are concerned, the kinds of development we need to be especially attentive to are developments of a historical character. And that means availing ourselves not only of "the youngest of all philosophical methods"—that is, those of natural-scientific inquiry—but also of other methods needed to comprehend such developments.

That is what Nietzsche spent much of his time exploring in the vast number of reflections of which the rest of *Human* consists, as well as the two other aphoristic volumes in his "free spirit" series that followed it (*Daybreak* and *Inquiry*). And that is what he continued to do in the books following *Zarathustra*, to the end. He at times avails himself of language that is "casual-causal" (as I would call it) in doing so; but few of the developments he discusses lend themselves at all well to nomological-causal[35] analysis and explanation more strictly speaking (on the model of the natural sciences). His proposed interpretations and explanations do certainly involve ideas of *influences* of many sorts. As a moment's reflection on the kinds of developments and phenomena we find him talking about makes clear, however, that sort of causalism is ill suited to many of those that he considers to have been most significant and deserving of attention. They include many social and cultural phenomena that are *normatively* structured or consequential, and that make a considerable difference in human lives when they are internalized. Indeed, the causalist model is ill suited to the understanding of the crucially important human phenomenon of such internalization itself.

In short: Nietzsche's "naturalistic project" may be characterized as *the reinterpretation of human reality*, in all of its complexity, in mundane terms he considered to be (broadly speaking) naturalistically respectable. And human reality, for him, includes what he considered to be modern-day Western morality, a variety of other sorts of morality, and a vast array of other (predominantly social, cultural, and psychological) phenomena and developments that have figured significantly in the shaping of human life at various junctures in the course of human events.

X

I shall develop this point in a manner that has significant implications for the understanding of Nietzsche's naturalism, by availing myself of the notion of "sensibilities" [*Sensibilitäten*] associated with human cultures and cultural formations, instances of which figure significantly in his writings. His naturalism must be conceived in a manner that takes account of his concern to do justice to, and make sense of, this phenomenon—which for him is central to human life and to the character of our attained human reality.

Nietzsche does not seem to have discovered the word *Sensibilität*—or its usefulness for his purposes did not occur to him—until quite late. He does use it, however, and in a relevant way, in his encomium to Bizet's opera *Carmen* in his late book *The Case of Wagner*. There he writes that "a different sensibility" [*eine andere Sensibilität*] than Wagner's finds expression in this work—and one that indeed had not previously found expression at all in European classical music. He refers to it and characterizes it as "this more southern, [sun-]browned, [sun-]burned sensibility" [*dieser südlicheren, bräuneren, verbrannteren Sensibilität*] (*CW* I:2).

Other instances of this kind of phenomenon had long attracted Nietzsche's attention; and he makes frequent use—in an extended and refined sense of the closely related term *Empfindung(en)*—sometimes also translated as "sensibility" and "sensibilities," but too often in one of the more usual (and oversimplifying) ways as "feeling(s)" or "emotion(s)." And "sentiment(s)" is not much better for Nietzsche's purposes. So, for example, in the aphorism on "What Remains of Art" in *Human*, he writes that art "has taught us [. . .] to cultivate our *Empfindung* so extensively that we at last cry: 'life, however it may be, is good!'" (*HH* I:222; "sensibilities" is Hollingdale's better rendering of the term in this instance). *Empfindung* here is no mere "feeling" or "emotion" and no mere "sentiment" either.

Sensibilities figure significantly in Nietzsche's understanding of how human conduct has come to differ from "behaving like an animal"—and also of how human life comes to be configured differently not only in different societies and cultures but also within them. So, for example, they are what he is getting at in much of his talk about various human "types," as well as about "peoples and fatherlands." A notable case in point occurs in *Twilight*, when, after observing "how naive it is altogether to say: '*Der Mensch ought* to be such and such,'" he continues: "Reality shows us an enchanting wealth of types, the abundance of a lavish play and change of forms" (*TI* "Morality," 6).

Nietzsche's interest in sensibility-phenomena—and in the conditions of their possibility, their variability, and their importance in human life—made its first appearance, in striking fashion, in *The Birth of Tragedy*. There he is concerned with the historical "birth" or emergence and development of "tragedy" not only as a dramatic-literary genre, but also (and, for him, more importantly) as a cultural and human-spiritual phenomenon—and with the "tragic" sensibility associated with it, that was both expressed in and cultivated by that genre and culture. He also is concerned in *Birth* (and subsequently) with the differing cultural phenomena and sensibilities that gave birth to tragedy that he calls by the names of their associated deities—"Apollinian" and "Dionysian." The very different sensibility of Socrates (and Stoicism), that resulted in tragedy's demise, is another case in point. And it prepared the way for the subsequent emergence of the sensibilities associated with the scientific spirit, on the one hand, and (implicitly, at any rate) with the subsequently emerging Christian sort of religiousness on the other.

This interest continues and becomes more self-conscious in Nietzsche's subsequent writings. It is central to the very project of *Thus Spoke Zarathustra*—the whole point of which is to cultivate a new life-affirming (post-nihilistic as well as post-Christian) sensibility. And it becomes ever more pronounced in the analyses and critiques of various cultural pathologies in the polemics of the last two years of his productive life.

Nietzsche's naturalizing project in effect—even if not explicitly—involves the recognition and examination of such sensibilities and associated forms of experience and activity, as very significant diverse forms of human spirituality that make a great difference in the character of human life. It further involves the attempt to show that they can plausibly be construed as neither more nor less than human-historical, sociocultural, and psychological phenomena, that have emerged and developed in ways that can be made sense of in entirely mundane terms. They may be developmentally related to basic human capacities and dispositions (as Apollinian and Dionysian arts and sensibilities are purported to have developed out of the human phenomena of dreaming and intoxication). They also may be related to each other—as tragedy and its associated sensibility are purported to have been "born out of the spirit of music," by way of the coupling of the Dionysian and the Apollinian. They also may emerge and take shape under the impact (upon prior sensibilities and dispositions) of certain social constraints, group dynamics, and the like.

XI

Sensibilities, of the sort I take Nietzsche to have in mind, are complex configurations of dispositions, attitudes, beliefs, valuations, and interpretive tendencies. They are powered (as it were) by affective resources, and may be channeled at least to some extent by inherited but humanly variable traits; but they are also strongly scripted culturally, reflecting elements of cultural formations to which one has been exposed and that one has internalized.

Sensibilities thus are typically bound up with *Lebensformen* and their associated formations (such as practices, traditions, institutions, artifacts, symbols, art forms, and texts), of which sensibilities are the internalization, and in which they are anchored—and yet which also are *their* expressions and elaborations, each informing and sustaining the other.

This dynamic relation is one of the hallmarks—and indeed is part of the very fabric—of our attained humanity. Its contingencies and endless mutability also serve to make it possible for human reality to branch out into the creative profusion of Nietzsche's "lavish play and change of forms" (*Twilight*), and to endow and enrich itself with historically emergent values and meanings—even though all such phenomena themselves are the products of transformations of originally merely nature-given or need-driven abilities and traits. It is always our affects that are expressing themselves in whatever we may do, for Nietzsche; but they do so *through our sensibilities*, which not only *in*form but also *trans*form our affects in their manner of expression. Such transformations can be particularly dramatic when other aspects of our human-psychological repertoire come into play, of which our capacities for what he calls the "internalization," "redirection," and "sublimation" of our basic drives and dispositions are of particular importance.

Sensibilities exist in the dynamic and highly differentiated medium of human languages, and so might usefully be thought of as involving distinctive "language games" within which their characterizing concepts, norms, and values are anchored. Because much of their content and configuration further has a historical character, it has the contingency of all things historical. Moreover, human beings are not simply passively and uniformly programmed by the cultural formations that provide them with basic scripting. They rather are actively responsive in nonidentical ways even as they internalize cultural constructions. For all of these reasons, sensibilities are resistant to natural-scientifically modeled causal analysis.

Human beings, for Nietzsche, are not merely *capable* of entering into broader and narrower historically developed, frequently socially contextual, and always culturally textured forms of life, and of acquiring the associated sensibilities and mentalities—just as they are not merely *capable* of learning a language, using it, and acquiring the sensibilities characteristic of it. They (we) *must* do so, having lost the ability to live otherwise precisely as these capacities have been gained. It is part of the price that had to be paid to gain them. That is both our unique strength as a species and our great vulnerability—for which reason Nietzsche constantly characterizes *der Mensch* by such phrases as "the most endangered animal," "the unfixed animal," "the most de-natured animal," and "the animal that has strayed most dangerously from its old instincts"—but also "the most *interesting* animal," through whose transformation "the aspect of the earth was fundamentally altered" (*GM* II:16).

Nietzsche delights in exploring the many sensibilities and mentalities he notices, many of which relate in significant ways to issues he pursues across the spectrum of his philosophical interests. His explorations of them in their historical (and occasionally even biographical) specificity are grist for the mill of his robust naturalism. His attention to the sensibility-phenomenon they exemplify is an important part of it—as is his concern to show that they can all be made sense of within the framework of what I am calling its Guiding Idea: all are to be conceived and accounted for as anchored in—and emerging out of—aspects of our human-animal nature, by way of historical developments of a social and cultural nature, and cultivated by associated forms of human life.

XII

It has been in something like this way, Nietzsche surmises, and in no small measure by these means, that humankind has bootstrapped itself from animality to human reality. *Lebensformen* and sensibilities have come to be as much a part of human reality as the use of the rich and complex forms of language they both require and continually modify. Moreover, Nietzsche would further seem to suppose that, just as they have been the means and medium of all previous "enhancements of life," versions of them will be needed to play the same sort of role in any to come. And just as they have long figured significantly in developments *detrimental* to human flourishing and enhancement, that (obviously) will continue to be possible as well.

Nietzsche considers the sensibilities acquired by individual human beings to be modifiable in the courses of their lives—both for the better (as, he believes, in his own case) and for the worse (as, for example, he considers to have happened in the case of Pascal) (*BGE* 46). The general human rule, however, is suggested to be that human beings tend to live their lives and conduct themselves in ways reflecting sensibilities they come to have through a combination of nature (that is, heredity) with specific sorts of nurture, under certain social circumstances. This, for Nietzsche, is only to be expected—and it is only infrequently to be lamented. Human beings for him also may—and perhaps even commonly do—have identities in which single comprehensive sensibilities are sufficiently dominant for it to be appropriate to characterize them in terms of those sensibilities, as he often does.

Nietzsche further considers it to be humanly possible, however, for a single human being to develop a multiplicity of sensibilities (rather in the manner of becoming multilingual), and to be able to shift from one to another in appropriate contexts, or even to play them off against each other, or draw upon various of them together when that proves advantageous, illuminating, or creative. That is an ability he takes to be of particular importance and value for a philosopher; but it also is needful for anyone who lives in a number of different social and cultural "worlds," each of which requires that one have and operate out of an appropriately different sensibility or mentality.

Expanding upon and extrapolating from this idea, Nietzsche envisions human possibilities associated with his idea of a "higher" humanity, anticipated and approximated here and there, consisting of human beings who have attained measures of self-mastery, autonomy, and creativity sufficient to enable them to fashion distinctive sensibilities of their own, out of and beyond those they have previously acquired and encountered, giving their own "styles" to their "characters," and becoming self-creating "artists of their own lives." His naturalism further must be conceived in such a way as to make provision for these possibilities, and make sense of the claims he makes with respect to their divergence from the human rule. It would seem to me that, as he conceives and speaks of them, even more than in cases of more ordinary (and pathological) humanity and sensibility, the kinds of scientific thinking and explanation pursued in or modeled on natural-scientific inquiry will be able to play no more than a supporting role.

It is just such a role—supporting, but not leading—that Nietzsche envisions for that sort of inquiry in an important passage in *Inquiry*, in which he at once celebrates and embraces it and also gently puts it in its place in this context. It bears the charming heading "*Hoch die Physik!*" ["Here's to Physics!"]. He writes, of the "higher humanity" to which he would have us join him in aspiring: "We, however, want to become those we are" (*JI* 335). This, for him, involves attaining both the autonomy of the "sovereign individual" of *GM* II:2 and the creativity of the "*Mensch* of the future" of *GM* II:24, as his explication of this line shows: "the new, the unique, the incomparable, the self-legislating, the self-creating!" He then immediately continues: "And to that end we must become the best learners and discoverers of everything law-like [*Gesetzlichen*] and necessary in the world: we must be *physicists* [*Physiker*, natural scientists] in order to be able to be creators [*Schöpfer sein zu können*] in this sense. And so: Here's to physics! [*Hoch die Physik!*] And even more [*höher noch*] to that which compels us to do so—our *Redlichkeit* [intellectual integrity]!" (*JI* 335).

Knowledge of "everything law-like and necessary in the world" will not suffice to enable one actually to live one's life autonomously and creatively, and certainly will not suffice to determine what someone doing so should actually do or create. Nietzsche clearly thinks that it can and will be importantly helpful. But it will not even suffice to enable one to *comprehend* such autonomy and creativity as human possibilities, let alone to *attain and live it*. The former, for Nietzsche, is the preliminary challenge and task of his kind of philosophy and his naturalizing reinterpretation of human reality. The latter is their ultimate aim. Both require a larger set of eyes and strategies of acquaintance and interpretation, more comprehensively attuned to all that human reality has become—and has become capable of becoming.

XIII

In sum: for Nietzsche no naturalism is worth taking seriously that ignores or is clumsy in dealing with all that gives depth and richness to human reality— such as the dimension and character of human reality I have been discussing in terms of "sensibilities" and what they make possible. It is undoubtedly at least in part for this reason that he is so scornful of some versions of naturalism. The naturalism that he envisions, calls for, attempts to inaugurate, and expects his "new philosophers" to embrace and develop thus cannot possibly be that of the crudely mechanistic naturalists whose "clumsiness" and "stupidity" he derides, or even that of their more sophisticated but still causalist scientistic cousins.

In relation to both such versions, Nietzsche's is an alternative sort of naturalism. It is appropriately attentive both to the kinds of phenomena and aspects of things that the natural sciences are good at describing and (in their fashion) explaining—and also (differently) to historical developments that resist causal-deterministic analysis, such as the vast profusion of human-cultural forms of life and the sorts of experience and activity they make possible. And it is further attentive to things like "what is '*music*' in a piece of music"; to what is going on in the "cases" of Wagner, Socrates, Christianity, and the like; and to the emergence of diverse valuations and sensibilities more generally that make differences in the lives of those who encounter and either internalize or resist them.

Nietzsche's naturalism is thus a naturalism in which, beyond the nexus of causes, allowance is made for the developmental emergence of "a space of reasons" in which "the activities of rational interpreters and agents" proceed differently, in ways appropriately described and understood in the language of the kind of normativity appropriate to them. Allowance is also made for the developmental emergence of what correspondingly might be called "a space of sensibilities." And in *that* "space" the activities of cultural interpreters, agents, and creators proceed in yet other ways, appropriately described and understood in the language of the kinds of affectivity, purposes, values, and normativities associated with historically developing sociocultural formations and their more individuated adaptations.

Nietzsche's "naturalizing" program is to be allied with but not restricted to and guided by the sciences—"scientian" but not scientistic. Those who "get with" that program, in the spirit of what we find him saying and doing as he attempts to get on with it, will take care not to be guilty of "losing 'the soul' the moment they touch it" (*BGE* 12), by being blind to or inept in dealing with what he is talking about when he uses this language.

Of course, for the Nietzschean naturalizing reinterpreter, *Seele*, like *Geist*, is *"nur ein Wort für Etwas am Leibe"* [only a word for something about the body] (*Z* I:4). But it is a word for what has become a very extraordinary *Etwas* [something]. It has become what it is as a human possibility phylogenetically. But it comes to be whatever is made of that possibility in particular instances ontogenetically, in the context of a host of human social, cultural, and interpersonal circumstances and relations that have themselves developed historically. This renders it imperative for us, if we are to be Nietzsche's kind of philosophers, to adapt our naturalism accordingly—both methodologically and substantively—as our comprehension of this *Etwas* develops.

In short: particularly where human reality is concerned, Nietzsche considers his kind of philosophy to be the proper senior partner in the alliance of philosophy with the sciences—and not only because that alliance needs to include other partners as well, and further needs coordination and direction. It is also, for Nietzsche, because there is much about human reality that the sciences are ill equipped and ill positioned to comprehend, and with respect to which they therefore are either oblivious or obtuse. This applies to much of what has a human-historical character, and to virtually the whole of human cultural reality, both outwardly and inwardly conceived.

Even here, the sciences have an important role to play and contribution to make. For there are undoubtedly causal stories to be told—about developments at the physiological, neurophysiological, evolutionary, and psychological levels in particular—that contributed to making such historical and cultural transformations and phenomena possible. And also about changes in the latter domains that may again be precipitated by further such developments at the former levels (or, for that matter, vice versa). Moreover, and no less importantly, the Nietzschean philosopher needs to be equipped with a scientific sensibility and conscience—even though with others as well.

But for Nietzsche it is his kind of multiperspectival and interpretively experimental philosophy—rather than any or even all of the various natural-scientific and natural-scientifically modeled *Wissenschaften* by themselves—that is needed to be able to make the most crucial assessments, raise the most important questions, and make the most promising interpretive responses to them. It is only his kind of philosopher that he deems capable of attaining "the height for a comprehensive look, for looking around, for looking *down*." And for him it is only the ability to rise to that sort of highest-level perspective on all merely partial perspectives that can give one the ability, responsibility, right, and the self-respect to "*lead* in the realm of knowledge" (*BGE* 205).

But all such "leading" can never be or reach a definitive final ending, where anything living rather than dead or inert is concerned. Its best efforts, conclusions, and convictions always remain provisional, open to reconsideration, and subject to challenges—including challenges prompted by developments in the sciences that may bear upon them. The "commanding" of which Nietzsche speaks, and expects of his "new philosophers," can never settle anything once and for all. It is commanding within never-ending contesting. So he continues: "But the genuine philosopher—as it seems to *us*, my friends?—lives [. . .] *imprudently*, and feels the burden and the duty of a hundred attempts and temptations of life—he risks *himself* constantly, he plays *the* nasty game [das *schlimme Spiel*]" (*BGE* 205).

I shall conclude by citing two telling passages, together displaying Nietzsche's two sides as a philosopher—one (as it were) rather Apollinian, the other more Dionysian. The first is an astute general observation he makes in *Daybreak*—at the very midpoint of his supposedly "positivistic" period—with respect to cognitive inquiry (*Wissenschaft*) in general. It applies not only to the various special *Wissenschaften* but also to his own philosophical *fröhliche Wissenschaft* both in principle and in practice, both at that time and subsequently—and also to his kind of naturalism, the adventuresome methodological character of which it nicely reflects and underscores.

In making the quip with which the first passage concludes, Nietzsche undoubtedly was thinking primarily of the (conventionally) moralistically minded. But it actually would apply just as well to the dim view that one would expect many—including the traditionally minded (philosophically speaking), the (strictly) analytically minded, and the (austerely) scientistically minded—to take of his own naturalism, as illuminated by his philosophical practice. (By all of which he would be equally undaunted.) And it nicely sums up the spirit that the German title of *Daybreak*—*Morgenröte*—both literally means and was meant to evoke: that of a "rosy dawn."

> *Investigators and experimenters* [*Forscher und Versucher*].—There are no exclusive knowledge-yielding methods of inquiry [*keine alleinwissendmachende Methode der Wissenschaft*]! We have to tackle things experimentally, now

angry with them and now kind, and be successively just, passionate and cold with them. This [inquirer] addresses things as a policeman, that one as a father confessor, a third as an inquisitive wanderer. It is sometimes by sympathy and sometimes by force that something can be wrung from them [. . .]. We investigators [*Forscher*] are—like all conquerors, discoverers, seafarers, adventurers—of an audacious [*verwegenen*] morality, and must reconcile ourselves to being generally considered evil! (*D* 432)

But—no matter, to Nietzsche's kind of *fröhliche Wissenschaftler*! And it is that Nietzsche, at his zenith commencing the 1887 fifth Book of *Joyful Inquiry*—as if to ready and rally any kindred spirits he might have, to proceed beyond both *Zarathustra* and *Beyond* itself—to whom I give the last word:

> We philosophers and "free spirits" feel, when we hear the news that "the old god is dead," as if a new dawn [*Morgenröte*] shone on us; our heart overflows with gratitude, amazement, premonitions, expectation. [. . .] All the daring of the pursuer of knowledge [*Erkennenden*] is permitted again; the sea, *our* sea, lies open again; perhaps there has never yet been such an "open sea." (*JI* 343)

Backstory and Acknowledgments

This book has been a long time in coming. Its origins and history warrant recounting and some explanation. In the 1960s (the era of the Cold War), at the outset of my career, philosophy as a discipline was riven and plagued by its own cold war that often became quite hot, between two camps. Philosophy as an academic discipline at that point, in the English-speaking world, consisted of an "analytic" mainstream and what might best be contrastingly called an "interpretive" undercurrent (commonly called "Continental," as it was Europe-centered). And that made life very difficult for those of my generation who were attracted to the latter but were also appreciative of the former (or vice versa), and yet in effect were forced to make a choice between them to survive in the discipline (or one's philosophy department, as a major or grad student—or untenured faculty member!).

I found that situation intolerable, for philosophy as well as for those like me who were attracted to aspects of both traditions, and wanted to make it their career. I resolved to make the overcoming of that division my goal, and to devote my career to attempting in various ways to further it.

To that end, I devoted myself to a series of "projects" (as I have thought of them). The first of them was to try to find a way to make figures like Hegel and Marx, and others like Heidegger and Sartre, seem less alien and more recognizably philosophical. (Doing that with Nietzsche was my dream; but at the time doing so in his case seemed not to be possible. So I had to try to prepare the way for him.) My strategy was to show how they contributed to the development of something that could be made intelligible to at least some Anglo-American "analytic" philosophers, particularly in social philosophy: namely, the topic of "alienation," and "alienation theory." Hence my first book, *Alienation* (1970), and other work in "alienation theory" in the years that followed.

But that was only an initial decade-long testing of the waters. Emboldened by its modest success (the bar for that was not high), I then decided to give it a try with Nietzsche. He had been my greatest interest all along, and posed an even greater challenge for me, owing to the fact that he was associated mainly with existentialism, and was dismissed by most analytic philosophers at the time as either a raving maniac or an insidious threat to all "we" hold dear, and in either case no real philosopher at all. My next project was to try to change that—and to make a strong case for his being not only a philosopher (even if an unorthodox one) but also one who could and should be of interest to analytic philosophers.

But how to do it? The answer to that question, for me, came when I had the good fortune to be offered the opportunity to write the Nietzsche volume in Routledge's Arguments of the Philosophers series, which gave me the chance I needed. Hence my next major book, and first Nietzsche book: *Nietzsche* (1983). In its eight chapters (and well over five hundred pages), I undertook to present his philosophical thinking across the range of philosophical issues that were of interest within the philosophical mainstream both traditionally and currently. That book turned out to be a ten-year undertaking. And somewhat to my surprise, it worked—at least as a significant beachhead. During the years following its appearance, mainstream philosophers began at least to be less hostile to him, and some even began to take him seriously. Some even began to write about him!

While Nietzsche was coming to be regarded no longer merely as a kind of nihilistic proto-existentialist, however, he was at that time (in the 1980s) coming to be regarded as something no less problematic in the eyes of most mainstream philosophers: namely, a kind of proto-poststructuralist—and therefore, once again, no real philosopher. My next project, therefore, was to try to make it clear that he was *not that* sort of quasi-philosopher (or anti-philosopher). That project preoccupied me for the next dozen years, culminating in another Nietzsche book, *Making Sense of Nietzsche* (1995).

But that led me to the realization that what actually needed to be done was something more important: to confront directly the question or issue of *what kind of philosopher Nietzsche actually was*, or was trying to be and calling for—in contrast to those kinds of which he was so critical, and those kinds that he was all too often being mistaken for. That then became my next major project. And I recognized that it was very likely to take me more than the ten years my *Nietzsche* had required—because to be convincing, it called for a different and more complex kind of case-making than even that had required, each piece of which would take a lengthy immersion in one or another of his various major philosophical texts, or confrontation with one or another of the standard ways of framing him.

What it called for, I concluded, was *both* of the kinds of exploration and reflection of which the two parts of this book consist—*plus* a comparable set of studies, across the broad range of matters that are of philosophical interest to him, exemplifying what I take to be his kind of philosophy. My original intent was for all of this to be done in a single large book or two-volume work, comparable to my *Nietzsche*. Realizing that works of either sort in philosophy on that order of magnitude are no longer considered feasible, however, I now conceive of them as two separate books, of which this is the first.

A project of this magnitude—certain to require at least as much time as my *Nietzsche* did—made it unwise for me to do nothing with any of it until all of it was done. For one thing, I would have disappeared in the interval. And I also wanted to be able to devote myself to whichever parts of the envisioned whole took my fancy, at any given time, or matched up with some professional opportunity, in any given year. That required my doing them in a disorderly fashion.

To complicate matters even further: this huge project, which was begun in earnest roughly twenty years ago, was interrupted in a major way. I was offered an irresistible opportunity—an opportunity of a lifetime, as I saw it—to make a substantial contribution to the larger cause I described at the outset of these remarks. I refer to the reconciliation of what I had come to think of as the two major traditions in Western philosophy after Kant: the analytic and the interpretive.

What happened was that I was invited to be the general editor of the new *Norton Anthology of Western Philosophy*, originally intended as a single massive tome but reconceived as five volumes, of which the last two were to be the "after Kant" volumes: *The Interpretive Tradition* and *The Analytic Tradition*. And I was to "edit" (actually to structure and create) the *Interpretive* volume myself. (For various reasons, the project was reduced to cover just the last two volumes.)

That was an offer I could not refuse (particularly in view of my "mission"). Little did I know what a long and rocky road it would be. I knew that it would slow me down in the completion of my Nietzsche project; but I never imagined how greatly it would—or that several other substantial but important projects of a time-sensitive nature would need to be undertaken and completed as well. But both volumes were finally finished, and came out in 2017.

At that point, since I also had the freedom of having "gone emeritus," I was at last able to devote my full attention to the Nietzsche project. That specifically meant filling the remaining gaps in the plan, and revisiting everything that was by then already in hand in preliminary or initial form, to rework, revise, and (in some cases) further develop and expand what I had previously done on and in it. This included not only the contents of the present book, but also those intended for the second book, to fill out the third part (and second half) of the project's plan.

So much for the "backstory" of this book (and of what I hope will be its sequel and complement). I now will conclude by describing and acknowledging what needs describing and acknowledging in this book's various chapters. It is my conviction that each piece of this book is the better for its having been given its own time and full attention on my part; that no book of this sort could possibly have been written in one fell swoop; and that the whole of it is greater than the simple sum of its original parts.

I will go one step further: it turns out that, in its present form and content, it realizes my original intention better than I could have realized it in any other way. And my deepening understanding of Nietzsche's kind of philosophy—in the course of these years of reflection on his philosophical thinking as viewed through these various prisms—has been of great benefit to me, as I have reworked them all in the course of the past few years of its finalization.

Personal Acknowledgments

There are many people to whom I am grateful for the contributions—and differences—they made in one way or another, to this book, to all that went into the writing of it, to the kind of philosopher and "Nietzsche person" I have become, and (in some cases) to the understanding of Nietzsche I have come to have. These contributions began with the development of my interest in philosophy and in him in the 1960s, and my first papers and first book on him in the 1970s and 1980s; and they have continued through the genesis and eventual completion and publication of this sixth book dealing with him that I have written or edited. I would like to take this occasion to mention some of these people, beginning well before the conception and planning of the book itself.

I am grateful to Raphael Demos, the grand old man of the Harvard Philosophy Department at the time, who in my first undergraduate year introduced me to philosophy (via a yearlong seminar, a majestic two-semester history of philosophy lecture course, and weekly Sunday afternoon teas in his home), and made me fall in love with it. To Paul Tillich, who in my second and third years introduced me to Nietzsche and the "interpretive tradition" (as he called it and I now call it) of European philosophy from Hegel to Heidegger and beyond, and who kindled the strong interest in it that has made it the focus of my career. And to Walter Kaufmann, through whose books and translations I became acquainted with Nietzsche in those years, and with whom I worked and wrote my dissertation (not on Nietzsche, but on Hegel and others in that tradition, in a way that helped to prepare me to begin writing on Nietzsche subsequently). I dedicated my second book, *Hegel and After*, to the two of them: to Tillich, "who showed me where to look," and to Kaufmann, "who showed me how to see."

I am also grateful to my more mainstream philosophy teachers at Harvard and Princeton—and to four of them in particular: John Rawls, Richard Rorty, Gil Harman, and Stuart Hampshire—who introduced me to the counterpart "analytic tradition" in philosophy, and convinced me that it, too, had value. They instilled in me a strong interest in their kinds of analytic philosophy that has served me in very good stead in my subsequent work on Nietzsche, Hegel, Heidegger, and others in the interpretive tradition. Thanks to them, I became the kind of (broadly) analytically minded interpretive-tradition philosopher I am, in my Nietzsche studies as in other work.

I further am grateful to Charles Taylor, whom I came to know at Princeton, in whom I found a kindred spirit, and who became a kind of "older brother" role model for me in my attempt to combine elements of both traditions. And to Bernard Williams, who turned out subsequently to have become a kindred spirit as well, and whose encouragement down the road was very meaningful to me. My gratitude of this sort further extends to Yeri Yovel, a prominent Israeli philosopher also somewhat my senior, and whom I also befriended at Princeton, for being another such spirit. Their commitment to this middle course was and remains important to me in undertakings such as this book, in which I continue to try to walk the same line.

I am grateful to the members of the Philosophische Seminar (Philosophy Department) at Tübingen University—and to Frithjof Rodi and Helmut Fahrenbach in particular—for welcoming me and introducing me so valuably to (pre-analytic) German philosophy from the inside during my two long stays there just before and after I began teaching. And I am grateful to Bill Diggs and the other then-senior members of the Philosophy Department at the University of Illinois who hired me sight unseen (while I was in Germany), at the high tide of analytic philosophy in the discipline (that department included) and the cold war between it and Continental philosophy; allowed me to teach it; and made the department there a most congenial and supportive place for me to go my own precarious line-walking way—even when it turned out that Nietzsche was becoming a major interest of mine. I am also grateful to Peter Winch, during whose subsequent years in that

BACKSTORY AND ACKNOWLEDGMENTS

department it became a model of balance and cordiality between the two traditions, and of their bridging.

I am grateful, moreover (and very differently), to two prominent mid-century analytic philosophers, who played crucial roles at the very time I was risking everything professionally in that way: Arthur Danto and (surprisingly) the fiercely analytic Ted Honderich. Danto's analytic-philosophical book on Nietzsche, actually taking him seriously, made it professionally respectable to write about him, thereby opening the way for me—and served as a model for me, as I began to write about Nietzsche myself. He was also a very valuable provocation for me—and was the best possible foil for me, not only because playing his game against him was legitimate, but also because he took no offense, and even welcomed my challenge to his take on Nietzsche.

I am grateful to Honderich, the veritable British pontiff of positivistic analytic philosophy at the time, for his decision (no doubt prompted by Danto's book) to want to include a book on Nietzsche in his highly visible Arguments of the Philosophers series, for giving me the opportunity to write it, and for allowing me to write the kind of book I did. His imprimatur enabled it to help open the door and prepare the way for a new mainstream generation of both analytic and tradition-bridging Nietzsche studies, to which new tradition this book belongs. I am further grateful to Bernd Magnus and the North American Nietzsche Society he organized and led during its crucial early years. It provided a mainstream identity, structure, and publication opportunity for Nietzsche studies of that sort, which was crucial to their survival and encouragement.

Finally, along these lines, I am grateful to like-minded colleagues who further have been both good friends and boon companions, in fostering and advancing the way of taking Nietzsche and his kind of philosophy seriously of which this book is my latest example. They include Alexander Nehamas, Jim Conant, Bob Pippin, Bob Solomon, Kathy Higgins, Maudemarie Clark, and Lanier Anderson. Most, like myself, have other major interests in addition to Nietzsche, and even beyond the interpretive tradition altogether; but I am grateful for their company in both respects, past and present.

I am also grateful for the valuable assistance with things having to do with this book, over the years, of a number of grad students: again inter alia, Ben Dykes, Nathalie Morasch, Justin Remhof, and most especially Matt Rukgaber, whose assistance with a number of my projects has continued long after his graduate program ended, and has been nothing less than extraordinary.

And I am now grateful to the University of Chicago Press for publishing this book, to my editor Kyle Wagner for his interest in doing it and for his efforts and wise counsel, and to his two assistants who have been so helpful: first Dylan Montanari, and then Kristin Rawlings.

Last but not least, and actually most of all: my gratitude to my wife, Judy, for everything relating to this book (as well as everything else), is beyond all measure.

Notes on Previously Published Material

CHAPTER 1: TOWARD UNDERSTANDING NIETZSCHE

An initial and shorter version of this first chapter (and prologue to the rest of the book) was presented as a keynote address at a 2019 conference of the Groupe international de recherche sur Nietzsche, at the University of Montreal. A version of this text then appeared as "Understanding Nietzsche's Kind of Philosophy" in *Nietzsche on Making Sense of Nietzsche / Comprendre Nietzsche selon Nietzsche*, ed. Martine Béland, Céline Defat, Chiara Piazzesi, and Patrick Wotling (Reims: Éditions et presses universitaires de Reims, 2021), 33–48.

CHAPTER 2: THE NIETZSCHE OF
HUMAN, ALL TOO HUMAN

This chapter incorporates material adapted from my introduction to the Cambridge edition of R. J. Hollingdale's translation of *Human, All Too Human: A Book for Free Spirits* (© Cambridge University Press, 1996; reprinted with permission). Modified portions of this text also derive from my contribution, under the title "Nietzsche on Cultur: Menschlich, Allzumenschlich, and Höher," to *Friedrich Nietzsche: Menschliches, Allzumenschliches*, ed. Eike Brock and Jutta Georg (Berlin: De Gruyter, 2020), 111–26.

CHAPTER 3: THE NIETZSCHE OF *JOYFUL INQUIRY*

This chapter incorporates material adapted from "Nietzsche Naturalizing," which appeared in *Friedrich Nietzsche: Die fröhliche Wissenschaft*, ed. Christian Benne and Jutta Georg (Berlin: De Gruyter, 2015), 88–106.

CHAPTER 4: THE NIETZSCHE OF
THUS SPOKE ZARATHUSTRA

This chapter derives from an earlier version, "Zarathustra/*Zarathustra* as Educator," which appeared in *Nietzsche: A Critical Reader*, ed. Peter R. Sedgwick (Oxford: Blackwell, 1995), 222–49.

CHAPTER 5: THE NIETZSCHE OF
BEYOND GOOD AND EVIL

This chapter is a modified and expanded version of "Friedrich Nietzsche, *Beyond Good and Evil*: Prelude to a Philosophy of the Future," which appeared in *The Classics of Western Philosophy*, ed. Jorge E. Garcia, Gregory Reichberg, and Bernard N. Schumacher (Oxford: Blackwell, 2003), 405–15.

CHAPTER 6: THE NIETZSCHE OF *ON THE GENEALOGY OF MORALITY*

This chapter derives from "Nietzsche's *Genealogy*," which appeared in *The Oxford Handbook of Nietzsche*, ed. Ken Gemes and John Richardson (Oxford: Oxford University Press, 2013; reproduced by permission of Oxford University Press), 363–87, and also draws from an earlier essay in German, "Moral und Mensch," which was first delivered in 2003 at a conference at Tübingen University and then appeared under that title in *Zur Genealogie der Moral*, ed. Otfried Höffe (Berlin: Akademie Verlag, 2004), 115–32. Portions of it also derive from my "Nietzsche and Philosophical Anthropology," in *A Companion to Nietzsche*, ed. Keith Ansell-Pearson (Oxford: Blackwell, 2006), 115–32.

CHAPTER 7: NIETZSCHE AS NIHILIST?

This chapter derives in part from a presentation originally delivered at the conference "Nietzsche, Nihilism and Naturalism" in Hiddensee, Germany, in 2012, which was subsequently published (along with other contributions) in German as "Was ist aus dem 'Nihilismus' geworden?" in *Nietzsche-Studien* 43 (2014): 19–41. A portion of it is also adapted from "Nietzschean Cognitivism," which appeared in *Nietzsche-Studien* 29 (2000): 12–40.

CHAPTER 8: NIETZSCHE AS EXISTENTIALIST?

An earlier version of this chapter appeared under the title "Nietzsche: After the Death of God" in *The Cambridge Companion to Existentialism*, ed. Steven Crowell (© Cambridge University Press, 2012; reprinted with permission), 111–36.

CHAPTER 9: NIETZSCHE AS INDIVIDUALIST?

This chapter is a revised and expanded version of what began as an invited contribution to a 2005 symposium of the North American Nietzsche Society called "Nietzsche and Individuality," and was subsequently published under that title in *International Studies in Philosophy* 38, no. 3 (2006): 131–51.

CHAPTER 10: NIETZSCHE AS "FREE SPIRIT"?

This chapter is a revised version of an essay that appeared as "Nietzsche's 'Free Spirit'" in *Nietzsche's Free Spirit Philosophy*, ed. Rebecca Bamford (London: Rowman and Littlefield, 2015; all rights reserved), 169–88.

CHAPTER 11: NIETZSCHE AS NATURALIST?

This chapter is adapted from "Nietzsche's Naturalism," *Journal of Nietzsche Studies* 43, no. 2 (2012): 185–212, © The Pennsylvania State University. This material is used by permission of The Pennsylvania State University Press.

Notes

Preface

1. Arthur Danto, *Nietzsche as Philosopher* (New York: Macmillan, 1965).

2. Philosophy after Kant moved in a number of different directions, as subsequent philosophers responded in different ways to various aspects of Kant's thought. They may very roughly be thought of as those who took the primary business of philosophy to be kinds of *analysis*, differing from those characteristic of the sciences but somewhat akin to them in spirit; and those who took it to be kinds of *interpretation* (and reinterpretation), attempting to develop ways of improving upon our ordinary, traditional religious and philosophical, and newer scientific understandings of ourselves, human reality, and the world in which we find ourselves.

In the English-speaking world these two kinds of philosophy are commonly called "analytic philosophy" and "Continental philosophy"—so called because the British philosophers who dominated its philosophical mainstream in the first half of the twentieth century were partisans of the first kind, whereas most of the philosophers of note who pursued the second were European, or, as the British derisively called them, "Continental," and the label stuck. I consider it far preferable to refer to them as two broad *traditions*, and to refer to the second of them as "interpretive" sorts of philosophical endeavor, which—together with "analytic"—better captures what characterizes the most salient difference of emphasis between the two "traditions."

In fact, however, it is only a difference of emphasis, the kinds of analysis and interpretation advocated and pursued, and philosophical style, idiom, and temperament. And there have been a fair number of philosophers since Kant who—like Kant himself—engage in forms of both analysis and interpretation. Nietzsche is one of them.

See my *Norton Anthology of Western Philosophy after Kant: The Interpretive Tradition* and *The Analytic Tradition* (New York: Norton, 2017).

3. Richard Schacht, *Nietzsche*, Arguments of the Philosophers series, ed. Ted Honderich (London: Routledge & Kegan Paul, 1983).

4. Richard Schacht, *Making Sense of Nietzsche* (Urbana: University of Illinois Press, 1995).

Introduction

1. My *Making Sense of Nietzsche* (1995) contains essays on *The Birth of Tragedy* (chapter 7), *Schopenhauer as Educator* (chapter 8)—and the "Nietzsches" who were their authors—as well

as previous such discussions of *Joyful Inquiry* (chapter 10, there referred to as *The Gay Science*) and *Genealogy* (chapter 11).

2. Nietzsche's kind of philosophical "inquirer" at this point.

Chapter One

1. This of course is something that many commentators have addressed in one way or another. They include (from the bibliography): Allison, Ansell-Pearson (2005), Clark and Dudrick, Cox, Danto, Del Caro, Dudley, Green, Lampert (2018), Leiter (2015, 2019), Moore, Pippin, Remhof, Richardson (1996), Schrift, Sedgwick, Solomon, Tanner, and Welshon (2004).

2. Throughout this chapter (and book), I will be referring to books of Nietzsche's using English renderings of his German titles, initially giving the complete titles, but for the most part thereafter by either shortened (usually one key word) versions of those renderings or by acronyms of key words in their titles, for reasons of economy and convenience. See the reference key at the front of the book. In citations I will be following the standard practice of using the work's acronym followed by his section numbers (preceded by his volume and part numbers or identifying part title words if his section numbers are not consecutive throughout).

3. In 1886 Nietzsche reissued all of his pre-*Inquiry* books, and provided them all with new prefaces, commenting on them in ways that are both interesting and helpful to understanding them—or rather, to how the Nietzsche of 1886 wished them to be understood. (He did not provide *Inquiry* with a new preface at the same time, because he saved what he wanted to say by way of a preface for the one he added to the expanded five-Book version of that work that he published the next year.) He continued this practice for what remained of his productive life.

4. See my note 2 to chapter 3 about my choice of the word "joyful" (rather than the more usual "gay") to render Nietzsche's *fröhliche* in this book's title. See also my description of my chapter on this book in the preface above, concerning my choice of the word "inquiry" (rather than "science") to render "*Wissenschaft*" in the title.

5. This work is of course a *book*, in the usual sense; but it is a work that Nietzsche divided into parts that he called "Books" [*Bücher*]—initially four of them in 1882, to which he added a "Fifth Book" in 1887. To avoid confusion, I refer to the whole volume as "the work" (rather than "the book"), and use "Book" (capitalized) as he did here—usually specifying which one is meant as he did, as the "first Book, second Book," etc., or as "Book 1, Book 2," etc.

6. "Behold the man!" These are the Latin words purported in the Bible to have been spoken by Pontius Pilate when he turned Jesus over to the mob calling for Jesus's crucifixion.

7. The word *Mensch* is commonly rendered as "man" in English; but "man" in English can mean either "human being" (male or female) or a male human being. In German, and for Nietzsche (who uses the word *Mensch* a great deal), it is *always* to be understood as "human being." The German word for "male human being" is *Mann*. It is very important to understand that when he talks about *der Mensch* and *Menschen*, and the translation given is "man" and "men," he is *not* talking about "the man" and "men" to the exclusion of women. I endeavor to avoid that rendering in the whole of this book.

8. Alexander Nehamas, *Nietzsche: Life as Literature* (Cambridge: Harvard University Press, 1985).

9. Richard Schacht, *Making Sense of Nietzsche* (Urbana: University of Illinois Press, 1995).

10. I discuss the meaning of *Wissenschaft* in German and for Nietzsche at length in chapter 3.

11. Kaufmann was a professor of mine, and my dissertation supervisor, at Princeton, in the mid-1960s; and here, as elsewhere in this book, I draw upon our conversations about this and other matters.

12. I discuss these matters at length in chapters 7 and 11. I discuss them briefly here because they serve very nicely as examples of what I am talking about.

Chapter Two

1. Undoubtedly Nietzsche's version of the disguised "Wanderer" identity of Wagner's character "Wotan" in *Siegfried* (the recently premiered third part of Wagner's operatic cycle *The Ring of the Nibelung*). That Wotan had been the greatest of the gods, but had been easily defeated by his imposing but naive son Siegfried, and had become wiser and a seeker of knowledge of life and the world.

2. See *JI* 108, 125, and 343.

3. *Human*, like *Daybreak*, Nietzsche's next book, attracted and was given little attention (compared to his other works) for quite some time, owing in no small measure to Walter Kaufmann's low opinion of their relative importance in relation to the rest of his writings, all of which Kaufmann translated. It was his translations and Nietzsche book that (selectively) stimulated and guided both popular and academic interest in Nietzsche for much of the last half of the twentieth century. That situation has begun to be corrected in the last few decades, as these two works and their sequel in Nietzsche's "free spirit" series—*Joyful Inquiry* (itself not translated by Kaufmann until seven years after the last batch of his other translations)—have been given increasing attention in the secondary literature. See (in the bibliography) Abbey, Ansell-Pearson (2018), Ansell-Pearson and Bamford, Cohen, Franco, Meyer, and Ure (2008).

4. In my identifications of passages from *Human*, those from its original and first volume will be identified by the volume number and Nietzsche's section or "aphorism" numbering of them. So, for example: "(*HH* I:252)." Those from the two parts of the second volume will be identified by volume number ("II"), to indicate that they are from that volume, and then by a second, *part* number (either "I" or "II"), to indicate which of the volume's two parts they are from, followed by their section or "aphorism" number in that part of the volume. So, in this instance: "(*HH* II:I:128)." In these citations "P" signifies "Preface."

5. For much information and discussion of matters of this sort, see William H. Schaberg's excellent *The Nietzsche Canon: A Publication History and Bibliography* (Chicago: University of Chicago Press, 1995).

6. Readers who are not familiar with this work and Schopenhauer's philosophical thinking more generally can get a helpful introduction to both from the selections and commentary on him in my *Norton Anthology of Western Philosophy after Kant: The Interpretive Tradition* (New York: Norton, 2017), pp. 637–84.

7. Schaberg, *Nietzsche Canon*, pp. 58ff.

8. See Walter Kaufmann's introduction to his translation of the book as *The Gay Science* (New York: Vintage, 1974), pp. 30 and 32.

9. "Voltaire" was the pen name of François-Marie Arouet (1694–1788), the most prominent French Enlightenment writer and thinker (philosopher, historian, and public intellectual).

10. The most common form of this word in German is *Kultur*; but this is the version Nietzsche chose to use at this point. They do not differ in meaning.

11. Hegel's fullest presentation of his "philosophy of *Geist*" is set forth in the third and final volume of his *Encyclopedia of the Philosophical Wissenschaften* (1830), translated as *Hegel's*

Philosophy of Mind, trans. William Wallace and A. V. Miller (Oxford: Oxford University Press, 1971).

12. The second of his *Unfashionable Reflections, On the Uses and Disadvantages of History for Life.*

13. The Greek Apollinian-Dionysian duality is central to Nietzsche's purposes in his remarkable first book, *The Birth of Tragedy*. The Greek god Apollo represented the artistic and human principle of self-control, order, beauty, perfection, and rationality; while the god Dionysus represented passion, emotion, frenzy, creation and destruction. See my chapter 7 on "Nietzsche on Art in *The Birth of Tragedy*," in my *Making Sense of Nietzsche*.

14. It is clear that Nietzsche (like Hegel) considers *Sittlichkeit*—which I suggest rendering as *ethicality* (or *ethic*)—to be importantly different from the sort of thing that morality (*Moralität*) has come to be. It is not clear whether he regards them both as kinds of "morals" (*die Moral*), and simply different varieties of the same sort of normative phenomena, or fundamentally different sorts of normative phenomena. That is one of the interesting and important issues in his moral philosophy.

Chapter Three

1. See William H. Schaberg, *The Nietzsche Canon: A Publication History and Bibliography* (Chicago: University of Chicago Press, 1995), pp. 85–86.

2. It is more commonly known by the title *The Gay Science* because that is how its most recent translator chose to translate the German title, to accord with the Italian phrase, despite the fact that what the word "science" now means is very different from what *scienza* meant back in the late Middle Ages, when the phrase was coined to refer to the distinctive admirable way the troubadours knew how to live. I consider "inquiry" to be a less misleading and more apt broader rendering of *Wissenschaft* in Nietzsche's title than "science."

3. Several words of explanation are in order. Until the publication of Walter Kaufmann's translation in 1974, with its title rendered as *The Gay Science*, this work was generally known in English as *The Joyful Wisdom*—the title of Thomas Common's translation, published a half century earlier. Kaufmann by then had become *the* modern-day translator of most of Nietzsche's major works; and his previous translations had completely captured the American market. His translation immediately replaced the Common translation—and with it, his different rendering of Nietzsche's German title, *Die fröhliche Wissenschaft*. Kaufmann argued that Nietzsche had chosen that title to render the Italian phrase *la gaya scienza*, and so in that sense *The Gay Science* was faithful to his intention, as well as preferable because *Wissenschaft* is the German word for *science*.

It is certainly true that *Wissenschaft* does not mean anything like "wisdom." It also is true, however, that in contemporary usage the standard rendering of it as "science" is very problematic, because that word has come to mean either natural science or something similar to it—that is, a discipline that either is or ought to try to be very much like it methodologically and theoretically. That has proven to have had unfortunate consequences for the disciplines known as the "social sciences"; and it also has unfortunate consequences when it is used to refer to other cognitive disciplines—as the German word *Wissenschaft* has been for the past several centuries. In German, it has always been recognized to be an umbrella term for "cognitive disciplines" generally, for many of which the natural sciences are understood not to be paradigmatic. In English, however, the use of the word *science* in the title of this book of

Nietzsche's is widely thought either to be some sort of joke or to be wildly inappropriate. But there has seemed to be no good alternative. I consider "inquiry" to be an acceptable (even if rather bland) one, and a much less problematic choice than "science."

The case of *fröhlich* in the title is different. There is an English rendering of it that is at least as appropriate as *gay* used to be: namely, *joyful*. And I believe it to be the case that it would be the first option that would come to mind for most speakers of both English and German when needing to translate *fröhlich* either in speech or in writing. Kaufmann's translation choices are no longer deemed to be binding. Moreover, *joyful* is the rendering chosen by the editors of the Stanford *Complete Works of Friedrich Nietzsche*. So with all of these considerations in mind, I have decided to alter my own long-standing practice, and make the change to *Joyful Inquiry*.

4. This work began to receive serious attention in the literature before its predecessors in Nietzsche's "free spirit" series did, as is witnessed by the studies dealing with it in the bibliography. See Abbey, Ansell-Pearson (2018), Franco, Higgins (2000), Langer, Meyer, and Ure (2019).

5. I have chosen to defer discussion of the 1887 fifth Book until after discussing *Zarathustra* and *Beyond Good and Evil*, because that is when he wrote it; and for my purposes in this book and discussion of "Nietzsche Becoming Nietzsche," that is where it belongs. It is one of the two significant things Nietzsche wrote after *Beyond Good and Evil* and before the final frantic year of his productive life preceding his collapse; and so it and *Genealogy* constitute most of what we really have to go on (among his published writings) in trying to get a sense of the philosophical Nietzsche he became, and how that relates to what he previously had been philosophically. It shows us, quite literally, what for Nietzsche was the first thing—and one of the last things—that was beyond *Beyond*!

6. Schopenhauer, whose discovery drew Nietzsche to philosophy, was both celebrated by Nietzsche as an inspiration in his earlier essay *Schopenhauer as Educator* [*Erzieher*], and excoriated by him for his utterly negative verdict upon life.

7. See my addendum to chapter 6.

8. See Schaberg, *Nietzsche Canon*, pp. 83ff.

9. In particular, this period saw the deterioration of his relationships with his closest intellectual companion and friend, Peter Gast, and with his sister and mother (his only family), with whom his relations had long been intense but fraught.

10. See Schaberg, *Nietzsche Canon*, chapter 4.

11. This, and not just the *comprehension* of human reality and of what these things involve, clearly matters greatly to Nietzsche. But what they actually and fully involve for him is not at all clear; and his ideas about them developed and changed significantly. It *is* clear that he does not consider them to be the same for everyone. "The great health" that he talks about in the penultimate section of Book 5, for example, is by no means for everyone (*JI* 382). But it very definitely is one of the foremost concerns of his kind of philosophy. And his *Zarathustra* is among the venues he chooses and creates through which he attempts to pursue it.

12. For an extended discussion of this matter, see chapter 11.

13. "Sensibility" (and "sensibilities") is a concept of which I will be making considerable use throughout this book. I discuss it toward the end of chapter 11 (sections X–XII). I suggest that readers take a look at those sections now. But I also suggest that they be attentive to the uses I make of the idea as I go along. That will be more helpful as a way of fleshing this important idea out than anything else I can think of.

14. On this matter, see chapter 4 below.

15. Nietzsche does consider several types of (naturalized) morality and ethicality to be deserving of a human future, as forms of normativity that have significant roles to play in the flourishing and enhancement of human life. For an elaboration of this point, see my "Nietzsche's Naturalism and Normativity," in *Nietzsche, Naturalism, and Normativity*, ed. Christopher Janaway and Simon Robertson (Oxford: Oxford University Press, 2012), pp. 236–57. But the same is true with respect to at least one type of (naturalized) religiousness. See my "After Transcendence: The Death of God and the Future of Religion," in *Religion without Transcendence*, ed. D. Z. Phillips (New York: Harvest Press, 2000).

16. Nietzsche tends to use the singular, *die Moral* [morality], in these titles, because it's what he considers the prevailing sort of modern-day European/Western morality to be that he is talking about; but he of course rejects the idea that it is the only sort of morality there is or has been or could be. And his underlying general point is that moralities always have had and always will have (different) "genealogies"—which, however, do not settle the question of their assessment (which needs to be contextual, and may well vary considerably). The same presumably applies in the case of different instances of the "*Sittlichkeit der Sitte*" ["ethic of custom"].

17. The question of the kinds of skepticism that do and do not accord with Nietzsche's kind of philosophy (at this point, previously, and subsequently), however, is a much more complicated one than this, as Jessica Berry has made clear in her *Nietzsche and the Ancient Skeptical Tradition* (Oxford: Oxford University Press, 2011).

18. *Zarathustra*'s part 4 moves toward its conclusion with Zarathustra's realization that his "final sin" is "Pity! Pity for the higher *Menschen*!" [Mitleiden! Das Mitleiden mit dem höheren Menschen!], and with his reaction to that realization, which is essentially: "Well—the time for that has come and gone!!" [Das—*hatte seine Zeit!*]

19. In this connection, recall Genesis 3:7, about Adam and Eve after having tasted of the tree of knowledge: "Then the eyes of both of them were opened, and they realized they were naked; so they sewed fig leaves together and made coverings for themselves."

20. In the language of *JI* 108.

21. In "*Die vier grossen Irrtümer*," section 8.

22. It ends with the proclamation: "*ich will irgendwann einmal noch ein Ja-sagender sein!*" That is: "I want someday once and for all to be an affirmer!"

23. Schaberg, *Nietzsche Canon*, pp. 83f.

24. See section XVI at the end of the previous chapter.

Chapter Four

1. *KGW* IV 1, 5[25].

2. Nietzsche's formerly close relationship with Wagner had at this point soured to the point of animosity and rivalry.

3. I am referring in particular to Gooding-Williams, Hatab (2005), Higgins (2010), Lampert (1987), Loeb, Rosen, Suong, and Whitlock, all listed in the bibliography.

4. Friedrich Schiller (1759–1805) and Johann Wolfgang von Goethe (1749–1832) were the great icons of German literature in the century prior to Nietzsche, and together made Weimar the cultural capital of Germany. Nietzsche's sister moved Nietzsche to Weimar for the last years of his life after his collapse, in the hope (in vain) that he would be entombed together with them.

5. Friedrich Schiller, *On the Aesthetic Education of Man*, trans. Reginald Snell (New York: Fredrick Ungar, 1965). For excerpts and commentary, see my *Norton Anthology of Western Philosophy after Kant: The Interpretive Tradition* (New York: Norton, 2017), pp. 41–70.

6. See my *Nietzsche*, Arguments of the Philosophers series, ed. Ted Honderich (London: Routledge and Kegan Paul, 1983), ch. 8.

7. As in the cases of other writings of Nietzsche's prior to *Human*, the numbers given in citation identifications are section numbers, and his sections are much longer than they are in his "aphoristic" books from *Human* onward. Page numbers are of no use, because of the existence of multiple translations, none of which is authoritative. So despite their length, Nietzsche's section numbers would seem to be the only solution with any utility for most readers.

8. This is Nietzsche's description of the "free spirit" series that he had printed on the back cover of the original version of *Inquiry*.

9. As in "seal of approval." Ratification; making something official.

10. See the last sections of chapter 11 for a discussion of this concept and how I mean it to be understood.

11. "The Tragedy Begins" is the heading Nietzsche gave to the final section of the concluding Book of the original four-Book version of *Joyful Inquiry*, which consists in a preview of the prologue to the first part of *Zarathustra*, published the next year but obviously already well underway.

12. See my *Nietzsche*, ch. 5 and 6, especially pp. 326–40 and 380–94.

13. I am here borrowing an apt phrase Paul Tillich used to use in connection with Nietzsche, in lectures at Harvard University in 1961–62 (in which, as an undergraduate, I first made Nietzsche's acquaintance).

14. It should be noted that Nietzsche returned to the project of *Joyful Inquiry* after finishing the four parts of *Zarathustra* and writing *Beyond*, bringing out an expanded second edition of *Inquiry* with a new fifth Book and new preface in 1887, just prior to *Genealogy*. *Zarathustra* thus did not mark the end or abandonment of that project, but rather only an extended intermission in it.

15. *Uses and Disadvantages of History* is now a part of *Unfashionable Reflections* (aka *Untimely Meditations*).

16. In these passage identification abbreviations, "P" refers to "Zarathustra's Prologue" (to the First Part).

17. As in the humorous episode of the mindless braying of an ass that is mistaken for the profundity of persistent affirmation (saying "*Ja*" [Yah, i.e., Yes] repeatedly), in a parody of Zarathustra's wisdom, that is made a laughing matter near the end of this fourth part (*Z* IV:17–18).

Chapter Five

1. See William Schaberg, *The Nietzsche Canon: A Publication History and Bibliography* (Chicago: University of Chicago Press, 1995), ch. 6. This is my source for other such information relating to Nietzsche's publication history as well.

2. In *Unfashionable Reflections*.

3. The word *einer* in Nietzsche's German subtitle, *Vorspiel einer Philosophie der Zukunft*, is usually translated as "of a" rather than "to a"; and that would yield a subtitle that would seem to have a somewhat different meaning: "Prelude *of* a Philosophy of the Future." (The prelude *of* something is usually considered to be the first part of it; whereas a prelude *to* something is usually considered to be something preliminary to it.) However, I am rendering it here as "of a" because that is what is always done in English translations. The relation of this book to its topic, however, is an interesting and important question.

4. It is not exactly a lighthearted intermission, however, and contains some of Nietzsche's most problematic and (I would say) lamentable comments about women. They happily are exceptional in both tone and content, but can only be partially explained by the all-too-human fact that he had not gotten over the devastation he had recently suffered when his sister contrived (with his mother's encouragement) to sabotage his relationship with a woman named Lou Salomé, with whom he had been madly in love, and had hoped to marry, and who had broken with him. His bitterness is understandable; but it seems to have gotten the better of his judgment.

5. See again Schaberg, *Nietzsche Canon*.

6. Ludwig Feuerbach (1804–72) was a leading member of the post-Hegelian next generation of German philosophers (Marx was another) who began as Hegelians and then sought to turn philosophy in a different, more down-to-earth direction, replacing Hegel's "philosophy of *Geist*" with a "philosophy of man." He and his main writings were certainly known to Nietzsche.

7. *BGE*, Kaufmann translation, p. 30.

8. See my "Nietzsche and Lamarckism," *Journal of Nietzsche Studies* 44, no. 2 (2013): 263–80.

9. For much more on this point, see chapter 7.

10. See my "Nietzsche's 'Will to Power,'" *International Studies in Philosophy* 32, no. 3 (2000): 83–94, and, in the same issue, the article by Maudemarie Clark, who disagrees: "Nietzsche's Doctrine of the Will to Power: Neither Ontological nor Biological," 119–135.

11. See chapter 10 below for much more on this topic and part of the book.

12. That is what I proposed in the previous chapter (chapter 4).

13. In chapter 10 below.

14. See note 4 above.

15. See the addendum to chapter 6 and the concluding sections of chapter 10.

16. "*Vornehm*" is difficult to translate. In ordinary usage it is often appropriately translated as "noble"; but it might just as appropriately—for Nietzsche—be rendered here as "distinguished," "superior," "outstanding," or "exceptional." As Nietzsche means it here, it would seem to be in the vicinity of all of these terms at various points, but isn't precisely captured by any of them.

17. Schaberg, *Nietzsche Canon*, p. 166.

18. For an introduction to Leibniz and Kant, see my *Classical Modern Philosophers* (London: Routledge, 1984). For an introduction to Hegel and Schopenhauer, see my *Norton Anthology of Western Philosophy after Kant: The Interpretive Tradition* (New York: Norton, 2017).

Chapter Six

1. The first modern translation of *Genealogy* into English was Francis Golffing's *The Genealogy of Morals* (with *The Birth of Tragedy*; New York: Doubleday, 1956). It was followed by Walter Kaufmann's and R. J. Hollingdale's *On the Genealogy of Morals* (with *Ecce Homo*; New York: Vintage, 1967). Their translation had canonical status for decades, and still is the one most commonly used and cited. It is the version used in this essay, but has been modified in places. A number of new translations have appeared in recent years: Carol Diethe's *On the Genealogy of Morality* (Cambridge: Cambridge University Press, 1994), Douglas Smith's *On the Genealogy of Morals* (Oxford: Oxford University Press, 1996), Maudemarie Clark's and Alan J. Swensen's *On the Genealogy of Morality* (Cambridge, MA: Hackett, 1998), and Horace Barnett Samuel's *The Genealogy of Morals* (Mineola, NY: Dover Publications, 2003).

2. *Genealogy* has attracted considerable attention in the literature in recent decades. It includes a number of good books: most notably Christopher Janaway's *Beyond Selflessness: Reading*

Nietzsche's "Genealogy" (Oxford: Oxford University Press, 2007), David Owen's *Nietzsche's "Genealogy of Morality"* (Chesham, UK: Acumen, 2007), and Lawrence J. Hatab's *Nietzsche's "On the Genealogy of Morality": An Introduction* (Cambridge: Cambridge University Press, 2008). Janaway's book is a particularly useful one. Essays *on Genealogy* are legion. A number of them may be found in my *Nietzsche, Genealogy, Morality* (Oakland: University of California Press, 1994). Another such collection is *Nietzsche's "On the Genealogy of Morals": Critical Essays*, edited by Christa Davis Acampora (Lanham, MD: Rowman and Littlefield, 2006). An essay that has influenced the poststructuralist reading of Nietzsche—and the "genealogy" of poststructuralism itself—is Michel Foucault's 1971 essay "Nietzsche, Genealogy, History," which may be found in translation in a collection of his writings entitled *Language, Counter-Memory, Practice*, edited by D. F. Bouchard (Ithaca, NY: Cornell University Press, 1977).

3. A volume of particular interest, in terms of the genesis of *Genealogy* itself, is a translation of Paul Rée's two genealogical-psychological studies of morality that were very much on Nietzsche's mind (as he himself admits in his preface to it): *Paul Rée: Basic Writings*, edited as well as translated by Robin Small (Urbana: University of Illinois Press, 2003).

4. The German word *vornehm* can and often should be translated as *noble*. However, that translation would be misleading here, because *noble* in English has strongly sociocultural connotations of being "upper class," highly cultivated and refined, and of high rank and "birth"; whereas Nietzsche employs the term much more broadly, to refer to a variety of sorts of superiority, including barbaric forms of it. It therefore is best rendered as something like *superior*, in one compelling way or another, whether as an individual or a group.

5. What Nietzsche is talking about is not the meanings of either the word *ascetic* or the words for various ascetic ideals specifically (such as "chastity" or "self-denial"), but rather what such ideals or values *show about* those who embrace them.

6. In this book it seems entirely appropriate to speak of "sections" rather than "aphorisms." None of Nietzsche's numbered sections in the entire book is anything like an aphorism, as at least some sections in his other books from *Human* onward are.

7. This is one of Nietzsche's clearest statements in his published writings regarding nihilism and his stand with respect to it. See the following chapter (chapter 7) for much more on this topic.

8. Pronounced *"more-aze."*

9. See my "Nietzsche and Lamarckism," *Journal of Nietzsche Studies* 44, no. 2 (2013): 263–80.

10. Nietzsche makes a great deal of use of the term *Züchten* and its variants in his post-*Zarathustra* writings. At times it is clear that he means the kind of breeding that is done at the genetic level, when animal breeders select for desired traits (eugenic breeding). At other times it is clear that he means the kind of breeding that is accomplished through behavior modification (as when dispositions to desired sorts of behavior are inculcated in young people as they are growing up). And at times it is not clear which model he has in mind. This is a matter that fairly obsessed him during his last few years, and concerning which he developed some clearly erroneous views, and some very problematic ideas. The best that can be said about all of this is that he was right to realize that this is an important issue, with major implications; and to recognize that philosophers need to give it careful scientifically as well as morally and valuationally sophisticated attention.

11. This is a very important point, which all too often is missed. These are, for Nietzsche, two very different phenomena, and two very different kinds of conscience.

12. The emphasis on "in the service of knowledge" is mine; but it actually is Nietzsche's as well, because that is one of the important points he is making here. It crucially qualifies what

might otherwise be supposed to be a subversion of the very idea of "knowledge" that is in any way deserving of the name.

13. See William Schaberg, *The Nietzsche Canon: A Publication History and Bibliography* (Chicago: University of Chicago Press, 1995), p. 166.

Chapter Seven

1. Arthur Danto, *Nietzsche as Philosopher* (New York: Macmillan, 1965).

2. This of course is a matter than has been and continues to be much debated. Significant contributions to the debate include such titles from the bibliography as those of Danto, Havas, Reginster, and Young (2003).

3. The German term *Sache* (plural *Sachen*) is a very useful one, because everything there is and everything that goes on is a *Sache* of some sort, and can be referred to as such without any question-begging implications with respect to its ontological or epistemological status—of the sort that words like *thing* and *object* have. Our term *matter* seems to be the best we can do in English (as in "matters of various sorts" and even "What's the matter?"). But it, too, suggests—in philosophical circles—the idea of a materiality of some sort (as does *stuff*). *Sache* does not. The best way to render it in a truly open way, and to refer in the least tendentious way possible to anything whatsoever, might be simply to use the convention X (and Xs in such cases.) But better *matter* and *matters* than *thing* and *things*.

4. This applies even to the English renderings of his language in translations of these works; but I mean to be referring in particular to the German originals that he actually uses.

5. It is well worth recalling that even at Nietzsche's end of the nineteenth century, *Wissenschaft* was not as strongly identified or considered to be as paradigmatically exemplified by the natural (and especially the physical) "sciences" as it has for some time been in English, having the more general sense of "cognitive discipline." And we are dealing, after all, with an author who entitled a book—devoted to a range of investigations and reflections far broader than these sciences—*Die fröhliche Wissenschaft*. He may be gesturing here to the so-called *gaya scienza* of the medieval poet-knights and troubadours; but it is part of the task of the book at once to illustrate its title and to contribute to the revitalization of its central concept, the *-schaft* of *Wissen*.

6. See my *Nietzsche*, Arguments of the Philosophers series, ed. Ted Honderich (London: Routledge and Kegan Paul, 1983), ch. 2, "Truth and Knowledge."

7. Giambattista Vico (1668–1744) was an Italian Renaissance philosopher who espoused this view.

8. In my citations from the *Nachlass* that are to be found in the collection published in English as *The Will to Power* (*WP*), I shall identify the material cited by giving both the section number in *WP* and the location in *KGW*.

9. One who engages in this sort of *Wissenschaft*.

10. It is both interesting and significant that Nietzsche here associates "justice" with "intellectual integrity." This supports my contention that for him "intellectual integrity" may be thought of as a determination to "do justice" to whatever it is that one is inquiring into, which in turn is how he thinks of humanly possible knowing and humanly attainable knowledge, which for him are matters of "greater or lesser" rather than "all or nothing."

11. Both Kaufmann and Hollingdale misleadingly translate *Erkenntnis* here as *perception*, no doubt to play on the phrase *immaculate conception*—which itself might have been a better rendering, although still misleading.

12. Note the plural, *Erkenntnisse*, which is to say: *knowledges*, which are as many as there are forms of inquiry.

13. The importance of the words with which this passage ends—*"useful for knowledge"*—can hardly be overstated. This shows that Nietzsche is here taking for granted the human possibility and reality of knowledge in various domains, in relation to the attainment of which such perspectives are "useful."

14. It should be observed that Nietzsche speaks quite comfortably of "sameness" here, and also that he does not speak of "things" (*Dinge*), but rather uses the ontologically and epistemologically much more neutral term *Sache*. Again, it would be best to render that term here as *X*, which is in effect what it means (and Nietzsche means) here. He is not just talking about material/physical objects of one sort or another (e.g., tree), or batches of such objects (e.g., forest). What he is saying applies to anything whatsoever (dog, human being, the game of baseball, Wagner's *Ring* cycle, Germany, World War II, the French horn, etc., ad infinitum).

Chapter Eight

1. This label is best laid to rest, because it was unfair to the French philosophical community even in the glory days of poststructuralism, and is even more unfair to it today.

2. Kierkegaard, *Concluding Unscientific Postscript*, excerpted in my *Norton Anthology of Western Philosophy after Kant: The Interpretive Tradition* (New York: Norton, 2017), pp. 422–51. It should be noted that, although this undoubtedly is what Kierkegaard himself thought, this not only is a translation of the Danish original, but also is from a work of his that he published (like most of his works) under a pseudonym (in this instance Johannes Climacus) rather than under his own name, claiming only (on the title page) to have been "Responsible for its publication."

3. In *Thus Spoke Zarathustra*, I:3. This was without his ever having read Kierkegaard. Nietzsche never had the opportunity to read him because he could not read Danish, and Kierkegaard had not yet been translated into German.

4. To mention just a few, they would include Karl Jaspers and Martin Buber in German, and Simone de Beauvoir, Albert Camus, Gabriel Marcel, and Maurice Merleau-Ponty in France. See my *Norton Anthology*, pp. 1122–1324, for discussions of and selections from many of them.

5. Sartre, "Existentialism is a Humanism," in my *Norton Anthology*, pp. 1214–31.

6. Heidegger, *Being and Time*, excerpted in my *Norton Anthology*, pp. 994–1084.

7. Sartre, *Search for a Method*, Preface, excerpted in my *Norton Anthology*, pp. 1278–88.

8. "Always Look on the Bright Side of Life," from Monty Python's movie *Life of Brian* (1979). Tune and lyrics by Eric Idle.

9. I shall stop italicizing "Existenz" in the remainder of this discussion, because, like Heidegger's *Dasein*—a common German word for the existence of something or something's existence—it has been incorporated into the English-language existential-philosophical vocabulary. "Existenz" is understood to designate existential-philosophical human "existing," and "Dasein" is understood to be a kind of shorthand invoking the conception of that manner of existing (in contrast to the ways in which other entities exist or do their existing while they do so).

10. Edmund Husserl was the founder of the kind of philosophical theory and analysis called "phenomenology," in which Existenz-philosophy had its philosophical origin, for both Heidegger and Sartre. See the discussion of and selections from Husserl in my *Norton Anthology*, pp. 923–87. Existential philosophy might be thought of as the issue of a strange coupling (which would not have been even conceivable to the two parents) of Kierkegaardian and Husserlian

ways of thinking—both of whose thought has nothing whatsoever in common with Nietzsche's (but some of whose thinking might be thought of as having catalyzed the match for some, including Heidegger, Sartre, and Camus).

11. These distinctions, unfortunately, are not widely observed; and it remains common for all of them to be referred to simply as "existentialism." That, for example, is the case in the instance of the rubric used in the title of an (otherwise) excellent volume of essays on the most prominent figures associated with this general philosophical development: Steven Crowell, ed., *The Cambridge Companion to Existentialism* (Cambridge: Cambridge University Press, 2012). It must be admitted, however, that "existentialism" is both catchier and simpler than any of the possible alternatives.

12. See my *Norton Anthology*, pp. 1325–1456.

13. See, again, my comments in note 10 above.

14. I generally cite the Kaufmann or Hollingdale translations but on occasion modify them where I consider different renderings to be desirable.

15. A good deal of what Nietzsche had to say about nihilism is to be found in notes from his notebooks of 1886–88 that are gathered in the first part of a volume of selections from these notebooks published posthumously under the title *The Will to Power*. The status and significance of the material in this volume and in his notebooks is much debated. See what I say about this in chapter 1, section IV, and in my *Making Sense of Nietzsche*, ch. 6, "Beyond Scholasticism: On Dealing with Nietzsche and His *Nachlaß*."

16. Made popular by John Wild, in his pathbreaking (in the English-speaking world) book *The Challenge of Existentialism* (Bloomington: Indiana University Press, 1955).

Chapter Nine

1. Ayn Rand (1905–82) was a Russian-born writer and self-styled philosopher and advocate of a radical sort of individualism, who has had a large and devoted following. She had a complex (first positive and later negative) intellectual relationship with Nietzsche, but sufficient to convince many people that they were kindred spirits. She was the author of two massive cult novels, *The Fountainhead* and *Atlas Shrugged*.

2. This topic has been the subject of a number of interesting studies, including those by Mikics, Pittz, Thiele, and White, listed in the bibliography.

3. See my discussion of Schopenhauer and relevant selections from his writings in my *Norton Anthology of Western Philosophy after Kant: The Interpretive Tradition* (New York: Norton, 2017), pp. 637–84.

4. Ralph Waldo Emerson (1803–82) was an American philosopher and public intellectual whom Nietzsche greatly admired, and by whom the pre–*Human, All Too Human* Nietzsche was significantly influenced. See my discussion of him with selections in my *Norton Anthology*.

5. This monograph is divided into numbered sections; but at this point Nietzsche had not yet begun to write in the quasi-aphoristic style that he continued in most of his writings from *Human, All Too Human* onward, in which his numbered sections were relatively short, and seldom more than a page or two. Here they run much longer, up to a half dozen pages. There is no standard edition or translation of this work, and so there is no good way of identifying citations more precisely than by using these section numbers, which makes locating them difficult. My apologies to readers who want to try to find them.

6. Johann Wolfgang von Goethe (1749–1832) was the very center of literary, intellectual, and cultural life in German-speaking Europe for much of his long life, and was revered as much for

his wisdom as for his many talents and creative abilities. His two-part epic telling and elaboration of the Faust legend is one of the greatest works of German literature. He embodied the German human and cultural ideal—or rather: he established that ideal by precisely what he was. He was one of the few German intellectuals whom Nietzsche truly respected; and he was one of the few figures Nietzsche discusses in his *Twilight of the Idols* to emerge unscathed.

7. Jacob Burckhardt, *The Civilization of the Renaissance in Italy*, trans. S. G. C. Middlemore (New York: Penguin, 1990).

8. Hegel's thinking about all matters of this sort is set out most systematically in *Hegel's Philosophy of Mind [Geist]*, part 3 of his *Encyclopedia of the Philosophical Sciences [Wissenschaften]*, trans. William Wallace and A. V. Miller (Oxford: Oxford University Press, 1971). See also my discussion of Hegel and selections from this and others of his works in my *Norton Anthology*.

9. See again note 6 above.

10. It seems to me that this important point is missed by too many of those who have been arguing about this passage and the status of the "sovereign individual" in Nietzsche's thinking during the past few decades. Here and in the next section of this chapter, I try to put this entire matter into its proper perspective.

Chapter Ten

1. As related by Walter Kaufmann in his translation of this work (New York: Vintage Books / Random House, 1974), pp. 28, 30.

2. Interest in this rubric that Nietzsche himself formulated has finally begun to receive the attention it deserves in Anglophone philosophical Nietzsche studies. See, for example, the books in the bibliography by Cohen, Meyer, and Pittz. And an earlier version of this chapter is among the contributions to a very nice volume of essays on *Nietzsche's Free Spirit Philosophy*, edited by Rebecca Bamford (London: Rowman & Littlefield, 2015).

3. See my "Nietzsche's 'Will to Power,'" in *International Studies in Philosophy* 32, no. 3 (2000): 83–94.

4. Stendhal is the pen name of Marie-Henri Beyle (1783–1842), a French writer and excellent novelist, who wrote astutely about many things, and for whom Nietzsche had a high regard.

5. Note that he does not say: "no one else is entitled to it." He says "no one else is *easily [nicht leicht]* entitled to it." To be entitled to share some interpretation or conclusion of his, one has to have *earned the right* (done the work warranting it) to do so.

6. The interpretation I am about to advance is not widely shared. In fact, I believe it to be rather novel. But it is one that I have arrived at after discussing and thinking about this question for many years; and I now find it not only convincing but the only one that makes sense of everything Nietzsche has to say about this matter. And the question at issue is obviously of the greatest importance for a full understanding of his kind of philosophy—even though, if I am right about it, the stand he takes may dissuade many who find his kind of philosophy appealing up to this point from accompanying him along this last step of his way.

7. The "Theses on Feuerbach" is a now famous early (1843) manuscript critique by the young Marx of the philosophy of his philosophical mentor and point of departure, Ludwig Feuerbach (1804–1872). Feuerbach was one of the "Young Hegelians" who attempted to turn Hegel's "philosophy of *Geist* [Spirit]" into a kind of naturalized secular humanism, about which Marx was initially enthusiastic but soon became increasingly critical—in this respect, among others.

8. See, for example, my *Norton Anthology of Western Philosophy after Kant: The Interpretive Tradition* (New York: Norton, 2017), p. 514.

9. This was in the preface he added to the 1887 edition of *Joyful Inquiry* the next year.

Chapter Eleven

1. Richard Schacht, *Nietzsche*, Arguments of the Philosophers, ed. Ted Honderich (London: Routledge and Kegan Paul, 1983), p. 271 (emphasis added). That was in 1983, when Nietzsche was largely shunned by mainstream analytic philosophers, for most of whom he was thought to be nothing of the sort (and no real philosopher at all).

See also my *Making Sense of Nietzsche* (Urbana: University of Illinois Press, 1995), ch. 10: "How to Naturalize Cheerfully: Nietzsche's *Fröhliche Wissenschaft*."

2. Needless to say, a great deal has been written on this subject in recent years, in both books and journals. Taking explicit account of what others have had to say about it would be impossible; so I have had to restrict myself to a relative few. Books listed in the bibliography in which it is discussed include Cox, Emden (2014), Janaway, Leiter (2015 and 2019), Lemm, Lightbody, Moore, and Stack.

3. *Sciential* is defined in the *New Shorter Oxford English Dictionary* as "Of or pertaining to knowledge or science." *Scientian* means the same thing, and is simply the form of the word I prefer. It refers to attentiveness to the sciences that stops well short of complete and exclusive adherence to the model and findings of the sciences, with the natural sciences taken as paradigmatic. *Scientistic*, by contrast, like the noun form *scientism*, means precisely such complete and exclusive adherence. One who is "scientistic" is eo ipso "scientian"; but one can be "scientian" without being "scientistic." I go on to explain the difference more fully in what follows.

4. Brian Leiter, *Nietzsche on Morality* (London: Routledge, 2002), pp. 2–3.

5. Leiter, p. 3.

6. Leiter, p. 5; emphasis added.

7. Leiter, p. 11.

8. Leiter, p. 4.

9. Maudemarie Clark and David Dudrick, in *A Companion to Nietzsche*, ed. Keith Ansell-Pearson (Oxford: Blackwell, 2006).

10. Clark and Dudrick, p. 152.

11. Clark and Dudrick, p. 164.

12. Clark and Dudrick, p. 165.

13. Clark and Dudrick, p. 164.

14. Clark and Dudrick, p. 165.

15. Clark and Dudrick, p. 165.

16. This idea is owing to the important twentieth-century American philosopher Wilfrid Sellars.

17. Immanuel Kant, *Critique of Practical Reason*, trans. Lewis White Beck, 3rd edition (New York: Macmillan, 1993).

18. Afrikan Spir was a Ukraine-born new-Kantian nineteenth-century philosopher who wrote mainly in German.

19. Clark and Dudrick, pp. 159–61.

20. Clark and Dudrick, p. 151; emphasis added.

21. Christopher Janaway, *Beyond Selflessness* (Oxford: Oxford University Press, 2007).

22. Janaway, p. 34.

23. Janaway, p. 39; emphasis added.

24. Janaway, p. 47.

25. Janaway, pp. 52–53.

26. Janaway, p. 52; emphasis added.

27. This was one of my main points in the first chapter.

28. Kaufmann often so translates it.

29. That reading is further put into practice in various ways in another book, on aspects of Nietzsche's philosophical thinking (anticipated soon to follow this one), that should further strengthen that case.

30. Sensualism is a philosophical doctrine according to which all knowledge is based upon and derives from sensations and perceptions. The name *sensualism* is rather misleading, because of the most common construal of the word *sensual*; so it might better be referred to (albeit awkwardly) as *sense-ism*—or better still, perhaps, as *radical empiricism*. Nietzsche found the doctrine attractive, at least as an approach.

31. This title is commonly rendered in English as *The Antichrist*. As its subtitle (*Fluch auf dem Christentum* [*Curse upon Christianity*]) indicates, however, this title would be better rendered—in accordance with the common German usage of the word *Christ* to mean "Christian" (rather than "the Christ")—as *The Antichristian*.

32. Kaufmann chose not to translate the world *schrecklich* at all, and instead to leave it out. This is an example of why consulting the German in cases in which translator decisions matter is a good idea. It also is not the only instance in which Kaufmann made problematic translation choices. See my "Translating Nietzsche: The Case of Kaufmann," *Journal of Nietzsche Studies*, 43, no. 1 (2012): 68–86.

33. The expression *Lebensformen*, more commonly associated with Wittgenstein, is occasionally used by Nietzsche as well, and is a very apt one in this context.

34. See note 5 above.

35. That is, analysis in terms of causal laws.

Bibliography of Related Nietzsche Studies

Abbey, Ruth. *Nietzsche's Middle Period*. Oxford: Oxford University Press, 2000.

Ahern, Daniel R. *Nietzsche as Cultural Physician*. University Park: Pennsylvania State University Press, 1995.

———. *The Smile of Tragedy: Nietzsche and the Art of Virtue*. University Park: Pennsylvania State University Press, 2012.

Alfano, Mark. *Nietzsche's Moral Psychology*. Cambridge: Cambridge University Press, 2019.

Allison, David B. *Reading the New Nietzsche*. Lanham, MD: Rowman and Littlefield, 2001.

Ansell-Pearson, Keith. *How to Read Nietzsche*. New York: Norton, 2005.

———. *Nietzsche's Search for Philosophy: On the Middle Writings*. New York: Bloomsbury Academic, 2018.

Ansell-Pearson, Keith, and Rebecca Bamford. *Nietzsche's "Dawn": Philosophy, Ethics, and the Passion of Knowledge*. Hoboken, NJ: Wiley Blackwell, 2021.

Berry, Jessica N. *Nietzsche and the Ancient Skeptical Tradition*. Oxford: Oxford University Press, 2011.

Blondel, Eric. *Nietzsche: The Body and Culture*. Translated by Sean Hand. Stanford: Stanford University Press, 1991.

Bornedal, Peter. *The Surface and the Abyss: Nietzsche as Philosopher of Mind and Knowledge*. Berlin: De Gruyter, 2010.

Church, Jeffrey. *Nietzsche's Culture of Humanity: Beyond Aristocracy and Democracy in the Early Period*. Cambridge: Cambridge University Press, 2015.

Clark, Maudemarie. *Nietzsche on Ethics and Politics*. Oxford: Oxford University Press, 2015.

———. *Nietzsche on Truth and Philosophy*. New York: Cambridge University Press, 1991.

Clark, Maudemarie, and David Dudrick. *The Soul of Nietzsche's "Beyond Good and Evil."* New York: Cambridge University Press, 2012.

Cohen, Jonathan. *Science, Culture and Free Spirits: A Study of Nietzsche's "Human, All Too Human."* Amherst, MA: Humanity Books, 2010.

Conway, Daniel. *Nietzsche and the Political*. London: Routledge, 1997.

———. *Nietzsche's "On the Genealogy of Morals."* London: Continuum, 2008.

Cox, Christoph. *Nietzsche: Naturalism and Interpretation*. Berkeley: University of California Press, 1999.

Danto, Arthur C. *Nietzsche as Philosopher.* Exp. ed. New York: Columbia University Press, 2005.

Del Caro, Adrian. *Nietzsche contra Nietzsche: Creativity and the Anti-Romantic.* Baton Rouge: Louisiana State University Press, 1989.

Dudley, Will. *Hegel, Nietzsche, and Philosophy: Thinking Freedom.* Cambridge: Cambridge University Press, 2002.

Emden, Christian. *Friedrich Nietzsche and the Politics of History.* Cambridge: Cambridge University Press, 2008.

———. *Nietzsche on Language, Consciousness, and the Body.* Urbana: University of Illinois Press, 2005.

———. *Nietzsche's Naturalism: Philosophy and the Life Sciences in the Nineteenth Century.* Cambridge: Cambridge University Press, 2014.

Franck, Didier. *Nietzsche and the Shadow of God.* Evanston: Northwestern University Press, 2012.

Franco, Paul. *Nietzsche's Enlightenment: The Free-Spirit Trilogy of the Middle Period.* Chicago: University of Chicago Press, 2011.

Gooding-Williams, Robert. *Zarathustra's Dionysian Modernism.* Stanford: Stanford University Press, 2001.

Green, Michael Steven. *Nietzsche and the Transcendental Tradition.* Urbana: University of Illinois Press, 2002.

Haar, Michel. *Nietzsche and Metaphysics.* Albany: State University of New York Press, 1996.

Hales, Steven, and Rex Welshon. *Nietzsche's Perspectivism.* Urbana: University of Illinois Press, 2000.

Hatab, Lawrence. *Nietzsche's Life Sentence: Coming to Terms with Eternal Recurrence.* London: Routledge, 2005.

———. *Nietzsche's "On the Genealogy of Morals": An Introduction.* Cambridge: Cambridge University Press, 2008.

Havas, Randall. *Nietzsche's Genealogy: Nihilism and the Will to Knowledge.* Ithaca, NY: Cornell University Press, 2015.

Higgins, Kathleen. *Comic Relief: Nietzsche's "Gay Science."* Oxford: Oxford University Press, 2000.

———. *Nietzsche's "Zarathustra."* Rev. ed. Lanham, MD: Lexington Books, 2010.

Huddleston, Andrew. *Nietzsche and the Decadence and Flourishing of Culture.* Oxford: Oxford University Press, 2019.

Hunt, Lester. *Nietzsche and the Origin of Virtue.* London: Routledge, 1991.

Janaway, Christopher. *Beyond Selflessness: Reading Nietzsche's "Genealogy."* Oxford: Oxford University Press, 2007.

Jensen, Anthony K. *Nietzsche's Philosophy of History.* Cambridge: Cambridge University Press, 2013.

Johnson, Dirk Robert. *Nietzsche's Anti-Darwinism.* Cambridge: Cambridge University Press, 2010.

Katsafanas, Paul. *Agency and the Foundations of Ethics: Nietzschean Constitutivism.* Oxford: Oxford University Press, 2013.

———. *The Nietzschean Self: Moral Psychology, Agency and the Unconscious.* Oxford: Oxford University Press, 2019.

Lampert, Laurence. *Nietzsche and Modern Times.* New Haven, CT: Yale University Press, 1993.

———. *Nietzsche's Task: An Interpretation of "Beyond Good and Evil."* New Haven, CT: Yale University Press, 2001.

———. *Nietzsche's Teaching: An Interpretation of "Thus Spoke Zarathustra."* New Haven, CT: Yale University Press, 1987.

———. *What a Philosopher Is: Becoming Nietzsche.* Chicago: University of Chicago Press, 2018.

Langer, Monika. *Nietzsche's "Gay Science": Dancing Coherence.* London: Palgrave Macmillan, 2010.

Leiter, Brian. *Moral Psychology with Nietzsche.* Oxford: Oxford University Press, 2019.

———. *Nietzsche on Morality.* London: Routledge, 2002. 2nd ed. 2015.

Lemm, Vanessa. *Homo Natura: Nietzsche, Philosophical Anthropology and Biopolitics.* Edinburgh: Edinburgh University Press, 2020.

Lightbody, Brian. *Nietzsche's Will to Power Naturalized: Translating the Human into Nature and Nature into the Human.* Lanham, MD: Lexington Books, 2017.

Loeb, Paul. *The Death of Nietzsche's Zarathustra.* Cambridge: Cambridge University Press, 2010.

May, Simon. *Nietzsche's Ethics and His War on "Morality."* Oxford: Oxford University Press, 1999.

Metzger, Jeffrey. *The Rise of Politics and Morality in Nietzsche's "Genealogy": From Chaos to Conscience.* Lanham, MD: Lexington Books, 2020.

Meyer, Matthew. *Nietzsche's Free Spirit Works: A Dialectical Reading.* Cambridge: Cambridge University Press, 2019.

Mikics, David. *The Romance of Individualism in Emerson and Nietzsche.* Athens: Ohio University Press, 2003.

Moles, Alistair. *Nietzsche's Philosophy of Nature and Cosmology.* New York: Lang, 1989.

Moore, Gregory. *Nietzsche, Biology and Metaphor.* Cambridge: Cambridge University Press, 2002.

Nehamas, Alexander. *Nietzsche: Life as Literature.* Cambridge, MA: Harvard University Press, 1985.

Owen, David. *Nietzsche's "Genealogy of Morality."* Chesham, UK: Acumen, 2007.

Parkes, Graham. *Composing the Soul: Reaches of Nietzsche's Psychology.* Chicago: University of Chicago Press, 1994.

Pippin, Robert M. *Nietzsche, Psychology, and First Philosophy.* Chicago: University of Chicago Press, 2010.

Pittz, Steven. *Recovering the Liberal Spirit: Nietzsche, Individuality, and Spiritual Freedom.* Albany: State University of New York Press, 2020.

Poellner, Peter. *Nietzsche and Metaphysics.* Oxford: Oxford University Press, 1995.

Reginster, Bernard. *The Affirmation of Life: Nietzsche on Overcoming Nihilism.* Cambridge, MA: Harvard University Press, 2006.

Remhof, Justin. *Nietzsche's Constructivism: A Metaphysics of Material Objects.* New York: Routledge, 2018.

Richardson, John. *Nietzsche's New Darwinism.* Oxford: Oxford University Press, 2004.

———. *Nietzsche's System.* Oxford: Oxford University Press, 1996.

———. *Nietzsche's Values.* Oxford: Oxford University Press, 2020.

Ridley, Aaron. *Nietzsche's Conscience: Six Character Studies from the "Genealogy."* Ithaca, NY: Cornell University Press, 1998.

Roberts, Tyler. *Contesting Spirit: Nietzsche, Affirmation, Religion.* Princeton, NJ: Princeton University Press, 1998.

Robertson, Ritchie. *Conflict and Contest in Nietzsche's Philosophy.* New York: Bloomsbury Academic, 2019.

Rosen, Stanley. *The Mask of Enlightenment: Nietzsche's "Zarathustra."* 2nd ed. New Haven, CT: Yale University Press, 2004.

Schacht, Richard. *Making Sense of Nietzsche.* Urbana: University of Illinois Press, 1995.

————. *Nietzsche*. Arguments of the Philosophers series, ed. Ted Honderich. London: Routledge and Kegan Paul, 1983.

————. *Norton Anthology of Western Philosophy after Kant: The Interpretive Tradition*. New York: Norton, 2017.

Schrift, Alan D. *Nietzsche and the Question of Interpretation*. New York: Routledge, 1990.

Sedgwick, Peter. *Nietzsche's Economy: Modernity, Normativity and Futurity*. London: Palgrave Macmillan, 2007.

————. *Nietzsche's Justice: Naturalism in Search of an Ethics*. Montreal: McGill-Queen's University Press, 2013.

Shapiro, Gary. *Nietzsche's Earth: Great Events, Great Politics*. Chicago: University of Chicago Press, 2016.

Shaw, Tamsin. *Nietzsche's Political Skepticism*. Princeton, NJ: Princeton University Press, 2007.

Sleinis, E. E. *Nietzsche's Revaluation of Values: A Study in Strategies*. Urbana: University of Illinois Press, 1994.

Small, Robin. *Time and Becoming in Nietzsche's Thought*. New York: Continuum, 2010.

Solomon, Robert. *Living with Nietzsche: What the Great Immoralist Has to Teach Us*. Oxford: Oxford University Press, 2003.

Solomon, Robert, and Kathleen Higgins. *What Nietzsche (Really) Said*. New York: Schocken / Random House, 2000.

Stack, George J. *Nietzsche's Anthropic Circle: Man, Science, and Myth*. Rochester, NY: University of Rochester Press, 2005.

Suong, T. K. *Nietzsche's Epic of the Soul: "Thus Spoke Zarathustra."* Lanham, MD: Lexington Books, 2005.

Swanton, Christine. *The Virtue Ethics of Hume and Nietzsche*. Chichester, UK: Wiley Blackwell, 2015.

Tanner, Michael. *Nietzsche: A (Very) Short Introduction*. Oxford: Oxford University Press, 2000.

Thiele, Leslie Paul. *Friedrich Nietzsche and the Politics of the Soul: A Study of Heroic Individualism*. Princeton, NJ: Princeton University Press, 1990.

Ure, Michael. *Nietzsche's "The Gay Science": An Introduction*. Cambridge: Cambridge University Press, 2019.

————. *Nietzsche's Therapy: Self-Cultivation in the Middle Works*. Lanham, MD: Lexington Books, 2008.

Welshon, Rex. *The Philosophy of Nietzsche*. Chesham, UK: Acumen, 2004.

White, Richard J. *Nietzsche and the Problem of Sovereignty*. Urbana: University of Illinois Press, 1997.

Whitlock, Greg. *Returning to Sils-Maria*. New York: Peter Lang, 1990.

Williams, Bernard. *Truth and Truthfulness: An Essay in Genealogy*. Princeton, NJ: Princeton University Press, 2002.

Williams, Robert W. *Tragedy, Recognition, and the Death of God: Studies in Hegel and Nietzsche*. Oxford: Oxford University Press, 2012.

Woodford, Peter. *The Moral Meaning of Nature: Nietzsche's Darwinian Religion and Its Critics*. Chicago: University of Chicago Press, 2018.

Young, Julian. *The Death of God and the Meaning of Life*. New York: Routledge, 2003.

————. *Friedrich Nietzsche: A Philosophical Biography*. Cambridge: Cambridge University Press, 2010.

————. *Nietzsche's Philosophy of Religion*. Cambridge: Cambridge University Press, 2006.

Index